802.11® Wireless Networks

The Definitive Guide

802.11® Wireless Networks
The Definitive Guide

Matthew S. Gast

O'REILLY®

Beijing · Cambridge · Farnham · Köln · Paris · Sebastopol · Taipei · Tokyo

802.11® Wireless Networks: The Definitive Guide
by Matthew S. Gast

Copyright © 2002 O'Reilly & Associates, Inc. All rights reserved.
Printed in the United States of America.

Published by O'Reilly & Associates, Inc., 1005 Gravenstein Highway North,
Sebastopol, CA 95472.

O'Reilly & Associates books may be purchased for educational, business, or sales promotional use. Online editions are also available for most titles (*safari.oreilly.com*). For more information contact our corporate/institutional sales department: (800) 998-9938 or *corporate@oreilly.com*.

Editor:	Mike Loukides
Production Editor:	Matt Hutchinson
Cover Designer:	Ellie Volckhausen

Printing History:

April 2002:	First Edition.

ISBN: 0-596-00183-5

[M]

Table of Contents

Preface

People move. Networks don't.

More than anything else, these two statements can explain the explosion of wireless LAN hardware. In just a few years, the projected revenues from wireless LAN products will be in the billions of dollars. The price of wireless LAN gear has plummeted and continues to fall dramatically. Wireless LANs are now a fixture on the networking landscape, which means you need to learn to deal with them.

Prometheus Untethered: The Possibilities of Wireless LANs

Wireless networks offer several advantages over fixed (or "wired") networks:

Mobility
> Users move, but data is usually stored centrally. Enabling users to access data while they are in motion can lead to large productivity gains.

Ease and speed of deployment
> Many areas are difficult to wire for traditional wired LANs. Older buildings are often a problem; running cable through the walls of an older stone building to which the blueprints have been lost can be a challenge. In many places, historic preservation laws make it difficult to carry out new LAN installations in older buildings. Even in modern facilities, contracting for cable installation can be expensive and time-consuming.

Flexibility
> No cables means no recabling. Wireless networks allow users to quickly form amorphous, small group networks for a meeting, and wireless networking makes moving between cubicles and offices a snap. Expansion with wireless networks is easy because the network medium is already everywhere. There are no cables to pull, connect, or trip over. Flexibility is the big selling point for the "hot spot" market, composed mainly of hotels, airports, train stations, libraries, and cafes.

Cost

In some cases, costs can be reduced by using wireless technology. As an example, 802.11® equipment can be used to create a wireless bridge between two buildings. Setting up a wireless bridge requires some initial capital cost in terms of outdoor equipment, access points, and wireless interfaces. After the initial capital expenditure, however, an 802.11-based, line-of-sight network will have only a negligible recurring monthly operating cost. Over time, point-to-point wireless links are far cheaper than leasing capacity from the telephone company.

Until the completion of the 802.11 standard in 1997, however, users wanting to take advantage of these attributes were forced to adopt single-vendor solutions with all of the risk that entailed. Once 802.11 started the ball rolling, speeds quickly increased from 2 Mbps to 11 Mbps to 54 Mbps. Standardized wireless interfaces and antennas have made it possible to build wireless networks. Several service providers have jumped at the idea, and enthusiastic bands of volunteers in most major cities have started to build public wireless networks based on 802.11.

Audience

This book is intended for readers who need to learn more about the technical aspects of wireless LANs, from operations to deployment to monitoring:

- Network architects contemplating rolling out 802.11 equipment onto networks or building networks based on 802.11
- Network administrators responsible for building and maintaining 802.11 networks
- Security professionals concerned about the exposure from deployment of 802.11 equipment and interested in measures to reduce the security headaches

The book assumes that you have a solid background in computer networks. You should have a basic understanding of IEEE 802 networks (particularly Ethernet), the OSI reference model, and the TCP/IP protocols, in addition to any other protocols on your network.

Overture for Book in Black and White, Opus 2

Part of the difficulty in writing a book on a technology that is evolving quickly is that you are never quite sure what to include. 2001 was a year of active development for 802.11, especially in the area of security. Several studies suggested that security concerns were delaying the widespread adoption of 802.11, so I made a particular effort to keep the security coverage in this book up-to-date. Undoubtedly, the benefits of that effort will quickly fade, but I certainly hope that I have described the basic components well enough to make this book useful no matter what final form the security-related standards take. This book has two main purposes: it is meant to teach the reader about the 802.11 standard itself, and it offers practical advice on building wireless LANs with 802.11 equipment. These two purposes are meant to be independent of each other so you can easily find what interests you. To help you decide what to read first and to give you a better idea of the layout, the following are brief summaries of all the chapters.

Chapter 1, *Introduction to Wireless Networks*, lists ways in which wireless networks are different from traditional wired networks and discusses the challenges faced when adapting to fuzzy boundaries and unreliable media. Wireless LANs are perhaps the most interesting illustration of Christian Huitema's assertion that the Internet has no center, just an ever-expanding edge. With wireless LAN technology becoming commonplace, that edge is now blurring.

Chapter 2, *Overview of 802.11 Networks*, describes the overall architecture of 802.11 wireless LANs. 802.11 is somewhat like Ethernet but with a number of new network components and a lot of new acronyms. This chapter introduces you to the network components that you'll work with. Broadly speaking, these components are stations (mobile devices with wireless cards), access points (glorified bridges between the stations and the distribution system), and the distribution system itself (the wired backbone network). Stations are grouped logically into Basic Service Sets (BSSs). When no access point is present, the network is a loose, ad-hoc confederation called an independent BSS (IBSS). Access points allow more structure by connecting disparate physical BSSs into a further logical grouping called an Extended Service Set (ESS).

Chapter 3, *The 802.11 MAC*, describes the Media Access Control (MAC) layer of the 802.11 standard in detail. 802.11, like all IEEE 802 networks, splits the MAC-layer functionality from the physical medium access. Several physical layers exist for 802.11, but the MAC is the same across all of them. The main mode for accessing the network medium is a traditional contention-based access method, though it employs collision avoidance (CSMA/CA) rather than collision detection (CSMA/CD). The chapter also discusses data encapsulation in 802.11 frames and helps network administrators understand the frame sequences used to transfer data.

Chapter 4, *802.11 Framing in Detail*, builds on the end of Chapter 3 by describing the various frame types and where they are used. This chapter is intended more as a reference than actual reading material. It describes the three major frame classes. Data frames are the workhorse of 802.11. Control frames serve supervisory purposes. Management frames assist in performing the extended operations of the 802.11 MAC. Beacons announce the existence of an 802.11 network, assist in the association process, and are used for authenticating stations.

Chapter 5, *Wired Equivalent Privacy (WEP)*, describes the Wired Equivalent Privacy protocol. By default, 802.11 networks do not provide any authentication or confidentiality functions. WEP is a part of the 802.11 standard that provides rudimentary authentication and confidentiality features. Unfortunately, it is severely flawed. This chapter discusses what WEP is, how it works, and why you can't rely on it for any meaningful privacy or security.

Chapter 6, *Security, Take 2: 802.1x*, describes 802.1x, which is a new attempt to solve the authentication and confidentiality problem on LANs. 802.1x will serve as the basis for an authentication framework for 802.11, but the adaptation is currently being carried out.

Chapter 7, *Management Operations*, describes the management operations on 802.11 networks. To find networks to join, stations scan for active networks announced by access points or the IBSS creator. Before sending data, stations must associate with an access point. This chapter also discusses the power-management features incorporated into the MAC that allow battery-powered stations to sleep and pick up buffered traffic at periodic intervals.

Chapter 8, *Contention-Free Service with the PCF*, describes the point coordination function. The PCF is not widely implemented, so this chapter can be skipped for most purposes. The PCF is the basis for contention-free access to the wireless medium. Contention-free access is like a centrally controlled, token-based medium, where access points provide the "token" function.

Chapter 9, *Physical Layer Overview*, describes the general architecture of the physical layer (PHY) in the 802.11 model. The PHY itself is broken down into two "sublayers." The Physical Layer Convergence Procedure (PLCP) adds a preamble to form the complete frame and its own header, while the Physical Medium Dependent (PMD) sublayer includes modulation details. The most common PHYs use radio frequency (RF) as the wireless medium, so the chapter closes with a short discussion on RF systems and technology that can be applied to any PHY discussed in the book.

Chapter 10, *The ISM PHYs: FH, DS, and HR/DS*, describes the three physical layers that have been used in 802.11 networks up through late 2001. These include the frequency hopping spread spectrum (FHSS) physical layer, the direct sequence spread spectrum (DSSS) physical layer, and the high-rate direct sequence spread spectrum (HR/DSSS) physical layer, which is defined by the 802.11b standard. Of these, the 11-Mbps HR/DSSS layer is most widely used at present.

Chapter 11, *802.11a: 5-GHz OFDM PHY*, describes the 5-GHz PHY standardized with 802.11a, which operates at 54 Mbps. This physical layer uses another modulation technique known as orthogonal frequency division multiplexing (OFDM). OFDM is also the basis for a 54-Mbps standard known as 802.11g, which operates in the same frequency bands as the other 802.11 physical layers. 802.11a products started to appear in late 2001; 802.11g products will probably appear in late 2002. It's a good bet that one of these standards will supplant 802.11b, just as 100BaseT Ethernet has supplanted 10BaseT.

Chapter 12, *Using 802.11 on Windows*, describes the basic driver installation procedure in Windows. It also illustrates how some drivers allow reconfiguration of the 802.11 MAC parameters discussed in Chapters 3–7.

Chapter 13, *Using 802.11 on Linux*, discusses how to install 802.11 support on a Linux system. It discusses the Linux-WLAN-NG project, which provides support for cards based on Intersil's PRISM and PRISM2 chip sets. It also discusses the wireless driver that Lucent provides for their wireless cards (Lucent goes under many names, including WaveLAN, Orinoco, and Agere), and it discusses how to install PCMCIA support.

Chapter 14, *Using 802.11 Access Points*, describes the equipment used on the infra-structure end of 802.11 networks. Commercial access point products have varying features. This chapter describes the common features of access points, offers buying advice, and presents two practical configuration examples.

Chapter 15, *802.11 Network Deployment*, suggests a process by which a wireless LAN could be installed. One of the key advantages of a wireless network is mobility. Mobility can be guaranteed only when all wireless stations reside on the same logical IP network. (This may require readdressing; it almost certainly requires renumbering to free a large contiguous address space.) Corporations deploying 802.11 must naturally be concerned with security. This chapter also discusses various aspects of network planning, including capacity management (how many users can you support, and what bandwidth can they expect?), site surveys, and physical details such as antennas and transmission lines.

Chapter 16, *802.11 Network Analysis*, teaches administrators how to recognize what's going on with their wireless LANs. Network analyzers have proven their worth time and time again on wired networks. Wireless network analyzers are just as valuable a tool for 802.11 networks. This chapter discusses how to use wireless network analyzers and what certain symptoms may indicate. It also describes how to build an analyzer using Ethereal. Finally, AirSnort is a tool that allows recovery of WEP keys and is something that readers should be aware of, if only for its security implications when used by others.

Chapter 17, *802.11 Performance Tuning*, describes how network administrators can change commonly exposed 802.11 parameters. It revisits each parameter and discusses what changing the parameter will do to the wireless network.

Chapter 18, *The Future, at Least for 802.11*, summarizes the standardization work pending in the 802.11 working group. After summarizing the work in progress, I get to prognosticate and hope that I don't have to revise this too extensively in future editions.

Appendix A, *802.11 MIB*, is a description of the MAC MIB. A number of parameters in the MAC can be changed by the network administrator using standard SNMP tools. This appendix follows the style I have used in my T1 book to show the parameters and call out the important parameters.

Appendix B, *802.11 on the Macintosh*, describes Apple's popular AirPort system. Apple's aggressive pricing of AirPort hardware was one of the most important events in the story of 802.11. AirPort base stations are fully compliant with 802.11 and can be used to build a network for any 802.11-compliant wireless device. Apple has also included a dedicated slot on all of their recent hardware for AirPort cards, which makes adding 802.11 interfaces to Apple hardware a snap. No book about 802.11 would be complete without a description of the AirPort.

Conventions Used in This Book

Italic is used for:

- Pathnames, filenames, class names, and directories
- New terms where they are defined
- Internet addresses, such as domain names and URLs

Bold is used for:

- GUI components

Constant Width is used for:

- Command lines and options that should be typed verbatim on the screen
- All code listings

Constant Width Italic is used for:

- General placeholders that indicate that an item should be replaced by some actual value in your own program

Constant Width Bold is used for:

- Text that is typed in code examples by the user

 Indicates a tip, suggestion, or general note

Indicates a warning or caution

How to Contact Us

Please address comments and questions concerning this book to the publisher:

O'Reilly & Associates, Inc.
1005 Gravenstein Highway North
Sebastopol, CA 95472

(800) 998-9938 (in the U.S. or Canada)
(707) 829-0515 (international/local)
(707) 829-0104 (fax)

There is a web site for the book, where errata and any additional information will be listed. You can access this page at:

http://www.oreilly.com/catalog/802dot11/

To comment or ask technical questions about this book, send email to:

bookquestions@oreilly.com

For more information about our books, conferences, software, Resource Centers, and the O'Reilly Network, see our web site at:

http://www.oreilly.com/

Acknowledgments

This book was made possible by a wide range of corporate support. I received Nokia hardware from Kelly Robertson, a Senior Sales Engineering Manager who appreciated the value of this book. O'Reilly & Associates was a tremendous help in marshalling the hardware I needed. In addition to loaning me some O'Reilly-owned 802.11 hardware, they helped me make the right connections at other companies. In particular, they were able to put me in touch with Brian Barton at Apple's Seeding Lab. Apple proved to be an easy company to work with, and they enthusiastically provided an iBook and an AirPort. While it is always gratifying to see hardware vendors "get it," I hope that Apple's work with the technical community pays dividends for them down the road.

As with many other projects, the scope of this book turned out wider than planned. One of the later additions to the text was the chapter on the 802.11a physical layer. I am indebted to James Chen and Tom Mahon of Atheros Communications for their assistance in understanding the complexities of OFDM and how they are applied by 802.11.

The large supporting cast at O'Reilly was tremendously helpful in a wide variety of ways. Ellie Volckhausen designed a stunning cover that adorned my cube for most of the time I was writing the book. I only hope that this book upholds the long tradition of bats on O'Reilly covers. The illustrators were once again in top form, handily converting my large batch of sketches into something that is worthy of public display. And, as always, I am thankful for the wisdom of Mike Loukides, the editor. Mike kept this project moving forward in the innumerable ways I have been accustomed to from our past collaborations, and his background as a ham radio operator proved especially useful when I started writing about the dark and forbidding world of antennas and RF transmission. (Among many, many other items, you have him to thank for the footnote on the gain of the Aricebo radio telescope!)

More than in any previous book, my thanks go out to my review team. My reviewers caught a great number of mistakes and helped improve the text in a number of areas. (Any remaining mistakes are, of course, my sole responsibility.) Debbie Fligor at the Computing and Communications Services Office of the University of Illinois provided a useful counterweight to my corporate-leaning view of the world, and her experience in the design of the campus-wide wireless LAN at the Champaign-Urbana campus proved especially useful. Jay Kreibich, of the Software Development Group at the Computing and Communications Services Office of the University of Illinois, is one of those reviewers authors like to get before the book goes to press (which means there is still time to fix it!). Jay's voluminous commentary led to revisions in every chapter, most notably in the deployment chapter. The VLAN discussion in the deployment chapter is the most notable improvement he helped to bring about, but there were countless others. Debbie and Jay were also strenuous advocates for inclusion of the Macintosh, and I hope they are satisfied with the result. Gian-Paolo Musumeci's review suggested a number of corrections to my discussions of security throughout the book. Professor Joseph Sloan at Lander University kept me honest in a number of places where I might otherwise have let things slide, especially with regard to using 802.11 on Linux.

As with many other tasks, the devil of writing is in the details. Getting it right means rewriting, and then probably rewriting some more. My initial proposal for this book went through several iterations before it was accepted by O'Reilly. After I began the book, I had to remain flexible to incorporate new details. Furthermore, wireless LAN technology is evolving rapidly and I fully expect this book to need several revisions in the future. I did not attempt a large writing project until college, when I took Brad Bateman's U.S. Financial System class. Although I certainly learned about the flow of money through the economy and the tools that the Federal Reserve uses in formulating policy, what I most valued in retrospect was the highly structured process of writing a lengthy paper throughout the semester. In addition to simply producing a large document, Dr. Bateman stressed the revision process, a skill that I had to use repeatedly in the preparation of this book. (Several innovations to wireless LANs came to the market during the writing process and needed to be incorporated.) It would be a mistake, however, for me to simply credit Dr. Bateman as an outstanding writing teacher or an economist gifted with the ability to explain complex subjects to his students. Not all professors teach to prepare students for graduate school, and not all professors confine their teaching to the classroom. I am a far better writer, economist, and citizen for his influence.

When writing a book, it is easy to acknowledge the tangible contributions of others. Behind every author, though, there is a supportive cast of relatives and friends. As always, my wife Ali continued to indulge my writing habit with extremely good humor, especially considering the number of weekends that were sacrificed to this book. Many of my friends informally supported this project with a great deal of encouragement and support; my thanks must go to (in alphabetical order) Annie, Aramazd, Brian, Dameon, Kevin, and Nick.

## CHAPTER 1

Introduction to Wireless Networks

Over the past five years, the world has become increasingly mobile. As a result, traditional ways of networking the world have proven inadequate to meet the challenges posed by our new collective lifestyle. If users must be connected to a network by physical cables, their movement is dramatically reduced. Wireless connectivity, however, poses no such restriction and allows a great deal more free movement on the part of the network user. As a result, wireless technologies are encroaching on the traditional realm of "fixed" or "wired" networks. This change is obvious to anybody who drives on a regular basis. One of the "life and death" challenges to those of us who drive on a regular basis is the daily gauntlet of erratically driven cars containing mobile phone users in the driver's seat.

We are on the cusp of an equally profound change in computer networking. Wireless telephony has been successful because it enables people to connect with each other regardless of location. New technologies targeted at computer networks promise to do the same for Internet connectivity. The most successful wireless networking technology this far has been 802.11.

Why Wireless?

To dive into a specific technology at this point is getting a bit ahead of the story, though. Wireless networks share several important advantages, no matter how the protocols are designed, or even what type of data they carry.

The most obvious advantage of wireless networking is *mobility*. Wireless network users can connect to existing networks and are then allowed to roam freely. A mobile telephone user can drive miles in the course of a single conversation because the phone connects the user through cell towers. Initially, mobile telephony was expensive. Costs restricted its use to highly mobile professionals such as sales managers and important executive decision makers who might need to be reached at a moment's notice regardless of their location. Mobile telephony has proven to be a useful service, however, and now it is relatively common in the United States and extremely common among Europeans.*

Likewise, wireless data networks free software developers from the tethers of an Ethernet cable at a desk. Developers can work in the library, in a conference room, in the parking lot, or even in the coffee house across the street. As long as the wireless users remain within the range of the base station, they can take advantage of the network. Commonly available equipment can easily cover a corporate campus; with some work, more exotic equipment, and favorable terrain, you can extend the range of an 802.11 network up to a few miles.

Wireless networks typically have a great deal of *flexibility*, which can translate into rapid deployment. Wireless networks use a number of base stations to connect users to an existing network. The infrastructure side of a wireless network, however, is qualitatively the same whether you are connecting one user or a million users. To offer service in a given area, you need base stations and antennas in place. Once that infrastructure is built, however, adding a user to a wireless network is mostly a matter of authorization. With the infrastructure built, it must be configured to recognize and offer services to the new users, but authorization does not require more infrastructure. Adding a user to a wireless network is a matter of configuring the infrastructure, but it does not involve running cables, punching down terminals, and patching in a new jack.†

Flexibility is an important attribute for service providers. One of the markets that many 802.11 equipment vendors have been chasing is the so-called "hot spot" connectivity market. Airports and train stations are likely to have itinerant business travelers interested in network access during connection delays. Coffeehouses and other public gathering spots are social venues in which network access is desirable. Many cafes already offer Internet access; offering Internet access over a wireless network is a natural extension of the existing Internet connectivity. While it is possible to serve a fluid group of users with Ethernet jacks, supplying access over a wired network is problematic for several reasons. Running cables is time-consuming and expensive and may also require construction. Properly guessing the correct number of cable drops is more an art than a science. With a wireless network, though, there is no need to suffer through construction or make educated (or wild) guesses about demand. A simple wired infrastructure connects to the Internet, and then the wireless network can

---

* While most of my colleagues, acquaintances, and family in the U.S. have mobile telephones, it is still possible to be a holdout. In Europe, it seems as if everybody has a mobile phone—one cab driver in Finland I spoke with while writing this book took great pride in the fact that his family of four had six mobile telephones!

† This simple example ignores the challenges of scale. Naturally, if the new users will overload the existing infrastructure, the infrastructure itself will need to be beefed up. Infrastructure expansion can be expensive and time-consuming, especially if it involves legal and regulatory approval. However, my basic point holds: adding a user to a wireless network can often be reduced to a matter of configuration (moving or changing bits) while adding a user to a fixed network requires making physical connections (moving atoms), and moving bits is easier than moving atoms.

accommodate as many users as needed. Although wireless LANs have somewhat limited bandwidth, the limiting factor in networking a small hot spot is likely to be the cost of WAN bandwidth to the supporting infrastructure.

Flexibility may be particularly important in older buildings because it reduces the need for constructions. Once a building is declared historical, remodeling can be particularly difficult. In addition to meeting owner requirements, historical preservation agencies must be satisfied that new construction is not desecrating the past. Wireless networks can be deployed extremely rapidly in such environments because there is only a small wired network to install.

Flexibility has also led to the development of grassroots community networks. With the rapid price erosion of 802.11 equipment, bands of volunteers are setting up shared wireless networks open to visitors. Community networks are also extending the range of Internet access past the limitations for DSL into communities where high-speed Internet access has been only a dream. Community networks have been particularly successful in out-of-the way places that are too rugged for traditional wireline approaches.

Like all networks, wireless networks transmit data over a network medium. The medium is a form of electromagnetic radiation.* To be well-suited for use on mobile networks, the medium must be able to cover a wide area so clients can move throughout a coverage area. The two media that have seen the widest use in local-area applications are infrared light and radio waves. Most portable PCs sold now have infrared ports that can make quick connections to printers and other peripherals. However, infrared light has limitations; it is easily blocked by walls, partitions, and other office construction. Radio waves can penetrate most office obstructions and offer a wider coverage range. It is no surprise that most, if not all, 802.11 products on the market use the radio wave physical layer.

Radio Spectrum: The Key Resource

Wireless devices are constrained to operate in a certain frequency band. Each band has an associated *bandwidth*, which is simply the amount of frequency space in the band. Bandwidth has acquired a connotation of being a measure of the data capacity of a link. A great deal of mathematics, information theory, and signal processing can be used to show that higher-bandwidth slices can be used to transmit more information. As an example, an analog mobile telephony channel requires a 20-kHz bandwidth. TV signals are vastly more complex and have a correspondingly larger bandwidth of 6 MHz.

---

* Laser light is also used by some wireless networking applications, but the extreme focus of a laser beam makes it suited only for applications in which the ends are stationary. "Fixed wireless" applications, in which lasers replace other access technology such as leased telephone circuits, are a common application.

The use of a radio spectrum is rigorously controlled by regulatory authorities through *licensing* processes. In the U.S., regulation is done by the Federal Communications Commission (FCC). Many FCC rules are adopted by other countries throughout the Americas. European allocation is performed by CEPT's European Radiocommunications Office (ERO). Other allocation work is done by the International Telecommunications Union (ITU). To prevent overlapping uses of the radio waves, frequency is allocated in bands, which are simply ranges of frequencies available to specified applications. Table 1-1 lists some common frequency bands used in the U.S.

Table 1-1. Common U.S. frequency bands

Band	Frequency range
UHF ISM	902–928 MHz
S-Band	2–4 GHz
S-Band ISM	2.4–2.5 GHz
C-Band	4–8 GHz
C-Band satellite downlink	3.7–4.2 GHz
C-Band Radar (weather)	5.25–5.925 GHz
C-Band ISM	5.725–5.875 GHz
C-Band satellite uplink	5.925–6.425 GHz
X-Band	8–12 GHz
X-Band Radar (police/weather)	8.5–10.55 GHz
Ku-Band	12–18 GHz
Ku-Band Radar (police)	13.4–14 GHz
	15.7–17.7 GHz

The ISM bands

In Table 1-1, there are three bands labeled ISM, which is an abbreviation for industrial, scientific, and medical. ISM bands are set aside for equipment that, broadly speaking, is related to industrial or scientific processes or is used by medical equipment. Perhaps the most familiar ISM-band device is the microwave oven, which operates in the 2.4-GHz ISM band because electromagnetic radiation at that frequency is particularly effective for heating water.

I pay special attention to the ISM bands because that's where 802.11 devices operate. The more common 802.11b devices operate in S-band ISM. The ISM bands are generally license-free, provided that devices are low-power. How much sense does it make to require a license for microwave ovens, after all? Likewise, you don't need a license to set up and operate a wireless network.

The Limits of Wireless Networking

Wireless networks do not replace fixed networks. The main advantage of mobility is that the network user is moving. Servers and other data center equipment must access data, but the physical location of the server is irrelevant. As long as the servers do not move, they may as well be connected to wires that do not move.

The speed of wireless networks is constrained by the available bandwidth. Information theory can be used to deduce the upper limit on the speed of a network. Unless the regulatory authorities are willing to make the unlicensed spectrum bands bigger, there is an upper limit on the speed of wireless networks. Wireless-network hardware tends to be slower than wired hardware. Unlike the 10-GB Ethernet standard, wireless-network standards must carefully validate received frames to guard against loss due to the unreliability of the wireless medium.

Using radio waves as the network medium poses several challenges. Specifications for wired networks are designed so that a network will work as long as it respects the specifications. Radio waves can suffer from a number of propagation problems that may interrupt the radio link, such as multipath interference and shadows.

Security on any network is a prime concern. On wireless networks, it is often a critical concern because the network transmissions are available to anyone within range of the transmitter with the appropriate antenna. On a wired network, the signals stay in the wires and can be protected by strong physical-access control (locks on the doors of wiring closets, and so on). On a wireless network, sniffing is much easier because the radio transmissions are designed to be processed by any receiver within range. Furthermore, wireless networks tend to have fuzzy boundaries. A corporate wireless network may extend outside the building. It is quite possible that a parked car across the street could be receiving the signals from your network. As an experiment on one of my trips to San Francisco, I turned on my laptop to count the number of wireless networks near a major highway outside the city. I found eight without expending any significant effort. A significantly more motivated investigator would undoubtedly have discovered many more networks by using a much more sensitive antenna mounted outside the steel shell of the car.

A Network by Any Other Name...

Wireless networking is a hot industry segment. Several wireless technologies have been targeted primarily for data transmission. Bluetooth is a standard used to build small networks between peripherals: a form of "wireless wires," if you will. Most people in the industry are familiar with the hype surrounding Bluetooth. I haven't met many people who have used devices based on the Bluetooth specification.

Third-generation (3G) mobile telephony networks are also a familiar source of hype. They promise data rates of megabits per cell, as well as the "always on" connections that have proven to be quite valuable to DSL and cable modem customers. In spite of the hype and press from 3G equipment vendors, the rollout of commercial 3G services has been continually pushed back.

In contrast to Bluetooth and 3G, equipment based on the IEEE 802.11 standard has been an astounding success. While Bluetooth and 3G may be successful in the future, 802.11 is a success *now*. Apple initiated the pricing moves that caused the market for 802.11 equipment to explode in 1999. Price erosion made the equipment affordable and started the growth that continues today.

This is a book about 802.11 networks. 802.11 goes by a variety of names, depending on who is talking about it. Some people call 802.11 *wireless Ethernet*, to emphasize its shared lineage with the traditional wired Ethernet (802.3). More recently, the Wireless Ethernet Compatibility Alliance (WECA) has been pushing its *Wi-Fi* ("wireless fidelity") certification program.[*] Any 802.11 vendor can have its products tested for interoperability. Equipment that passes the test suite can use the Wi-Fi mark. For newer products based on the 802.11a standard, WECA will allow use of the *Wi-Fi5* mark. The "5" reflects the fact that 802.11a products use a different frequency band of around 5 GHz.

Table 1-2 is a basic comparison of the different 802.11 standards. Products based on 802.11 were initially released in 1997. 802.11 included an infrared (IR) layer that was never widely deployed, as well as two spread-spectrum radio layers: frequency hopping (FH) and direct sequence (DS). (The differences between these two radio layers is described in Chapter 10.) Initial 802.11 products were limited to 2 Mbps, which is quite slow by modern network standards. The IEEE 802.11 working group quickly began working on faster radio layers and standardized both 802.11a and 802.11b in 1999. Products based on 802.11b were released in 1999 and can operate at speeds of up to 11 Mbps. 802.11a uses a third radio technique called orthogonal frequency division multiplexing (OFDM). 802.11a operates in a different frequency band entirely and currently has regulatory approval only in the United States. As you can see from the table, 802.11 already provides speeds faster than 10BASE-T Ethernet and is reasonably competitive with Fast Ethernet.

Table 1-2. Comparison of 802.11 standards

IEEE standard	Speed	Frequency band	Notes
802.11	1 Mbps 2 Mbps	2.4 GHz	First standard (1997). Featured both frequency-hopping and direct-sequence modulation techniques.
802.11a	up to 54 Mbps	5 GHz	Second standard (1999), but products not released until late 2000.
802.11b	5.5 Mbps 11 Mbps	2.4 GHz	Third standard, but second wave of products. The most common 802.11 equipment as this book was written.
802.11g	up to 54 Mbps	2.4 GHz	Not yet standardized.

---

[*] More details on WECA and the Wi-Fi certification can be found at *http://www.wi-fi.org/*.

## CHAPTER 2

Overview of 802.11 Networks

Before studying the details of anything, it often helps to get a general "lay of the land." A basic introduction is often necessary when studying networking topics because the number of acronyms can be overwhelming. Unfortunately, 802.11 takes acronyms to new heights, which makes the introduction that much more important. To understand 802.11 on anything more than a superficial basis, you must get comfortable with some esoteric terminology and a herd of three-letter acronyms. This chapter is the glue that binds the entire book together. Read it for a basic understanding of 802.11, the concepts that will likely be important to users, and how the protocol is designed to provide an experience as much like Ethernet as possible. After that, move on to the low-level protocol details or deployment, depending on your interests and needs.

Part of the reason why this introduction is important is because it introduces the acronyms used throughout the book. With 802.11, the introduction serves another important purpose. 802.11 is superficially similar to Ethernet. Understanding the background of Ethernet helps slightly with 802.11, but there is a host of additional background needed to appreciate how 802.11 adapts traditional Ethernet technology to a wireless world. To account for the differences between wired networks and the wireless media used by 802.11, a number of additional management features were added. At the heart of 802.11 is a white lie about the meaning of media access control (MAC). Wireless network interface cards are assigned 48-bit MAC addresses, and, for all practical purposes, they look like Ethernet network interface cards. In fact, the MAC address assignment is done from the same address pool so that 802.11 cards have unique addresses even when deployed into a network with wired Ethernet stations.

To outside network devices, these MAC addresses appear to be fixed, just as in other IEEE 802 networks; 802.11 MAC addresses go into ARP tables alongside Ethernet addresses, use the same set of vendor prefixes, and are otherwise indistinguishable from Ethernet addresses. The devices that comprise an 802.11 network (access points and other 802.11 devices) know better. There are many differences between an 802.11 device and an Ethernet device, but the most obvious is that 802.11 devices are mobile; they can easily move from one part of the network to another. The 802.11 devices on your network understand this and deliver frames to the current location of the mobile station.

IEEE 802 Network Technology Family Tree

802.11 is a member of the IEEE 802 family, which is a series of specifications for local area network (LAN) technologies. Figure 2-1 shows the relationship between the various components of the 802 family and their place in the OSI model.

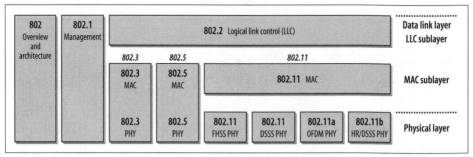

Figure 2-1. The IEEE 802 family and its relation to the OSI model

IEEE 802 specifications are focused on the two lowest layers of the OSI model because they incorporate both physical and data link components. All 802 networks have both a MAC and a Physical (PHY) component. The MAC is a set of rules to determine how to access the medium and send data, but the details of transmission and reception are left to the PHY.

Individual specifications in the 802 series are identified by a second number. For example, 802.3 is the specification for a Carrier Sense Multiple Access network with Collision Detection (CSMA/CD), which is related to (and often mistakenly called) Ethernet, and 802.5 is the Token Ring specification. Other specifications describe other parts of the 802 protocol stack. 802.2 specifies a common link layer, the Logical Link Control (LLC), which can be used by any lower-layer LAN technology. Management features for 802 networks are specified in 802.1. Among 802.1's many provisions are bridging (802.1d) and virtual LANs, or VLANs (802.1q).

802.11 is just another link layer that can use the 802.2/LLC encapsulation. The base 802.11 specification includes the 802.11 MAC and two physical layers: a frequency-hopping spread-spectrum (FHSS) physical layer and a direct-sequence spread-spectrum (DSSS) link layer. Later revisions to 802.11 added additional physical layers. 802.11b specifies a high-rate direct-sequence layer (HR/DSSS); products based on 802.11b hit the marketplace in 1999 and make up the bulk of the installed base. 802.11a describes a physical layer based on orthogonal frequency division multiplexing (OFDM); products based on 802.11a were released as this book was completed.

To say that 802.11 is "just another link layer for 802.2" is to omit the details in the rest of this book, but 802.11 is exciting precisely because of these details. 802.11 allows for mobile network access; in accomplishing this goal, a number of additional features were incorporated into the MAC. As a result, the 802.11 MAC may seem baroquely complex compared to other IEEE 802 MAC specifications.

The use of radio waves as a physical layer requires a relatively complex PHY, as well. 802.11 splits the PHY into two generic components: the Physical Layer Convergence Procedure (PLCP), to map the MAC frames onto the medium, and a Physical Medium Dependent (PMD) system to transmit those frames. The PLCP straddles the boundary of the MAC and physical layers, as shown in Figure 2-2. In 802.11, the PLCP adds a number of fields to the frame as it is transmitted "in the air."

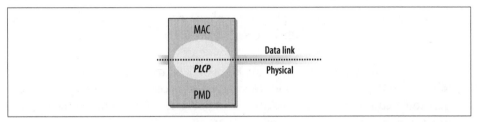

Figure 2-2. PHY components

All this complexity begs the question of how much you actually need to know. As with any technology, the more you know, the better off you will be. The 802.11 protocols have many knobs and dials that you can tweak, but most 802.11 implementations hide this complexity. Many of the features of the standard come into their own only when the network is congested, either with a lot of traffic or with a large number of wireless stations. Today's networks tend not to push the limits in either respect. At any rate, I can't blame you for wanting to skip the chapters about the protocols and jump ahead to the chapters about planning and installing an 802.11 network. After you've read this chapter, you can skip ahead to Chapters 12–17 and return to the chapters on the protocol's inner workings when you need (or want) to know more.

802.11 Nomenclature and Design

802.11 networks consist of four major physical components, which are summarized in Figure 2-3. The components are:

Distribution system

> When several access points are connected to form a large coverage area, they must communicate with each other to track the movements of mobile stations. The distribution system is the logical component of 802.11 used to forward frames to their destination. 802.11 does not specify any particular technology for

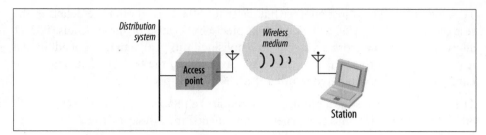

Figure 2-3. Components of 802.11 LANs

> the distribution system. In most commercial products, the distribution system is implemented as a combination of a bridging engine and a distribution system medium, which is the backbone network used to relay frames between access points; it is often called simply the backbone network. In nearly all commercially successful products, Ethernet is used as the backbone network technology.

Access points

> Frames on an 802.11 network must be converted to another type of frame for delivery to the rest of the world. Devices called access points perform the wireless-to-wired bridging function. (Access points perform a number of other functions, but bridging is by far the most important.)

Wireless medium

> To move frames from station to station, the standard uses a wireless medium. Several different physical layers are defined; the architecture allows multiple physical layers to be developed to support the 802.11 MAC. Initially, two radio frequency (RF) physical layers and one infrared physical layer were standardized, though the RF layers have proven far more popular.

Stations

> Networks are built to transfer data between stations. Stations are computing devices with wireless network interfaces. Typically, stations are battery-operated laptop or handheld computers. There is no reason why stations must be portable computing devices, though. In some environments, wireless networking is used to avoid pulling new cable, and desktops are connected by wireless LANs.

Types of Networks

The basic building block of an 802.11 network is the *basic service set* (BSS), which is simply a group of stations that communicate with each other. Communications take place within a somewhat fuzzy area, called the *basic service area*, defined by the propagation characteristics of the wireless medium.* When a station is in the basic

---

* All of the wireless media used will propagate in three dimensions. From that perspective, the service area should perhaps be called the service *volume*. However, the term area is widely used and accepted.

service area, it can communicate with the other members of the BSS. BSSs come in two flavors, both of which are illustrated in Figure 2-4.

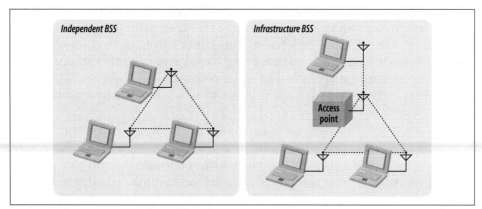

Figure 2-4. Independent and infrastructure BSSs

Independent networks

On the left is an *independent BSS* (IBSS). Stations in an IBSS communicate directly with each other and thus must be within direct communication range. The smallest possible 802.11 network is an IBSS with two stations. Typically, IBSSs are composed of a small number of stations set up for a specific purpose and for a short period of time. One common use is to create a short-lived network to support a single meeting in a conference room. As the meeting begins, the participants create an IBSS to share data. When the meeting ends, the IBSS is dissolved.* Due to their short duration, small size, and focused purpose, IBSSs are sometimes referred to as *ad hoc BSSs* or *ad hoc networks*.

Infrastructure networks

On the right side of Figure 2-4 is an *infrastructure BSS* (never called an IBSS). Infrastructure networks are distinguished by the use of an access point. Access points are used for all communications in infrastructure networks, including communication between mobile nodes in the same service area. If one mobile station in an infrastructure BSS needs to communicate with a second mobile station, the communication must take two hops. First, the originating mobile station transfers the frame to the access point. Second, the access point transfers the frame to the destination station. With all communications relayed through an access point, the basic service area corresponding to an infrastructure BSS is defined by the points in which transmissions from the access point can be received. Although the multihop transmission takes

---

* IBSSs have found a similar use at LAN parties throughout the world.

more transmission capacity than a directed frame from the sender to the receiver, it has two major advantages:

- An infrastructure BSS is defined by the distance from the access point. All mobile stations are required to be within reach of the access point, but no restriction is placed on the distance between mobile stations themselves. Allowing direct communication between mobile stations would save transmission capacity but at the cost of increased physical layer complexity because mobile stations would need to maintain neighbor relationships with all other mobile stations within the service area.

- Access points in infrastructure networks are in a position to assist with stations attempting to save power. Access points can note when a station enters a power-saving mode and buffer frames for it. Battery-operated stations can turn the wireless transceiver off and power it up only to transmit and retrieve buffered frames from the access point.

In an infrastructure network, stations must *associate* with an access point to obtain network services. Association is the process by which mobile station joins an 802.11 network; it is logically equivalent to plugging in the network cable on an Ethernet. It is not a symmetric process. Mobile stations always initiate the association process, and access points may choose to grant or deny access based on the contents of an association request. Associations are also exclusive on the part of the mobile station: a mobile station can be associated with only one access point.* The 802.11 standard places no limit on the number of mobile stations that an access point may serve. Implementation considerations may, of course, limit the number of mobile stations an access point may serve. In practice, however, the relatively low throughput of wireless networks is far more likely to limit the number of stations placed on a wireless network.

Extended service areas

BSSs can create coverage in small offices and homes, but they cannot provide network coverage to larger areas. 802.11 allows wireless networks of arbitrarily large size to be created by linking BSSs into an *extended service set* (ESS). An ESS is created by chaining BSSs together with a backbone network. 802.11 does not specify a particular backbone technology; it requires only that the backbone provide a specified set of services. In Figure 2-5, the ESS is the union of the four BSSs (provided that all the access points are configured to be part of the same ESS). In real-world deployments, the degree of overlap between the BSSs would probably be much greater than

---

* One reviewer noted that a similar restriction was present in traditional Ethernet networks until the development of VLANs and specifically asked how long this restriction was likely to last. I am not intimately involved with the standardization work, so I cannot speak to the issue directly. I do, however, agree that it is an interesting question.

the overlap in Figure 2-5. In real life, you would want to offer continuous coverage within the extended service area; you wouldn't want to require that users walk through the area covered by BSS3 when en route from BSS1 to BSS2.

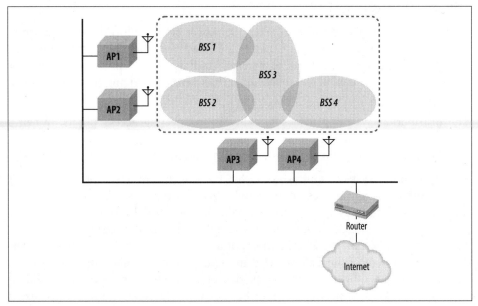

Figure 2-5. Extended service set

Stations within the same ESS may communicate with each other, even though these stations may be in different basic service areas and may even be moving between basic service areas. For stations in an ESS to communicate with each other, the wireless medium must act like a single layer 2 connection. Access points act as bridges, so direct communication between stations in an ESS requires that the backbone network also be a layer 2 connection. Any link-layer connection will suffice. Several access points in a single area may be connected to a single hub or switch, or they can use virtual LANs if the link-layer connection must span a large area.

 802.11 supplies link-layer mobility within an ESS but only if the backbone network is a single link-layer domain, such as a shared Ethernet or a VLAN. This important constraint on mobility is often a major factor in 802.11 network design.

Extended service areas are the highest-level abstraction supported by 802.11 networks. Access points in an ESS operate in concert to allow the outside world to use a single MAC address to talk to a station somewhere within the ESS. In Figure 2-5, the router uses a single MAC address to deliver frames to a mobile station; the access point with which that mobile station is associated delivers the frame. The router remains ignorant of the location of the mobile station and relies on the access points to deliver the frame.

The Distribution System, Revisited

With an understanding of how an extended service set is built, I'd like to return to the concept of the distribution system. 802.11 describes the distribution system in terms of the services it provides to wireless stations. While these services will be described in more detail later in this chapter, it is worth describing their operation at a high level.

The distribution system provides mobility by connecting access points. When a frame is given to the distribution system, it is delivered to the right access point and relayed by that access point to the intended destination.

The distribution system is responsible for tracking where a station is physically located and delivering frames appropriately. When a frame is sent to a mobile station, the distribution system is charged with the task of delivering it to the access point serving the mobile station. As an example, consider the router in Figure 2-5. The router simply uses the MAC address of a mobile station as its destination. The distribution system of the ESS pictured in Figure 2-5 must deliver the frame to the right access point. Obviously, part of the delivery mechanism is the backbone Ethernet, but the backbone network cannot be the entire distribution system because it has no way of choosing between access points. In the language of 802.11, the backbone Ethernet is the *distribution system medium*, but it is not the entire distribution system.

To find the rest of the distribution system, we need to look to the access points themselves. Most access points currently on the market operate as bridges. They have at least one wireless network interface and at least one Ethernet network interface. The Ethernet side can be connected to an existing network, and the wireless side becomes an extension of that network. Relaying frames between the two network media is controlled by a bridging engine.

Figure 2-6 illustrates the relationship between the access point, backbone network, and the distribution system. The access point has two interfaces connected by a bridging engine. Arrows indicate the potential paths to and from the bridging engine. Frames may be sent by the bridge to the wireless network; any frames sent by the bridge's wireless port are transmitted to all associated stations. Each associated station can transmit frames to the access point. Finally, the backbone port on the bridge can interact directly with the backbone network. The distribution system in Figure 2-6 is composed of the bridging engine plus the wired backbone network..

Every frame sent by a mobile station in an infrastructure network must use the distribution system. It is easy to understand why interaction with hosts on the backbone network must use the distribution system. After all, they are connected to the distribution

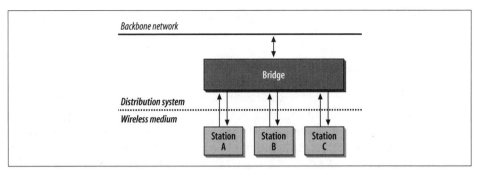

Figure 2-6. Distribution system in common 802.11 access point implementations

system medium. Wireless stations in an infrastructure network depend on the distribution system to communicate with each other because they are not directly connected to each other. The only way for station A to send a frame to station B is by relaying the frame through the bridging engine in the access point. However, the bridge is a component of the distribution system. While what exactly makes up the distribution system may seem like a narrow technical concern, there are some features of the 802.11 MAC that are closely tied to its interaction with the distribution system.

Inter-access point communication as part of the distribution system

Included with this distribution system is a method to manage associations. A wireless station is associated with only one access point at a time. If a station is associated with one access point, all the other access points in the ESS need to learn about that station. In Figure 2-5, AP4 must know about all the stations associated with AP1. If a wireless station associated with AP4 sends a frame to a station associated with AP1, the bridging engine inside AP4 must send the frame over the backbone Ethernet to AP1 so it can be delivered to its ultimate destination. To fully implement the distribution system, access points must inform other access points of associated stations. Naturally, many access points on the market use an *inter-access point protocol* (IAPP) over the backbone medium. There is, however, no standardized method for communicating association information to other members of an ESS. Proprietary technology is giving way to standardization, however. One of the major projects in the IEEE 802.11 working group is the standardization of the IAPP.

Wireless bridges and the distribution system

Up to this point, I have tacitly assumed that the distribution system was an existing fixed network. While this will often be the case, the 802.11 specification explicitly supports using the wireless medium itself as the distribution system. The wireless distribution system configuration is often called a "wireless bridge" configuration because it allows network engineers to connect two LANs at the link layer. Wireless bridges can be used to quickly connect distinct physical locations and are well-suited for use by access providers. Most 802.11 access points on the market now support the wireless bridge configuration, though it may be necessary to upgrade the firmware on older units.

Network Boundaries

Because of the nature of the wireless medium, 802.11 networks have fuzzy boundaries. In fact, some degree of fuzziness is desirable. As with mobile telephone networks, allowing basic service areas to overlap increases the probability of successful transitions between basic service areas and offers the highest level of network coverage. The basic service areas on the right of Figure 2-7 overlap significantly. This means that a station moving from BSS2 to BSS4 is not likely to lose coverage; it also means that AP3 (or, for that matter, AP4) can fail without compromising the network too badly. On the other hand, if AP2 fails, the network is cut into two disjoint parts, and stations in BSS1 lose connectivity when moving out of BSS1 and into BSS3 or BSS4.

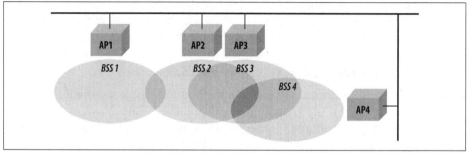

Figure 2-7. Overlapping BSSs in an ESS

Different types of 802.11 networks may also overlap. Independent BSSs may be created within the basic service area of an access point. Figure 2-8 illustrates spatial overlap. An access point appears at the top of the figure; its basic service area is shaded. Two stations are operating in infrastructure mode and communicate only with the access point. Three stations have been set up as an independent BSS and communicate with each other. Although the five stations are assigned to two different BSSs, they may share the same wireless medium. Stations may obtain access to the medium only by using the rules specified in the 802.11 MAC; these rules were carefully designed to enable multiple 802.11 networks to coexist in the same spatial area. Both BSSs must share the capacity of a single radio channel, so there may be adverse performance implications from co-located BSSs.

802.11 Network Operations

From the outset, 802.11 was designed to be just another link layer to higher-layer protocols. Network administrators familiar with Ethernet will be immediately comfortable

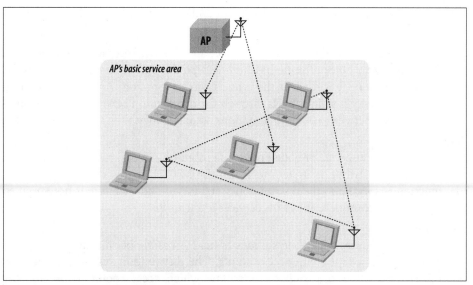

Figure 2-8. Overlapping network types

with 802.11. The shared heritage is deep enough that 802.11 is sometimes referred to as "wireless Ethernet."

The core elements present in Ethernet are present in 802.11. Stations are identified by 48-bit IEEE 802 MAC addresses. Conceptually, frames are delivered based on the MAC address. Frame delivery is unreliable, though 802.11 incorporates some basic reliability mechanisms to overcome the inherently poor qualities of the radio channels it uses.*

From a user's perspective, 802.11 might just as well be Ethernet. Network administrators, however, need to be conversant with 802.11 at a much deeper level. Providing MAC-layer mobility while following the path blazed by previous 802 standards requires a number of additional services and more complex framing.

Network Services

One way to define a network technology is to define the services it offers and allow equipment vendors to implement those services in whatever way they see fit. 802.11 provides nine services. Only three of the services are used for moving data; the remaining six are management operations that allow the network to keep track of the mobile nodes and deliver frames accordingly.

---

* I don't mean "poor" in an absolute sense. But the reliability of wireless transmission is really not comparable to the reliability of a wired network.

The services are described in the following list and summarized in Table 2-1:

Distribution

This service is used by mobile stations in an infrastructure network every time they send data. Once a frame has been accepted by an access point, it uses the distribution service to deliver the frame to its destination. Any communication that uses an access point travels through the distribution service, including communications between two mobile stations associated with the same access point.

Integration

Integration is a service provided by the distribution system; it allows the connection of the distribution system to a non-IEEE 802.11 network. The integration function is specific to the distribution system used and therefore is not specified by 802.11, except in terms of the services it must offer.

Association

Delivery of frames to mobile stations is made possible because mobile stations register, or associate, with access points. The distribution system can then use the registration information to determine which access point to use for any mobile station. Unassociated stations are not "on the network," much like workstations with unplugged Ethernet cables. 802.11 specifies the function that must be provided by the distribution system using the association data, but it does not mandate any particular implementation.

Reassociation

When a mobile station moves between basic service areas within a single extended service area, it must evaluate signal strength and perhaps switch the access point with which it is associated. Reassociations are initiated by mobile stations when signal conditions indicate that a different association would be beneficial; they are never initiated by the access point. After the reassociation is complete, the distribution system updates its location records to reflect the reachability of the mobile station through a different access point.

Disassociation

To terminate an existing association, stations may use the disassociation service. When stations invoke the disassociation service, any mobility data stored in the distribution system is removed. Once disassociation is complete, it is as if the station is no longer attached to the network. Disassociation is a polite task to do during the station shutdown process. The MAC is, however, designed to accommodate stations that leave the network without formally disassociating.

Authentication

Physical security is a major component of a wired LAN security solution. Network attachment points are limited, often to areas in offices behind perimeter access control devices. Network equipment can be secured in locked wiring closets, and data jacks in offices and cubicles can be connected to the network only when needed. Wireless networks cannot offer the same level of physical security, however, and therefore must depend on additional authentication routines to ensure that users accessing the network are authorized to do so. Authentication is a necessary prerequisite to association because only authenticated users are authorized to use the network. (In practice, though, many access points are configured for "open-system" authentication and will authenticate any station.)

Deauthentication

Deauthentication terminates an authenticated relationship. Because authentication is needed before network use is authorized, a side effect of deauthentication is termination of any current association.

Privacy

Strong physical controls can prevent a great number of attacks on the privacy of data in a wired LAN. Attackers must obtain physical access to the network medium before attempting to eavesdrop on traffic. On a wired network, physical access to the network cabling is a subset of physical access to other computing resources. By design, physical access to wireless networks is a comparatively simpler matter of using the correct antenna and modulation methods. To offer a similar level of privacy, 802.11 provides an optional privacy service called Wired Equivalent Privacy (WEP). WEP is not ironclad security—in fact, it has been proven recently that breaking WEP is easily within the capabilities of any laptop (for more information, see Chapter 5). Its purpose is to provide roughly equivalent privacy to a wired network by encrypting frames as they travel across the 802.11 air interface. Depending on your level of cynicism, you may or may not think that WEP achieves its goal; after all, it's not that hard to access the Ethernet cabling in a traditional network. In any case, do not assume that WEP provides more than minimal security. It prevents other users from casually appearing on your network, but that's about all.*

MSDU delivery

Networks are not much use without the ability to get the data to the recipient. Stations provide the MAC Service Data Unit (MSDU) delivery service, which is responsible for getting the data to the actual endpoint.

Table 2-1. Network services

Service	Station or distribution service?	Description
Distribution	Distribution	Service used in frame delivery to determine destination address in infrastructure networks
Integration	Distribution	Frame delivery to an IEEE 802 LAN outside the wireless network

---

* One of O'Reilly's offices had a strange situation in which apparent "interlopers" appeared on the network. They eventually discovered that their ESS overlapped a company in a neighboring office building, and "foreign" laptops were simply associating with the access point that had the strongest signal. WEP solves problems like this but will not withstand a deliberate attack on your network.

Table 2-1. Network services (continued)

Service	Station or distribution service?	Description
Association	Distribution	Used to establish the AP which serves as the gateway to a particular mobile station
Reassociation	Distribution	Used to change the AP which serves as the gateway to a particular mobile station
Disassociation	Distribution	Removes the wireless station from the network
Authentication	Station	Establishes identity prior to establishing association
Deauthentication	Station	Used to terminate authentication, and by extension, association
Privacy	Station	Provides protection against eavesdropping
MSDU delivery	Station	Delivers data to the recipient

Station services

Station services are part of every 802.11-compliant station and must be incorporated by any product claiming 802.11 compliance. Station services are provided by both mobile stations and the wireless interface on access points. Stations provide frame delivery services to allow message delivery, and, in support of this task, they may need to use the authentication services to establish associations. Stations may also wish to take advantage of privacy functions to protect messages as they traverse the vulnerable wireless link.

Distribution system services

Distribution system services connect access points to the distribution system. The major role of access points is to extend the services on the wired network to the wireless network; this is done by providing the distribution and integration services to the wireless side. Managing mobile station associations is the other major role of the distribution system. To maintain association data and station location information, the distribution system provides the association, reassociation, and disassociation services.

Mobility Support

Mobility is the major motivation for deploying an 802.11 network. Stations can move while connected to the network and transmit frames while in motion. Mobility can cause one of three types of transition:

No transition

When stations do not move out of their current access point's service area, no transition is necessary. This state occurs because the station is not moving or it is moving within the basic service area of its current access point.* (Arguably, this isn't a transition so much as the absence of a transition, but it is defined in the specification.)

BSS transition

Stations continuously monitor the signal strength and quality from all access points administratively assigned to cover an extended service area. Within an extended service area, 802.11 provides MAC layer mobility. Stations attached to the distribution system can send out frames addressed to the MAC address of a mobile station and let the access points handle the final hop to the mobile station. Distribution system stations do not need to be aware of a mobile station's location as long as it is within the same extended service area.

Figure 2-9 illustrates a BSS transition. The three access points in the picture are all assigned to the same ESS. At the outset, denoted by *t=1*, the laptop with an 802.11 network card is sitting within AP1's basic service area and is associated with AP1. When the laptop moves out of AP1's basic service area and into AP2's at *t=2*, a BSS transition occurs. The mobile station uses the reassociation service to associate with AP2, which then starts sending frames to the mobile station.

BSS transitions require the cooperation of access points. In this scenario, AP2 needs to inform AP1 that the mobile station is now associated with AP2. 802.11 does not specify the details of the communications between access points during BSS transitions. A standardized IAPP is a likely result of future work within the 802.11 working group.

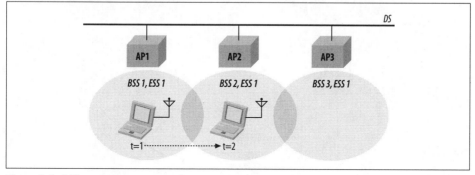

Figure 2-9. BSS transition

---

* Although my explanation makes it sound as if the "no motion" and "local motion" substates are easily distinguishable, they are not. The underlying physics of RF propagation can make it impossible to tell whether a station is moving because the signal strength can vary with the placement of objects in the room, which, of course, includes the people who may be walking around.

Because inter-access point communications are not standardized, mobility between access points supplied by different vendors is not guaranteed.

ESS transition

An ESS transition refers to the movement from one ESS to a second distinct ESS. 802.11 does not support this type of transition, except to allow the station to associate with an access point in the second ESS once it leaves the first. Higher-layer connections are almost guaranteed to be interrupted. It would be fair to say that 802.11 supports ESS transitions only to the extent that it is relatively easy to attempt associating with an access point in the new extended service area. Maintaining higher-level connections requires support from the protocol suites in question. In the case of TCP/IP, Mobile IP is required to seamlessly support an ESS transition.

Figure 2-10 illustrates an ESS transition. Four basic service areas are organized into two extended service areas. Seamless transitions from the lefthand ESS to the righthand ESS are not supported. ESS transitions are supported only because the mobile station will quickly associate with an access point in the second ESS. Any active network connections are likely to be dropped when the mobile station leaves the first ESS.

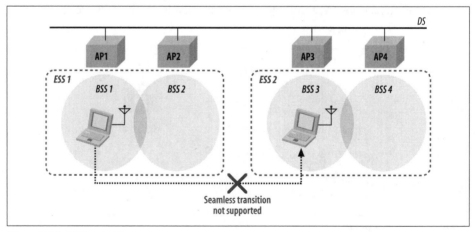

Figure 2-10. ESS transition

## CHAPTER 3

The 802.11 MAC

This chapter begins our exploration of the 802.11 standard in depth. Chapter 2 provided a high-level overview of the standard and discussed some of its fundamental attributes. You are now at a fork in the book. Straight ahead lies a great deal of information on the 802.11 specifications. It is possible, however, to build a wired network without a thorough and detailed understanding of the protocols, and the same is true for wireless networks. However, there are a number of situations in which you may need a deeper knowledge of the machinery under the hood:

- Although 802.11 has been widely and rapidly adopted, security issues have continued to grab headlines. Network managers will undoubtedly be asked to comment on security issues, especially in any wireless LAN proposals. To understand and participate in these discussions, read Chapter 5. As I write this, WEP has been fully broken and the IEEE is forging a successor to it based on 802.1x.* Though the final form of the new and improved security framework has not yet become apparent, it will almost surely be based on 802.1x, which is described in Chapter 6.

- Troubleshooting wireless networks is similar to troubleshooting wired networks but can be much more complex. As always, a trusty packet sniffer can be an invaluable aid. To take full advantage of a packet sniffer, though, you need to understand what the packets mean to interpret your network's behavior.

- Tuning a wireless network is tied intimately to a number of parameters in the specification. To understand the behavior of your network and what effect the optimizations will have requires a knowledge of what those parameters really do.

- Device drivers may expose low-level knobs and dials for you to play with. Most drivers provide good defaults for all of the parameters, but some give you freedom to experiment. Open source software users have the source code and are free to experiment with any and all settings.

---

* And as we go to press, 802.1x has reportedly been broken.

- A number of interesting features of the standard have not been implemented by the current products, but they may be implemented later. As these features are rolled out, you may need to know what they are and how to use them.

As with many other things in life, the more you know, the better off you are. Ethernet is usually trouble-free, but serious network administrators have long known that when you do run into trouble, there is no substitute for thorough knowledge of how the network is working. To some extent, 802.11 networks have had a "free ride" the past few years. Because they were cool, users were forgiving when they failed; wireless connectivity was a privilege, not a right. And since there were relatively few networks and relatively few users on those networks, the networks were rarely subjected to severe stresses. An Ethernet that has only a half dozen nodes is not likely to be a source of problems; problems occur when you add a few high-capacity servers, a few hundred users, and the associated bridges and routers to glue everything together. There is no reason to believe that wireless will be any different. A couple of access points serving a half dozen users will not reveal any problems. But when the user community grows to a few dozen, and you have several overlapping wireless networks, each with its own set of access points, you can expect to see the effects of stress.

That is why you should read this chapter. Now on to the details.

The key to the 802.11 specification is the MAC. It rides on every physical layer and controls the transmission of user data into the air. It provides the core framing operations and the interaction with a wired network backbone. Different physical layers may provide different transmission speeds, all of which are supposed to interoperate.

802.11 does not depart from the previous IEEE 802 standards in any radical way. The standard successfully adapts Ethernet-style networking to radio links. Like Ethernet, 802.11 uses a carrier sense multiple access (CSMA) scheme to control access to the transmission medium. However, collisions waste valuable transmission capacity, so rather than the collision detection (CSMA/CD) employed by Ethernet, 802.11 uses collision avoidance (CSMA/CA). Also like Ethernet, 802.11 uses a distributed access scheme with no centralized controller. Each 802.11 station uses the same method to gain access to the medium. The major differences between 802.11 and Ethernet stem from the differences in the underlying medium.

This chapter provides some insight into the motivations of the MAC designers by describing some challenges they needed to overcome and describes the rules used for access to the medium, as well as the basic frame structure. If you simply want to understand the basic frame sequences that you will see on an 802.11 network, skip ahead to the end of this chapter. For further information on the MAC, consult its formal specification in Clause 9 of the 802.11 standard; detailed MAC state diagrams are in Annex C.

Challenges for the MAC

Differences between the wireless network environment and the traditional wired environment create challenges for network protocol designers. This section examines a number of the hurdles that the 802.11 designers faced.

RF Link Quality

On a wired Ethernet, it is reasonable to transmit a frame and assume that the destination receives it correctly. Radio links are different, especially when the frequencies used are unlicensed ISM bands. Even narrowband transmissions are subject to noise and interference, but unlicensed devices must assume that interference will exist and work around it. The designers of 802.11 considered ways to work around the radiation from microwave ovens and other RF sources. In addition to the noise, multipath fading may also lead to situations in which frames cannot be transmitted because a node moves into a dead spot.

Unlike many other link layer protocols, 802.11 incorporates positive acknowledgments. All transmitted frames must be acknowledged, as shown in Figure 3-1. If any part of the transfer fails, the frame is considered lost.

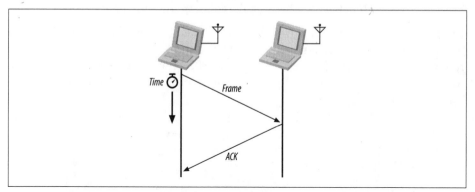

Figure 3-1. Positive acknowledgment of data transmissions

The sequence in Figure 3-1 is an *atomic* operation. 802.11 allows stations to lock out contention during atomic operations so that atomic sequences are not interrupted by other stations attempting to use the transmission medium.

The Hidden Node Problem

In Ethernet networks, stations depend on the reception of transmissions to perform the carrier sensing functions of CSMA/CD. Wires in the physical medium contain the signals and distribute them to network nodes. Wireless networks have fuzzier boundaries, sometimes to the point where each node may not be able to communicate with every other node in the wireless network, as in Figure 3-2.

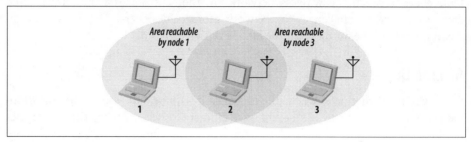

Figure 3-2. Nodes 1 and 3 are "hidden"

In the figure, node 2 can communicate with both nodes 1 and 3, but something prevents nodes 1 and 3 from communicating directly. (The obstacle itself is not relevant; it could be as simple as nodes 1 and 3 being as far away from 2 as possible, so the radio waves cannot reach the full distance from 1 to 3.) From the perspective of node 1, node 3 is a "hidden" node. If a simple transmit-and-pray protocol was used, it would be easy for node 1 and node 3 to transmit simultaneously, thus rendering node 2 unable to make sense of anything. Furthermore, nodes 1 and 3 would not have any indication of the error because the collision was local to node 2.

Collisions resulting from hidden nodes may be hard to detect in wireless networks because wireless transceivers are generally half-duplex; they don't transmit and receive at the same time. To prevent collisions, 802.11 allows stations to use Request to Send (RTS) and Clear to Send (CTS) signals to clear out an area. Figure 3-3 illustrates the procedure.

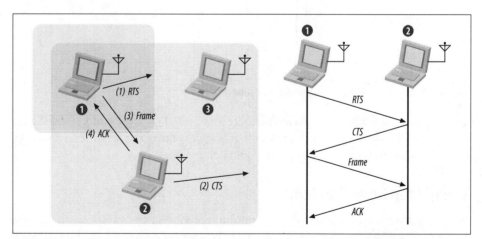

Figure 3-3. RTS/CTS clearing

In Figure 3-3, node 1 has a frame to send; it initiates the process by sending an RTS frame. The RTS frame serves several purposes: in addition to reserving the radio link for transmission, it silences any stations that hear it. If the target station receives an RTS, it responds with a CTS. Like the RTS frame, the CTS frame silences stations in the immediate vicinity. Once the RTS/CTS exchange is complete, node 1 can transmit its frames without worry of interference from any hidden nodes. Hidden nodes beyond the range of the sending station are silenced by the CTS from the receiver. When the RTS/CTS clearing procedure is used, any frames must be positively acknowledged.

The multiframe RTS/CTS transmission procedure consumes a fair amount of capacity, especially because of the additional latency incurred before transmission can commence. As a result, it is used only in high-capacity environments and environments with significant contention on transmission. For lower-capacity environments, it is not necessary.

You can control the RTS/CTS procedure by setting the *RTS threshold* if the device driver for your 802.11 card allows you to adjust it. The RTS/CTS exchange is performed for frames larger than the threshold. Frames shorter than the threshold are simply sent.

MAC Access Modes and Timing

Access to the wireless medium is controlled by coordination functions. Ethernet-like CSMA/CA access is provided by the distributed coordination function (DCF). If contention-free service is required, it can be provided by the point coordination function (PCF), which is built on top of the DCF. Contention-free services are provided only in infrastructure networks. The coordination functions are described in the following list and illustrated in Figure 3-4:

DCF

The DCF is the basis of the standard CSMA/CA access mechanism. Like Ethernet, it first checks to see that the radio link is clear before transmitting. To avoid collisions, stations use a random backoff after each frame, with the first transmitter seizing the channel. In some circumstances, the DCF may use the CTS/RTS clearing technique to further reduce the possibility of collisions.

PCF

Point coordination provides contention-free services. Special stations called *point coordinators* are used to ensure that the medium is provided without contention. Point coordinators reside in access points, so the PCF is restricted to infrastructure networks. To gain priority over standard contention-based services, the PCF allows stations to transmit frames after a shorter interval. The PCF is not widely implemented and is described in Chapter 8.

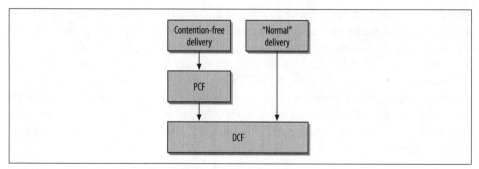

Figure 3-4. MAC coordination functions

Carrier-Sensing Functions and the Network Allocation Vector

Carrier sensing is used to determine if the medium is available. Two types of carrier-sensing functions in 802.11 manage this process: the physical carrier-sensing and virtual carrier-sensing functions. If either carrier-sensing function indicates that the medium is busy, the MAC reports this to higher layers.

Physical carrier-sensing functions are provided by the physical layer in question and depend on the medium and modulation used. It is difficult (or, more to the point, expensive) to build physical carrier-sensing hardware for RF-based media, because transceivers can transmit and receive simultaneously only if they incorporate expensive electronics. Furthermore, with hidden nodes potentially lurking everywhere, physical carrier-sensing cannot provide all the necessary information.

Virtual carrier-sensing is provided by the Network Allocation Vector (NAV). Most 802.11 frames carry a duration field, which can be used to reserve the medium for a fixed time period. The NAV is a timer that indicates the amount of time the medium will be reserved. Stations set the NAV to the time for which they expect to use the medium, including any frames necessary to complete the current operation. Other stations count down from the NAV to 0. When the NAV is nonzero, the virtual carrier-sensing function indicates that the medium is busy; when the NAV reaches 0, the virtual carrier-sensing function indicates that the medium is idle.

By using the NAV, stations can ensure that atomic operations are not interrupted. For example, the RTS/CTS sequence in Figure 3-3 is atomic. Figure 3-5 shows how the NAV protects the sequence from interruption. (This is a standard format for a number of diagrams in this book that illustrate the interaction of multiple stations with the corresponding timers.) Activity on the medium by stations is represented by the shaded bars, and each bar is labeled with the frame type. Interframe spacing is depicted by the lack of any activity. Finally, the NAV timer is represented by the bars on the NAV line at the bottom of the figure. The NAV is carried in the frame headers on the RTS and CTS frames; it is depicted on its own line to show how the NAV relates to actual transmissions in the air. When a NAV bar is present on the NAV line, stations should defer access to the medium because the virtual carrier-sensing mechanism will indicate a busy medium.

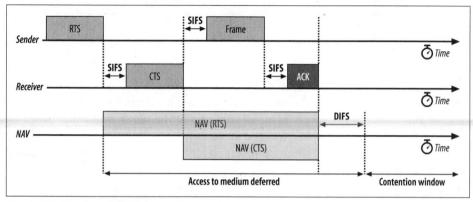

Figure 3-5. Using the NAV for virtual carrier sensing

To ensure that the sequence is not interrupted, node 1 sets the NAV in its RTS to block access to the medium while the RTS is being transmitted. All stations that hear the RTS defer access to the medium until the NAV elapses.

RTS frames are not necessarily heard by every station in the network. Therefore, the recipient of the intended transmission responds with a CTS that includes a shorter NAV. This NAV prevents other stations from accessing the medium until the transmission completes. After the sequence completes, the medium can be used by any station after distributed interframe space (DIFS), which is depicted by the contention window beginning at the right side of the figure.

RTS/CTS exchanges may be useful in crowded areas with multiple overlapping networks. Every station on the same physical channel receives the NAV and defers access appropriately, even if the stations are configured to be on different networks.

Interframe Spacing

As with traditional Ethernet, the interframe spacing plays a large role in coordinating access to the transmission medium. 802.11 uses four different interframe spaces. Three are used to determine medium access; the relationship between them is shown in Figure 3-6.

We've already seen that as part of the collision avoidance built into the 802.11 MAC, stations delay transmission until the medium becomes idle. Varying interframe spacings create different priority levels for different types of traffic. The logic behind this is simple: high-priority traffic doesn't have to wait as long after the medium has become idle. Therefore, if there is any high-priority traffic waiting, it grabs the network before low-priority frames have a chance to try. To assist with interoperability

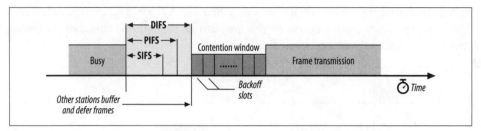

Figure 3-6. Interframe spacing relationships

between different data rates, the interframe space is a fixed amount of time, independent of the transmission speed. (This is only one of the many problems caused by having different physical layers use the same radio resources, which are different modulation techniques.) Different physical layers, however, can specify different interframe space times.

Short interframe space (SIFS)

> The SIFS is used for the highest-priority transmissions, such as RTS/CTS frames and positive acknowledgments. High-priority transmissions can begin once the SIFS has elapsed. Once these high-priority transmissions begin, the medium becomes busy, so frames transmitted after the SIFS has elapsed have priority over frames that can be transmitted only after longer intervals.

PCF interframe space (PIFS)

> The PIFS, sometimes erroneously called the priority interframe space, is used by the PCF during contention-free operation. Stations with data to transmit in the contention-free period can transmit after the PIFS has elapsed and preempt any contention-based traffic.

DCF interframe space (DIFS)

> The DIFS is the minimum medium idle time for contention-based services. Stations may have immediate access to the medium if it has been free for a period longer than the DIFS.

Extended interframe space (EIFS)

> The EIFS is not illustrated in Figure 3-6 because it is not a fixed interval. It is used only when there is an error in frame transmission.

Interframe spacing and priority

Atomic operations start like regular transmissions: they must wait for the DIFS before they can begin. However, the second and any subsequent steps in an atomic operation take place using the SIFS, rather than during the DIFS. This means that the second (and subsequent) parts of an atomic operation will grab the medium before another type of frame can be transmitted. By using the SIFS and the NAV, stations can seize the medium for as long as necessary.

In Figure 3-5, for example, the short interframe space is used between the different units of the atomic exchange. After the sender gains access to the medium, the receiver replies with a CTS after the SIFS. Any stations that might attempt to access the medium at the conclusion of the RTS would wait for one DIFS interval. Partway through the DIFS interval, though, the SIFS interval elapses, and the CTS is transmitted.

Contention-Based Access Using the DCF

Most traffic uses the DCF, which provides a standard Ethernet-like contention-based service. The DCF allows multiple independent stations to interact without central control, and thus may be used in either IBSS networks or in infrastructure networks.

Before attempting to transmit, each station checks whether the medium is idle. If the medium is not idle, stations defer to each other and employ an orderly exponential backoff algorithm to avoid collisions.

In distilling the 802.11 MAC rules, there is a basic set of rules that are always used, and additional rules may be applied depending on the circumstances. Two basic rules apply to all transmissions using the DCF:

1. If the medium has been idle for longer than the DIFS, transmission can begin immediately. Carrier sensing is performed using both a physical medium-dependent method and the virtual (NAV) method.

   a. If the previous frame was received without errors, the medium must be free for at least the DIFS.

   b. If the previous transmission contained errors, the medium must be free for the amount of the EIFS.

2. If the medium is busy, the station must wait for the channel to become idle. 802.11 refers to the wait as *access deferral*. If access is deferred, the station waits for the medium to become idle for the DIFS and prepares for the exponential backoff procedure.

Additional rules may apply in certain situations. Many of these rules depend on the particular situation "on the wire" and are specific to the results of previous transmissions.

1. Error recovery is the responsibility of the station sending a frame. Senders expect acknowledgments for each transmitted frame and are responsible for retrying the transmission until it is successful.

   a. Positive acknowledgments are the only indication of success. Atomic exchanges must complete in their entirety to be successful. If an acknowledgment is expected and does not arrive, the sender considers the transmission lost and must retry.

   b. All unicast data must be acknowledged.

c. Any failure increments a retry counter, and the transmission is retried. A failure can be due to a failure to gain access to the medium or a lack of an acknowledgment. However, there is a longer congestion window when transmissions are retried (see next section).

2. Multiframe sequences may update the NAV with each step in the transmission procedure. When a station receives a medium reservation that is longer than the current NAV, it updates the NAV. Setting the NAV is done on a frame-by-frame basis and is discussed in much more detail in the next chapter.

3. The following types of frames can be transmitted after the SIFS and thus receive maximum priority: acknowledgments, the CTS in an RTS/CTS exchange sequence, and fragments in fragment sequences.

    a. Once a station has transmitted the first frame in a sequence, it has gained control of the channel. Any additional frames and their acknowledgments can be sent using the short interframe space, which locks out any other stations.

    b. Additional frames in the sequence update the NAV for the expected additional time the medium will be used.

4. Extended frame sequences are required for higher-level packets that are larger than configured thresholds.

    a. Packets larger than the RTS threshold must have RTS/CTS exchange.

    b. Packets larger than the fragmentation threshold must be fragmented.

Error Recovery with the DCF

Error detection and correction is up to the station that begins an atomic frame exchange. When an error is detected, the station with data must resend the frame. Errors must be detected by the sending station. In some cases, the sender can infer frame loss by the lack of a positive acknowledgment from the receiver. Retry counters are incremented when frames are retransmitted.

Each frame or fragment has a single retry counter associated with it. Stations have two retry counters: the *short retry count* and the *long retry count*. Frames that are shorter than the RTS threshold are considered to be short; frames longer than the threshold are long. Depending on the length of the frame, it is associated with either a short or long retry counter. Frame retry counts begin at 0 and are incremented when a frame transmission fails.

The short retry count is reset to 0 when:

- A CTS frame is received in response to a transmitted RTS
- A MAC-layer acknowledgment is received after a nonfragmented transmission
- A broadcast or multicast frame is received

The long retry count is reset to 0 when:

- A MAC-layer acknowledgment is received for a frame longer than the RTS threshold
- A broadcast or multicast frame is received

In addition to the associated retry count, fragments are given a maximum "lifetime" by the MAC. When the first fragment is transmitted, the lifetime counter is started. When the lifetime limit is reached, the frame is discarded and no attempt is made to transmit any remaining fragments.

Using the retry counters

Like most other network protocols, 802.11 provides reliability through retransmission. Data transmission happens within the confines of an atomic sequence, and the entire sequence must complete for a transmission to be successful. When a station transmits a frame, it must receive an acknowledgment from the receiver or it will consider the transmission to have failed. Failed transmissions increment the retry counter associated with the frame (or fragment). If the retry limit is reached, the frame is discarded, and its loss is reported to higher-layer protocols.

One of the reasons for having short frames and long frames is to allow network administrators to customize the robustness of the network for different frame lengths. Large frames require more buffer space, so one potential application of having two separate retry limits is to decrease the long retry limit to decrease the amount of buffer space required.

Backoff with the DCF

After frame transmission has completed and the DIFS has elapsed, stations may attempt to transmit congestion-based data. A period called the *contention window* or *backoff window* follows the DIFS. This window is divided into slots. Slot length is medium-dependent; higher-speed physical layers use shorter slot times. Stations pick a random slot and wait for that slot before attempting to access the medium; all slots are equally likely selections. When several stations are attempting to transmit, the station that picks the first slot (the station with the lowest random number) wins.

As in Ethernet, the backoff time is selected from a larger range each time a transmission fails. Figure 3-7 illustrates the growth of the contention window as the number of transmissions increases, using the numbers from the direct-sequence spread-spectrum (DSSS) physical layer. Other physical layers use different sizes, but the principle is identical. Contention window sizes are always 1 less than a power of 2 (e.g., 31, 63, 127, 255). Each time the retry counter increases, the contention window moves to the next greatest power of two. The size of the contention window is limited by the physical layer. For example, the DS physical layer limits the contention window to 1023 transmission slots.

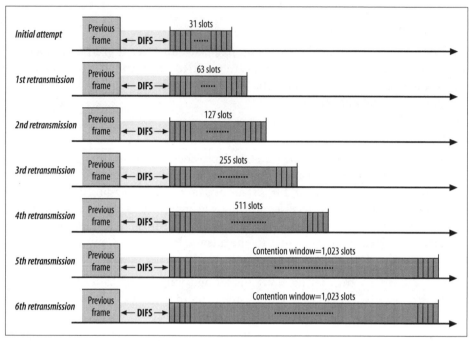

Figure 3-7. DSSS contention window size

When the contention window reaches its maximum size, it remains there until it can be reset. Allowing long contention windows when several competing stations are attempting to gain access to the medium keeps the MAC algorithms stable even under maximum load. The contention window is reset to its minimum size when frames are transmitted successfully, or the associated retry counter is reached, and the frame is discarded.

Fragmentation and Reassembly

Higher-level packets and some large management frames may need to be broken into smaller pieces to fit through the wireless channel. Fragmentation may also help improve reliability in the presence of interference. The primary sources of interference with 802.11 LANs are microwave ovens, with which they share the 2.4-GHz ISM band. Electromagnetic radiation is generated by the magnetron tube during its ramp-up and ramp-down, so microwaves emit interference half the time.*

---

* In the US, appliances are powered by 60-Hz alternating current, so microwaves interfere for about 8 milliseconds (ms) out of every 16-ms cycle. Much of the rest of the world uses 50-Hz current, and interference takes place for 10 ms out of the 20-ms cycle.

Wireless LAN stations may attempt to fragment transmissions so that interference affects only small fragments, not large frames. By immediately reducing the amount of data that can be corrupted by interference, fragmentation may result in a higher effective throughput.

Fragmentation takes place when a higher-level packet's length exceeds the fragmentation threshold configured by the network administrator. Fragments all have the same frame sequence number but have ascending fragment numbers to aid in reassembly. Frame control information also indicates whether more fragments are coming. All of the fragments that comprise a frame are normally sent in a *fragmentation burst*, which is shown in Figure 3-8. This figure also incorporates an RTS/CTS exchange, because it is common for the fragmentation and RTS/CTS thresholds to be set to the same value. The figure also shows how the NAV and SIFS are used in combination to control access to the medium.

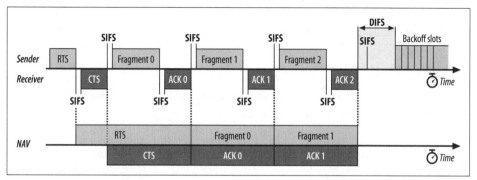

Figure 3-8. Fragmentation burst

Fragments and their acknowledgments are separated by the SIFS, so a station retains control of the channel during a fragmentation burst. The NAV is also used to ensure that other stations don't use the channel during the fragmentation burst. As with any RTS/CTS exchange, the RTS and CTS both set the NAV from the expected time to the end of the first fragments in the air. Subsequent fragments then form a chain. Each fragment sets the NAV to hold the medium until the end of the acknowledgment for the next frame. Fragment 0 sets the NAV to hold the medium until ACK 1, fragment 1 sets the NAV to hold the medium until ACK 2, and so on. After the last fragment and its acknowledgment have been sent, the NAV is set to 0, indicating that the medium will be released after the fragmentation burst completes.

Frame Format

To meet the challenges posed by a wireless data link, the MAC was forced to adopt several unique features, not the least of which was the use of four address fields. Not all frames use all the address fields, and the values assigned to the address fields may change depending on the type of MAC frame being transmitted. Details on the use of address fields in different frame types are presented in Chapter 4.

Figure 3-9 shows the generic 802.11 MAC frame. All diagrams in this section follow the IEEE conventions in 802.11. Fields are transmitted from left to right, and the most significant bits appear last.

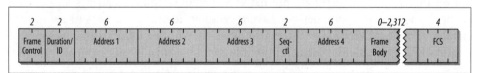

Figure 3-9. Generic 802.11 MAC frame

802.11 MAC frames do not include some of the classic Ethernet frame features, most notably the type/length field and the preamble. The preamble is part of the physical layer, and encapsulation details such as type and length are present in the header on the data carried in the 802.11 frame.

Frame Control

Each frame starts with a two-byte Frame Control subfield, shown in Figure 3-10. The components of the Frame Control subfield are:

Protocol version
    Two bits indicate which version of the 802.11 MAC is contained in the rest of the frame. At present, only one version of the 802.11 MAC has been developed; it is assigned the protocol number 0. Other values will appear when the IEEE standardizes changes to the MAC that render it incompatible with the initial specification.

Type and subtype fields
    Type and subtype fields identify the type of frame used. To cope with noise and unreliability, a number of management functions are incorporated into the 802.11 MAC. Some, such as the RTS/CTS operations and the acknowledgments, have already been discussed. Table 3-1 shows how the type and subtype identifiers are used to create the different classes of frames.

    In Table 3-1, bit strings are written most-significant bit first, which is the reverse of the order used in Figure 3-10. Therefore, the frame type is the third bit in the frame control field followed by the second bit (b3 b2), and the subtype is the seventh bit, followed by the sixth, fifth, and fourth bits (b7 b6 b5 b4).

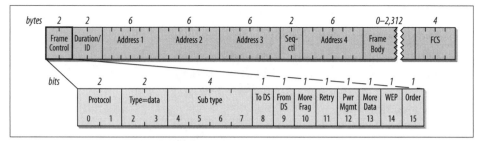

Figure 3-10. Frame control field

Table 3-1. Type and subtype identifiers

Subtype value	Subtype name
Management frames (type=00)[a]	
0000	Association request
0001	Association response
0010	Reassociation request
0011	Reassociation response
0100	Probe request
0101	Probe response
1000	Beacon
1001	Announcement traffic indication message (ATIM)
1010	Disassociation
1011	Authentication
1100	Deauthentication
Control frames (type=01)[b]	
1010	Power Save (PS)-Poll
1011	RTS
1100	CTS
1101	Acknowledgment (ACK)
1110	Contention-Free (CF)-End
1111	CF-End+CF-Ack
Data frames (type=10)[c]	
0000	Data
0001	Data+CF-Ack
0010	Data+CF-Poll
0011	Data+CF-Ack+CF-Poll
0100	Null data (no data transmitted)

Table 3-1. Type and subtype identifiers (continued)

Subtype value	Subtype name
0101	CF-Ack (no data transmitted)
0110	CF-Poll (no data transmitted)
0111	Data+CF-Ack+CF-Poll
(Frame type 11 is reserved)	

[a]Management subtypes 0110–0111 and 1101–1111 are reserved and not currently used.
[b]Control subtypes 0000–1001 are reserved and not currently used.
[c]Data subtypes 1000–1111 are reserved and not currently used.

ToDS and FromDS bits

These bits indicate whether a frame is destined for the distribution system. All frames on infrastructure networks will have one of the distribution system's bits set. Table 3-2 shows how these bits are interpreted. As Chapter 4 will explain, the interpretation of the address fields depends on the setting of these bits.

Table 3-2. Interpreting the ToDS and FromDS bits

	To DS=0	To DS=1
From DS=0	All management and control frames Data frames within an IBSS (never infrastructure data frames)	Data frames transmitted from a wireless station in an infrastructure network
From DS=1	Data frames received for a wireless station in an infrastructure network	Data frames on a "wireless bridge"

More fragments bit

This bit functions much like the "more fragments" bit in IP. When a higher-level packet has been fragmented by the MAC, the initial fragment and any following nonfinal fragments set this bit to 1. Some management frames may be large enough to require fragmentation; all other frames set this bit to 0.

Retry bit

From time to time, frames may be retransmitted. Any retransmitted frames set this bit to 1 to aid the receiving station in eliminating duplicate frames.

Power management bit

Network adapters built on 802.11 are often built to the PC Card form factor and used in battery-powered laptop or handheld computers. To conserve battery life, many small devices have the ability to power down parts of the network interface. This bit indicates whether the sender will be in a power-saving mode after the completion of the current atomic frame exchange. One indicates that the station will be in power-save mode, and 0 indicates that the station will be active. Access points perform a number of important management functions and are not allowed to save power, so this bit is always 0 in frames transmitted by an access point.

More data bit

To accommodate stations in a power-saving mode, access points may buffer frames received from the distribution system. An access point sets this bit to indicate that at least one frame is available and is addressed to a dozing station.

WEP bit

Wireless transmissions are inherently easier to intercept than transmissions on a fixed network. 802.11 defines a set of encryption routines called Wired Equivalent Privacy (WEP) to protect and authenticate data. When a frame has been processed by WEP, this bit is set to 1, and the frame changes slightly. WEP is described in more detail in Chapter 5.

Order bit

Frames and fragments can be transmitted in order at the cost of additional processing by both the sending and receiving MACs. When the "strict ordering" delivery is employed, this bit is set to 1.

Duration/ID Field

The Duration/ID field follows the frame control field. This field has several uses and takes one of the three forms shown in Figure 3-11.

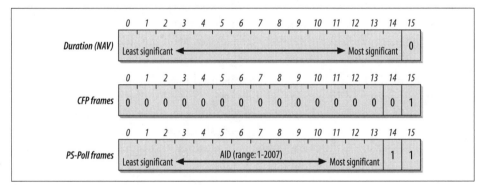

Figure 3-11. Duration/ID field

Duration: setting the NAV

When bit 15 is 0, the duration/ID field is used to set the NAV. The value represents the number of microseconds that the medium is expected to remain busy for the transmission currently in progress. All stations must monitor the headers of all frames they receive and update the NAV accordingly. Any value that extends the amount of time the medium is busy updates the NAV and blocks access to the medium for additional time.

Frames transmitted during contention-free periods

During the contention-free periods, bit 14 is 0 and bit 15 is 1. All other bits are 0, so the duration/ID field takes a value of 32,768. This value is interpreted as a NAV. It allows any stations that did not receive the Beacon* announcing the contention-free period to update the NAV with a suitably large value to avoid interfering with contention-free transmissions.

PS-Poll frames

Bits 14 and 15 are both set to 0 in PS-Poll frames. Mobile stations may elect to save battery power by turning off antennas. Dozing stations must wake up periodically. To ensure that no frames are lost, stations awaking from their slumber transmit a PS-Poll frame to retrieve any buffered frames from the access point. Along with this request, waking stations incorporate the association ID (AID) that indicates which BSS they belong to. The AID is included in the PS-Poll frame and may range from 1–2,007. Values from 2,008–16,383 are reserved and not used.

Address Fields

An 802.11 frame may contain up to four address fields. The address fields are numbered because different fields are used for different purposes depending on the frame type (details are found in Chapter 4). The general rule of thumb is that Address 1 is used for the receiver, Address 2 for the transmitter, with the Address 3 field used for filtering by the receiver.

Addressing in 802.11 follows the conventions used for the other IEEE 802 networks, including Ethernet. Addresses are 48 bits long. If the first bit sent to the physical medium is a 0, the address represents a single station (unicast). When the first bit is a 1, the address represents a group of physical stations and is called a *multicast* address. If all bits are 1s, then the frame is a *broadcast* and is delivered to all stations connected to the wireless medium.

48-bit addresses are used for a variety of purposes:

Destination address
> As in Ethernet, the destination address is the 48-bit IEEE MAC identifier that corresponds to the final recipient: the station that will hand the frame to higher protocol layers for processing.

Source address
> This is the 48-bit IEEE MAC identifier that identifies the source of the transmission. Only one station can be the source of a frame, so the Individual/Group bit is always 0 to indicate an individual station.

---

* Beacon frames are a subtype of management frames, which is why "Beacon" is capitalized.

Receiver address

> This is a 48-bit IEEE MAC identifier that indicates which wireless station should process the frame. If it is a wireless station, the receiver address is the destination address. For frames destined to a node on an Ethernet connected to an access point, the receiver is the wireless interface in the access point, and the destination address may be a router attached to the Ethernet.

Transmitter address

> This is a 48-bit IEEE MAC address to identify the wireless interface that transmitted the frame onto the wireless medium. The transmitter address is used only in wireless bridging.

Basic Service Set ID (BSSID)

> To identify different wireless LANs in the same area, stations may be assigned to a BSS. In infrastructure networks, the BSSID is the MAC address used by the wireless interface in the access point. Ad hoc networks generate a random BSSID with the Universal/Local bit set to 1 to prevent conflicts with officially assigned MAC addresses.

The number of address fields used depends on the type of frame. Most data frames use three fields for source, destination, and BSSID. The number and arrangement of address fields in a data frame depends on how the frame is traveling relative to the distribution system. Most transmissions use three addresses, which is why only three of the four addresses are contiguous in the frame format.

Sequence Control Field

This 16-bit field is used for both defragmentation and discarding duplicate frames. It is composed of a 4-bit fragment number field and a 12-bit sequence number field, as shown in Figure 3-12.

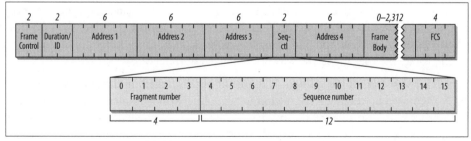

Figure 3-12. Sequence Control field

Higher-level frames are each given a sequence number as they are passed to the MAC for transmission. The sequence number subfield operates as a modulo-4096 counter of the frames transmitted. It begins at 0 and increments by 1 for each higher-level packet handled by the MAC. If higher-level packets are fragmented, all fragments will have the same sequence number. When frames are retransmitted, the sequence number is not changed.

What differs between fragments is the fragment number. The first fragment is given a fragment number of 0. Each successive fragment increments the fragment number by one. Retransmitted fragments keep their original sequence numbers to assist in reassembly.

Frame Body

The frame body, also called the Data field, moves the higher-layer payload from station to station. 802.11 can transmit frames with a maximum payload of 2,304 bytes of higher-level data. (Implementations must support frame bodies of 2,312 bytes to accommodate WEP overhead.) 802.2 LLC headers use 8 bytes for a maximum network protocol payload of 2,296 bytes. Preventing fragmentation must be done at the protocol layer. On IP networks, Path MTU Discovery (RFC 1191) will prevent the transmission of frames with Data fields larger than 1,500 bytes.

Frame Check Sequence

As with Ethernet, the 802.11 frame closes with a frame check sequence (FCS). The FCS is often referred to as the cyclic redundancy check (CRC) because of the underlying mathematical operations. The FCS allows stations to check the integrity of received frames. All fields in the MAC header and the body of the frame are included in the FCS. Although 802.3 and 802.11 use the same method to calculate the FCS, the MAC header used in 802.11 is different from the header used in 802.3, so the FCS must be recalculated by access points.

When frames are sent to the wireless interface, the FCS is calculated before those frames are sent out over the RF or IR link. Receivers can then calculate the FCS from the received frame and compare it to the received FCS. If the two match, there is a high probability that the frame was not damaged in transit.

On Ethernets, frames with a bad FCS are simply discarded, and frames with a good FCS are passed up the protocol stack. On 802.11 networks, frames that pass the integrity check may also require the receiver to send an acknowledgment. For example, data frames that are received correctly must be positively acknowledged, or they are retransmitted. 802.11 does not have a negative acknowledgment for frames that fail the FCS; stations must wait for the acknowledgment timeout before retransmitting.

Encapsulation of Higher-Layer Protocols Within 802.11

Like all other 802 link layers, 802.11 can transport any network-layer protocol. Unlike Ethernet, 802.11 relies on 802.2 logical-link control (LLC) encapsulation to carry higher-level protocols. Figure 3-13 shows how 802.2 LLC encapsulation is used to carry an IP packet. In the figure, the "MAC headers" for 802.1h and RFC 1042 might be the 12 bytes of source and destination MAC address information on Ethernet or the long 802.11 MAC header from the previous section.

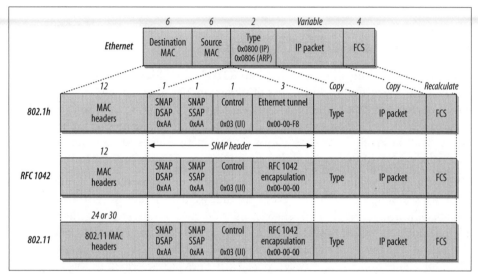

Figure 3-13. IP encapsulation in 802.11

Two different methods can be used to encapsulate LLC data for transmission. One is described in RFC 1042, and the other in 802.1h. As you can see in Figure 3-13, though, the two methods are quite similar. An Ethernet frame is shown in the top line of Figure 3-13. It has a MAC header composed of source and destination MAC addresses, a type code, the embedded packet, and a frame check field. In the IP world, the Type code is either 0x0800 (2048 decimal) for IP itself, or 0x0806 (2054 decimal) for the Address Resolution Protocol (ARP).

Both RFC 1042 and 802.1h are derivatives of 802.2's *sub-network access protocol* (SNAP). The MAC addresses are copied into the beginning of the encapsulation frame, and then a SNAP header is inserted. SNAP headers begin with a *destination service access point* (DSAP) and a *source service access point* (SSAP). After the addresses, SNAP includes a Control header. Like high-level data link control (HDLC) and its progeny, the Control field is set to 0x03 to denote unnumbered information (UI), a category that maps well to the best-effort delivery of IP datagrams. The last field inserted by SNAP is an organizationally unique identifier (OUI). Initially, the IEEE hoped that the 1-byte service access points would be adequate to handle the number of network protocols, but this proved to be an overly optimistic assessment of the state of the world. As a result, SNAP copies the type code from the original Ethernet frame.

 Products usually have a software option to toggle between the two encapsulation types. Of course, products on the same network must use the same type of encapsulation.

Contention-Based Data Service

The additional features incorporated into 802.11 to add reliability lead to a confusing tangle of rules about which types of frames are permitted at any point. They also make it more difficult for network administrators to know which frame exchanges they can expect to see on networks. This section clarifies the atomic exchanges that move data on an 802.11 LAN. (Most management frames are announcements to interested parties in the area and transfer information in only one direction.)

The exchanges presented in this section are atomic, which means that they should be viewed as a single unit. As an example, unicast data is always acknowledged to ensure delivery. Although the exchange spans two frames, the exchange itself is a single operation. If any part of it fails, the parties to the exchange retry the operation. Two distinct sets of atomic exchanges are defined by 802.11. One is used by the DCF for contention-based service; those exchanges are described in this chapter. A second set of exchanges is specified for use with the PCF for contention-free services. Frame exchanges used with contention-free services are intricate and harder to understand. Since very few (if any) commercial products implement contention-free service, these exchanges are not described.

Frame exchanges under the DCF dominate the 802.11 MAC. According to the rules of the DCF, all products are required to provide best-effort delivery. To implement the contention-based MAC, stations process MAC headers for every frame while they are active. Exchanges begin with a station seizing an idle medium after the DIFS.

Broadcast and Multicast Data or Management Frames

Broadcast and multicast frames have the simplest frame exchanges because there is no acknowledgment. Framing and addressing are somewhat more complex in 802. 11, so the types of frames that match this rule are the following:

- Broadcast data frames with a broadcast address in the Address1 field
- Multicast data frames with a multicast address in the Address1 field
- Broadcast management frames with a broadcast address in the Address1 field (Beacon, Probe Request, and IBSS ATIM frames)

Frames destined for group addresses cannot be fragmented and are not acknowledged. The entire atomic sequence is a single frame, sent according to the rules of the contention-based access control. After the previous transmission concludes, all stations wait for the DIFS and begin counting down the random delay intervals in the contention window.

Because the frame exchange is a single-frame sequence, the NAV is set to 0. With no further frames to follow, there is no need to use the virtual carrier-sense mechanism to lock other stations out of using the medium. After the frame is transmitted, all stations wait through the DIFS and begin counting down through the contention window for any deferred frames. See Figure 3-14.

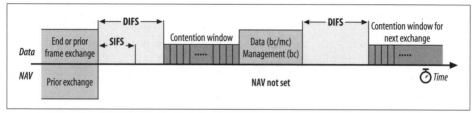

Figure 3-14. Broadcast/multicast data and broadcast management atomic frame exchange

Depending on the environment, frames sent to group addresses may have lower service quality because the frames are not acknowledged. Some stations may therefore miss broadcast or multicast traffic, but there is no facility built into the MAC for retransmitting broadcast or multicast frames.

Unicast Frames

Frames that are destined for a single station are called *directed* data by the 802.11 standard. This book uses the more common term *unicast*. Unicast frames must be acknowledged to ensure reliability, which means that a variety of mechanisms can be used to improve efficiency. All the sequences in this section apply to any unicast frame and thus can apply to management frames and data frames. In practice, these operations are usually observed only with data frames.

Basic positive acknowledgment (final fragment)

Reliable transmission between two stations is based on simple positive acknowledgments. Unicast data frames must be acknowledged, or the frame is assumed to be lost. The most basic case is a single frame and its accompanying acknowledgment, as shown in Figure 3-15.

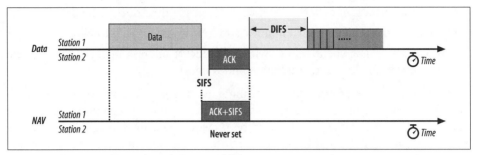

Figure 3-15. Basic positive acknowledgment of data

The frame uses the NAV to reserve the medium for the frame, its acknowledgment, and the intervening SIFS. By setting a long NAV, the sender locks the virtual carrier for the entire sequence, guaranteeing that the recipient of the frame can send the acknowledgment. Because the sequence concludes with the ACK, no further virtual carrier locking is necessary, and the NAV in the ACK is set to 0.

Fragmentation

Many higher-layer network protocols, including IP, incorporate fragmentation. The disadvantage of network-layer fragmentation is that reassembly is performed by the final destination; if any of the fragments are lost, the entire packet must be retransmitted. Link layers may incorporate fragmentation to boost speed over a single hop with a small MTU.* 802.11 can also use fragmentation to help avoid interference. Radio interference is often in the form of short, high-energy bursts and is frequently synchronized with the AC power line. Breaking a large frame into small frames allows a larger percentage of the frames to arrive undamaged. The basic fragmentation scheme is shown in Figure 3-16.

The last two frames exchanged are the same as in the previous sequence, and the NAV is set identically. However, all previous frames use the NAV to lock the medium for the next frame. The first data frame sets the NAV for a long enough period to accommodate its ACK, the next fragment, and the acknowledgment following the next fragment. To indicate that it is a fragment, the MAC sets the More Fragments bit in the frame control field to 1. All nonfinal ACKs continue to extend the lock for the next data fragment and its ACK. Subsequent data frames then continue to lengthen the NAV to include successive acknowledgments until the final data frame, which sets the More Fragments bit to 0, and the final ACK, which sets the NAV to 0. No limit is placed on the number of fragments, but the total frame length must be shorter than any constraint placed on the exchange by the PHY.

Fragmentation is controlled by the fragmentation threshold parameter in the MAC. Most network card drivers allow you to configure this parameter. Any frames larger

---

* This is the approach used by Multi-link PPP (RFC 1990).

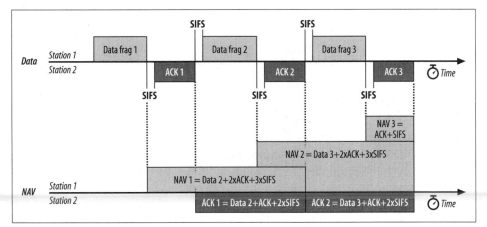

Figure 3-16. Fragmentation

than the fragmentation threshold are fragmented in an implementation-dependent way. Network administrators can change the fragmentation threshold to tune network behavior. Higher fragmentation thresholds mean that frames are delivered with less overhead, but the cost to a lost or damaged frame is much higher because more data must be discarded and retransmitted. Low fragmentation thresholds have much higher overhead, but they offer increased robustness in the face of hostile conditions.

RTS/CTS

To guarantee reservation of the medium and uninterrupted data transmission, a station can use the RTS/CTS exchange. Figure 3-17 shows this process. The RTS/CTS exchange acts exactly like the initial exchange in the fragmentation case, except that the RTS frame does not carry data. The NAV in the RTS allows the CTS to complete, and the CTS is used to reserve access for the data frame.

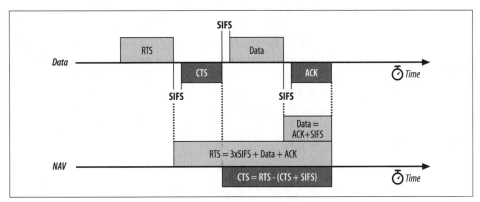

Figure 3-17. RTS/CTS lockout

RTS/CTS can be used for all frame exchanges, none of them, or something in between. Like fragmentation, RTS/CTS behavior is controlled by a threshold set in the driver software. Frames larger than the threshold are preceded by an RTS/CTS exchange to clear the medium, while smaller frames are simply transmitted.

RTS/CTS with fragmentation

In practice, the RTS/CTS exchange is often combined with fragmentation (Figure 3-18). Fragmented frames are usually quite long and thus benefit from the use of the RTS/CTS procedure to ensure exclusive access to the medium, free from contention from hidden nodes. Some vendors set the default fragmentation threshold to be identical to the default RTS/CTS threshold.

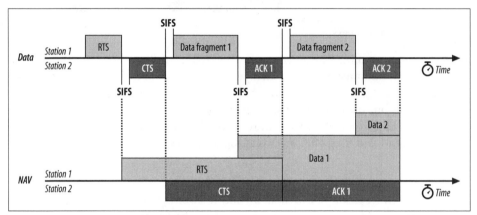

Figure 3-18. RTS/CTS with fragmentation

Power-Saving Sequences

The most power-hungry components in RF systems are the amplifiers used to boost a signal immediately prior to transmission and to boost the received signal to an intelligible level immediately after its reception. 802.11 stations can maximize battery life by shutting down the radio transceiver and sleeping periodically. During sleeping periods, access points buffer any unicast frames for sleeping stations. These frames are announced by subsequent Beacon frames. To retrieve buffered frames, newly awakened stations use PS-Poll frames.

Immediate response

Access points can respond immediately to the PS-Poll. After a short interframe space, an access point may transmit the frame. Figure 3-19 shows an implied NAV as a result of the PS-Poll frame. The PS-Poll frame contains an Association ID in the Duration/ID field so that the access point can determine which frames were buffered for the mobile station. However, the MAC specification requires all stations receiving a

PS-Poll to update the NAV with an implied value equal to a short interframe space and one ACK. Although the NAV is too short for the data frame, the access point acquires that the medium and all stations defer access for the entire data frame. At the conclusion of the data frame, the NAV is updated to reflect the value in the header of the data frame.

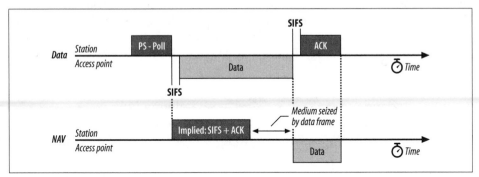

Figure 3-19. Immediate PS-Poll response

If the buffered frame is large, it may require fragmentation. Figure 3-20 illustrates an immediate PS-Poll response requiring fragmentation. Like all other stations, access points typically have a configurable fragmentation threshold.

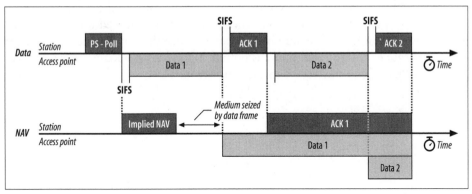

Figure 3-20. Immediate PS-Poll response with fragmentation

Deferred response

Instead of an immediate response, access points can also respond with a simple acknowledgment. This is called a *deferred response* because the access point acknowledges the request for the buffered frame but does not act on it immediately. A station requesting a frame with a PS-Poll must stay awake until it is delivered. Under contention-based service, however, the access point can deliver a frame at any point. A station cannot return to a low-power mode until it receives a Beacon frame in which its bit in the traffic indication map (TIM) is clear.

Figure 3-21 illustrates this process. In this figure, the station has recently changed from a low-power mode to an active mode, and it notes that the access point has buffered frames for it. It transmits a PS-Poll to the access point to retrieve the buffered frames. However, the access point may choose to defer its response by transmitting only an ACK. At this point, the access point has acknowledged the station's request for buffered frames and promised to deliver them at some point in the future. The station must wait in active mode, perhaps through several atomic frame exchanges, before the access point delivers the data. A buffered frame may be subject to fragmentation, although Figure 3-21 does not illustrate this case.

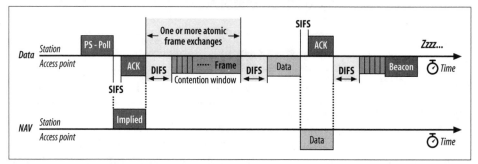

Figure 3-21. Deferred PS-Poll response example

After receiving a data frame, the station must remain awake until the next Beacon is transmitted. Beacon frames only note whether frames are buffered for a station and have no way of indicating the number of frames. Once the station receives a Beacon frame indicating that no more traffic is buffered, it can conclude that it has received the last buffered frame and return to a low-power mode.

## CHAPTER 4

802.11 Framing in Detail

Chapter 3 presented the basic frame structure and the fields that comprise it, but it did not go into detail about the different frame types. Ethernet framing is a simple matter: add a preamble, some addressing information, and tack on a frame check at the end. 802.11 framing is much more involved because the wireless medium requires several management features and corresponding frame types not found in wired networks.

Three major frame types exist. Data frames are the pack horses of 802.11, hauling data from station to station. Several different data frame flavors can occur, depending on the network. Control frames are used in conjunction with data frames to perform area clearing operations, channel acquisition and carrier-sensing maintenance functions, and positive acknowledgment of received data. Control and data frames work in conjunction to deliver data reliably from station to station. Management frames perform supervisory functions; they are used to join and leave wireless networks and move associations from access point to access point.

This chapter is intended to be a reference. There is only so much life any author can breathe into framing details, no matter how much effort is expended to make the details interesting. Please feel free to skip this chapter in its entirety and flip back when you need in-depth information about frame structure. With rare exception, detailed framing relationships generally do not fall into the category of "something a network administrator needs to know." This chapter tends to be a bit acronym-heavy as well, so refer to the glossary at the back of the book if you do not recognize an acronym.

Data Frames

Data frames carry higher-level protocol data in the frame body. Figure 4-1 shows a generic data frame. Depending on the particular type of data frame, some of the fields in the figure may not be used.

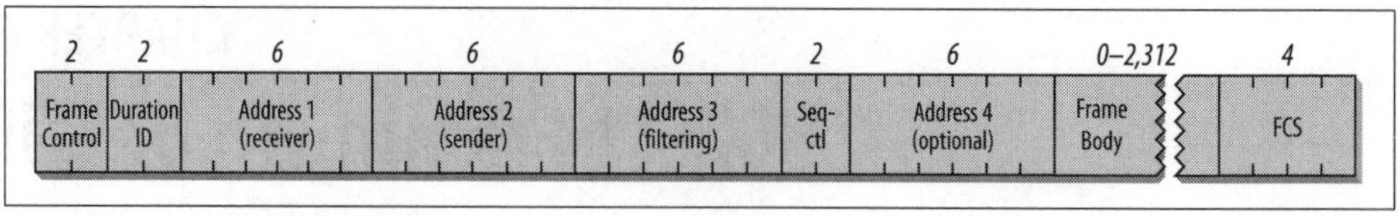

Figure 4-1. Generic data frame

The different data frame types can be categorized according to function. One such distinction is between data frames used for contention-based service and those used for contention-free service. Any frames that appear only in the contention-free period can never be used in an IBSS. Another possible division is between frames that carry data and frames that perform management functions. Table 4-1 shows how frames may be divided along these lines. Frames used in contention-free service are discussed in detail in Chapter 8.

Table 4-1. Categorization of data frame types

Frame type	Contention-based service	Contention-free service	Carries data	Does not carry data
Data	✓		✓	
Data+CF-Ack		✓	✓	
Data+CF-Poll		AP only	✓	
Data+CF-Ack+CF-Poll		AP only	✓	
Null	✓	✓		✓
CF-Ack		✓		✓
CF-Poll		AP only		✓
CF-Ack+CF-Poll		AP only		✓

Frame Control

All the bits in the Frame Control field are used according to the rules described in Chapter 3. Frame Control bits may affect the interpretation of other fields in the MAC header, though. Most notable are the address fields, which depend on the value of the ToDS and FromDS bits.

Duration

The Duration field carries the value of the Network Allocation Vector (NAV). Access to the medium is restricted for the time specified by the NAV. Four rules specify the setting for the Duration field in data frames:

1. Any frames transmitted during the contention-free period set the Duration field to 32,768. Naturally, this applies to any data frames transmitted during this period.

2. Frames transmitted to a broadcast or multicast destination (Address 1 has the group bit set) have a duration of 0. Such frames are not part of an atomic exchange and are not acknowledged by receivers, so contention-based access to the medium can begin after the conclusion of a broadcast or multicast data frame. The NAV is used to protect access to the transmission medium for a frame exchange sequence. With no link-layer acknowledgment following the transmission of a broadcast or multicast frame, there is no need to lock access to the medium for subsequent frames.

3. If the More Fragments bit in the Frame Control field is 0, no more fragments remain in the frame. The final fragment need only reserve the medium for its own ACK, at which point contention-based access resumes. The Duration field is set to the amount of time required for one short interframe space and the fragment acknowledgment. Figure 4-2 illustrates this process. The penultimate fragment's Duration field locks access to the medium for the transmission of the last fragment.

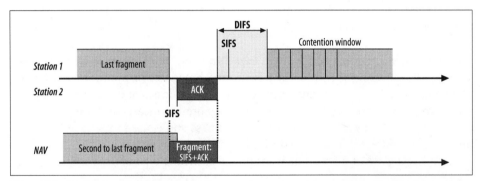

Figure 4-2. Duration setting on final fragment

4. If the More Fragments bit in the Frame Control field is set to 1, more fragments remain. The Duration field is set to the amount of time required for transmission of two acknowledgments, plus three short interframe spaces, plus the time required for the next fragment. In essence, nonfinal fragments set the NAV just like an RTS would (Figure 4-3); for this reason, they are referred to as a *virtual RTS*.

Addressing and DS Bits

The number and function of the address fields depends on which of the distribution system bits are set, so the use of the address fields indirectly depends on the type of network deployed. Table 4-2 summarizes the use of the address fields in data frames.

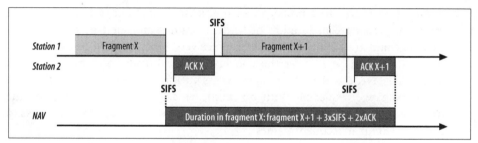

Figure 4-3. Duration settings on nonfinal fragment

Table 4-2. Use of the address fields in data frames

Function	ToDS	FromDS	Address 1 (receiver)	Address 2 (transmitter)	Address 3	Address 4
IBSS	0	0	DA	SA	BSSID	not used
To AP (infra.)	1	0	BSSID	SA	DA	not used
From AP (infra.)	0	1	DA	BSSID	SA	not used
WDS (bridge)	1	1	RA	TA	DA	SA

Address 1 indicates the receiver of the frame. In many cases, the receiver is the destination, but not always. If Address 1 is set to a broadcast or multicast address, the BSSID is also checked. Stations respond only to broadcasts and multicasts originating in the same basic service set (BSS); they ignore broadcasts and multicasts from different BSSs. Address 2 is the transmitter address and is used to send acknowledgments. The Address 3 field is used for filtering by access points and the distribution system, but the use of the field depends on the particular type of network used.

In the case of an IBSS, no access points are used, and no distribution system is present. The transmitter is the source, and the receiver is the destination. All frames carry the BSSID so that stations may check broadcasts and multicasts; only stations that belong to the same BSS will process broadcasts and multicasts. In an IBSS, the BSSID is created by a random-number generator.

802.11 draws a distinction between the source and transmitter and a parallel distinction between the destination and the receiver. The transmitter sends a frame on to the wireless medium but does not necessarily create the frame. A similar distinction holds for destination addresses and receiver addresses. A receiver may be an intermediate destination, but frames are processed by higher protocol levels only when they reach the destination.

To expand on these distinctions, consider the use of the address fields in infrastructure networks. Figure 4-4 shows a simple network in which a wireless client is connected to a server through an 802.11 network. Frames sent by the client to the server use the address fields as specified in the second line of Table 4-2.

The BSSID

Each BSS is assigned a BSSID, a 48-bit binary identifier that distinguishes it from other BSSs throughout the network. The major advantage of the BSSID is filtering. Several distinct 802.11 networks may overlap physically, and there is no reason for one network to receive link-layer broadcasts from a physically overlapping network.

In an infrastructure BSS, the BSSID is the MAC address of the wireless interface in the access point creating the BSS. IBSSs must create BSSIDs for networks brought into existence. To maximize the probability of creating a unique address, 46 random bits are generated for the BSSID. The Universal/Local bit for the new BSSID is set to 1, indicating a local address, and the Individual/Group bit is set to 0. For two distinct IBSSs to create the same BSSID, they would need to generate an identical random 46 bits.

One BSSID is reserved. The all-1s BSSID is the *broadcast BSSID*. Frames that use the broadcast BSSID pass through any BSSID filtering in the MAC. BSSID broadcasts are used only when mobile stations try to locate a network by sending probe requests. In order for probe frames to detect the existence of a network, they must not be filtered by the BSSID filter. Probe frames are the only frames allowed to use the broadcast BSSID.

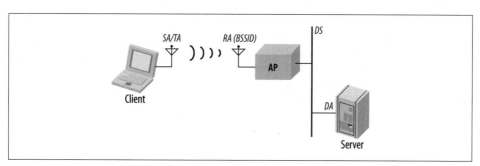

Figure 4-4. Address field usage in frames to the distribution system

In the case of frames bound for a destination on the distribution system, the client is both source and transmitter. The receiver of the wireless frame is the access point, but the access point is only an intermediate destination. When the frame reaches the access point, it is relayed to the distribution system to reach the server. Thus, the access point is the receiver, and the (ultimate) destination is the server. In infrastructure networks, access points create associated BSSs with the address of their wireless interfaces, which is why the receiver address (Address 1) is set to the BSSID.

When the server replies to the client, frames are transmitted to the client through the access point, as in Figure 4-5. This scenario corresponds to the third line in Table 4-2.

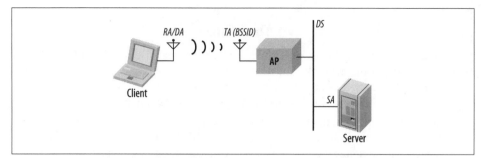

Figure 4-5. Address field usage in frames from the distribution system

Frames are created by the server, so the server's MAC address is the source address for frames. When frames are relayed through the access point, the access point uses its wireless interface as the transmitter address. As in the previous case, the access point's interface address is also the BSSID. Frames are ultimately sent to the client, which is both the destination and receiver.

The fourth line in Table 4-2 shows the use of the address fields in a *wireless distribution system (WDS)*, which is sometimes called a *wireless bridge*. In Figure 4-6, two wired networks are joined by access points acting as wireless bridges. Frames bound from the client to the server traverse the 802.11 WDS. The source and destination addresses of the wireless frames remain the client and server addresses. These frames, however, also identify the transmitter and receiver of the frame on the wireless medium. For frames bound from the client to the server, the transmitter is the client-side access point, and the receiver is the server-side access point. Separating the source from the transmitter allows the server-side access point to send required 802.11 acknowledgments to its peer access point without interfering with the wired link layer.

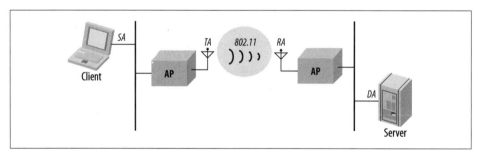

Figure 4-6. Wireless distribution system

Variations on the Data Frame Theme

802.11 uses several different data frame types. Variations depend on whether the service is contention-based or contention-free. Contention-free frames can incorporate several functions for the sake of efficiency. Data may be transmitted, but by changing the frame subtype, data frames in the contention-free period may be used to acknowledge other frames, saving the overhead of interframe spaces and separate acknowledgments. Here are the different data frame types that are commonly used:

Data
> Frames of the Data subtype are transmitted only during the contention-based access periods. They are simple frames with the sole purpose of moving the frame body from one station to another.

Null
> Null frames* are a bit of an oddity. They consist of a MAC header followed by the FCS trailer. In a traditional Ethernet, empty frames would be extraneous overhead; in 802.11 networks, they are used by mobile stations to inform the access point of changes in power-saving status. When stations sleep, the access point must begin buffering frames for the sleeping station. If the mobile station has no data to send through the distribution system, it can use a Null frame with the Power Management bit in the Frame Control field set. Access points never enter power-saving mode and do not transmit Null frames. Usage of Null frames is shown in Figure 4-7.

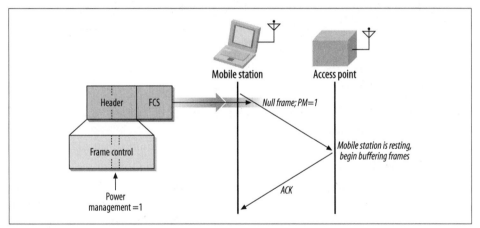

Figure 4-7. Data frame of subtype Null

Several other frame types exist for use within the contention-free period. However, contention-free service is not widely implemented, so the discussion of the contention-free frames (Data+CF-Ack, Data+CF-Poll, Data+CF-Ack+CF-Poll, CF-Ack, CF-Poll, and CF-Ack+CF-Poll) can be found in Chapter 8.

---

* To indicate that Null is used as the frame type from the specification rather than the English word, it is capitalized. This convention will be followed throughout the chapter.

Applied Data Framing

The form of a data frame can depend on the type of network. The actual subtype of the frame is determined solely by the subtype field, not by the presence or absence of other fields in the frame.

IBSS frames

In an IBSS, three address fields are used, as shown in Figure 4-8. The first address identifies the receiver, which is also the destination address in an IBSS. The second address is the source address. After the source and destination addresses, data frames in an IBSS are labeled with the BSSID. When the wireless MAC receives a frame, it checks the BSSID and passes only frames in the station's current BSSID to higher protocol layers.

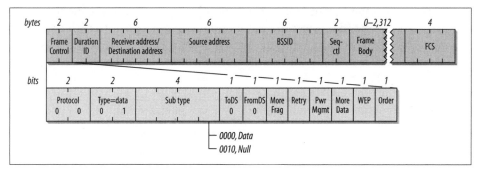

Figure 4-8. IBSS data frame

IBSS data frames have the subtype data or Null; the latter is used only to communicate power management state.

Frames from the AP

Figure 4-9 shows the format of a frame sent from an access point to a mobile station. As in all data frames, the first address field indicates the receiver of the frame on the wireless network, which is the frame's destination. The second address holds the transmitter address. On infrastructure networks, the transmitter address is the address of the station in the access point, which is also the BSSID. Finally, the frame indicates the source MAC address of the frame. The split between source and transmitter is necessary because the 802.11 MAC sends acknowledgments to the frame's transmitter (the access point), but higher layers send replies to the frame's source.

Nothing in the 802.11 specification forbids an access point from transmitting Null frames, but there is no reason to transmit them. Access points are forbidden from using the power-saving routines, and they can acknowledge Null frames from stations without using Null frames in response. In practice, access points send Data

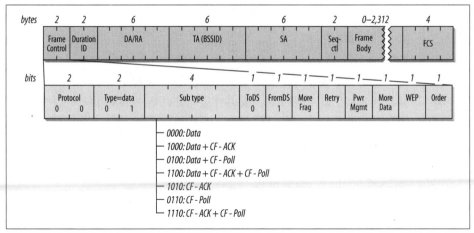

Figure 4-9. Data frames from the AP

frames during the contention-based access period, and they send frames incorporating the CF-Poll feature during the contention-free period.

Frames to the AP

Figure 4-10 shows the format of a frame sent from a mobile station in an infrastructure network to the access point currently serving it. The receiver address is the BSSID. In infrastructure networks, the BSSID is taken from the MAC address of the network station in the access point. Frames destined for an access point take their source/transmitter address from the network interface in the wireless station. Access points do not perform filtering, but instead use the third address to forward data to the appropriate location in the distribution system.

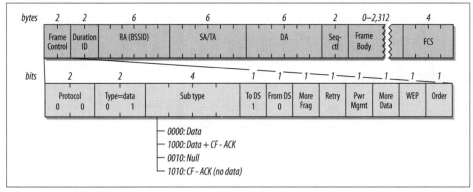

Figure 4-10. Data frames to the AP

Frames from the distribution system have the ToDS bit set, but the FromDS bit is 0. Mobile stations in an infrastructure network cannot become the point coordinator, and thus never send frames that incorporate the contention-free polling (CF-Poll) functions.

Frames in a WDS

When access points are deployed in a wireless bridge, or WDS, topology, all four address fields are used, as shown in Figure 4-11. Like all other data frames, WDS frames use the first address for the receiver of the frame and the second address for the transmitter. The MAC uses these two addresses for acknowledgments and control traffic, such as RTS, CTS, and ACK frames. Two more address fields are necessary to indicate the source and destination of the frame and distinguish them from the addresses used on the wireless link.

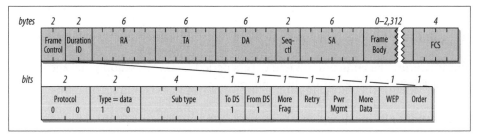

Figure 4-11. WDS frames

On a wireless bridging link, there are usually no mobile stations, and the contention-free period is not used. Access points are forbidden to enter power-saving modes, so the power management bit is always set to 0.

Frames using WEP

Frames protected by WEP are not new frame types. When a frame is handled by WEP, the WEP bit in the Frame Control field is set to 1, and the Frame Body field begins with the WEP header described in Chapter 5.

Control Frames

Control frames assist in the delivery of data frames. They administer access to the wireless medium (but not the medium itself) and provide MAC-layer reliability functions.

Common Frame Control Field

All control frames use the same Frame Control field, which is shown in Figure 4-12.

Protocol version
> The protocol version is shown as 0 in Figure 4-12 because that is currently the only version. Other versions may exist in the future.

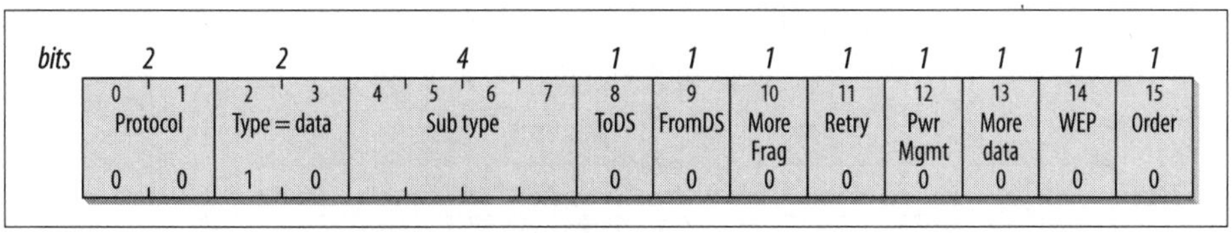

bits	2		2		4			1	1	1	1	1	1	1	1
	0	1	2	3	4	5	6	7	8	9	10	11	12	13	14	15
	Protocol		Type = data		Sub type				ToDS	FromDS	More Frag	Retry	Pwr Mgmt	More data	WEP	Order
	0	0	1	0					0	0	0	0	0	0	0	0

Figure 4-12. Frame Control field in control frames

Type

Control frames are assigned the Type identifier 01. By definition, all control frames use this identifier.

Subtype

This field indicates the subtype of the control frame that is being transmitted.

ToDS and FromDS bits

Control frames arbitrate access to the wireless medium and thus can only originate from wireless stations. The distribution system does not send or receive control frames, so these bits are always 0.

More Fragments bit

Control frames are not fragmented, so this bit is always 0.

Retry bit

Control frames are not queued for retransmission like management or data frames, so this bit is always 0.

Power Management bit

This bit is set to indicate the power management state of the sender after conclusion of the current frame exchange.

More Data bit

The More Data bit is used only in management and data frames, so this bit is set to 0 in control frames.

WEP bit

Control frames may not be encrypted by WEP, which may be used only for data frames and association requests. Thus, for control frames, the WEP bit is always 0.

Order bit

Control frames are used as components of atomic frame exchange operations and thus cannot be transmitted out of order. Therefore, this bit is set to 0.

Request to Send (RTS)

RTS frames are used to gain control of the medium for the transmission of "large" frames, in which "large" is defined by the RTS threshold in the network card driver. Access to the medium can be reserved only for unicast frames; broadcast and multicast frames are simply transmitted. The format of the RTS frame is shown in

Figure 4-13. Like all control frames, the RTS frame is all header. No data is transmitted in the body, and the FCS immediately follows the header.

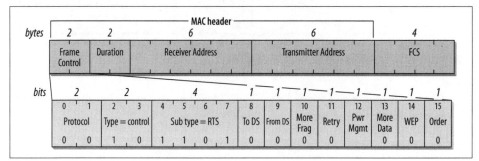

Figure 4-13. RTS frame

Four fields make up the MAC header of an RTS:

Frame Control

There is nothing special about the Frame Control field. The frame subtype is set to 1011 to indicate an RTS frame, but otherwise, it has all the same fields as other control frames. (The most significant bits in the 802.11 specification come at the end of fields, so bit 7 is the most significant bit in the subtype field.)

Duration

An RTS frame attempts to reserve the medium for an entire frame exchange, so the sender of an RTS frame calculates the time needed for the frame exchange sequence after the RTS frame ends. The entire exchange, which is depicted in Figure 4-14, requires three SIFS periods, the duration of one CTS, the final ACK, plus the time needed to transmit the frame or first fragment. (Fragmentation bursts use subsequent fragments to update the Duration field.) The number of microseconds required for the transmission is calculated and placed in the Duration field. If the result is fractional, it is rounded up to the next microsecond.

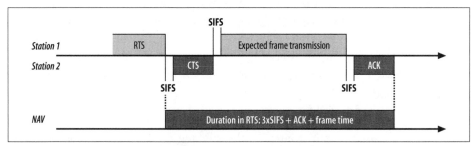

Figure 4-14. Duration field in RTS frame

Address 1: Receiver Address
The address of the station that is the intended recipient of the large frame.

Address 2: Transmitter Address
The address of the sender of the RTS frame.

Clear to Send (CTS)

The CTS frame answers the RTS frame. Its format is shown in Figure 4-15.

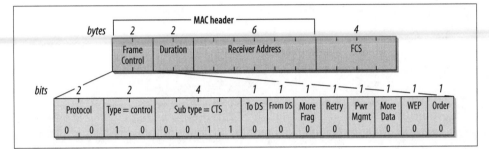

Figure 4-15. CTS frame

Three fields make up the MAC header of a CTS frame:

Frame Control
The frame subtype is set to 1100 to indicate a CTS frame.

Duration
The sender of a CTS frame uses the duration from the RTS frame as the basis for its duration calculation. RTS frames reserve the medium for the entire RTS-CTS-frame-ACK exchange. By the time the CTS frame is transmitted, though, only the pending frame or fragment and its acknowledgment remain. The sender of a CTS frame subtracts the time required for the CTS frame and the short inter-frame space that preceded the CTS from the duration in the RTS frame, and places the result of that calculation in the Duration field. Figure 4-16 illustrates the relationship between the CTS duration and the RTS duration.

Address 1: Receiver Address
The receiver of a CTS frame is the transmitter of the previous RTS frame, so the MAC copies the transmitter address of the RTS frame into the receiver address of the CTS frame.

Acknowledgment (ACK)

ACK frames are used to send the positive acknowledgments required by the MAC and are used with any data transmission, including plain transmissions; frames preceded by an RTS/CTS handshake; and fragmented frames (see Figure 4-17).

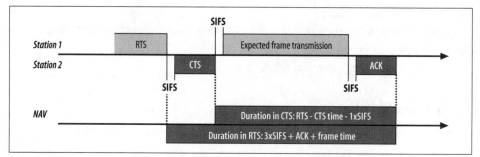

Figure 4-16. CTS duration

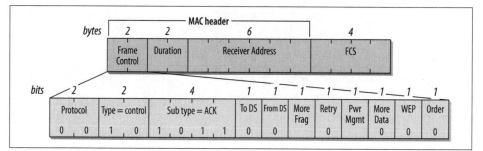

Figure 4-17. ACK frame

Three fields make up the MAC header of an ACK frame:

Frame Control

The frame subtype is set to 1101 to indicate an ACK frame.

Duration

The duration may be set in one of two ways, depending on the position of the ACK within the frame exchange. ACKs for complete data frames and final fragments in a fragment burst set the duration to 0. The data sender indicates the end of a data transmission by setting the More Fragments bit in the Frame Control header to 0. If the More Fragments bit is 0, the transmission is complete, and there is no need to extend control over the radio channel for additional transmissions. Thus, the duration is set to 0.

If the More Fragments bit is 1, a fragment burst is in progress. The Duration field is used like the Duration field in the CTS frame. The time required to transmit the ACK and its short interframe space is subtracted from the duration in the most recent fragment (Figure 4-18). The duration calculation in nonfinal ACK frames is similar to the CTS duration calculation. In fact, the 802.11 specification refers to the duration setting in the ACK frames as a *virtual CTS*.

Address 1: Receiver Address

The receiver address is copied from the transmitter of the frame being acknowledged. Technically, it is copied from the Address 2 field of the frame being

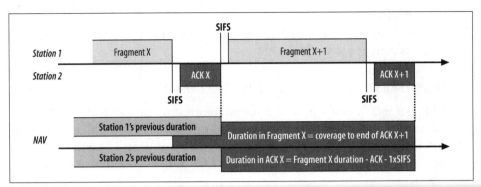

Figure 4-18. Duration in non-final ACK frames

acknowledged. Acknowledgments are transmitted in response to directed data frames, management frames, and PS-Poll frames.

Power-Save Poll (PS-Poll)

When a mobile station wakes from a power-saving mode, it transmits a PS-Poll frame to the access point to retrieve any frames buffered while it was in power-saving mode. The format of the PS-Poll frame is shown in Figure 4-19.

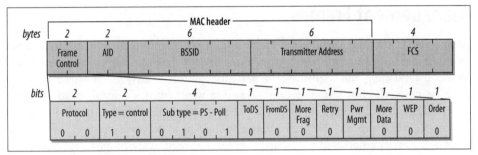

Figure 4-19. PS-Poll frame

Four fields make up the MAC header of a PS-Poll frame:

Frame Control
The frame subtype is set to 1010 to indicate a PS-Poll frame.

Association ID (AID)
Instead of a Duration field, the PS-Poll frame uses the third and fourth bytes in the MAC header for the association ID. This is a numeric value assigned by the access point to identify the association. Including this ID in the frame allows the access point to find any frames buffered for the now-awakened mobile station.

Address 1: BSSID
> This field contains the BSSID of the BSS created by the access point that the sender is currently associated with.

Address 2: Transmitter Address
> This is the address of the sender of the PS-Poll frame.

The PS-Poll frame does not include duration information to update the NAV. However, all stations receiving a PS-Poll frame update the NAV by the short interframe space plus the amount of time required to transmit an ACK. The automatic NAV update allows the access point to transmit an ACK with a small probability of collision with a mobile station.

Association ID (AID)

In the PS-Poll frame, the Duration/ID field is an association ID rather than a value used by the virtual carrier-sensing function. When mobile stations associate with an access point, the access point assigns a value called the Association ID (AID) from the range 1–2,007. The AID is used for a variety of purposes that appear throughout this book.

Management Frames

Management is a large component of the 802.11 specification. Several different types of management frames are used to provide services that are simple on a wired network. Establishing the identity of a network station is easy on a wired network because network connections require dragging wires from a central location to the new workstation. In many cases, patch panels in the wiring closet are used to speed up installation, but the essential point remains: new network connections can be authenticated by a personal visit when the new connection is brought up.

Wireless networks must create management features to provide similar functionality. 802.11 breaks the procedure up into three components. Mobile stations in search of connectivity must first locate a compatible wireless network to use for access. With wired networks, this step is typically finding the appropriate data jack on the wall. Next, the network must authenticate mobile stations to establish that the authenticated identity is allowed to connect to the network. The wired-network equivalent is provided by the network itself. If signals cannot leave the wire, obtaining physical access is at least something of an authentication process. Finally, mobile stations must associate with an access point to gain access to the wired backbone, a step equivalent to plugging the cable into a wired network.

The Structure of Management Frames

802.11 management frames share the structure shown in Figure 4-20.

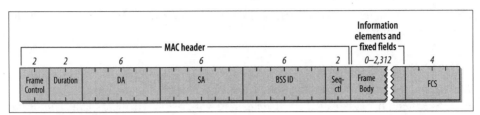

Figure 4-20. Generic management frame

The MAC header is the same in all management frames; it does not depend on the frame subtype. Some management frames use the frame body to transmit information specific to the management frame subtype.

Address fields

As with all other frames, the first address field is used for the frame's destination address. Some management frames are used to maintain properties within a single BSS. To limit the effect of broadcast and multicast management frames, stations inspect the BSSID after receiving a mangement frame. Only broadcast and multicast frames from the BSSID that a station is currently associated with are passed to MAC management layers. The one exception to this rule is Beacon frames, which are used to announce the existence of an 802.11 network.

BSSIDs are assigned in the familiar manner. Access points use the MAC address of the wireless network interface as the BSSID. Mobile stations adopt the BSSID of the access point they are currently associated with. Stations in an IBSS use the randomly generated BSSID from the BSS creation. One exception to the rule: frames sent by the mobile station seeking a specific network may use the BSSID of the network they are seeking, or they may use the broadcast BSSID to find all networks in the vicinity.

Duration calculations

Management frames use the Duration field in the same manner that other frames do:

1. Any frames transmitted in the contention-free period set the duration to 32,768.
2. Frames transmitted during the contention-based access periods using only the DCF use the Duration field to block access to the medium to allow any atomic frame exchanges to complete.
   a. If the frame is a broadcast or multicast (the destination address is a group address), the duration is 0. Broadcast and multicast frames are not acknowledged, so the NAV is not needed to block access to the medium.

b. If a nonfinal fragment is part of a multiframe exchange, the duration is set to the number of microseconds taken up by three SIFS intervals plus the next fragment and its acknowledgment.

c. Final fragments use a duration that is the time required for one acknowledgment plus one SIFS.

Frame body

Management frames are quite flexible. Most of the data contained in the frame body uses fixed-length fields called *fixed fields* and variable-length fields called *information elements*. Information elements are blobs of data of varying size. Each data blob is tagged with a type number and a size, and it is understood that an information element of a certain type has its data field interpreted in a certain way. New information elements can be defined by newer revisions to the 802.11 specification; implementations that predate the revisions can ignore newer elements. Old implementations depend on backward-compatible hardware and frequently can't join networks based on the newer standards. Fortunately, new options usually can be easily turned off for compatibility.

This section presents the fixed fields and information elements as building blocks and shows how the building blocks are assembled into management frames. 802.11 mandates the order in which information elements appear, but not all elements are mandatory. This book shows all the frame building blocks in the specified order, and the discussion of each subtype notes which elements are rare and which are mutually exclusive.

Fixed-Length Management Frame Components

Ten fixed-length fields may appear in management frames. Fixed-length fields are often referred to simply as *fields* to distinguish them from the variable-length information elements.

Authentication Algorithm Number

Two bytes are used for the Authentication Algorithm Number field, shown in Figure 4-21. This field identifies the type of authentication used in the authentication process. (The authentication process is discussed more thoroughly in Chapter 7.) The values permitted for this field are shown in Table 4-3. Only two values are currently defined. Other values are reserved for future standardization work.

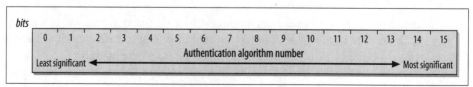

Figure 4-21. Authentication Algorithm Number field

Table 4-3. Values of the Authentication Algorithm Number field

Value	Meaning
0	Open System authentication
1	Shared Key authentication
2–65,535	Reserved

Authentication Transaction Sequence Number

Authentication is a multistep process that consists of a challenge from the access point and a response from the mobile station attempting to associate. The Authentication Transaction Sequence Number, shown in Figure 4-22, is a two-byte field used to track progress through the authentication exchange. It takes values from 1 to 65,535; it is never set to 0. Use of this field is discussed in Chapter 7.

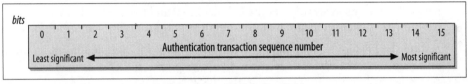

Figure 4-22. Authentication Transaction Sequence Number field

Beacon interval

Beacon transmissions announce the existence of an 802.11 network at regular intervals. Beacon frames carry information about the BSS parameters and the frames buffered by access points, so mobile stations must listen to Beacons. The Beacon Interval, shown in Figure 4-23, is a 16-bit field set to the number of *time units* between Beacon transmissions. One time unit, which is often abbreviated TU, is 1,024 microseconds (μs), which is about 1 millisecond. Time units may also be called kilo-microseconds in various documentation (Kμs or kμs). It is common for the Beacon interval to be set to 100 time units, which corresponds to an interval between Beacon transmissions of approximately 100 milliseconds or 0.1 seconds.

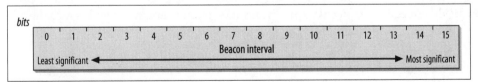

Figure 4-23. Beacon Interval field

Capability Information

The 16-bit Capability Information field, shown in Figure 4-24, is used in Beacon transmissions to advertise the network's capabilities. Capability Information is also used in Probe Request and Probe Response frames. In this field, each bit is used as a flag to advertise a particular function of the network. Stations use the capability advertisement to determine whether they can support all the features in the BSS. Stations that do not implement all the features in the capability advertisement are not allowed to join.

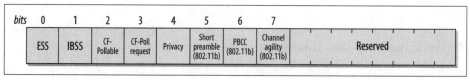

Figure 4-24. Capability Information field

ESS/IBSS
These two bits are mutually exclusive. Access points set the ESS field to 1 and the IBSS field to 0 to indicate that the access point is part of an infrastructure network. Stations in an IBSS set the ESS field to 0 and the IBSS field to 1.

Privacy
Setting the Privacy bit to 1 requires the use of WEP for confidentiality. In infrastructure networks, the transmitter is an access point. In IBSSs, Beacon transmission must be handled by a station in the IBSS.

Short Preamble
This field was added to 802.11b to support the high-rate DSSS PHY. Setting it to 1 indicates that the network is using the short preamble as described in Chapter 10. Zero means the option is not in use and is forbidden in the BSS.

PBCC
This field was added to 802.11b to support the high-rate DSSS PHY. When it is set to 1, it indicates that the network is using the packet binary convolution coding modulation scheme described in Chapter 10. Zero means that the option is not in use and is forbidden in the BSS.

Channel Agility
This field was added to 802.11b to support the high rate DSSS PHY. When it is set to one, it indicates that the network is using the Channel Agility option described in Chapter 10. Zero means the option is not in use and is forbidden in the BSS.

Contention-free polling bits
Stations and access points use these two bits as a label. The meanings of the labels are shown in Table 4-4.

Table 4-4. Interpretation of polling bits in Capability Information

CF-Pollable	CF-Poll Request	Interpretation
Station usage		
0	0	Station does not support polling
0	1	Station supports polling but does not request to be put on the polling list

CF-Pollable	CF-Poll Request	Interpretation
1	0	Station supports polling and requests a position on the polling list
1	1	Station supports polling and requests that it never be polled (results in station treated as if it does not support contention-free operation)
Access point usage		
0	0	Access point does not implement the point coordination function
0	1	Access point uses PCF for delivery but does not support polling
1	0	Access point uses PCF for delivery and polling
1	1	Reserved; unused

Current AP Address

Mobile stations use the Current AP Address field, shown in Figure 4-25, to indicate the MAC address of the access point with which they are associated. This field is used to ease associations and reassociations. Stations transmit the address of the access point that handled the last association with the network. When an association is established with a different access point, this field can be used to transfer the association and retrieve any buffered frames.

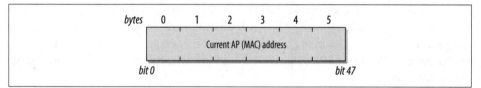

Figure 4-25. Current AP Address field

Listen interval

To save battery power, stations may shut off the antenna units in 802.11 network interfaces. While stations are sleeping, access points must buffer frames for them. Dozing stations periodically wake up to listen to traffic announcements to determine whether the access point has any buffered frames. When stations associate with an access point, part of the saved data is the *Listen Interval*, which is the number of Beacon intervals that stations wait between listening for Beacon frames. The Listen Interval, shown in Figure 4-26, allows mobile stations to indicate how long the access point must retain buffered frames. Higher listen intervals require more access point memory for frame buffering. Access points may use this feature to estimate the resources that will be required and may refuse resource-intensive associations. The Listen Interval is described in Chapter 7.

Association ID

The Association ID, shown in Figure 4-27, is a 16-bit field. When stations associate with an access point, they are assigned an Association ID to assist with control and

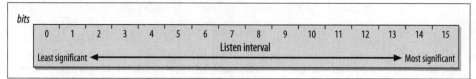

Figure 4-26. Listen Interval field

management functions. Even though 14 bits are available for use in creating Association IDs, they range only from 1–2,007. To maintain compatibility with the Duration/ID field in the MAC header, the two most significant bits are set to 1.

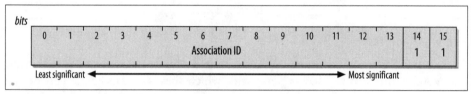

Figure 4-27. Association ID field

Timestamp

The Timestamp field, shown in Figure 4-28, allows synchronization between the stations in a BSS. The master timekeeper for a BSS periodically transmits the number of microseconds it has been active. When the counter reaches its maximum value, it wraps around. (Counter wraps are unlikely given the length of time it takes to wrap a 64-bit counter. At over 580,000 years, I would bet on a required patch or two before the counter wrap.)

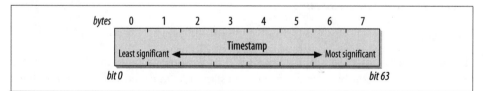

Figure 4-28. Timestamp field

Reason Code

Stations may send Disassociation or Deauthentication frames in response to traffic when the sender has not properly joined the network. Part of the frame is a 16-bit Reason Code field, shown in Figure 4-29, to indicate what the sender has done incorrectly. Table 4-5 shows why certain reason codes are generated. Fully understanding the use of reason codes requires an understanding of the different classes of frames and states of the 802.11 station, which is discussed in the section "Frame Transmission and Association and Authentication States."

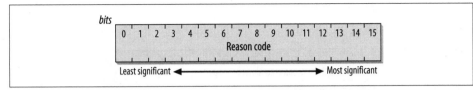

Figure 4-29. Reason Code field

Table 4-5. Reason codes

Code	Explanation
0	Reserved; unused
1	Unspecified
2	Prior authentication is not valid
3	Station has left the basic service area or extended service area and is deauthenticated
4	Inactivity timer expired and station was disassociated
5	Disassociated due to insufficient resources at the access point
6	Incorrect frame type or subtype received from unauthenticated station
7	Incorrect frame type or subtype received from unassociated station
8	Station has left the basic service area or extended service area and is disassociated
9	Association or reassociation requested before authentication is complete
10–65,535	Reserved; unused

Status Code

Status codes indicate the success or failure of an operation. The Status Code field, shown in Figure 4-30, is 0 when an operation succeeds and nonzero on failure. Table 4-6 shows the status codes that have been standardized.

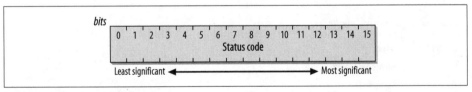

Figure 4-30. Status Code field

Table 4-6. Status codes

Code	Explanation
0	Operation completed successfully
1	Unspecified failure
2–9	Reserved; unused
10	Requested capability set is too broad and cannot be supported
11	Reassociation denied; prior association cannot be identified and transferred

Table 4-6. Status codes (continued)

Code	Explanation
12	Association denied for a reason not specified in the 802.11 standard
13	Requested authentication algorithm not supported
14	Unexpected authentication sequence number
15	Authentication rejected; the response to the challenge failed
16	Authentication rejected; the next frame in the sequence did not arrive in the expected window
17	Association denied; the access point is resource-constrained
18	Association denied; the mobile station does not support all of the data rates required by the BSS
19 (802.11b)	Association denied; the mobile station does not support the Short Preamble option
20 (802.11b)	Association denied; the mobile station does not support the PBCC modulation option
21 (802.11b)	Association denied; the mobile station does not support the Channel Agility option
22–65,535	Reserved for future standardization work

Management Frame Information Elements

Information elements are variable-length components of management frames. A generic information element has an ID number, a length, and a variable-length component, as shown in Figure 4-31. Standardized values for the element ID number are shown in Table 4-7.

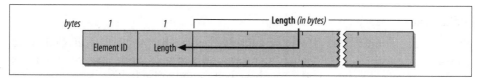

Figure 4-31. Generic management frame information element

Table 4-7. Information elements

Element ID	Name
0	Service Set Identity (SSID)
1	Supported Rates
2	FH Parameter Set
3	DS Parameter Set
4	CF Parameter Set
5	Traffic Indication Map (TIM)
6	IBSS Parameter Set
7–15	Reserved; unused
16	Challenge text
17–31	Reserved for challenge text extension
32–255	Reserved; unused

Service Set Identity (SSID)

Network managers are only human, and they usually prefer to work with letters, numbers, and names rather than 48-bit identifiers. 802.11 networks, in the broadest sense, are either extended service sets or independent BSSs. The SSID, shown in Figure 4-32, allows network managers to assign an identifier to the service set. Stations attempting to join a network may scan an area for available networks and join the network with a specified SSID. The SSID is the same for all the basic service areas composing an extended service area.

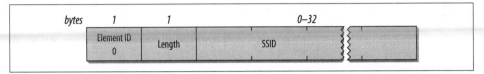

Figure 4-32. Service Set Identity information element

Some documentation refers to the SSID as the *network name* because network administrators frequently assign a character string to it. Most products require that the string be a garden variety, null-terminated ASCII string. In all cases, the length of the SSID ranges between 0 and 32 bytes. The zero-byte case is a special case called the *broadcast SSID*; it is used only in Probe Request frames when a station attempts to discover all the 802.11 networks in its area.

Supported Rates

Several data rates have been standardized for wireless LANs. The Supported Rates information element allows an 802.11 network to specify the data rates it supports. When mobile stations attempt to join the network, they check the data rates used in the network. Some rates are mandatory and must be supported by the mobile station, while others are optional.

The Supported Rates information element is shown in Figure 4-33. It consists of a string of bytes. Each byte uses the seven low-order bits for the data rate; the most significant bit indicates whether the data rate is mandatory. Mandatory rates are encoded with the most significant bit set to 1 and optional rates have a 0. Up to eight rates may be encoded in the information element.

In the initial revision of the 802.11 specification, the seven bits encoded the data rate as a multiple of 500 kbps. New technology, especially ETSI's HIPERLAN efforts, required a change to the interpretation. When seven bits are used to have a multiple of 500 kbps, the maximum data rate that can be encoded is 63.5 Mbps. Research and development on wireless LAN technology has made this rate achievable in the near future. As a result, the IEEE changed the interpretation from a multiple of 500 kbps to a simple label in 802.11b. Previously standardized rates were given labels corresponding to

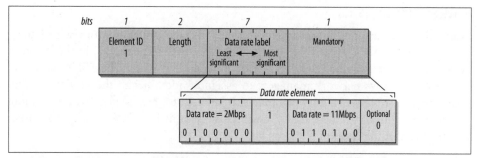

Figure 4-33. Supported Rates information element

the multiple of 500 kbps, but future standards may use any value. Currently standardized values are shown in Table 4-8.

Table 4-8. Supported Rate labels

Binary value	Corresponding rate
2	1 Mbps
4	2 Mbps
11	5.5 Mbps
22	11 Mbps

As an example, Figure 4-33 shows the encoding of two data rates. Two-Mbps service is mandatory, and 11-Mbps service is supported. This is encoded as a mandatory 2-Mbps rate and an optional 11-Mbps rate.

FH Parameter Set

The FH Parameter Set information element, shown in Figure 4-34, contains all parameters necessary to join a frequency-hopping 802.11 network.

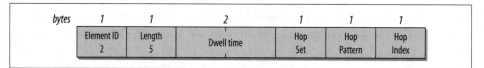

Figure 4-34. FH Parameter Set information element

The FH Parameter Set has four fields that uniquely specify an 802.11 network based on frequency hopping. Chapter 10 describes these identifiers in depth.

Dwell Time
> 802.11 FH networks hop from channel to channel. The amount of time spent on each channel in the hopping sequence is called the *dwell time*. It is expressed in time units (TUs).

Hop Set

Several hopping patterns are defined by the 802.11 frequency-hopping PHY. This field, a single byte, identifies the set of hop patterns in use.

Hop Pattern

Stations select one of the hopping patterns from the set. This field, also a single byte, identifies the hopping pattern in use.

Hop Index

Each pattern consists of a long sequence of channel hops. This field, a single byte, identifies the current point in the hop sequence.

DS Parameter Set

Direct-sequence 802.11 networks have only one parameter: the channel number used by the network. High-rate, distribution ststem networks use the same channels and thus can use the same parameter set. The channel number is encoded as a single byte, as shown in Figure 4-35.

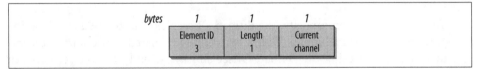

Figure 4-35. DS Parameter Set information element

Traffic Indication Map (TIM)

Access points buffer frames for mobile stations sleeping in low-power mode. Periodically, the access point attempts to deliver buffered frames to sleeping stations. A practical reason for this arrangement is that much more power is required to power up a transmitter than to simply turn on a receiver. The designers of 802.11 envisioned battery-powered mobile stations; the decision to have buffered frames delivered to stations periodically was a way to extend battery life for low-power devices.

Part of this operation is to send the Traffic Indication Map (TIM) information element (Figure 4-36) to the network to indicate which stations have buffered traffic waiting to be picked up.

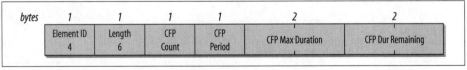

Figure 4-36. Traffic Indication Map information element

The meat of the traffic indication map is the *virtual bitmap*, a logical structure composed of 2,008 bits. Each bit is tied to the Association ID. When traffic is buffered for that Association ID, the bit is 1. If no traffic is buffered, the bit tied to the Association ID is 0.

Four fields make up the body of the TIM information element:

DTIM Count

This one-byte field is the number of Beacons that will be transmitted before the next DTIM frame. DTIM frames indicate that buffered broadcast and multicast frames will be delivered shortly. Not all Beacon frames are DTIM frames.

DTIM Period

This one-byte field indicates the number of Beacon intervals between DTIM frames. Zero is reserved and is not used. The DTIM count cycles through from the period down to 0.

Bitmap Control and Partial Virtual Bitmap

The Bitmap Control field is divided into two subfields. Bit 0 is used for the traffic indication status of Association ID 0, which is reserved for multicast traffic. The remaining seven bits of the Bitmap Control field are used for the Bitmap Offset field.

To save transmission capacity, the Bitmap Offset field can be used to transmit a portion of the virtual bitmap. The Bitmap Offset is related to the start of the virtual bitmap. By using the Bitmap Offset and the Length, 802.11 stations can infer which part of the virtual bitmap is included.

CF Parameter Set

The CF Parameter Set information element is transmitted in Beacons by access points that support contention-free operation. Contention-free service is discussed in Chapter 8 because of its optional nature.

IBSS Parameter Set

IBSSs currently have only one parameter, the announcement traffic indication map (ATIM) window, shown in Figure 4-37. This field is used only in IBSS Beacon frames. It indicates the number of time units (TUs) between ATIM frames in an IBSS.

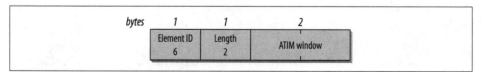
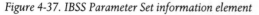

Figure 4-37. IBSS Parameter Set information element

Challenge Text

The shared-key authentication system defined by 802.11 requires that the mobile station successfully decrypt an encrypted challenge. The challenge is sent using the Challenge Text information element, which is shown in Figure 4-38.

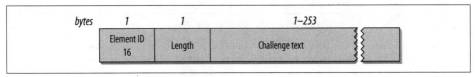

Figure 4-38. Challenge Text information element

Types of Management Frames

The fixed fields and information elements are used in the body of management frames to convey information. Several types of management frames exist and are used for various link-layer maintenance functions.

Beacon

Beacon frames announce the existence of a network and are an important part of many network maintenance tasks. They are transmitted at regular intervals to allow mobile stations to find and identify a network, as well as match parameters for joining the network. In an infrastructure network, the access point is responsible for transmitting Beacon frames. The area in which Beacon frames appear defines the basic service area. All communication in an infrastructure network is done through an access point, so stations on the network must be close enough to hear the Beacons.

Figure 4-39 shows all the fields that can be used in a Beacon frame in the order in which they appear. Not all of the elements are present in all Beacons. Optional fields are present only when there is a reason for them to be used. The FH and DS Parameter Sets are used only when the underlying physical layer is based on frequency hopping or direct-sequence techniques. Only one physical layer can be in use at any point, so the FH and DS Parameter Sets are mutually exclusive.

The CF Parameter Set is used only in frames generated by access points that support the PCF, which is optional. The TIM element is used only in Beacons generated by access points, because only access points perform frame buffering.

Probe Request

Mobile stations use Probe Request frames to scan an area for existing 802.11 networks. The format of the Probe Request frame is shown in Figure 4-40. All fields are mandatory.

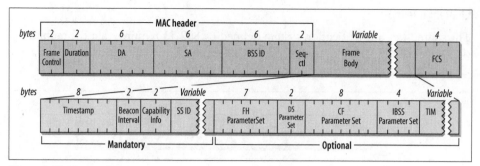

Figure 4-39. Beacon frame

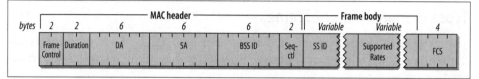

Figure 4-40. Probe Request frame

A Probe Request frame contains two fields: the SSID and the rates supported by the mobile station. Stations that receive Probe Requests use the information to determine whether the mobile station can join the network. To make a happy union, the mobile station must support all the data rates required by the network and must want to join the network identified by the SSID. This may be set to the SSID of a specific network or set to join any compatible network. Drivers that allow cards to join any network use the broadcast SSID in Probe Requests.

Probe Response

If a Probe Request encounters a network with compatible parameters, the network sends a Probe Response frame. The station that sent the last Beacon is responsible for responding to incoming probes. In infrastructure networks, this station is the access point. In an IBSS, responsibility for Beacon transmission is distributed. After a station transmits a Beacon, it assumes responsibility for sending Probe Response frames for the next Beacon interval. The format of the Probe Response frame is shown in Figure 4-41. Some of the fields in the frame are mutually exclusive; the same rules apply to Probe Response frames as to Beacon frames.

The Probe Response frame carries all the parameters in a Beacon frame, which enables mobile stations to match parameters and join the network. Probe Response frames can safely leave out the TIM element because stations sending probes are not yet associated and thus would not need to know which associations have buffered frames waiting at the access point.

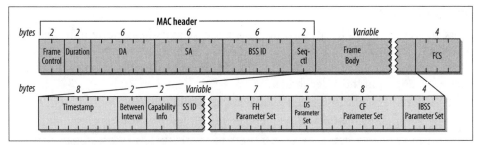

Figure 4-41. Probe Response frame

IBSS announcement traffic indication map (ATIM)

IBSSs have no access points and therefore cannot rely on access points for buffering. When a station in an IBSS has buffered frames for a receiver in low-power mode, it sends an ATIM frame during the delivery period to notify the recipient it has buffered data. See Figure 4-42.

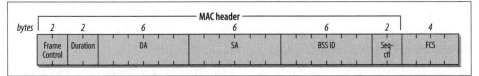

Figure 4-42. ATIM frame

Disassociation and Deauthentication

Disassociation frames are used to end an association relationship, and Deauthentication frames are used to end an authentication relationship. Both frames include a single fixed field, the Reason Code, as shown in Figure 4-43. Of course, the Frame Control fields differ because the subtype distinguishes between the different types of management frames.

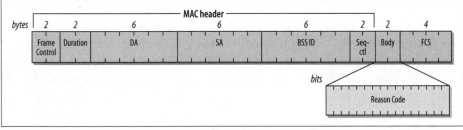

Figure 4-43. Disassociation and Deauthentication frames

Association Request

Once mobile stations identify a compatible network and authenticate to it, they may attempt to join the network by sending an Association Request frame. The format of the Association Request frame is shown in Figure 4-44. All fields are mandatory, and they must appear in the order shown.

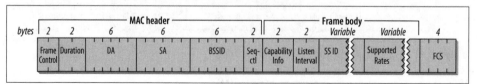

Figure 4-44. Association Request frame

The Capability Information field is used to indicate the type of network the mobile station wants to join. Before an access point accepts an association request, it verifies that the Capability Information, SSID, and Supported Rates all match the parameters of the network. Access points also note the Listen Interval, which describes how often a mobile station listens to Beacon frames to monitor the TIM.

Reassociation Request

Mobile stations moving between basic service areas within the same extended service area need to reassociate with the network before using the distribution system again. Stations may also need to reassociate if they leave the coverage area of an access point temporarily and rejoin it later. See Figure 4-45.

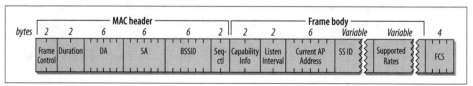

Figure 4-45. Reassociation Request frame

Association and Reassociation Requests differ only in that a Reassociation Request includes the address of the mobile station's current access point. Including this information allows the new access point to contact the old access point and transfer the association data. The transfer may include frames that were buffered at the old access point.

Association Response and Reassociation Response

When mobile stations attempt to associate with an access point, the access point replies with an Association Response or Reassociation Response frame, shown in Figure 4-46. The two differ only in the subtype field in the Frame Control field. All fields are mandatory. As part of the response, the access point assigns an Association ID. How an access point assigns the association ID is implementation-dependent.

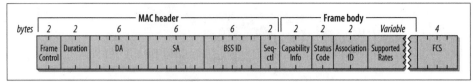

Figure 4-46. (Re)Association Response frame

Authentication

To authenticate to the access point, mobile stations exchange Authentication frames, which are shown in Figure 4-47.

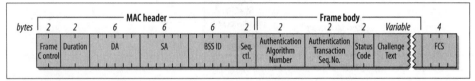

Figure 4-47. Authentication frames

Different authentication algorithms may co-exist. The Authentication Algorithm Number field is used for algorithm selection. The authentication process may involve a number of steps (depending on the algorithm), so there is a sequence number for each frame in the authentication exchange. The Status Code and Challenge Text are used in different ways by different algorithms; details are discussed in Chapter 7.

Frame Transmission and Association and Authentication States

Allowed frame types vary with the association and authentication states. Stations are either authenticated or unauthenticated and can be associated or unassociated. These two variables can be combined into three allowed states, resulting in the 802.11 Hierarchy of Network Development:

1. Initial state; not authenticated and not associated
2. Authenticated but not yet associated
3. Authenticated and associated

Each state is a successively higher point in the development of an 802.11 connection. All mobile stations start in State 1, and data can be transmitted through a distribution system only in State 3. (IBSSs do not have access points or associations and thus only reach Stage 2.) Figure 4-48 is the overall state diagram for frame transmission in 802.11.

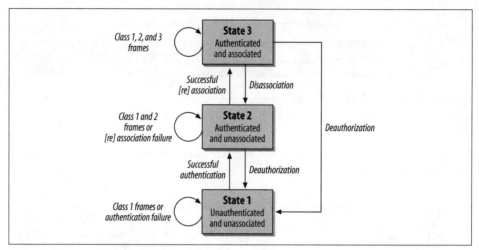

Figure 4-48. Overall 802.11 state diagram

Frame Classes

Frames are also divided into different classes. Class 1 frames can be transmitted in State 1; Class 1 and 2 frames in State 2; and Class 1, 2, and 3 frames in State 3.

Class 1 frames

Class 1 frames may be transmitted in any state and are used to provide the basic operations used by 802.11 stations. Control frames are received and processed to provide basic respect for the CSMA/CA "rules of the road" and to transmit frames in an IBSS. Class 1 frames also allow stations to find an infrastructure network and authenticate to it. Table 4-9 shows a list of the frames that belong to the Class 1 group.

Table 4-9. Class 1 frames

Control	Management	Data
Request to Send (RTS)	Probe Request	Any frame with ToDS and FromDS false (0)
Clear to Send (CTS)	Probe Response	
Acknowledgment (ACK)	Beacon	
CF-End	Authentication	
CF-End+CF-Ack	Deauthentication	
	Announcement Traffic Indication Message (ATIM)	

Class 2 frames

Class 2 frames can be transmitted only after a station has successfully authenticated to the network, and they can be used only in States 2 and 3. Class 2 frames manage associations. Successful association or reassociation requests move a station to State 3; unsuccessful association attempts cause the station to stay in State 2. When a station receives a Class 2 frame from a nonauthenticated peer, it responds with a Deauthentication frame, dropping the peer back to State 1.* Table 4-10 shows the Class 2 frames.

Table 4-10. Class 2 frames

Control	Management	Data
None	Association Request/Response	None
	Reassociation Request/Response	
	Disassociation	

Class 3 frames

Class 3 frames are used when a station has been successfully authenticated and associated with an access point. Once a station has reached State 3, it is allowed to use distribution system services and reach destinations beyond its access point. Stations may also use the power-saving services provided by access points in State 3 by using the PS-Poll frame. Table 4-11 lists the different types of Class 3 frames.

Table 4-11. Class 3 frames

Control	Management	Data
PS-Poll	Deauthentication	Any frames, including those with either the ToDS or FromDS bits set

If an access point receives frames from a mobile station that is authenticated but not associated, the access point responds with a Disassociation frame to bump the mobile station back to State 2. If the mobile station is not even authenticated, the access point responds with a Deauthentication frame to force the mobile station back into State 1.

---

* This rejection action takes place only for frames that are not filtered. Filtering prevents frames from a different BSS from triggering a rejection.

## CHAPTER 5

Wired Equivalent Privacy (WEP)

Anyone who is not shocked by quantum
theory has not understood it.
—Niels Bohr

In wireless networks, the word "broadcast" takes on an entirely new meaning. Security concerns have haunted 802.11 deployments since the standardization effort began. IEEE's attempt to address snooping concerns culminated in the optional Wired Equivalent Privacy (WEP) standard, which is found in clause 8.2 of 802.11. WEP can be used by stations to protect data as it traverses the wireless medium, but it provides no protection past the access point.

Many of the headlines about 802.11 over the past year were due to WEP. As networks become important to doing business, security has become an increasingly prominent worry. WEP was initially marketed as the security solution for wireless LANs, though its design was so flawed as to make that impossible.

WEP is so flawed that it is not worth using in many cases. Some of the flaws are severe design flaws, and the complete break of WEP in late 2001 was caused by a latent problem with the cryptographic cipher used by WEP. To understand WEP and its implications for the security of your network, this chapter presents some background on WEP's cryptographic heritage, lists the design flaws, and discusses the final straw. It closes with recommendations on the use of WEP. To make a long chapter much shorter, the basic recommendation is to think very, very carefully before relying on WEP because it has been soundly defeated.

Cryptographic Background to WEP

Before discussing the design of WEP, it's necessary to cover some basic cryptographic concepts. I am not a cryptographer, and a detailed discussion of the cryptography involved would not be appropriate in this book, so this chapter is necessarily brief.[*]

To protect data, WEP requires the use of the RC4 cipher, which is a symmetric (secret-key) stream cipher. RC4 shares a number of properties with all stream ciphers. Generally speaking, a stream cipher uses a stream of bits, called the *keystream*. The keystream is then combined with the message to produce the *ciphertext*. To recover the original message, the receiver processes the ciphertext with an identical keystream. RC4 uses the exclusive OR (XOR) operation to combine the keystream and the ciphertext. Figure 5-1 illustrates the process.

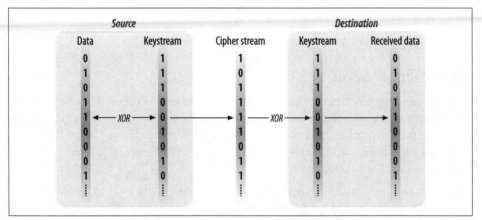

Figure 5-1. Generic stream cipher operation

Most stream ciphers operate by taking a relatively short secret key and expanding it into a pseudorandom keystream the same length as the message. This process is illustrated in Figure 5-2. The pseudorandom number generator (PRNG) is a set of rules used to expand the key into a keystream. To recover the data, both sides must share the same secret key and use the same algorithm to expand the key into a pseudorandom sequence.

Because the security of a stream cipher rests entirely on the randomness of the keystream, the design of the key-to-keystream expansion is of the utmost importance. When RC4 was selected by the 802.11 working group, it appeared to be quite secure. But once RC4 was selected as the ciphering engine of WEP, it spurred research that ultimately found an exploitable flaw in the RC4 cipher that will be discussed later.

---

[*] Readers interested in more detailed explanations of the cryptographic algorithms involved should consult *Applied Cryptography* by Bruce Schneier (Wiley, 1996).

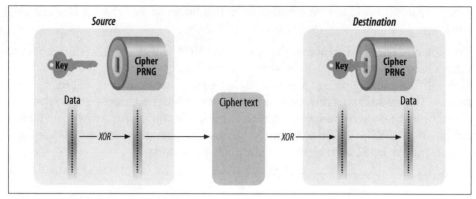

Figure 5-2. Keyed stream cipher operation

Stream Cipher Security

A totally random keystream is called a *one-time pad* and is the only known encryption scheme that is mathematically proven to protect against certain types of attacks. One-time pads are not commonly used because the keystream must be perfectly random and the same length as the data that will be protected, and it can never be reused.

Attackers are not limited to attacking the underlying cipher. They can choose to exploit any weak point in a cryptographic system. One famous Western intelligence effort, code-named VENONA, broke Soviet messages encrypted with one-time pads that were reused. The National Security Agency has made some information on the project public at *http://www.nsa.gov/docs/venona*. It is easy to understand the temptation to reuse the one-time pads. Huge volumes of keying material are necessary to protect even a small amount of data, and those keying pads must be securely distributed, which in practice proves to be a major challenge.

Stream ciphers are a compromise between security and practicality. The perfect randomness (and perfect security) of a one-time pad is attractive, but the practical difficulties and cost incurred in generating and distributing the keying material is worthwhile only for short messages that require the utmost security. Stream ciphers use a less random keystream but one that is random enough for most applications.

Cryptographic Politics

Three major nontechnical concerns may impact the use of WEP:

1. RC4 is the intellectual property of RSA Security, Inc., and must be licensed. RSA would almost certainly file suit against any unlicensed RC4 implementation. For

most end users, this is a minor point because wireless LAN equipment vendors would need to license RC4. In the past, this has been a problem for Linux users because some early wireless cards didn't include WEP on the card, and patents prevented open source developers from implementing it in the device driver. The latest generation of wireless cards solves this problem by implementing WEP on the card itself; all the device driver has to do is load the card with the keys.

2. Products must be exportable from U.S. locations to compete across the world. The 802.11 project committee specifically designed WEP to meet with approval from the U.S. export regulations at the time; as a consequence, WEP implementations were restricted to a maximum key length of 40 bits. Rules have been relaxed since then, and longer keys are allowed. Unfortunately, longer key lengths were never formally specified and may not be interoperable between products from different vendors.

3. Some governments impose restrictions on the importation of cryptographic hardware and software, which may prevent the use of encryption to protect the wireless LAN link. Without even the minimal protection provided by WEP, it may not be worth the risk to use wireless LAN technology in such locations.

WEP Cryptographic Operations

Communications security has three major objectives. Any protocol that attempts to secure data as it travels across a network must help network managers to achieve these goals. *Confidentiality* is the term used to describe data that is protected against interception by unauthorized parties. *Integrity* means that the data has not been modified. *Authentication* underpins any security strategy because part of the reliability of data is based on its origin. Users must ensure that data comes from the source it purports to come from. Systems must use authentication to protect data appropriately. Authorization and access control are both implemented on top of authentication. Before granting access to a piece of data, systems must find out who the user is (authentication) and whether the access operation is allowed (authorization).

WEP provides operations that attempt to help meet these objectives. Frame body encryption supports confidentiality. An integrity check sequence protects data in transit and allows receivers to validate that the received data was not altered in transit. WEP also enables stronger shared-key authentication of stations for access points, a feature discussed in Chapter 7. In practice, WEP falls short in all of these areas. Confidentiality is compromised by flaws in the RC4 cipher; the integrity check was poorly designed; and authentication is of users' MAC addresses, not users themselves.

WEP also suffers from the approach it takes. It encrypts frames as they traverse the wireless medium. Nothing is done to protect frames on a wired backbone, where they are subject to any attack. Furthermore, WEP is designed to secure the network from external intruders. Once an intruder discovers the WEP key, though, the wireless medium becomes the equivalent of a big shared wired network.

WEP Data Processing

Confidentiality and integrity are handled simultaneously, as illustrated in Figure 5-3. Before encryption, the frame is run through an integrity check algorithm, generating a hash called an integrity check value (ICV). The ICV protects the contents against tampering by ensuring that the frame has not changed in transit. The frame and the ICV are both encrypted, so the ICV is not available to casual attackers.

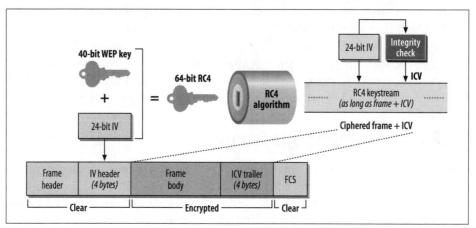

Figure 5-3. WEP operations

WEP specifies the use of a 40-bit secret key. The secret WEP key is combined with a 24-bit initialization vector (IV) to create a 64-bit RC4 key; the first 24 bits of the RC4 key are the IV, followed by the 40-bit WEP key. RC4 takes the 64 input bits and generates a keystream equal to the length of the frame body plus the IV. The keystream is then XORed with the frame body and the IV to cipher it. To enable the receiver to decrypt the frame, the IV is placed in the header of the frame.

WEP keying

To protect traffic from brute-force decryption attacks, WEP uses a set of up to four *default keys*, and it may also employ pairwise keys, called *mapped keys*, when allowed. Default keys are shared among all stations in a service set. Once a station has obtained the default keys for its service set, it may communicate using WEP.

Key reuse is often a weakness of cryptographic protocols. For this reason, WEP has a second class of keys used for pairwise communications. These keys are shared only

WEP Key Lengths

Standardized WEP implementations use 64-bit shared RC4 keys. Of the 64 bits, 40 are a shared secret. Vendors use a variety of names for the standard WEP mode: "standard WEP," "802.11-compliant WEP," "40-bit WEP," "40+24-bit WEP," or even "64-bit WEP." I personally feel that the last term is a stretch, based on hoodwinking the consumer with the length of the shared key and not the size of the shared secret, but it has become somewhat standard throughout the industry.

Concerns about the key length used in WEP have dogged it since its inception. Products that use 40-bit secret keys have always been exportable from the United States, which has served to cast doubt on the security provided by such a key. In a well-designed cryptographic system, additional security can be obtained by using a longer key. Each additional bit doubles the number of potential keys and, in theory, doubles the amount of time required for a successful attack.

To buy time for the standardization of a better solution than WEP, most of the industry moved to a 128-bit shared RC4 key. After subtracting 104 bits for the shared secret component of the RC4 key, only 104 bits are secret. Even though only 104 bits are secret, vendors refer to this as "128-bit WEP." Longer key-length implementations are not guaranteed to be compatible because no standard for them exists. At least one vendor uses 128 secret bits, plus the 24 in the initialization vector, for a total of 152 bits.

WEP, however, is not a well-designed cryptographic system, and the extra bits in the key buy you very little. The best publicly disclosed attack against WEP can recover the key in seconds, no matter what its length is. This book explores the use of the AirSnort tool to recover WEP keys in Chapter 16.

between the two stations communicating. The two stations sharing a key have a *key mapping relationship*; the key mapping relationship is part of the 802.11 MIB, which is presented in detail in Appendix A.

WEP framing

When WEP is in use, the frame body expands by eight bytes. Four bytes are used for a frame body IV header, and four are used for the ICV trailer. See Figure 5-4.

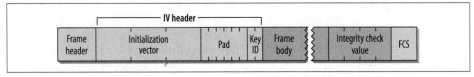

Figure 5-4. WEP frame extensions

The IV header uses 3 bytes for the 24-bit IV, with the fourth byte used for padding and key identification. When a default key is used, the Key ID subfield identifies the default key that was used to encrypt the frame. If a key mapping relationship is used, the Key ID subfield is 0. The 6 padding bits of the last byte must be 0. The integrity check is a 32-bit CRC of the data frame; it is appended to the frame body and protected by RC4.

Cryptographic Properties

Reuse of the keystream is the major weakness in any stream cipher–based cryptosystem. When frames are encrypted with the same RC4 keystream, the XOR of the two encrypted packets is equivalent to the XOR of the two plaintext packets. By analyzing differences between the two streams in conjunction with the structure of the frame body, attackers can learn about the contents of the plaintext frames themselves. To help prevent the reuse of the keystream, WEP uses the IV to encrypt different packets with different RC4 keys. However, the IV is part of the packet header and is not encrypted, so eavesdroppers are tipped off to packets that are encrypted with the same RC4 key.

Implementation problems can contribute to the lack of security. 802.11 admits that using the same IV for a large number of frames is insecure and should be avoided. The standard allows for using a different IV for each frame, but it is not required.

WEP incorporates an integrity check, but the algorithm used is a cyclic redundancy check (CRC). CRCs can catch single-bit alterations with high probability, but they are not *cryptographically secure*. Cryptographically secure integrity checks are based on hash functions, which are unpredictable. With unpredictable functions, if the attacker changes even one bit of the frame, the integrity check will change in unpredictable ways. The odds of an attacker finding an altered frame with the same integrity check are so slim that it cannot be done in real time. CRCs are not cryptographically secure. CRC calculations are straightforward mathematics, and it is easy to predict how changing a single bit will affect the result of the CRC calculation. (This property is often used by compressed data files for repair! If just a few bits are bad, they can sometimes be identified and corrected based on a CRC value.)

Key Distribution

Like so many other cryptographic protocols based on symmetric keys, WEP suffers from the Achilles heel of key distribution. The secret bits of the WEP key must be distributed to all stations participating in an 802.11 service set secured by WEP. The 802.11 standard, however, fails to specify the key distribution mechanism. The result is that vendors haven't done anything; you typically type keys into your device drivers or access points by hand. Unfortunately, manual configuration by the system administrator is the most nonscalable "protocol" in use.

Setting aside the system management headaches for a minute, consider the difficulties inherent in a cryptographic system requiring manual key distribution:

- Keys cannot be considered secret: all keys must be statically entered into either the driver software or the firmware on the wireless card. Either way, the key cannot be protected from a local user who wants to discover it.*

- If keys are accessible to users, then all keys must be changed whenever staff members leave the organization. Knowledge of WEP keys allows a user to set up an 802.11 station and passively monitor and decrypt traffic using the secret key for the network. WEP cannot protect against authorized insiders who also have the key.

- Organizations with large numbers of authorized users must publish the key to the user population, which effectively prevents it from being a secret. In the course of doing research for this book, I found network documentation at one major research university that described how to use the campus wireless network, including the WEP key.

Problems with WEP

Cryptographers have identified many flaws in WEP. The designers specified the use of RC4, which is widely accepted as a strong cryptographic cipher. Attackers, however, are not limited to a full-frontal assault on the cryptographic algorithms—they can attack any weak point in the cryptographic system. Methods of defeating WEP have come from every angle. One vendor shipped access points that exposed the secret WEP keys through SNMP, allowing an attacker to ask for just the key. Most of the press, though, has been devoted to flaws beyond implementation errors, which are much harder to correct.

Design Flaws

WEP's design flaws initially gained prominence when the Internet Security, Applications, Authentication and Cryptography (ISAAC) group at the University of California, Berkeley, published preliminary results based on their analysis of the WEP standard.† None of the problems identified by researchers depend on breaking RC4.

---

* Anecdotal evidence suggests that this may be commonplace. Power users who prefer to use Linux or FreeBSD may attempt to recover the key simply to allow access to the network from an otherwise unsupported operating system.

† The report is available on the Web at *http://www.isaac.cs.berkeley.edu/isaac/wep-faq.html*. Items 3–6 on the following list are summarized from that report.

Here's a summary of the problems they found; I've already touched on some of them:

1. Manual key management is a minefield of problems. Setting aside the operational issues with distributing identical shared secrets to the user population, the security concerns are nightmarish. New keying material must be distributed on a "flag day" to all systems simultaneously, and prudent security practices would lean strongly toward rekeying whenever anybody using WEP leaves the company (the administrative burden may, however, preclude doing this). Widely distributed secrets tend to become public over time. Passive sniffing attacks require obtaining only the WEP keys, which are likely to be changed infrequently. Once a user has obtained the WEP keys, sniffing attacks are easy. Market-leading sniffers are now starting to incorporate this capability for system administrators, claiming that after entering the network's WEP keys, all the traffic is readable!

2. In spite of vendor claims to the contrary, standardized WEP offers a shared secret of only 40 bits. Security experts have long questioned the adequacy of 40-bit private keys, and many recommend that sensitive data be protected by at least 128-bit keys.* Unfortunately, no standard has been developed for longer keys, so interoperability on multivendor networks with long WEP keys is not guaranteed without future work by the IEEE.

3. Stream ciphers are vulnerable to analysis when the keystream is reused. WEP's use of the IV tips off an attacker to the reuse of a keystream. Two frames that share the same IV almost certainly use the same secret key and keystream. This problem is made worse by poor implementations, which may not pick random IVs. The Berkeley team identified one implementation that started with an IV of 0 when the card was inserted and simply incremented the IV for each frame. Furthermore, the IV space is quite small (less than 17 million), so repetitions are guaranteed on busy networks.

4. Infrequent rekeying allows attackers to assemble what the Berkeley team calls *decryption dictionaries*—large collections of frames encrypted with the same keystreams. As more frames with the same IV pile up, more information is available about the unencrypted frames even if the secret key is not recovered. Given how overworked the typical system and network administration staff is, infrequent rekeying is the rule.

5. WEP uses a CRC for the integrity check. Although the value of the integrity check is encrypted by the RC4 keystream, CRCs are not cryptographically

---

* To be fair, WEP was originally developed with the goal of being exportable under the then current U.S. regulations for export of cryptographic systems. A longer key could not have been used without jeopardizing the commercial viability of U.S.-built 802.11 products.

secure. Use of a weak integrity check does not prevent determined attackers from transparently modifying frames.[*]

6. The access point is in a privileged position to decrypt frames. Conceptually, this feature can be attacked by tricking the access point into retransmitting frames that were encrypted by WEP. Frames received by the access point would be decrypted and then retransmitted to the attacker's station. If the attacker is using WEP, the access point would helpfully encrypt the frame using the attacker's key.

The Complete Break

In August 2001, Scott Fluhrer, Itsik Mantin, and Adi Shamir published a paper titled "Weaknesses in the Key Scheduling Algorithm of RC4." At the end of the paper, the authors describe a theoretical attack on WEP. At the heart of the attack is a weakness in the way that RC4 generates the keystream. All that is assumed is the ability to recover the first byte of the encrypted payload. Unfortunately, 802.11 uses LLC encapsulation, and the cleartext value of the first byte is known to be 0xAA (the first byte of the SNAP header). Because the first cleartext byte is known, the first byte of the keystream can be easily deduced from a trivial XOR operation with the first encrypted byte.

The paper's attacks are focused on a class of weak keys written in the form (B+3):ff: N. Each weak IV is used to attack a particular byte of the secret portion of the RC4 key. Key bytes are numbered from zero. Therefore, the weak IV corresponding to byte zero of the secret key has the form 3:FF:N. The second byte must be 0xFF; knowledge of the third byte in the key is required, but it need not be any specific value.

A standard WEP key is 40 secret bits, or 5 bytes numbered consecutively from 0 to 4. Weak IVs on a network protected by standard WEP must have a first byte that ranges from 3 (B=0) to 7 (B=4) and a second byte of 255. The third byte must be noted but is not constrained to any specific value. There are $5 \times 1 \times 256 = 1{,}280$ weak IVs in a standard WEP network.

It is interesting to note that the number of weak keys depends partly on the length of the RC4 key used. If the WEP key size is increased for added protection, the weak key net pulls in more data for use in the attack. Most commercial products use a 128-bit shared RC4 key, so there are more than twice as many weak IVs. Table 5-1 shows the number of weak IVs as a function of the secret key length.

---

[*] 802.11 requires frame retransmissions in the case of loss, so it may be possible for an attacker to retransmit a frame and cause a replacement injected frame to be accepted as legitimate.

Table 5-1. Number of weak IVs as a function of key length

Secret key length	Values of B+3 in weak IV (B+3:FF:N)	Number of weak IVs	Fraction of IV space
40 bits	3 <= B+3 < 8 (0 <= B < 5)	1,280	0.008%
104 bits	3 <= B+3 < 16 (0 <= B < 13)	3,328	0.020%
128 bits	3 <= B+3 < 19 (0 <= B < 16)	4,096	0.024%

Applying probability theory, Fluhrer, Mantin, and Shamir predict that about 60 resolved cases are needed to determine a key byte. Furthermore, and perhaps worst of all, the attack gains speed as more key bytes are determined; overall, it works in linear time. Doubling the key length only doubles the time for the attack to succeed.

With such a tantalizing result, it was only a matter of time before it was used to attack a real system. In early August 2001, Adam Stubblefield, John Ioannidis, and Avi Rubin applied the Fluhrer/Mantin/Shamir attack to an experimental, but real, network with devastating effect.[*] In their testing, 60 resolved cases usually determined a key byte, and 256 resolved cases always yielded a full key. It took less than a week to implement the attack, from the ordering of the wireless card to the recovery of the first full key. Coding the attack took only a few hours. Key recovery was accomplished between five and six million packets, which is a small number for even a moderately busy network.

Reporting on a successful attack, however, is nothing compared to having a public code base available to use at will. The hard part of the Fluhrer/Mantin/Shamir attack was finding the RC4 weakness. Implementing their recommendations is not too difficult. In late August 2001, Jeremy Bruestle and Blake Hegerle released AirSnort, an open source WEP key recovery program. Use of AirSnort is discussed in Chapter 16.

Conclusions and Recommendations

WEP was designed to provide relatively minimal protection to frames in the air. It was not designed for environments demanding a high level of security and therefore offers a comparatively smaller level of protection. The IEEE 802.11 working group has devoted an entire task group to security. The task group is actively working on a revised security standard. In the meantime, some vendors are offering proprietary approaches that allow stronger public-key authentication and random session keys, but these approaches are a single-vendor solution and only a stopgap. Better solutions can be built from off-the-shelf standardized components. Specific topology

[*] This work is described more fully in AT&T Labs Technical Report TD-4ZCPZZ.

deployments are discussed in Chapter 15. To close, I offer the following list of conclusions and recommendations.

1. WEP is not useful for anything other than protecting against casual traffic capture attacks. With the total break in August 2001 and the subsequent release of public implementation code, security administrators should assume that WEP on its own offers no confidentiality. Furthermore, 802.11 networks announce themselves to the world. On a recent trip through San Francisco, I configured a laptop to scan for area networks and found half a dozen. I was not making a serious effort to do this, either. My laptop was placed on the front passenger seat of my car, and I was using a PC Card 802.11 interface, which does not have particularly high gain. Had I been serious, I would have used a high-gain antenna to pick up fainter Beacon frames, and I would have mounted the antenna higher up so the radio signals were not blocked by the steel body of the car. Obscurity plus WEP may meet some definition of "wired equivalent" because frames on wired networks may be delivered to a number of users other than the intended recipient. However, defining "wired equivalent" is a semantic argument that is not worth getting bogged down in.

2. Manual key management is a serious problem. Peer-to-peer networking systems all have problems in the area of management scalability, and WEP is no different. Deploying pairwise keys is a huge burden on system administrators and does not add much, if any, security.

3. When a secret is widely shared, it quickly ceases to become a secret. WEP depends on widely sharing a secret key. Users may come and go, and WEP keys must be changed with every departure to ensure the protection provided by WEP.

4. Data that must be kept confidential should use strong cryptographic systems designed from the ground up with security in mind. The obvious choices are IPSec or SSH. The choice can be based on technical evaluation, product availability, user expertise, and nontechnical factors (institutional acceptance, pricing and licensing, and so on).

5. Varying levels of concern are appropriate for different locations. When using 802.11 for LAN extension, greater threats are likely to be found in large offices.

   a. Remote teleworkers should be protected by strong VPN systems such as IPSec. Using 802.11 in remote locations may increase the risk of interception, but any transmissions from a client to a central site should already be protected using a strong VPN system. Attackers may be able to capture packets traveling over a wireless network more easily, but IPSec was designed to operate in an environment where attackers had large amounts of encrypted traffic to analyze.

b. Large offices pose a much greater concern. VPNs to branch offices are typically site-to-site, protecting only from the edge of the branch office to the access link at the headquarters offices. Anything inside the remote office is not protected by IPSec and is vulnerable to sniffing if other measures are not taken.

6. Stopping anything more casual than packet sniffing requires client software that implements strong cryptographic protection. However, it requires extra system integration work and testing.

a. A higher-security, point-to-point tunneling technology may be all that is required for your organization. Unix systems can run PPP over SSH tunnels, and some IPSec solutions can be used to create point-to-point tunnels across the access point.

b. IPSec also protects across the LAN, which may be important. It is possible that a determined attacker can obtain access to the wired backbone LAN where traffic is no longer protected by WEP.

7. WEP does not protect users from each other. When all users have the WEP key, any traffic can be decrypted easily. Wireless networks that must protect users from each other should use VPN solutions or applications with strong built-in security.

It is dangerous to assume that protocols such as IPSec and SSH are magic bullets that can solve your security problems. But the bottom line for wireless networks is that you can't count on WEP to provide even minimal security, and using IPSec or SSH to encrypt your traffic goes a long way to improve the situation.

## CHAPTER 6

Security, Take 2: 802.1x

If at first you don't succeed, try again.
—Anonymous
(from the motivational poster
in breakrooms everywhere)

Security is a common thread linking many of the wireless LAN stories in the news throughout the past year, and several polls have shown that network managers consider security to be a significant obstacle to wider deployment of wireless LANs. Many of the security problems that have prevented stronger acceptance of 802.11 are caused by flaws in the design of WEP. WEP attempts to serve as both an authentication mechanism and a privacy mechanism. I hope Chapter 5 showed that it effectively serves as neither.

To address the shortcomings of WEP for authentication, the industry is working towards solutions based on the 802.1x specification, which is itself based on the IETF's Extensible Authentication Protocol (EAP). EAP was designed with flexibility in mind, and it has been used as the basis for a number of network authentication extensions. (Cisco's lightweight EAP, LEAP, also is based on EAP.)

802.1x is not without its problems, however. A recent research report identified several problems with the specification.[*] The first major problem is that 802.11 does not provide a way to guarantee the authenticity and integrity of any frames on the wireless network. Frames on wireless networks can easily be tampered with or forged outright, and the protocol does not provide a way to easily stop or even detect such attacks. The second major problem is that 802.1x was designed to allow the network to authenticate the user. Implicit in the protocol design is the assumption that users will connect to only the "right" network. On wireline networks, connecting to the right network can be as simple as following the wires. Access to the wiring helps

---

[*] "An Initial Analysis of the 802.1x Standard" by Arunesh Mishra and Bill Arbaugh; available at *http://www. cs.umd.edu/~waa/1x.pdf*.

the users identify the "right" network. On a wireless network, clear physical connections do not exist, so other mechanims must be designed for networks to prove their identity (or, more precisely, the identity of their owners) to users. 802.1x was designed to collect authentication information from users and grant or deny access based on that information. It was not designed to help networks provide credentials to users, so that function is not addressed by the 802.1x. The specter for rogue access points will not be put to rest by 802.1x.

How 802.1x will be applied to wireless networks is a matter for task group I (TGi) of the 802.11 working group. With no standard available, I have elected to describe how 802.1x works on LANs to provide a basic understanding of how the future 802.11i specification is likely to work. Some modifications will undoubtedly be made to adapt 802.1x to the wireless world, but the fundamental ideas will remain the same. Before talking about 802.1x, though, it is best to gain a solid understanding of the protocol that started it all: EAP.

The Extensible Authentication Protocol

802.1x is based on EAP. EAP is formally specified in RFC 2284 and was initially developed for use with PPP. When PPP was first introduced, there were two protocols available to authenticate users, each of which required the use of a PPP protocol number. Authentication is not a "one size fits all" problem, and it was an active area of research at the time. Rather than burn up PPP protocol numbers for authentication protocols that might become obsolete, the IETF standardized EAP. EAP used a single PPP protocol number while supporting a wide variety of authentication mechanisms. EAP is a simple encapsulation that can run over any link layer, but it has been most widely deployed on PPP links. Figure 6-1 shows the basic EAP architecture, which is designed to run over any link layer and use any number of authentication methods.

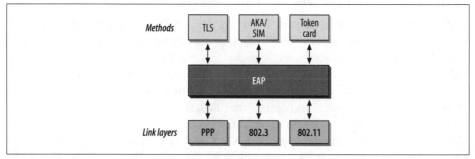

Figure 6-1. EAP architecture

EAP Packet Format

Figure 6-2 shows the format of an EAP packet. When used on PPP links, EAP is carried in PPP frames with a protocol number of 0xC227. There is no strict requirement that EAP run on PPP; the packet shown in Figure 6-2 can be carried in any type of frame. The fields in an EAP packet are:

Code

The Code field, the first field in the packet, is one byte long and identifies the type of EAP packet. It is used to interpret the Data field of the packet.

Identifier

The Identifier field is one byte long. It contains an unsigned integer used to match requests with responses to them. Retransmissions reuse the same identifier numbers, but new transmissions use new identifier numbers.

Length

The Length field is two bytes long. It is the number of bytes in the entire packet, which includes the Code, Identifier, Length, and Data fields. On some link layer protocols, padding may be required. EAP assumes that any data in excess of the Length field is link-layer padding and can be ignored.

Data

The last field is the variable-length Data field. Depending on the type of packet, the Data field may be zero bytes long. Interpretation of the Data field is based on the value of the Code field.

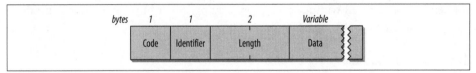

Figure 6-2. EAP packet format

EAP Requests and Responses

EAP exchanges are composed of requests and responses. The authenticator sends requests to the system seeking access, and based on the responses, access may be granted or denied. The format of request and response packets is shown in Figure 6-3.

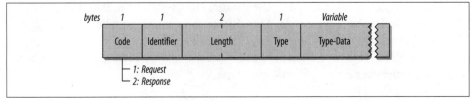

Figure 6-3. EAP Request and EAP Response packets

The Code field is set to 1 for requests and 2 for responses. The Identifier and Length fields are used as described in the previous section on the generic format. The Data field carries the data used in requests and responses. Each Data field carries one type of data, broken down into a type identifier code and the associated data:

Type

The Type field is a one-byte field that indicates the type of request or response. Only one type is used in each packet. With one exception, the Type field of the response matches the corresponding request. That exception is that when a request is unacceptable, the peer may send a NAK to suggest an alternative type. Types greater than or equal to 4 indicate authentication methods.

Type-Data

The Type-Data field is a variable field that must be interpreted according to the rules for each type.

Type code 1: Identity

The authenticator generally uses the Identity type as the initial request. After all, identifying the user is the first step in authentication. Naturally, most implementations of EAP prompt the user for input to determine the user identity. The Type-Data field may contain text used to prompt the user; the length of the string is computed from the Length field in the EAP packet itself.

Some EAP implementations may attempt to look up the user identity in a Response even before issuing the authentication challenge. If the user does not exist, the authentication can fail without further processing. Most implementations automatically reissue the identity request to correct typos.

Type Code 2: Notification

The authenticator can use the Notification type to send a message to the user. The user's system can then display the message for the user's benefit. Notification messages are used to provide messages to the user from the authentication system, such as a password about to expire. Responses must be sent in reply to Notification requests. However, they serve as simple acknowledgments, and the Type-Data field has a zero length.

Type code 3: NAK

NAKs are used to suggest a new authentication method. The authenticator issues a challenge, encoded by a type code. Authentication types are numbered 4 and above. If the end user system does not support the authentication type of the challenge, it can issue a NAK. The Type-Data field of a NAK message includes a single byte corresponding to the suggested authentication type.

Type code 4: MD-5 Challenge

The MD-5 Challenge is used to implement the EAP analog of the CHAP protocol, specified in RFC 1994. Requests contain a challenge to the end user. For successful authentication, CHAP requires that the challenge be successfully encoded with a shared secret. All EAP implementations must support the MD-5 Challenge, but they are free to NAK it in favor of another authentication method.

Type code 5: One-time password (OTP)

The one-time password system used by EAP is defined in RFC 1938. The Request issued to the user contains the OTP challenge string. In an OTP (type 5) response, the Type-Data field contains the words from the OTP dictionary in RFC 1938. Like all authentication types, responses may be NAKs (type 3).

Type code 6: Generic Token Card

Token cards such as RSA's SecurID and Secure Computing's Safeword are popular with many institutions because they offer the security of "random" one-time passwords without the hassle of an OTP rollout. The Request contains the Generic Token Card information necessary for authentication. The Type-Data field of the request must be greater than zero bytes in length. In the Response, the Type-Data field is used to carry the information copied from the token card by the user. In both Request and Response packets, the Length field of the EAP packet is used to compute the length of the Type-Data request.

Type code 13: TLS

In its initial form, EAP does not protect transmissions from eavesdropping. In a way, this is an understandable posture, given the origins of the protocol. When EAP is used over dial-up or dedicated links, there is a small chance of interception, but many administrators feel comfortable that the link is reasonably protected against eavesdropping.

For some links, however, assuming the existence of security may not be appropriate. RFC 2716 describes the use of Transport Layer Security (TLS) for authentication. TLS is the standardized successor to the widely deployed Secure Socket Layer (SSL), and TLS authentication inherits a number of useful characteristics from SSL. Most notably, mutual authentication is possible with TLS. Rather than issuing a one-sided challenge to the client ("Who are you?"), EAP-TLS can ensure that the client is communicating with a legitimate authenticator. In addition to mutual authentication, TLS provides a method to protect the authentication between the client and authenticator. It also provides a method to exchange a session key securely between the client and authenticator.

EAP-TLS is likely to become popular on wireless networks. In the current 802.11 authentication regime, access points are implicitly trusted by the clients. EAP-TLS could ensure clients that they are sending sensitive authentication data to legitimate access points instead of "rogue" access points set up by attackers seeking to collect data for a later attack on the network. EAP-TLS also enables the exchange of session keys, which limits the impact of a compromised WEP key.

Additional type codes in draft format

Several additional authentication types are currently in Internet-Draft form and may be standardized after this book is printed. Two of the most notable concepts are Kerberos authentication and cell-phone authentication (SIM cards on second-generation networks and AKA on third-generation networks).

EAP Success and Failure

At the conclusion of an EAP exchange, the user has either authenticated successfully or has failed to authenticate (Figure 6-4). Once the authenticator determines that the exchange is complete, it can issue a Success (code 3) or Failure (code 4) frame to end the EAP exchange. Implementations are allowed to send multiple requests before failing the authentication to allow a user to get the correct authentication data.

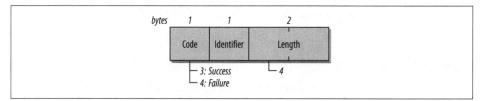

Figure 6-4. EAP Success and Failure frames

A Sample EAP Exchange

A sample EAP exchange is shown in Figure 6-5. It is unnecessarily complex to illustrate several features of the protocol. The EAP exchange is a series of steps beginning with a request for identity and ending with a success or failure message:

1. The authenticator issues a Request/Identity packet to identify the user.

2. The end user system prompts for input, collects the user identifier, and sends the user identifier in a Response/Identity message.

3. With the user identified, the authenticator can issue authentication challenges. In step 3 in the figure, the authenticator issues an MD-5 Challenge to the user with a Request/MD-5 Challenge packet.

4. The user system is configured to use a token card for authentication, so it replies with a Response/NAK, suggesting the use of Generic Token Card authentication.

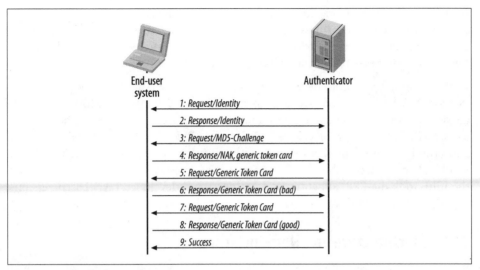

End-user system / Authenticator

1: Request/Identity
2: Response/Identity
3: Request/MD5-Challenge
4: Response/NAK, generic token card
5: Request/Generic Token Card
6: Response/Generic Token Card (bad)
7: Request/Generic Token Card
8: Response/Generic Token Card (good)
9: Success

Figure 6-5. Sample EAP exchange

5. The authenticator issues a Request/Generic Token Card challenge, prompting for the numerical sequence on the card.

6. The user types a response, which is passed along in a Response/Generic Token Card.

7. The user response was not correct, so authentication is not possible. However, the authenticator EAP implementation allows for multiple authentication Requests, so a second Request/Generic Token Card is issued.

8. Once again, the user types a response, which is passed along in a Response/ Generic Token Card.

9. On the second try, the response is correct, so the authenticator issues a Success message.

802.1x: Network Port Authentication

As LAN acceptance mushroomed in the 1990s, LAN ports popped up everywhere. Some types of organizations, such as universities, were further hampered by a need for openness. Network resources must be made available to a user community, but that community is fluid. Students are not like many network users. They frequently move from computer to computer and do not have a fixed network address; they may also graduate, transfer, enroll, leave campus, work on staff, or undergo any number of changes that may require changes in access privileges. Although network access must be extended to this fluid community, academic budgets are frequently tight, so it is important to prevent unauthorized use by outsiders.

In short, a generic network sign-on was required. Academic environments would not be the sole beneficiaries, however. Authentication to access network resources is common among Internet service providers, and corporations found the idea attractive because of the increasing flexibility of staffing plans.

Authentication to network devices at the link layer is not new. Network port authentication has been required by dial-up access servers for years. Most institutions already have a wide range of deployed infrastructure to support user authentication, such as RADIUS servers and LDAP directories. PPP over Ethernet (PPPoE) could conceivably be used to require user authentication to access an Ethernet, but it would add an unacceptable level of encapsulation overhead and complexity. Instead, the IEEE took the PPP authentication protocols and developed LAN-based versions. The resulting standard was 802.1x, "Port-Based Network Access Control."

802.1x Architecture and Nomenclature

802.1x defines three components to the authentication conversation, which are all shown in Figure 6-6. The *supplicant* is the end user machine that seeks access to network resources. Network access is controlled by the *authenticator*; it serves the same role as the access server in a traditional dial-up network. Both the supplicant and the authenticator are referred to as *Port Authentication Entities* (PAEs) in the specification. The authenticator terminates only the link-layer authentication exchange. It does not maintain any user information. Any incoming requests are passed to an *authentication server*, such as a RADIUS server, for actual processing.

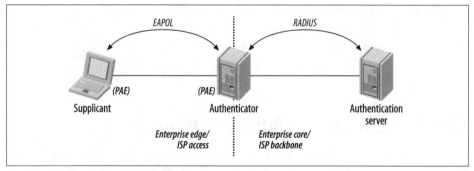

Figure 6-6. 802.1x architecture

Ports on an 802.1x-capable device are in an *authorized* state, in which the port is enabled, or an *unauthorized* state, in which it is disabled. Even while in the unauthorized state, however, the specification allows DHCP and other initialization traffic if permitted by a network manager.

The authentication exchange is logically carried out between the supplicant and the authentication server, with the authenticator acting only as a bridge. A derivation of EAP is used by the authenticator to pass challenges and responses back and forth.

From the supplicant to the authenticator (the "front end"), the protocol is EAP over LANs (EAPOL) or EAP over wireless (EAPOW). On the "back end," the protocol used is RADIUS. Some documentation may refer to it as "EAP over RADIUS." Figure 6-6 can be read as two different scenarios. In the enterprise scenario, the supplicant is a corporate host on the edge of the enterprise network, and the RADIUS server is located in the enterprise core. The figure also depicts an ISP using 802.1x to authenticate users, in which case the lefthand side of the figure is an ISP access area, and the righthand side is the ISP backbone.

802.1x is a framework, not a complete specification in and of itself. The actual authentication mechanism is implemented by the authentication server. 802.1x supplies a mechanism for issuing challenges and confirming or denying access, but it does not pass judgment on the offered credentials. Changes to the authentication method do not require complex changes to the end user devices or the network infrastructure. The authentication server can be reconfigured to "plug in" a new authentication service without changes to the end user driver software or switch firmware.

EAPOL Encapsulation

The basic format of an EAPOL frame is shown in Figure 6-7. EAPOL encapsulation is now analyzed by many popular network analyzers, including Ethereal. The frame's components are:

MAC header
Figure 6-7 shows the encapsulation on a wired Ethernet, so the MAC header consists of the destination MAC address and the source MAC address. On a wireless network, the MAC header would be the 24- to 30-byte header described in Chapter 3.

Ethernet Type
As with any other Ethernet frame, the Ethernet Type field contains the two-byte type code assigned to EAPOL: 88-8e.

Version
At this point, only Version 1 is standardized.

Packet Type
EAPOL is an extension of EAP. In addition to the EAP messages described in the previous section, EAPOL adds some messages to adapt EAP to the port-based LAN environment. Table 6-1 lists the packet types and their descriptions.

Table 6-1. EAPOL message types

Packet type	Name	Description
0000 0000	EAP-Packet	Contains an encapsulated EAP frame. Most frames are EAP-Packet frames.
0000 0001	EAPOL-Start	Instead of waiting for a challenge from the authenticator, the supplicant can issue an EAPOL-Start frame. In response, the authenticator sends an EAP-Request/Identity frame.

Table 6-1. EAPOL message types (continued)

Packet type	Name	Description
0000 0010	EAPOL-Logoff	When a system is done using the network, it can issue an EAPOL-Logoff frame to return the port to an unauthorized state.
0000 0011	EAPOL-Key	EAPOL can be used to exchange cryptographic keying information.
0000 0100	EAPOL-Encapsulated-ASF-Alert	The Alerting Standards Forum (ASF) has defined a way of allowing alerts, such as SNMP traps, to be sent to an unauthorized port using this frame type.

Packet Body Length

> This two-byte field is the length of the Packet Body field in bytes. It is set to 0 when no packet body is present.

Packet Body

> This variable-length field is present in all EAPOL frames except the EAPOL-Start and EAPOL-Logoff messages. It encapsulates one EAP packet in EAP-Packet frames, one key descriptor in EAPOL-Key frames, and one alert in EAPOL-Encapsulated-ASF-Alert frames.

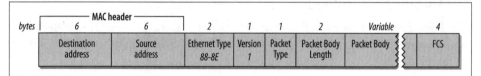

Figure 6-7. EAPOL frame format

Addressing

In shared-media LANs such as Ethernet, supplicants send EAPOL messages to the group address of 01:80:C2:00:00:03. On 802.11 networks, ports do not exist as such, and EAPOL can proceed only after the association process has allowed both the supplicant (mobile wireless station) and the authenticator (access point) to exchange MAC addresses. In environments such as 802.11, EAPOL requests use station addresses.

Sample 802.1x Exchange

EAPOL exchanges look almost exactly like EAP exchanges. The main difference is that supplicants can issue EAPOL-Start frames to trigger the EAP exchange, and they can use EAPOL-Logoff messages to deauthorize the port when the station is done using the network. The examples in this section assume that a RADIUS server is used as the back-end authentication server, and therefore they show the authenticator performing translation from EAP on the front end to RADIUS on the back end. EAP authentication in RADIUS packets is specified in RFC 2869.

The most common case, successful authentication, is shown in Figure 6-8. In the beginning, the port is unauthorized, so access to the network is blocked. The steps in this typical EAPOL exchange are:

1. The supplicant starts the 802.1x exchange with an EAPOL-Start message.

2. The "normal" EAP exchange begins. The authenticator (network switch) issues an EAP-Request/Identity frame.

3. The supplicant replies with an EAP-Response/Identity frame, which is passed on to the RADIUS server as a Radius-Access-Request packet.

4. The RADIUS server replies with a Radius-Access-Challenge packet, which is passed on to the supplicant as an EAP-Request of the appropriate authentication type containing any relevant challenge information.

5. The supplicant gathers the reply from the user and sends an EAP-Response in return. The response is translated by the authenticator into a Radius-Access-Request with the response to the challenge as a data field.

6. The RADIUS server grants access with a Radius-Access-Accept packet, so the authenticator issues an EAP-Success frame. The port is authorized, and the user can begin accessing the network. DHCP configuration may take place at this point.

7. When the supplicant is done accessing the network, it sends an EAPOL-Logoff message to put the port back into an authorized station.

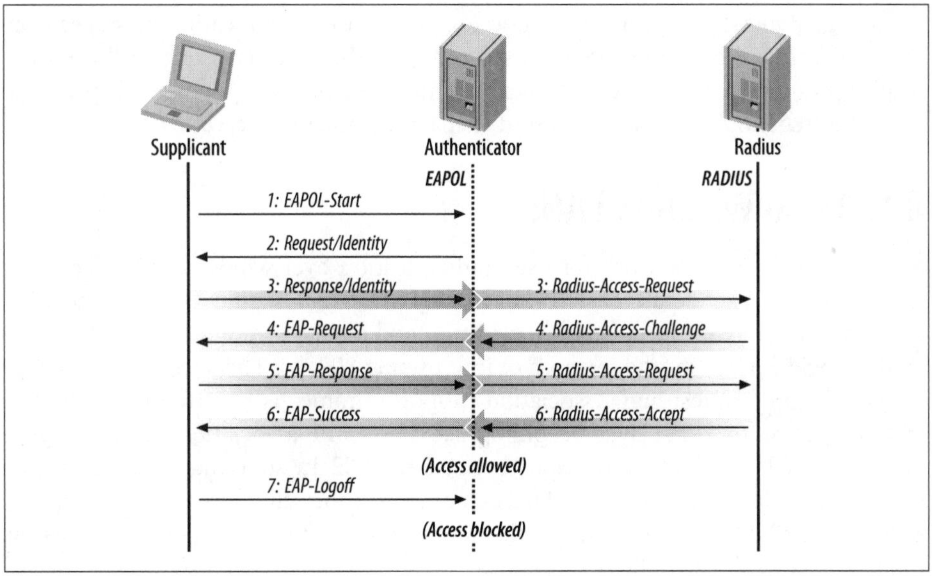

Figure 6-8. Typical EAPOL exchange

Exchanges similar to Figure 6-8 may be used at any point. It is not necessary for the user to begin an EAPOL exchange with the EAPOL-Start message. At any point, the authenticator can begin an EAPOL exchange by issuing an EAP-Request/Identity frame to refresh the authentication data.

802.1x Implementation and the User Experience

802.1x is naturally implemented in the device driver. No change to the hardware itself is necessary. Microsoft has implemented 802.1x as an operating system feature in Windows XP. With no additional software required, XP is likely to be a widely deployed 802.1x client. Cisco has made 802.1x clients available for Windows 9x, NT, 2000, MacOS, and Linux.

EAP is a generic authentication framework, so it does not require any particular authentication method. The first task is to decide on the type of authentication for wireless users. EAP-TLS is attractive because it enables mutual authentication and protects against rogue access points, but it requires that the RADIUS server support EAP-TLS. Use of EAP-TLS also requires that a certificate authority be deployed to manage certificates for wireless network users.

On the client side, authentication is configured in the driver. On XP, 802.1x authentication is configured along with other interface properties. Other implementations allow configuration in the driver. Certificate authentication may take place without any user interaction or may require the user to input a passphrase to unlock the certificate. EAP messages can result in pop ups to the user. Notification messages from the authenticator are immediately displayed, and the identity request allows for a display prompt. If the user is challenged to enter credentials, a pop up is displayed to enter the credentials that will be passed to the authentication server.

802.1x on Wireless LANs

802.1x provides a framework for user authentication over wireless LANs. The only minor change is to define how a "network port" exists within 802.11. The IEEE decided that an association between a station and an access point would be considered a "logical port" for the purpose of interpreting 802.1x. The successful exchange of Association Request and Association Response frames is reported to the 802.1x state engine as the link layer becoming active. 802.11 association must complete before the 802.1x negotiation begins because the 802.1x state machine requires an active link. Prior to a successful 802.1x authentication, the access point drops all non-802.1x traffic. Once the authentication succeeds, the access point removes the filter and allows traffic to flow normally.

The second change made possible by 802.1x is that the EAPOL-Key frame can be used to distribute keying information dynamically for WEP. Figure 6-9 shows a sample EAPOL exchange on an 802.11 network. The only differences from the previous figure are the requirements of the 802.11 Association Request and Response before beginning the EAPOL exchange and the EAPOL-Key frame that follows the EAP-Success frame. The figure also omits the closing EAPOL-Logoff message.

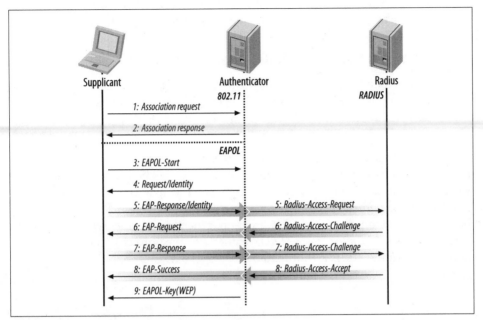

Figure 6-9. EAPOL exchange on an 802.11 network

Association Transfer

802.1x was designed for stations that attach to a port, use it, and then finish. 802.11 poses additional complexities for 802.1x because the association can move from access point to access point. Nothing in 802.1x describes how to move an authentication relationship from one port to another, because 802.1x was designed for a wired world. Transfer of the association and authentication information is an active area of standards development, and it should be addressed in the final 802.11i specification. Several proposals for a "fast handoff" between access points have been submitted, but their development and standardization will require cooperating with the task group developing the Inter-Access Point Protocol.

Keying

The EAPOL-Key frame allows keys to be sent from the access point to the client and vice versa. One commercial implementation uses two WEP keys for each associated station. One key encrypts downstream traffic to the client, and the other encrypts traffic from the client to the access point. Key exchange frames are sent only if the authentication succeeds; this prevents the compromise of key information. EAPOL-Key frames can be used periodically to update keys dynamically as well. Several of the weaknesses in WEP stem from the long lifetime of the keys. When it is difficult to rekey every station on the network, keys tend to be used for long periods of time. Several experts have recommended changing WEP keys on a regular basis, but no practical mechanism to do so has existed until now, with the development of 802.1x.

Enhancements to 802.11 Made Possible by 802.1x

802.1x brings a number of enhancements to 802.11 networks. Instead of deploying of Mobile IP, it might be possible for user-specific VLANs to be dynamically assigned using the RADIUS tunnel attributes specified in RFC 2868. Dynamic VLANs are clearly not an Internet-scale solution, but they may be a feasible enterprise solution.

Public Ethernet ports are much more attractive in an 802.1x world because they can tie in to a centralized billing infrastructure using RADIUS accounting, defined in RFCs 2866 and 2867 (Figure 6-10). When a user attempts to use a public Ethernet port, he can be authenticated by a corporate RADIUS server, and the company can be billed based on accounting information generated by the service provider's RADIUS server. "Routing" of RADIUS requests to the correct home server can be done if the user identifiers are formatted according to RFC 2486.

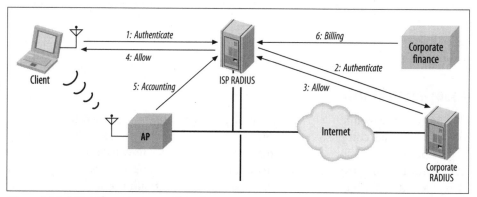

Figure 6-10. 802.11x supporting public Ethernet ports

One further advantage that 802.1x could bring to the build-out of 802.11 networks is a multiprovider access point. The idea is simple. Wireless networks are difficult and costly to build because of the extensive survey work required to avoid sources of interference. If the infrastructure could be built once and shared by a number of service providers, the overall network costs would be much lower.

As an example, airports are a popular wireless LAN "hot spot." Several service providers have attempted to build nationwide networks to allow roaming, and the airlines themselves may want to access an airport-wide wireless LAN. Multiprovider access points could be shared between several users, such as a few different wireless service providers plus airline kiosks and baggage workers. Multiprovider access points would need to support multiple wireless networks (multiple SSIDs) and multiple VLANs. 802.1x plays a key role in allowing the access point to implement only polices configured on external servers. Airlines are likely to have much more stringent access controls for their internal networks than a wireless service provider.

CHAPTER 7
Management Operations

While being untethered from a wired network can be an advantage, it can lead to problems: the medium is unreliable, unauthorized users can take advantage of the lack of physical boundaries, and power consumption is critical when devices are running on batteries. The management features of the 802.11 protocol were designed to reduce the effect of these problems.

Some device drivers allow you to customize the management features discussed in this chapter. Keep in mind, though, that the capabilities of the device driver vary from one product to another, and the state of wireless networking is such that some vendors are trying to produce the most feature-rich products possible, while others are aiming at the home market and trying to produce the simplest products. The only way to know what's possible is to understand the capabilities that have been built into the protocol. Then you'll be in a good position to work with whatever hardware drops in your lap.

Management Architecture

Conceptually, the 802.11 management architecture is composed of three components: the MAC layer management entity (MLME), a physical-layer management entity (PLME), and a system management entity (SME). The relation between the different management entities and the related parts of 802.11 is shown in Figure 7-1.

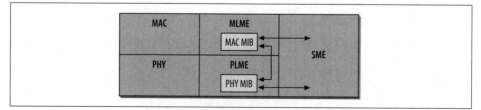

Figure 7-1. Relationship between management entities and components of the 802.11 specification

802.11 does not formally specify the SME. It is the method by which users and device drivers interact with the 802.11 network interface and gather information about its status. Both the MAC and PHY layers have access to a management information base (MIB). The MIB has objects that can be queried to gain status information, as well as objects that can cause certain actions to take place. A full description of the 802.11 MIB is found in Appendix A.

There are three defined interfaces between the management components. The station management entity may alter both the MAC and PHY MIBs through the MLME and PLME service interfaces. Additionally, changes to the MAC may require corresponding changes in the PHY, so an additional interface between the MLME and PLME allows the MAC to make changes to the PHY.

Scanning

Before using any network, you must first find it. With wired networks, finding the network is easy: look for the cable or a jack on the wall. In the wireless world, stations must identify a compatible network before joining it. The process of identifying existing networks in the area is called *scanning*.

Several parameters are used in the scanning procedure. These parameters may be specified by the user; many implementations have default values for these parameters in the driver.

BSSType (independent, infrastructure, or both)
> Scanning can specify whether to seek out independent ad hoc networks, infrastructure networks, or all networks.

BSSID (individual or broadcast)
> The device can scan for a specific network to join (individual) or for any network that is willing to allow it to join (broadcast). When 802.11 devices are moving, setting the BSSID to broadcast is a good idea because the scan results will include all BSSs in the area.

SSID ("network name")
> The SSID assigns a string of bits to an extended service set. Most products refer to the SSID as the network name because the string of bits is commonly set to a human-readable string. Clients wishing to find any network should set this to the broadcast SSID.

ScanType (active or passive)
> Active scanning uses the transmission of Probe Request frames to identify networks in the area. Passive scanning saves battery power by listening for Beacon frames.

ChannelList
> Scans must either transmit a Probe Request or listen on a channel for the existence of a network. 802.11 allows stations to specify a list of channels to try.

Products allow configuration of the channel list in different ways. What exactly constitutes a channel depends on the physical layer in use. With direct-sequence products, it is a list of channels. With frequency-hopping products, it is a hop pattern.

ProbeDelay

This is the delay, in microseconds, before the procedure to probe a channel in active scanning begins. This delay ensures that an empty or lightly loaded channel does not completely block the scan.

MinChannelTime and MaxChannelTime

These values, specified in time units (TUs), specify the minimum and maximum amount of time that the scan works with any particular channel.

Passive Scanning

Passive scanning saves battery power because it does not require transmitting. In passive scanning, a station moves to each channel on the channel list and waits for Beacon frames. Any Beacons received are buffered to extract information about the BSS that sent them.

In the passive scanning procedure, the station sweeps from channel to channel and records information from any Beacons it receives. Beacons are designed to allow a station to find out everything it needs to match parameters with the basic service set (BSS) and begin communications. In Figure 7-2, the mobile station uses a passive scan to find BSSs in its area; it hears Beacon frames from the first three access points. If it does not hear Beacons from the fourth access point, it reports that only three BSSs were found.

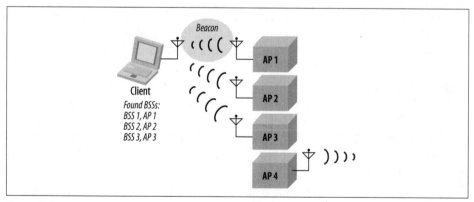

Figure 7-2. Passive scanning

Active Scanning

In active scanning, a station takes a more assertive role. On each channel, Probe Request frames are used to solicit responses from a network with a given name.

Rather than listening for that network to announce itself, an active scan attempts to find the network. Stations using active scanning employ the following procedure for each channel in the channel list:

1. Move to the channel and wait for either an indication of an incoming frame or for the ProbeDelay timer to expire. If an incoming frame is detected, the channel is in use and can be probed. The timer prevents an empty channel from blocking the entire procedure; the station won't wait indefinitely for incoming frames.

2. Gain access to the medium using the basic DCF access procedure and send a Probe Request frame.

3. Wait for the minimum channel time, MinChannelTime, to elapse.

    a. If the medium was never busy, there is no network. Move to the next channel.

    b. If the medium was busy during the MinChannelTime interval, wait until the maximum time, MaxChannelTime, and process any Probe Response frames.

Probe Response frames are generated by networks when they hear a Probe Request that is searching for the extended service set to which the network belongs. At a party, you might look for a friend by wandering around the dance floor shouting out his or her name. (It's not polite, but if you really want to find your friend, you may not have much choice.) If your friend hears you, he or she will respond—others will (you hope) ignore you. Probe Request frames function similarly, but they can also use a broadcast SSID, which triggers a Probe Response from all 802.11 networks in the area. (It's like shouting "Fire!" at the party—that's sure to result in a response from everybody!)

One station in each BSS is responsible for responding to Probe Requests. The station that transmitted the last Beacon frame is also responsible for transmitting any necessary Probe Response frames. In infrastructure networks, the access points transmit Beacons and thus are also responsible for responding to itinerant stations searching the area with Probe Requests. IBSSs may pass around the responsibility of sending Beacon frames, so the station that transmits Probe Response frames may vary. Probe Responses are unicast management frames and are therefore subject to the positive acknowledgment requirement of the MAC.

It is common for multiple Probe Responses to be transmitted as a result of a single Probe Request. The purpose of the scanning procedure is to find every basic service area that the scanning station can join, so a broadcast Probe Request results in a response from every access point within range. Any overlapping independent BSSs may also respond.

Figure 7-3 shows the relationship between the transmission of Probe frames and the various timing intervals that can be configured as part of a scan.

In Figure 7-3a, a mobile station transmits a probe request to which two access points respond. The activity on the medium is shown in Figure 7-3b. The scanning station transmits the Probe Request after gaining access to the medium. Both access points

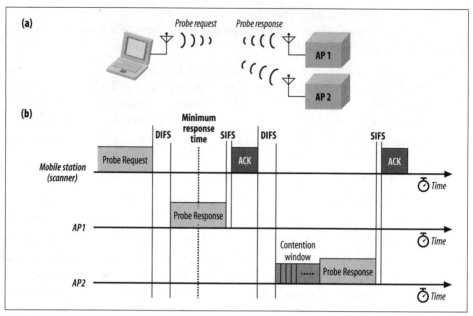

Figure 7-3. Active scanning procedure and medium access

respond with a Probe Response that reports their network's parameters. Note that the second Probe Response is subject to the rules of the distributed coordination function and must wait for the congestion window to elapse before transmitting. The first response is transmitted before the minimum response time elapses, so the station waits until the maximum response time has elapsed before collating the results. In areas with a large number of networks, it may be necessary to adjust the maximum channel time so the responses from all the access points in the area can be processed.

Scan Report

A scan report is generated at the conclusion of a scan. The report lists all the BSSs that the scan discovered and their parameters. The complete parameter list enables the scanning station to join any of the networks that it discovered. In addition to the BSSID, SSID, and BSSType, the parameters also include:[*]

Beacon interval (integer)
    Each BSS can transmit Beacon frames at its own specific interval, measured in TUs.

DTIM period (integer)
    DTIM frames are used as part of the power-saving mechanism.

---

[*] The items actually exposed by any particular software vary.

Timing parameters

Two fields assist in synchronizing the station's timer to the timer used by a BSS. The Timestamp field indicates the value of the timer received by the scanning station; the other field is an offset to enable a station to match timing information to join a particular BSS.

PHY parameters, CF parameters, and IBSS parameters

These three facets of the network have their own parameter sets, each of which was discussed in detail in Chapter 4. Channel information is included in the physical-layer parameters.

BSSBasicRateSet

The basic rate set is the list of data rates that must be supported by any station wishing to join the network. Stations must be able to receive data at all the rates listed in the set. The basic rate set is composed of the mandatory rates in the Supported Rates information element of management frames, as presented in Chapter 4.

Joining

After compiling the scan results, a station can elect to *join* one of the BSSs. Joining is a precursor to association; it is analogous to aiming a weapon. It does not enable network access. Before this can happen, both authentication and association are required.

Choosing which BSS to join is an implementation-specific decision and may even involve user intervention. BSSs that are part of the same ESS are allowed to make the decision in any way they choose; common criteria used in the decision are power level and signal strength. Observers cannot tell when a station has joined a network because the joining process is internal to a node; it involves matching local parameters to the parameters required by the selected BSS. One of the most important tasks is to synchronize timing information between the mobile station and the rest of the network, a process discussed in much more detail in the section "Timer Synchronization."

The station must also match the PHY parameters, which guarantees that any transmissions with the BSS are on the right channel. (Timer synchronization also guarantees that frequency-hopping stations hop at the correct time, too.) Using the BSSID ensures that transmissions are directed to the correct set of stations and ignored by stations in another BSS.* Capability information is also taken from the scan result, which matches the use of WEP and any high-rate capabilities. Stations must also adopt the Beacon interval and DTIM period of the BSS, though these parameters are not as important as the others for enabling communication.

---

* Technically, this is true only for stations obeying the filtering rules for received frames. Malicious attackers intent on compromising network security can easily choose to disobey these rules and capture frames.

Authentication

On a wired network, authentication is implicitly provided by physical access; if you're close enough to the network to plug in a cable, you must have gotten by the receptionist at the front door. While this is a weak definition of authentication, and one that is clearly inappropriate for high-security environments, it works reasonably well as long as the physical access control procedures are strong. Wireless networks are attractive in large part because physical access is not required to use network resources. Therefore, a major component of maintaining network security is ensuring that stations attempting to associate with the network are allowed to do so. Two major approaches are specified by 802.11: *open-system* authentication and *shared-key* authentication. Shared-key authentication is based on WEP and requires that both stations implement WEP.

802.11 does not restrict authentication to any particular scenario. Any station can authenticate with any other station. In practice, authentication is most useful in infrastructure networks. The usefulness of authentication for infrastructure networks is due in part to the design of the authentication methods, which do not really result in mutual authentication. As a matter of design, the authentication process really only proves the identity of one station. 802.11 implicitly assumes that access points are in a privileged position by virtue of the fact that they are typically under control of network administrators. Network administrators may wish to authenticate mobile stations to ensure that only authorized users access the 802.11 network, but mobile stations can't authenticate the access point. For this reason, the examples in this section assume that a mobile station such as an 802.11-equipped PC is attempting to authenticate to an access point. The standard, however, does not restrict authentication to infrastructure networks.

802.11 authentication is currently a one-way street. Stations wishing to join a network must authenticate to it, but networks are under no obligation to authenticate themselves to a station. The designers of 802.11 probably felt that access points were part of the network infrastructure and thus in a more privileged position, but this curious omission makes a man-in-the-middle attack possible. A rogue access point could certainly send Beacon frames for a network it is not a part of and attempt to steal authentication credentials.

Open-System Authentication

Open-system authentication is the only method required by 802.11. Calling it authentication is stretching the meaning of the term a great deal. In open-system authentication, the access point accepts the mobile station at face value without verifying its identity. (Imagine a world where similar authentication applied to bank withdrawals!) An open-system authentication exchange consists of two frames, shown in Figure 7-4.

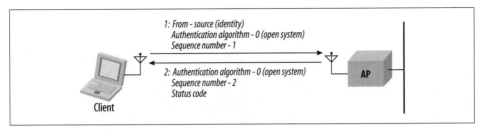

Figure 7-4. Open-system authentication exchange

The first frame from the mobile station is a management frame of subtype authentication. 802.11 does not formally refer to this frame as an authentication request, but that is its practical purpose. In 802.11, the identity of any station is its MAC address. Like Ethernet networks, MAC addresses must be unique throughout the network and can readily double as station identifiers. Access points use the source address of frames as the identity of the sender; no fields within the frame are used to further identify the sender.

There are two information elements in the body of the authentication request. First, the Authentication Algorithm Identification is set to 0 to indicate that the open-system method is in use. Second, the Authentication Transaction Sequence number is set to 1 to indicate that the first frame is in fact the first frame in the sequence.

The access point then processes the authentication request and returns its response. Like the first frame, the response frame is a management frame of subtype authentication. Three information elements are present: the Authentication Algorithm Identification field is set to 0 to indicate open-system authentication, the Sequence Number is 2, and a Status Code indicates the outcome of the authentication request. Values for the Status Code are shown in Table 4-6.

Shared-Key Authentication

Shared-key authentication makes use of WEP and therefore can be used only on products that implement WEP. Furthermore, 802.11 requires that any stations implementing WEP also implement shared-key authentication. Shared-key authentication, as its name implies, requires that a shared key be distributed to stations before attempting authentication. A shared-key authentication exchange consists of four management frames of subtype authentication, shown in Figure 7-5.

The first frame is nearly identical to the first frame in the open-system authentication exchange. Like the open-system frame, it has information elements to identify the authentication algorithm and the sequence number; the Authentication Algorithm Identification is set to 1 to indicate shared-key authentication.

Instead of blindly allowing admission to the network, the second frame in a shared-key exchange serves as a challenge. Up to four information elements may be present

Address Filtering

WEP is not required by 802.11, and a number of earlier products implement only open-system authentication. To provide more security than straight open-system authentication allows, many products offer an "authorized MAC address list." Network administrators can enter a list of authorized client addresses, and only clients with those addresses are allowed to connect.

While address filtering is better than nothing, it leaves a great deal to be desired. MAC addresses are generally software- or firmware-programmable and can easily be overridden by an attacker wishing to gain network access. Furthermore, distributing lists of allowed addresses to multiple access points is a painful process. Some access points implement trivial file transfer protocol (TFTP) servers that allow administrators to push out the address lists, but TFTP is fraught with its own security perils.

Authorized address filtering may be part of a security solution, but it should not be the linchpin. Shared-key authentication is currently the strongest standardized solution available. Once network administrators have made the effort to distribute the WEP keys, authentication will be as secure as standards provide for, and address filtering will only add complexity without significant additional security benefits.

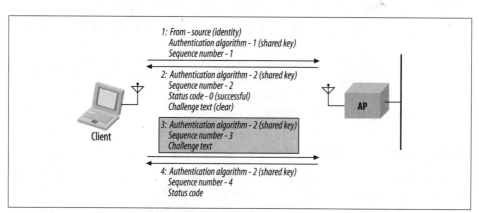

Figure 7-5. Shared-key authentication exchange

in the second frame. Naturally, the Authentication Algorithm Identification, Sequence Number, and Status Code are present. The access point may deny an authentication request in the second frame, ending the transaction. To proceed, however, the Status Code should be set to 0 (success), as shown in Figure 7-5. When the Status Code is successful, the frame also includes a fourth information element, the Challenge Text. The Challenge Text is composed of 128 bytes generated using the WEP keystream generator with a random key and initialization vector.

The third frame is the mobile station's response to the challenge. To prove that it is allowed on the network, the mobile station constructs a management frame with three information elements: the Authntication Algorithm Identifier, a Sequence Number of 3, and the Challenge Text. Before transmitting the frame, the mobile station processes the frame with WEP. The header identifying the frame as an authentication frame is preserved, but the information elements are hidden by WEP.

After receiving the third frame, the access point attempts to decrypt it and verify the WEP integrity check. If the frame decrypts to the Challenge Text, and the integrity check is verified, the access point will respond with a status code of successful. Successful decryption of the challenge text proves that the mobile station has been configured with the WEP key for the network and should be granted access. If any problems occur, the access point returns an unsuccessful status code.

Preauthentication

Stations must authenticate with an access point before associating with it, but nothing in 802.11 requires that authentication take place immediately before association. Stations can authenticate with several access points during the scanning process so that when association is required, the station is already authenticated. This is called preauthentication. As a result of preauthentication, stations can reassociate with access points immediately upon moving into their coverage area, rather than having to wait for the authentication exchange.

In both parts of Figure 7-6, there is an extended service set composed of two access points. Only one mobile station is shown for simplicity. Assume the mobile station starts off associated with AP1 at the left side of the diagram because it was powered on in AP1's coverage area. As the mobile station moves towards the right, it must eventually associate with AP2 as it leaves AP1's coverage area.

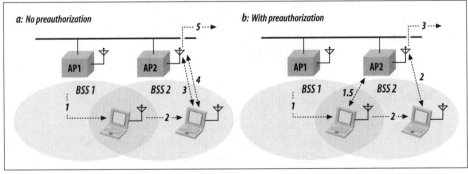

Figure 7-6. Time savings of preauthentication

Preauthentication is not used in the most literal interpretation of 802.11, shown in Figure 7-6a. As the mobile station moves to the right, the signal from AP1 weakens. The station continues monitoring Beacon frames corresponding to its ESS, and will eventually note the existence of AP2. At some point, the station may choose to disassociate from AP1, and then authenticate and reassociate with AP2. These steps are identified in the figure, in which the numbers are the time values from Table 7-1.

Table 7-1. Chronology for Figure 7-6

Step	Action without preauthentication (Figure 7-6a)	Action with preauthentication (Figure 7-6b)
0	Station is associated with AP1	Station is associated with AP1
1	Station moves right into the overlap between BSS1 and BSS2	Station moves right into the overlap between BSS1 and BSS2 and detects the presence of AP2
1.5		Station preauthenticates to AP2
2	AP2's signal is stronger, so station decides to move association to AP2	AP2's signal is stronger, so station decides to move association to AP2
3	Station authenticates to AP2	Station begins using the network
4	Station reassociates with AP2	
5	Station begins using the network	

Figure 7-6b shows what happens when the station is capable of preauthentication. With this minor software modification, the station can authenticate to AP2 as soon as it is detected. As the station is leaving AP1's coverage area, it is authenticated with both AP1 and AP2. The time savings become apparent when the station leaves the coverage area of AP1: it can immediately reassociate with AP2 because it is already authenticated. Preauthentication makes roaming a smoother operation because authentication can take place before it is needed to support an association. All the steps in Figure 7-6b are identified by time values from Table 7-1.Proprietary Authentication Approaches

The shared-key authentication method has its drawbacks. It is stronger than open-system authentication with address filtering, but it inherits all of WEP's security weaknesses. In response, some vendors have developed proprietary public-key authentication algorithms, many of which are based on 802.1x. Some of these proprietary approaches may serve as the basis for future standards work.

Association

Once authentication has completed, stations can associate with an access point (or reassociate with a new access point) to gain full access to the network. Association is a recordkeeping procedure that allows the distribution system to track the location of each mobile station, so frames destined for the mobile station can be forwarded to the correct access point. After association completes, an access point must register the mobile station on the network so frames for the mobile station are delivered to the access point. One method of registering is to send a gratuitous ARP so the station's MAC address is associated with the switch port connected to the access point.

Association is restricted to infrastructure networks and is logically equivalent to plugging into a wired network. Once the procedure is complete, a wireless station can use the distribution system to reach out to the world, and the world can respond through the distribution system. 802.11 explicitly forbids associating with more than one access point.

Association Procedure

The basic association procedure is shown in Figure 7-7.

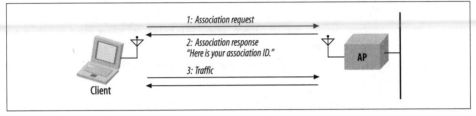

Figure 7-7. Association procedure

Like authentication, association is initiated by the mobile station. No sequence numbers are needed because the association process is a three-step exchange. The two frames are management frame subtypes defined by the specification. As unicast management frames, both steps in the association procedure are composed of an association frame and the required link-layer acknowledgment:

1. Once a mobile station has authenticated to an access point, it can issue an Association Request frame. Stations that have not yet authenticated receive a Deauthentication frame from the access point in response.

2. The access point then processes the association request. 802.11 does not specify how to determine whether an association should be granted; it is specific to the access point implementation. One common consideration is the amount of space required for frame buffering. Rough estimates are possible based on the Listen Interval in the Association Request frame.

   a. When the association request is granted, the access point responds with a status code of 0 (successful) and the Association ID (AID). The AID is a numerical identifier used to logically identify the mobile station to which buffered frames need to be delivered. More detail on the process can be found in the "Power Conservation" section of this chapter.

   b. Unsuccessful association requests include only a status code, and the procedure ends.

3. The access point begins processing frames for the mobile station. In all commonly used products, the distribution system medium is Ethernet. When an access point receives a frame destined for an associated mobile station, that

frame can be bridged from the Ethernet to the wireless medium or buffered if the mobile station is in a power-saving state. In shared Ethernets, the frame will be sent to all the access points and will be bridged by the correct one. In switched Ethernets, the station's MAC address will be associated with a particular switch port. That switch port is, of course, connected to the access point currently providing service for the station.

Reassociation Procedure

Reassociation is the process of moving an association from an old access point to a new one. Over the air, it is almost the same as an association; on the backbone network, however, access points may interact with each other to move frames. When a station moves from the coverage area of one access point to another, it uses the reassociation process to inform the 802.11 network of its new location. The procedure is shown in Figure 7-8.

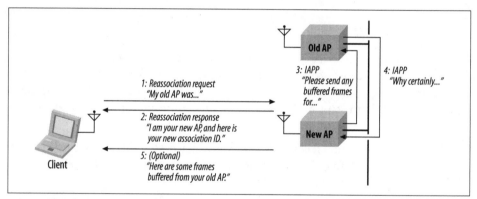

Figure 7-8. Reassociation procedure

The mobile station begins the procedure associated with an access point. The station monitors the quality of the signal it receives from that access point, as well as the signal quality from other access points in the same ESS. When the mobile station detects that another access point would be a better choice, it initiates the reassociation procedure. The factors used to make that decision are product-dependent. Received signal strength can be used on a frame-by-frame basis, and the constant Beacon transmissions provide a good baseline for signal strength from an access point. Before the first step, the mobile station must authenticate to the new access point if it has not done so already.

Figure 7-8 depicts the following steps:

1. The mobile station issues a Reassociation Request to the new access point. Reassociation Requests have content similar to Association Requests. The only difference is that Reassociation Request frames contain a field with the address of the

old access point. The new access point must communicate with the old access point to determine that a previous association did exist. The content of the inter-access point messages is proprietary, though the 802.11 working group is in the process of standardizing the inter-access point protocol. If the new access point cannot verify that the old access point authenticated the station, the new access point responds with a Deauthentication frame and ends the procedure.

2. The access point processes the Reassociation Request. Processing Reassociation Requests is similar to processing Association Requests; the same factors may be used in deciding whether to allow the reassociation:

   a. If the Reassociation Request is granted, the access point responds with a Status Code of 0 (successful) and the AID.

   b. Unsuccessful Reassociation Requests include just a Status Code, and the procedure ends.

3. The new access point contacts the old access point to finish the reassociation procedure. This communication is part of the IAPP.

4. The old access point sends any buffered frames for the mobile station to the new access point. 802.11 does not specify the communication between access points; filling in this omission is one of the major standardization efforts in the 802.11 working group. At the conclusion of the buffered frame transfer:

   a. Any frames buffered at the old access point are transferred to the new access point so they can be delivered to the mobile station.

   b. The old access point terminates its association with the mobile station. Mobile stations are allowed to associate with only one access point at any given time.

5. The new access point begins processing frames for the mobile station. When it receives a frame destined for the mobile station, that frame is bridged from the Ethernet to the wireless medium or buffered for a mobile station in a power-saving mode.

Reassociation is also used to rejoin a network if the station leaves the coverage area and returns later to the same access point. Figure 7-9 illustrates this scenario.

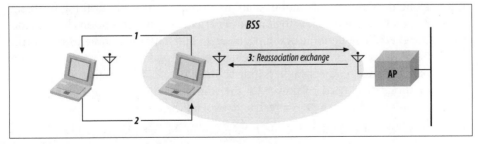

Figure 7-9. Reassociation with the same access point

Power Conservation

The major advantage of wireless networks is that network access does not require nodes to be in any particular location. To take full advantage of mobility, nothing can constrain the location of a node, including the availability of electrical power. Mobility therefore implies that most mobile devices can run on batteries. But battery power is a scarce resource; batteries can run only so long before they need to be recharged. Requiring mobile users to return frequently to commercial power is inconvenient, to say the least. Many wireless applications require long battery life without sacrificing network connectivity.

As with any other network interface, powering down the transceiver can lead to great power savings in wireless networks. When the transceiver is off, it is said to be *sleeping*, *dozing*, or in *power-saving mode* (PS). When the transceiver is on, it is said to be *awake*, *active*, or simply *on*. Power conservation in 802.11 is achieved by minimizing the time spent in the latter stage and maximizing the time in the former. However, 802.11 accomplishes this without sacrificing connectivity.

Power Management in Infrastructure Networks

Power management can achieve the greatest savings in infrastructure networks. All traffic for mobile stations must go through access points, so they are an ideal location to buffer traffic. There is no need to work on a distributed buffer system that must be implemented on every station; the bulk of the work is left to the access point. By definition, access points are aware of the location of mobile stations, and a mobile station can communicate its power management state to its access point. Furthermore, access points must remain active at all times; it is assumed that they have access to continuous power. Combining these two facts allows access points to play a key role in power management on infrastructure networks.

Access points have two power management–related tasks. First, because an access point knows the power management state of every station that has associated with it, it can determine whether a frame should be delivered to the wireless network because the station is active or buffered because the station is asleep. But buffering frames alone does not enable mobile stations to pick up the data waiting for them. An access point's second task is to announce periodically which stations have frames waiting for them. The periodic announcement of buffer status also helps to contribute to the power savings in infrastructure networks. Powering up a receiver to listen to the buffer status requires far less power than periodically transmitting polling frames. Stations only need to power up the transmitter to transmit polling frames after being informed that there is a reason to expend the energy.

Power management is designed around the needs of the battery-powered mobile stations. Mobile stations can sleep for extended periods to avoid using the wireless network interface. Part of the association request is the Listen Interval parameter, which is the number of Beacon periods for which the mobile station may choose to sleep. Longer listen intervals require more buffer space on the access point; therefore, the Listen Interval is one of the key parameters used in estimating the resources required to support an association. The Listen Interval is a contract with the access point. In agreeing to buffer any frames while the mobile station is sleeping, the access point agrees to wait for at least the listen interval before discarding frames. If a mobile station fails to check for waiting frames after each listen interval, they may be discarded without notification.

Unicast frame buffering and delivery using the Traffic Indication Map (TIM)

When frames are buffered, the destination node's AID provides the logical link between the frame and its destination. Each AID is logically connected to frames buffered for the mobile station that is assigned that AID. Multicast and broadcast frames are buffered and linked to an AID of zero. Delivery of buffered multicast and broadcast frames is treated in the next section.

Buffering is only half the battle. If stations never pick up their buffered frames, saving the frames is a rather pointless exercise. To inform stations that frames are buffered, access points periodically assemble a traffic indication map (TIM) and transmit it in Beacon frames. The TIM is a virtual bitmap composed of 2,008 bits; offsets are used so that the access point needs to transmit only a small portion of the virtual bitmap. This conserves network capacity when only a few stations have buffered data. Each bit in the TIM corresponds to a particular AID; setting the bit indicates that the access point has buffered unicast frames for the station with the AID corresponding to the bit position.

Mobile stations must wake up and enter the active mode to listen for Beacon frames to receive the TIM. By examining the TIM, a station can determine if the access point has buffered traffic on its behalf. To retrieve buffered frames, mobile stations use PS-Poll Control frames. When multiple stations have buffered frames, all stations with buffered data must use the random backoff algorithm before transmitting the PS-Poll.

Each PS-Poll frame is used to retrieve one buffered frame. That frame must be positively acknowledged before it is removed from the buffer. Positive acknowledgment is required to keep a second, retried PS-Poll from acting as an implicit acknowledgment. Figure 7-10 illustrates the process.

If multiple frames are buffered for a mobile station, then the More Data bit in the Frame Control field is set to 1. Mobile stations can then issue additional PS-Poll requests to the access point until the More Data bit is set to 0, though no time constraint is imposed by the standard.

After transmitting the PS-Poll, a mobile station must remain awake until either the polling transaction has concluded or the bit corresponding to its AID is no longer set in the TIM. The reason for the first case is obvious: the mobile station has successfully

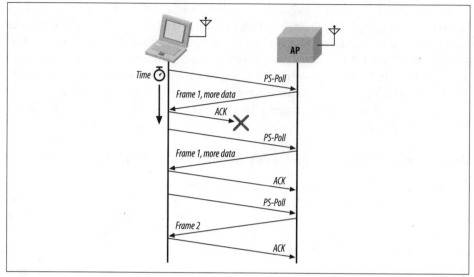

Figure 7-10. PS-Poll frame retrieval

polled the access point; part of that transaction was a notification that the mobile station will be returning to a sleeping mode. The second case allows the mobile station to return to a power conservation mode if the access point discards the buffered frame. Once all the traffic buffered for a station is delivered or discarded, the station can resume sleeping.

The buffering and delivery process is illustrated in Figure 7-11, which shows the medium as it appears to an access point and two associated power-saving stations. The hash marks on the timeline represent the beacon interval. Every beacon interval, the access point transmits a Beacon frame with a TIM information element. (This figure is somewhat simplified. A special kind of TIM is used to deliver multicast traffic; it will be described in the next section.) Station 1 has a listen interval of 2, so it must wake up to receive every other TIM, while station 2 has a listen interval of 3, so it wakes up to process every third TIM. The lines above the station base lines indicate the ramp-up process of the receiver to listen for the TIM.

At the first beacon interval, there are frames buffered for station 1. No frames are buffered for station 2, though, so it can immediately return to sleep. At the second beacon interval, the TIM indicates that there are buffered frames for stations 1 and 2, though only station 1 woke up to listen to the TIM. Station 1 issues a PS-Poll and receives the frame in response. At the conclusion of the exchange, station 1 returns to sleep. Both stations are asleep during the third beacon. At the fourth beacon, both wake up to listen to the TIM, which indicates that there are frames buffered for both. Both station 1 and station 2 prepare to transmit PS-Poll frames after the expiration of a contention window countdown as described in Chapter 3. Station 1 wins because

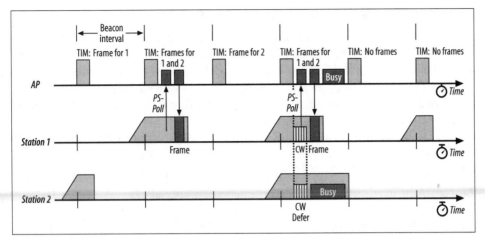

Figure 7-11. Buffered frame retrieval process

its random delay was shorter. Station 1 issues a PS-Poll and receives its buffered frame in response. During the transmission, station 2 defers. If, at the end of that frame transmission, a third station, which is not illustrated, seizes the medium for transmission, station 2 must continue to stay awake until the next TIM. If the access point has run out of buffer space and has discarded the buffered frame for station 2, the TIM at the fifth beacon indicates that no frames are buffered, and station 2 can finally return to a low-power mode.

Stations may switch from a power conservation mode to active mode at any time. It is common for laptop computers to operate with full power to all peripherals when connected to AC power and conserve power only when using the battery. If a mobile station switches to the active mode from a sleeping mode, frames can be transmitted without waiting for a PS-Poll. PS-Poll frames indicate that a power-saving mobile station has temporarily switched to an active mode and is ready to receive a buffered frame. By definition, active stations have transceivers operating continuously. After a switch to active mode, the access point can assume that the receiver is operational, even without receiving explicit notification to that effect.

Access points must retain frames long enough for mobile stations to pick them up, but buffer memory is a finite resource. 802.11 mandates that access points use an *aging function* to determine when buffered frames are old enough to be discarded. The standard leaves a great deal to the discretion of the developer because it specifies only one constraint. Mobile stations depend on access points to buffer traffic for at least the listen interval specified with the association, and the standard forbids the aging function from discarding frames before the listen interval has elapsed. Beyond that, however, there is a great deal of latitude for vendors to develop different buffer management routines.

Delivering multicast and broadcast frames: the Delivery TIM (DTIM)

Frames with a group address cannot be delivered using a polling algorithm because they are, by definition, addressed to a group. Therefore, 802.11 incorporates a mechanism for buffering and delivering broadcast and multicast frames. Buffering is identical to the unicast case, except that frames are buffered whenever any station associated with the access point is sleeping. Buffered broadcast and multicast frames are saved using AID 0. Access points indicate whether any broadcast or multicast frames are buffered by setting the first bit in the TIM to 0; this bit corresponds to AID 0.

Each BSS has a parameter called the DTIM Period. TIMs are transmitted with every Beacon. At a fixed number of Beacon intervals, a special type of TIM, a Delivery Traffic Indication Map (DTIM), is sent. The TIM element in Beacon frames contains a counter that counts down to the next DTIM; this counter is zero in a DTIM frame. Buffered broadcast and multicast traffic is transmitted after a DTIM Beacon. Multiple buffered frames are transmitted in sequence; the More Data bit in the Frame Control field indicates that more frames must be transmitted. Normal channel acquisition rules apply to the transmission of buffered frames. The access point may choose to defer the processing of incoming PS-Poll frames until the frames in the broadcast and multicast transmission buffers have been transmitted.

Figure 7-12 shows an access point and one associated station. The DTIM interval of the access point is set to 3, so every third TIM is a DTIM. Station 1 is operating in a sleep mode with a listen interval of 3. It will wake up on every third beacon to receive buffered broadcast and multicast frames. After a DTIM frame is transmitted, the buffered broadcast and multicast frames are transmitted, followed by any PS-Poll exchanges with associated stations. At the second beacon interval, only broadcast and multicast frames are present in the buffer, and they are transmitted to the BSS. At the fifth beacon interval, a frame has also been buffered for station 1. It can monitor the map in the DTIM and send a PS-Poll after the transmission of buffered broadcast and multicast frames has concluded.

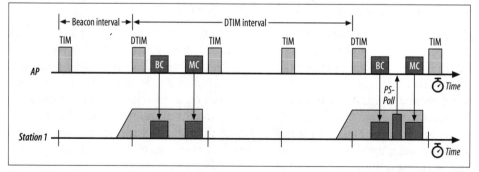

Figure 7-12. Multicast and broadcast buffer transmission after DTIMs

To receive broadcast and multicast frames, a mobile station must be awake for DTIM transmissions. Nothing in the specification, however, keeps power-saving stations in infrastructure networks from waking up to listen to DTIM frames. Some products that implement power-saving modes will attempt to align their awakenings with DTIM transmissions. If the system administrator determines that battery life is more important than receiving broadcast and multicast frames, a station can be configured to sleep for its listen period without regard to DTIM transmissions. Some documentation may refer to this as *extremely low power*, *ultra power-saving mode*, *deep sleep*, or something similar.

Several products allow configuration of the DTIM interval. Lengthening the DTIM interval allows mobile stations to sleep for longer periods and maximizes battery life at the expense of timely delivery. Shorter DTIM intervals emphasize quick delivery at the expense of more frequent power-up and power-down cycles. You can use a longer DTIM when battery life is at a premium and delivery of broadcast and multicast frames is not important. Whether this is appropriate depends on the applications you are using and how they react to long link-layer delays.

IBSS Power Management

Power management in an IBSS is not as efficient as power management in an infrastructure network. In an IBSS, far more of the burden is placed on the sender to ensure that the receiver is active. Receivers must also be more available and cannot sleep for the same lengths of time as in infrastructure networks.

As in infrastructure networks, power management in independent networks is based on traffic indication messages. Independent networks must use a distributed system because there is no logical central coordinator. Stations in an independent network use *announcement traffic indication messages* (ATIMs), which are sometimes called *ad hoc traffic indication messages*, to preempt other stations from sleeping. All stations in an IBSS listen for ATIM frames during specified periods after Beacon transmissions.

If a station has buffered data for another station, it can send an ATIM frame as notification. In effect, the ATIM frame is a message to keep the transceiver on because there is pending data. Stations that do not receive ATIM frames are free to conserve power. In Figure 7-13a, station A has buffered a frame for station C, so it sends a unicast ATIM frame to station C during the ATIM transmission window, which has the effect of notifying station C that it should not enter power-saving mode. Station B, however, is free to power down its wireless interface. Figure 7-13b shows a multicast ATIM frame in use. This frame can be used to notify an entire group of stations to avoid entering low-power modes.

A time window called the *ATIM window* follows the Beacon transmission. This window is the period during which nodes must remain active. No stations are permitted to power down their wireless interfaces during the ATIM window. It starts at the

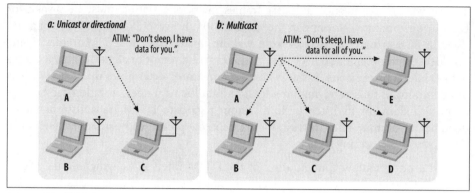

Figure 7-13. ATIM usage

time when the beacon is expected and ends after a period specified when the IBSS is created. If the beacon is delayed due to a traffic overrun, the usable portion of the ATIM window shrinks by the same amount.

The ATIM window is the only IBSS-specific parameter required to create an IBSS. Setting it to 0 avoids using any power management. Figure 7-14 illustrates the ATIM window and its relation to the beacon interval. In the figure, the fourth beacon is delayed due to a busy medium. The ATIM window remains constant, starting at the target beacon interval and extending the length of the ATIM window. Of course, the usable period of the ATIM window shrinks by the length of the delay in beacon transmission.

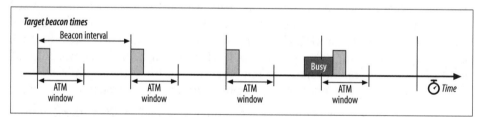

Figure 7-14. ATIM window

To monitor the entire ATIM window, stations must wake up before the target beacon transmission. Four situations are possible: the station has transmitted an ATIM, received an ATIM, neither transmitted nor received, or both transmitted and received. Stations that transmit ATIM frames must not sleep. Transmitting an ATIM indicates an intent to transmit buffered traffic and thus an intent to stay active. Stations to which ATIM frames are addressed must also avoid sleeping so they can receive any frames transmitted by the ATIM's sender. If a station both transmits and receives ATIM frames, it stays up. A station is permitted to sleep only if it neither transmits nor receives an ATIM. When a station stays up due to ATIM traffic, it remains active until the conclusion of the *next* ATIM window, as shown in

Figure 7-15. In the figure, the station goes active for the first ATIM window. If it does not send or receive any ATIM frames, it sleeps at the end of the ATIM window. If it sends or receives an ATIM frame, as in the second ATIM window, the station stays active until the conclusion of the third ATIM window.

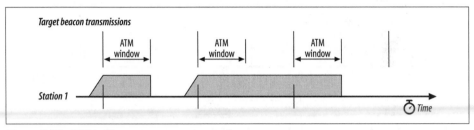

Figure 7-15. ATIM effects on power-saving modes

Only certain control and management frames can be transmitted during the ATIM window: Beacons, RTS, CTS, ACK, and, of course, ATIM frames. Transmission takes place according to the rules of the DCF. ATIM frames may be transmitted only during the ATIM window because stations may be sleeping outside the ATIM window. Sending an ATIM frame is useless if other stations in the IBSS are sleeping. In the same vein, acknowledgments are required for unicast ATIM frames because that is the only guarantee that the ATIM was received and that the frame destination will be active for the remainder of the beacon interval. Acknowledgments are not required for multicast ATIM frames because multicast frames cannot be efficiently acknowledged by a large group of stations. If all potential recipients of an ATIM frame were required to acknowledge it, the mass of acknowledgments could potentially interrupt network service.

Buffered broadcast and multicast frames are transmitted after the conclusion of the ATIM window, subject to DCF constraints. Following the transmission of broadcast and multicast frames, a station may attempt to transmit unicast frames that were announced with an ATIM and for which an acknowledgment was received. Following all transmissions announced with an ATIM, stations may transmit unbuffered frames to other stations that are known to be active. Stations are active if they have transmitted the Beacon, an ATIM, or are not capable of sleeping. If contention is severe enough to prevent a station from sending the buffered frame it announced with an ATIM, the station must reannounce the transmission with an ATIM at the start of the next ATIM window.

Figure 7-16 illustrates several of these rules. In the first beacon interval, the first station transmits a multicast ATIM to stations 2, 3, and 4. Multicast ATIM frames need not be acknowledged, but the transmission of the ATIM means that all stations must remain active for the duration of the first beacon window to receive multicast frames from station 1. When the ATIM window ends, station 1 can transmit its multicast frame to the other three stations. After doing so, station 4 can take advantage of the remaining time before the beacon to transmit a frame to station 1. It was not cleared with an ATIM, but it is known to be active.

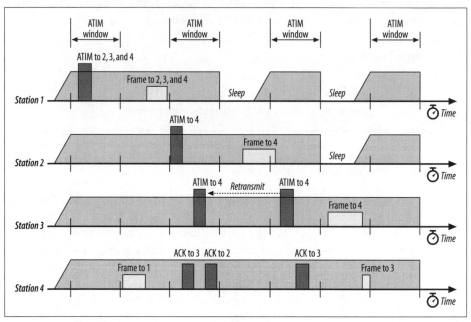

Figure 7-16. Effect of ATIM on power-saving modes in an IBSS network

In the second beacon interval, stations 2 and 3 have both buffered a frame for station 4, so each transmits an ATIM. Station 4 acknowledges both. At the conclusion of the ATIM window, station 1 has neither transmitted nor received an ATIM and can enter a low-power state until the next beacon interval. However, station 2's frame is extremely long and robs station 3 of the opportunity to transmit its frame.

Station 3 still has a buffered frame for station 4 when the third beacon interval opens. It therefore retransmits its ATIM frame to station 4, which is acknowledged. Station 2 is not involved in any ATIM exchanges and can enter a low-power state when the ATIM window ends. At that time, no broadcast or multicast frames have been buffered, and the ATIM-cleared frame from station 3 to station 4 can be transmitted. After the frame from 3 to 4 is transmitted, station 4 can again take advantage of the remaining time before the beacon frame to transmit a frame of its own to station 3, which is known to be active because of the ATIM exchange.

Stations are responsible for maintaining sufficient memory to buffer frames, but the buffer size must be traded off against the use of that memory for other purposes. The standard allows a station in an independent network to discard frames that have been buffered for an "excessive" amount of time, but the algorithm used to make that determination is beyond the scope of the standard. The only requirement placed on any buffer management function is that it retain frames for at least one beacon period.

Timer Synchronization

Like other wireless network technologies, 802.11 depends a great deal on the distribution of timing information to all the nodes. It is especially important in frequency-hopping networks because all stations on the network must change frequency channels in a coordinated pattern. Timing information is also used by the medium reservation mechanisms.

In addition to local station timing, each station in a basic service area maintains a copy of the *timing synchronization function* (TSF), which is a local timer synchronized with the TSF of every other station in the basic service area. The TSF is based on a 1-MHz clock and "ticks" in microseconds. Beacon frames are used to periodically announce the value of the TSF to other stations in the network. The "now" in a timestamp is when the first bit of the timestamp hits the PHY for transmission.

Infrastructure Timing Synchronization

The ease of power management in an infrastructure network is based on the use of access points as central coordinators for data distribution and power management functions. Timing in infrastructure networks is quite similar. Access points are responsible for maintaining the TSF time, and any stations associated with an access point must simply accept the access point's TSF as valid.

When access points prepare to transmit a Beacon frame, the access point timer is copied into the Beacon's timestamp field. Stations associated with an access point accept the timing value in any received Beacons, but they may add a small offset to the received timing value to account for local processing by the antenna and transceiver. Associated stations maintain local TSF timers so they can miss a Beacon frame and still remain roughly synchronized with the global TSF. The wireless medium is expected to be noisy, and Beacon frames are unacknowledged. Therefore, missing a Beacon here and there is to be expected, and the local TSF timer mitigates against the occasional loss of Beacon frames.

To assist active scanning stations in matching parameters with the BSS, timing values are also distributed in Probe Response frames. When a station finds a network by scanning, it saves the timestamp from the Beacon or Probe Response and the value of the local timer when it was received. To match the local timer to the network timer, a station then takes the timestamp in the received network advertisement and adds the number of microseconds since it was received. Figure 7-17 illustrates this process.

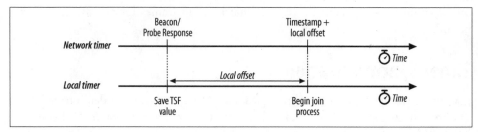

Figure 7-17. Matching the local timer to a network timer

IBSS Timing Synchronization

IBSSs lack a central coordination point, so the Beacon process is distributed. TSF maintenance is a subset of the Beacon generation process. Time is divided into segments equivalent to the interbeacon timing period. Beacon frames are supposed to be transmitted exactly as the beacon interval ends, at the so-called *target Beacon transmission time* (TBTT). Independent networks take the TBTT as a guideline.

All stations in the IBSS prepare to transmit a Beacon frame at the target time. As it approaches, all other traffic is suspended. Timers for the transmission of frames other than Beacon frames or ATIM frames are stopped and held to clear the medium for the important management traffic. All stations in the IBSS generate a *backoff timer* for Beacon transmission; the backoff timer is a random delay between 0 and twice the minimum contention window for the medium. After the target beacon interval, all stations begin to count the Beacon backoff timer down to 0. If a Beacon is received before the station's transmission time, the pending Beacon transmission is canceled.

In Figure 7-18, each station selects a random delay; station 2 has randomly generated the shortest delay. When station 2's timer expires, it transmits a Beacon, which is received by stations 1 and 3. Both stations 1 and 3 cancel their Beacon transmissions as a result. Because timer synchronization ensures that all stations have synchronized timers, multiple Beacon frames do not pose a problem. Receivers simply process multiple Beacon frames and perform multiple updates to the TSF timer.

Beacon generation interacts closely with power management. Beacon frames must be generated during the active period around each Beacon interval so that all stations are available to process the Beacon. Furthermore, the Beacon sender is not allowed to enter a low-power state until the end of the next active period. The latter rule ensures that at least one station is awake and can respond to probes from new stations scanning to discover networks.

Rules for adopting the received timestamp are more complex in an independent network. No centralized timer exists, so the goal of the standard is to synchronize all timers to the timer of the fastest-running clock in the BSS. When a Beacon is received, the timestamp is adjusted for processing delays and compared to the local

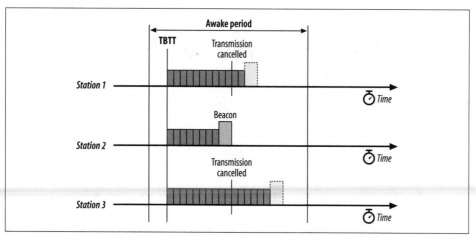

Figure 7-18. Distributed Beacon generation

TSF. The received timestamp updates the local timer only if it is later than the local timer.

## CHAPTER 8

Contention-Free Service with the PCF

To support applications that require near real-time service, the 802.11 standard includes a second coordination function to provide a different way of accessing the wireless medium. The point coordination function (PCF) allows an 802.11 network to provide an enforced "fair" access to the medium. In some ways, access to the medium under the PCF resembles token-based medium access control schemes, with the access point holding the token. This chapter describes medium access under the PCF, detailed frame diagrams for the PCF frames, and how power management operations interact with the PCF.

The PCF has not been widely implemented. This chapter is included for two reasons. Readers interested in the standard itself may also be interested in how the PCF works. It is also possible that products based on the PCF may someday hit the market, in which case, network engineers will need to understand the PCF so they can implement it. But most readers can skip this chapter safely.

Contention-Free Access Using the PCF

If contention-free delivery is required, the PCF may be used. The PCF is an optional part of the 802.11 specification; products are not required to implement it. However, the IEEE designed the PCF so stations that implement only the distributed coordination function (DCF) will interoperate with point coordinators.

Contention-free service is not provided full-time. Periods of contention-free service arbitrated by the point coordinator alternate with the standard DCF-based service. The relative size of the contention-free period can be configured. 802.11 describes the contention-free periods as providing "near isochronous" services because the contention-free periods will not always start at the expected time, as described in the section "Contention-Free Period Duration."

Contention-free service uses a centralized access control method. Access to the medium is restricted by the point coordinator, a specialized function implemented in access points. Associated stations can transmit data only when they are allowed to do so by the point coordinator. In some ways, contention-free access under the PCF resembles token-based networking protocols, with the point coordinator's polling taking the place of a token. Fundamentals of the 802.11 model remain in place, however. Although access is under the control of a central entity, all transmissions must be acknowledged.

PCF Operation

Figure 8-1 shows a transfer using the PCF. When the PCF is used, time on the medium is divided into the contention-free period (CFP) and the contention period. Access to the medium in the former case is controlled by the PCF, while access to the medium in the latter case is controlled by the DCF and the rules from Chapter 7. The contention period must be long enough for the transfer of at least one maximum-size frame and its associated acknowledgment. Alternating periods of contention-free service and contention-based service repeat at regular intervals, which are called the contention-free repetition interval.

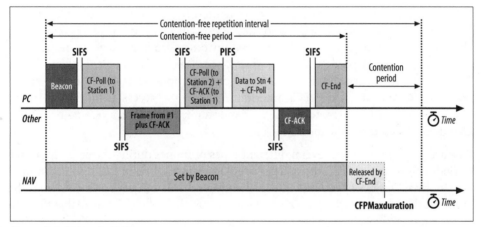

Figure 8-1. Using the PCF

Reserving the medium during the contention-free period

At the beginning of the contention-free period, the access point transmits a Beacon frame. One component of the beacon announcement is the maximum duration of the contention-free period, *CFPMaxDuration*. All stations receiving the Beacon set the NAV to the maximum duration to lock out DCF-based access to the wireless medium.

As an additional safeguard to prevent interference, all contention-free transmissions are separated only by the short interframe space and the PCF interframe space. Both are shorter than the DCF interframe space, so no DCF-based stations can gain access to the medium using the DCF.

The polling list

After the access point has gained control of the wireless medium, it polls any associated stations on a *polling list* for data transmissions. During the contention-free period, stations may transmit only if the access point solicits the transmission with a polling frame. Contention-free polling frames are often abbreviated CF-Poll. Each CF-Poll is a license to transmit one frame. Multiple frames can be transmitted only if the access point sends multiple poll requests.

The polling list is the list of privileged stations solicited for frames during the contention-free period. Stations get on the polling list when they associate with the access point. The Association Request includes a field that indicates whether the station is capable of responding to polls during the contention-free period.

Transmissions from the Access Point

Generally, all transmissions during the contention-free period are separated by only the short interframe space. To ensure that the point coordinator retains control of the medium, it may send to the next station on its polling list if no response is received after an elapsed PCF interframe space. (Such a situation is illustrated in Figure 8-1.) The access point polled the second station on its list but received no response. After waiting one PCF interframe space, the access point moves to the third station on the list. By using the PCF interframe space, the access point ensures that it retains access to the medium.

The access point may use several different types of frames during the contention-free period. During this period, the point coordinator has four major tasks. In addition to the "normal" tasks of sending buffered frames and acknowledging frames from the stations, the point coordinator can poll stations on the polling list to enable them to send frames; it may also need to transmit management frames.

Time in the contention-free period is precious, so acknowledgments, polling, and data transfer may be combined to improve efficiency. When any subset of these functions are combined into a single frame, the result is a bit strange. A single frame could, for example, acknowledge the receipt of the previous frame, poll a different station for buffered data, and send its own data to the station on the polling list.

Several different frame types can be used in the contention free period:

Data
> The standard vanilla Data frame is used when the access point is sending a frame to a station and does not need to acknowledge a previous transmission. The standard Data frame does not poll the recipient and thus does not allow the recipient

to transmit any data in return. The Data-Only frame used in the contention-free period is identical to the Data frame used in contention-based periods.

CF-Ack

This frame is used by stations to acknowledge the receipt of a frame when no data needs to be transmitted. Contention-free acknowledgments are longer than the standard control frame acknowledgment, so this frame may not be used in actual implementations.

CF-Poll

CF-Poll frames are sent by the access point to a mobile station to give the mobile station the right to transmit a single buffered frame. It is used when the access point does not have any data for the mobile station. When a frame for the mobile station is available, the access point uses the Data+CF-Poll frame type.

Data+CF-Ack

This frame combines data transmission with an acknowledgment. Data is directed to the frame recipient; the acknowledgment is for the previous frame transmitted and usually is not for the recipient of the data.

Data+CF-Poll

This frame is used by access points to transmit data to a mobile station and request one pending frame from the mobile station. The Data+CF-Poll can only be sent by the access point during the contention-free period.

CF-ACK+CF-Poll

This frame acknowledges the last frame from one of the access point's clients and requests a buffered frame from the next station on the polling list. It is directed to the next station on the polling list, though the acknowledgment may be intended for any mobile station associated with the access point.

Data+CF-ACK+CF-Poll

This frame brings together the data transmission, polling feature, and acknowledgment into one frame for maximum efficiency.

CF-End

This frame ends the contention-free period and returns control of the medium to the contention-based mechanisms of the DCF.

CF-End+CF-Ack

This is the same as the CF-End frame but also acknowledges the previously transmitted Data frame.

Any Management

No restriction is placed by the standard on which management frames can be transmitted during the contention-free period. If the rules applying to a particular frame type allow its transmission, the access point may transmit it.

Contention-Free Period Duration

The minimum length of the contention period is the time required to transmit and acknowledge one maximum-size frame. It is possible for contention-based service to overrun the end of the contention period, however. When contention-based service runs past the expected beginning of the contention-free period, the contention-free period is *foreshortened*, as in Figure 8-2.

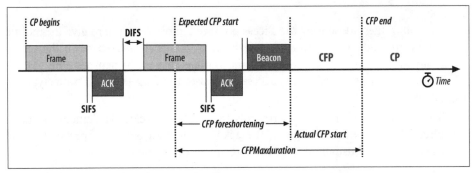

Figure 8-2. Data+CF-Ack and Data+CF-Poll usage

When the contention-free period is foreshortened, the existing frame exchange is allowed to complete before the beacon announcing the start of contention-free operation is transmitted. The contention-free period is shortened by the amount of the delay. Contention-free service ends no later than the maximum duration from the expected beginning point, which is referred to as the Target Beacon Transmission Time (TBTT).

The point coordinator may also terminate the contention-free period prior to its maximum duration by transmitting a CF-End frame. It can base this decision on the size of the polling list, the traffic load, or any other factor that the access point considers important.

Detailed PCF Framing

Several frame types are used exclusively within the contention-free period. They combine, in various states, data transmission, acknowledgment, and polling. This section describes when various frames are used and how the different functions interact during frame exchanges.

Data+CF-Ack

> The Data+CF-Ack frame combines two different functions for transmission efficiency. Data is transmitted in the frame payload, and the frame implicitly acknowledges the receipt of data received one short interframe space previously. Generally, the data and the acknowledgment are intended for two separate stations. In Figure 8-3, the contention-free acknowledgment is coupled with the

data for transmission to the access point in the previous frame, but the data may be intended for any station on the 802.11 network.

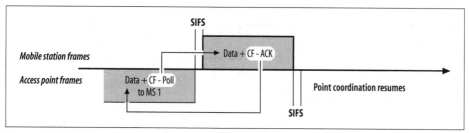

Figure 8-3. Data+CF-Ack usage

This frame is used only in infrastructure networks because it is transmitted during the contention-free period. It may be transmitted by either the access point or a mobile station. During the contention-free period, however, the access point is responsible for polling, and it is unlikely that it would transmit this frame subtype because it does not include a poll.

Data+CF-Poll

The Data+CF-Poll frame is used by access points in infrastructure networks during the contention-free period. When the access point does not need to acknowledge any outstanding frames, it sends a Data+CF-Poll to transmit data to the recipient and allows the recipient to send one buffered frame in response. The data in the frame body must be intended for the recipient of the poll; the two operations cannot be "split" across two different receivers. In Figure 8-3, the access point uses a Data+CF-Poll frame to send one frame to the mobile station and to solicit the response.

Data+CF-Ack+CF-Poll

The Data+CF-Ack+CF-Poll frame is used by access points in infrastructure networks during the contention-free period. When the access point has data to transmit, must acknowledge a frame, and needs to poll a station on the polling list, all the functions can be combined into one frame. Figure 8-4 illustrates the usage of Data+CF-Ack+CF-Poll. As with Data+CF-Ack, the components of the Data+CF-Ack+CF-Poll frame are generally intended for different stations. The data transmission and polling must be intended for the same station, but the acknowledgment is for the previous transmission.

The figure begins with mobile station 1 (MS1) transmitting a Data+CF-Ack frame. The Data must go to the access point, but the CF-Ack is used to acknowledge the previous Data frame transmitted by the access point. (That frame is not shown in the figure.) Moving down the polling list, the access point then polls mobile station 2 (MS2). However, the access point must acknowledge the data from MS1, which it does by transmitting a frame with a CF-Ack component. When the access point also has data to transmit, all three features can be combined into one

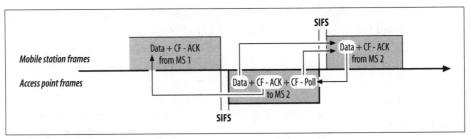

Figure 8-4. Usage of Data+CF-Ack+CF-Poll

omnibus frame. The Data and CF-Poll components are intended for the recipient of the frame, but the CF-Ack is intended for the transmitter of the *previous* frame. MS1 must listen to the access point frames to note the acknowledgment.

CF-Ack (no data)

When only an acknowledgment is required, a header-only frame with just the CF-Ack function can be transmitted. In Figure 8-4, if MS2 had no data to transmit, it would have responded with a CF-Ack frame.

CF-Poll (no data)

CF-Poll can also be transmitted by itself. Naturally, only access points perform this function, so the CF-Poll frame is transmitted only by access points in infrastructure networks during the contention-free period.

"Naked" CF-Polls are transmitted when the access point has no buffered data for the recipient and does not need to acknowledge the receipt of previous frames. One common situation in which no acknowledgment is necessary is when the access point transmits a CF-Poll and the polled station has no data and does not respond. If the access point has no data for the next station on the polling list, it transmits a CF-Poll, as in Figure 8-5.

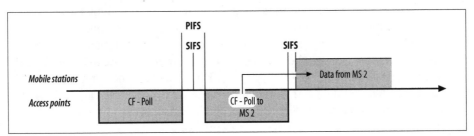

Figure 8-5. CF-Poll framing usage

In Figure 8-5, the access point attempts to transmit data to MS1 but does not receive a response. After the PCF interframe space has elapsed, the access point can proceed down the polling list to MS2. No frame from MS1 needs to be acknowledged, and if the access point has no data for MS2, it can use a CF-Poll to allow MS2 to send data.

CF-Ack+CF-Poll (no data)

The final subtype of Data frame is the CF-Ack+CF-Poll, which is also transmitted by access points. Like all CF-Poll frames, it is used only during the contention-free period and only by access points. It incorporates the acknowledgment function and the polling function into a frame with no data. Figure 8-6 illustrates its usage.

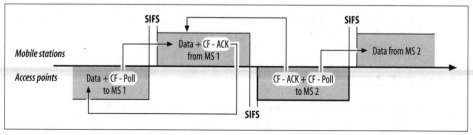

Figure 8-6. CF-Ack+CF-Poll usage

The scenario is a slight variation on the previous setting. Instead of a timeout waiting for MS1 to respond, MS1 returns a frame. When the access point takes control of the medium, it uses a CF-Ack+CF-Poll to acknowledge receipt of the frame from MS1 and notifies MS2 that it is allowed to send a frame.

Contention-Free End (CF-End)

When the contention-free period ends, the access point transmits a CF-End frame to release stations from the PCF access rules and begin contention-based service. The format of the CF-End frame is shown in Figure 8-7. Four fields make up the MAC header of the CF-End frame:

Frame Control
The frame subtype is set to 1110 to indicate a CF-End frame.

Duration
CF-End announces the end of the contention-free period and thus does not need to extend the virtual carrier sense. Duration is set to 0. Stations that receive the CF-End frame cut the virtual carrier sense short to resume contention-based access.

Address 1: Receiver Address
CF-End is relevant to the operation of all mobile stations, so the receiver address is the broadcast address.

Address 2: BSSID
CF-End is announced by the access point to all the stations associated with its BSS, so the second address field is the BSSID. In infrastructure networks, the BSSID is the address of the wireless interface in the access point, so the BSSID is also the transmitter address.

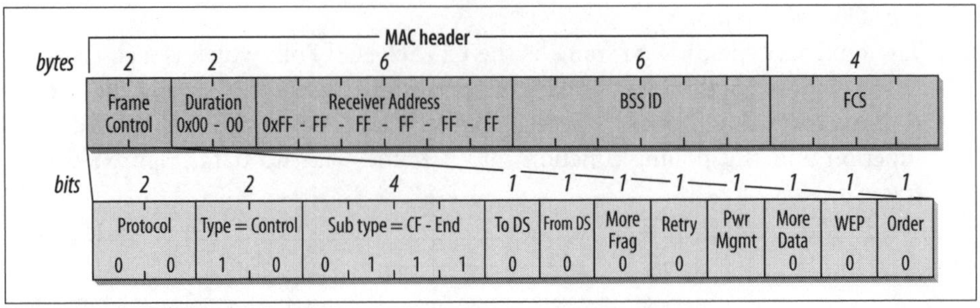

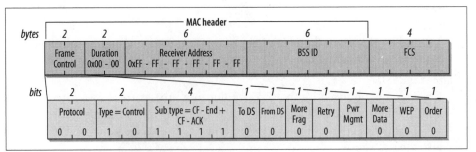

Figure 8-7. CF-End frame

CF-End+CF-Ack

When the contention-free period ends, the access point transmits a CF-End frame to release stations from the PCF access rules and then begins contention-based service using the DCF. If the access point must also acknowledge receipt of data, it may simultaneously end the contention-free period and acknowledge the previous frame by using the CF-End+CF-Ack frame, which combines both functions. The format of the CF-End+CF-Ack frame is shown in Figure 8-8. Four fields make up the MAC header of the CF-End+CF-Ack frame:

Frame Control
   The frame subtype is set to 1111 to indicate a CF-End+CF-Ack frame.

Duration
   CF-End+CF-Ack announces the end of the contention-free period and thus does not need to extend the virtual carrier sense. Duration is set to 0.

Address 1: Receiver Address
   CF-End+CF-Ack is relevant to the operation of all mobile stations, so the receiver address is the broadcast address.

Address 2: BSSID
   CF-End+CF-Ack is announced by the access point to all the stations associated with its BSS, so the second address field is the BSSID. In infrastructure networks, the BSSID is the address of the wireless interface in the access point, so the BSSID is also the transmitter address.

Figure 8-8. CF-End+CF-Ack frame

CF Parameter Set

Access points that support contention-free operation may include the CF Parameter Set information element, which is shown in Figure 8-9. CF Parameter Set elements are included in Beacon frames to keep all mobile stations apprised of contention-free operations. They are also included in Probe Response frames to allow stations to learn about contention-free options supported by a BSS. Four fields make up the CF Parameter Set information element:

CFP Count
This field, which is one byte in length, tells how many DTIM frames will be transmitted before the start of the next contention-free period. Zero indicates that the current frame is the start of contention-free service.

CFP Period
This one-byte field indicates the number of DTIM intervals between the start of contention-free periods.

CFP MaxDuration
This value is the maximum duration of the contention-free period as measured in time units (TUs). Mobile stations use this value to set the NAV to busy for the entire contention-free period.

CFP DurRemaining
This value is the number of TUs remaining in the current contention-free period. Mobile stations use it to update the NAV throughout the contention-free period. When DCF-based contention-free service is provided, it is set to 0.

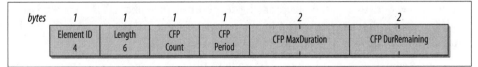

bytes	1	1	1	1	2	2
	Element ID 4	Length 6	CFP Count	CFP Period	CFP MaxDuration	CFP DurRemaining

Figure 8-9. CF Parameter Set information element

Power Management and the PCF

Power conservation during the contention-free period is similar to power conservation during the contention-based period, with a few minor exceptions. The basic distinction between the two is that frame delivery must obey the PCF rules, so buffered frames can be delivered only to CF-Pollable stations. Stations that do not support PCF operations must wait until contention-based service resumes before retrieving buffered frames.

Stations on the polling list are not allowed to sleep during the contention-free period. When the access point is performing its point coordination functions, it may poll any station on the polling list at any time. Frames destined for stations on the polling list do not need to be buffered during the contention-free period because those stations do not sleep.

Frame buffering is identical under contention-free and contention-based service. By maintaining power-saving status for each station, the access point can buffer frames for any station in a low-power mode. Broadcast and multicast frames are buffered whenever an associated station is in a low-power mode.

In addition to the buffer status associated with contention-free service, the access point also sets bits in the TIM for any station it intends to poll. The reason for setting these bits is related to how buffered frames are delivered. Like contention-based service, DTIM frames trigger the transmission of broadcast and multicast frames. If the total time required to transmit multicast and broadcast frames exceeds the Beacon interval, the access point will transmit one Beacon interval's worth of buffered frames and stop. Remaining frames will, however, cause the access point to keep the bit corresponding to AID 0 set.

After transmitting the buffered broadcast and multicast frames, the access point goes through the list of AIDs whose TIM bits are set in increasing order and transmits any pending data. Transmissions are conducted according to the rules of the PCF, so it is not necessary to include a delay before beginning transmission. Stations on the polling list are added to the TIM, so they will be included in this process. Multiple buffered frames can be transmitted, but this is entirely up to the access point implementation—in contention-free service, mobile stations can transmit only when given permission by the access point. A station is not allowed to resume sleeping until all frames have been delivered to it, as indicated by a 0 More Data bit. When a station is cleared to resume sleeping, it sleeps until the next DTIM transmission. DTIM frames signal the beginning of the contention-free period, so all stations that implement the PCF are required to wake up for every DTIM.

If a station switches from a low-power mode to the active mode, any frames buffered for it are transferred to the point coordination function for delivery during the contention-free period. The transfer does not result in immediate delivery, but the access point can place the frames into a queue for transmission as soon as the point coordination function permits.

## CHAPTER 9

Physical Layer Overview

*Any girl can be glamorous. All you have
to do is stand still and look stupid.*
—Hedy Lamarr

Protocol layering allows for research, experimentation, and improvement on different parts of the protocol stack. The second major component of the 802.11 architecture is the physical layer, which is often abbreviated PHY. This chapter introduces the common themes and techniques that appear in each of the radio-based physical layers and describes the problems common to all radio-based physical layers; it is followed by more detailed explanations of each of the physical layers that are standardized for 802.11.

Physical-Layer Architecture

The physical layer is divided into two sublayers: the *Physical Layer Convergence Procedure* (PLCP) sublayer and the *Physical Medium Dependent* (PMD) sublayer. The PLCP (Figure 9-1) is the glue between the frames of the MAC and the radio transmissions in the air. It adds its own header. Normally, frames include a preamble to help synchronize incoming transmissions. The requirements of the preamble may depend on the modulation method, however, so the PLCP adds its own header to any transmitted frames. The PMD is responsible for transmitting any bits it receives from the PLCP into the air using the antenna. The physical layer also incorporates a *clear channel assessment* (CCA) function to indicate to the MAC when a signal is detected.

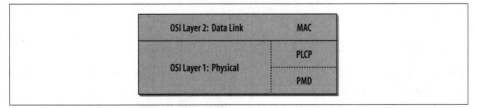

Figure 9-1. Physical layer logical architecture

The Radio Link

Three physical layers were standardized in the initial revision of 802.11, which was published in 1997:

- Frequency-hopping (FH) spread-spectrum radio PHY
- Direct-sequence (DS) spread-spectrum radio PHY
- Infrared light (IR) PHY

In 1999, two further physical layers based on radio technology were developed:

- 802.11a: Orthogonal Frequency Division Multiplexing (OFDM) PHY
- 802.11b: High-Rate Direct Sequence (HR/DS or HR/DSSS) PHY

This book discusses the four physical layers based on radio waves in detail; it does not discuss the infrared physical layer, which isn't widely used.

The IR PHY

802.11 also includes a specification for a physical layer based on infrared (IR) light. Using infrared light instead of radio waves seems to have several advantages. IR ports are less expensive than radio transceivers—in fact, the cost is low enough that IR ports are standard on practically every laptop.

IR is extremely tolerant of radio frequency (RF) interference because radio waves operate at a totally different frequency. This leads to a second advantage: IR is unregulated. Product developers do not need to investigate and comply with directives from several regulatory organizations throughout the world.

Security concerns regarding 802.11 are largely based on the threat of unauthorized users connecting to a network. Light can be confined to a conference room or office by simply closing the door. IR-based LANs can offer some of the advantages of flexibility and mobility but with fewer security concerns. This comes at a price. IR LANs rely on scattering light off the ceiling, so range is much shorter.

This discussion is academic, however. No products have been created based on the IR PHY. The infrared ports on laptops comply with a set of standards developed by the Infrared Data Association (IrDA), not 802.11. Even if products were created around the IR PHY, the big drivers to adopt 802.11 are flexibility and mobility, which are better achieved by radio's longer range and ability to penetrate solid objects.

Licensing

The classic approach to radio communications is to confine an information-carrying signal to a narrow frequency band and pump as much power as possible (or legally allowed) into the signal. Noise is simply the naturally present distortion in the frequency band. Transmitting a signal in the face of noise relies on brute force—you simply ensure that the power of the transmitted signal is much greater than the noise.

In the classic transmission model, avoiding interference is a matter of law, not physics. With high power output in narrow bands, a legal authority must impose rules on how the RF spectrum is used. In the United States, the Federal Communications Commission (FCC) is responsible for regulating the use of the RF spectrum. Many FCC rules are adopted by other countries throughout the Americas. European allocation is performed by CEPT's European Radiocommunications Office (ERO) and the European Telecommunications Standards Institute (ETSI). Other allocation work is performed by the International Telecommunications Union (ITU).

For the most part, an institution must have a license to transmit at a given frequency. Licenses can restrict the frequencies and transmission power used, as well as the area over which radio signals can be transmitted. For example, radio broadcast stations must have a license from the FCC. Likewise, mobile telephone networks must obtain licenses to use the radio spectrum in a given market. Licensing guarantees the exclusive use of a particular set of frequencies. When licensed signals are interfered with, the license holder can demand that a regulatory authority step in and resolve the problem, usually by shutting down the source of interference.

Frequency allocation and unlicensed frequency bands

Radio spectrum is allocated in bands dedicated to a particular purpose. A band defines the frequencies that a particular application may use. It often includes guard bands, which are unused portions of the overall allocation that prevent extraneous leakage from the licensed transmission from affecting another allocated band.

Several bands have been reserved for unlicensed use. For example, microwave ovens operate at 2.45 GHz, but there is little sense in requiring homeowners to obtain permission from the FCC to operate microwave ovens in the home. To allow consumer markets to develop around devices built for home use, the FCC (and its counterparts in other countries) designated certain bands for the use of "industrial, scientific, and medical" equipment. These frequency bands are commonly referred to as the *ISM bands*. The 2.4-GHz band is available worldwide for unlicensed use.* Unlicensed use, however, is not the same as unlicensed sale. Building, manufacturing, and designing 802.11 equipment does require a license; every 802.11 card legally sold in the U.S. carries an FCC identification number. The licensing process requires the manufacturer to file a fair amount of information with the FCC. All this information is a matter of public record and can be looked up online by using the FCC identification number.

---

* The 2.4-GHz ISM band is reserved by the FCC rules (Title 47 of the Code of Federal Regulations), part 15.247. ETSI reserved the same spectrum in ETSI Technical Specifications (ETS) 300-328.

The Nonexistent Microwave Absorption Peak of Water

It is often said that microwave ovens operate at 2.45 GHz because it corresponds to a particular excitation mode of water molecules. This is sometimes even offered as a reason why 802.11 cannot be used over long distances. Atmospheric water vapor would severely attenuate any microwave signals in rain or in humid climates.

The existence of a water excitation mode in the microwave range is a myth. If there was an excitation mode, water would absorb a significant amount of the microwave energy. And if that energy was absorbed effectively by water, microwave ovens would be unable to heat anything other than the water near the surface of food, which would absorb all the energy, leaving the center cold and raw. An absorption peak would also mean that atmospheric water vapor would disrupt satellite communications, which is not an observed phenomenon. NASA Reference Publication 1108(02), *Propagation Effects on Satellite Systems at Frequencies Below 10 GHz*, discusses the expected signal loss due to atmospheric effects, and the loss is much more pronounced at frequencies above 10 GHz. The microwave absorption peak for water, for example, is at 22.2 GHz.

Microwave ovens do not work by moving water molecules into an excited state. Instead, they exploit the unusually strong dipole moment of water. Although electrically neutral, the dipole moment allows a water molecule to behave as if it were composed of small positive and negative charges at either end of a rod. In the cavity of a microwave oven, the changing electric and magnetic fields twist the water molecules back and forth. Twisting excites the water molecules by adding kinetic energy to the entire molecule but does not change the excitation state of the molecule or any of its components.

Use of equipment in the ISM bands is generally license-free, provided that devices operating in them do not emit significant amounts of radiation. Microwave ovens are high-powered devices, but they have extensive shielding to restrict radio emissions. Unlicensed bands have seen a great deal of activity in the past three years as new communications technologies have been developed to exploit the unlicensed band. Users can deploy new devices that operate in the ISM bands without going through any licensing procedure, and manufacturers do not need to be familiar with the licensing procedures and requirements. At the time this book was written, a number of new communications systems were being developed for the 2.4-GHz ISM band:

- The variants of 802.11 that operate in the band (the frequency-hopping layer and both spread spectrum layers)

- Bluetooth, a short-range wireless communications protocol developed by an industry consortium led by Ericsson

- Spread-spectrum cordless phones introduced by several cordless phone manufacturers

- X10, a protocol used in home automation equipment that can use the ISM band for video transmission

Unfortunately, "unlicensed" does not necessarily mean "plays well with others." All that unlicensed devices must do is obey limitations on transmitted power. No regulations specify coding or modulation, so it is not difficult for different vendors to use the spectrum in incompatible ways. As a user, the only way to resolve this problem is to stop using one of the devices; because the devices are unlicensed, regulatory authorities will not step in.

Other unlicensed bands

Additional spectrum is available in the 5-GHz range. In the United States, the following three bands are called the Unlicensed National Information Infrastructure (UNII) bands:[*]

- 5.15–5.25 GHz
- 5.25–5.35 GHz
- 5.725–5.825 GHz

Devices operating in the UNII bands must obey limitations on radiated power, but there are no further constraints imposed on them. European regulatory authorities have set aside the same frequency bands, but the first two bands are dedicated to HiperLAN technology; the third band is the only one potentially available for 802.11 networks.

Spread Spectrum

Spread-spectrum technology is the foundation used to reclaim the ISM bands for data use. Traditional radio communications focus on cramming as much signal as possible into as narrow a band as possible. Spread spectrum works by using mathematical functions to diffuse signal power over a large range of frequencies. When the receiver performs the inverse operation, the smeared-out signal is reconstituted as a narrow-band signal, and, more importantly, any narrow-band noise is smeared out so the signal shines through clearly.

Use of spread-spectrum technologies is a requirement for unlicensed devices. In some cases, it is a requirement imposed by the regulatory authorities; in other cases, it is the only practical way to meet regulatory requirements. As an example, the FCC requires that devices in the ISM band use spread-spectrum transmission and impose acceptable ranges on several parameters.

Spreading the transmission over a wide band makes transmissions look like noise to a traditional narrowband receiver. Some vendors of spread-spectrum devices claim that the spreading adds security because narrowband receivers cannot be used to pick up the full signal. Any standardized spread-spectrum receiver can easily be used, though, so additional security measures are mandatory in nearly all environments.

---

[*] The UNII bands are defined by FCC part 15.407.

This does not mean that spread spectrum is a "magic bullet" that eliminates interference problems. Spread-spectrum devices can interfere with other communications systems, as well as with each other; and traditional narrow-spectrum RF devices can interfere with spread spectrum. Although spread spectrum does a better job of dealing with interference within other modulation techniques, it doesn't make the problem go away. As more RF devices (spread spectrum or otherwise) occupy the area that your wireless network covers, you'll see the noise level go up, the signal-to-noise ratio decrease, and the range over which you can reliably communicate drop.

To minimize interference between unlicenced devices, the FCC imposes limitations on the power of spread-spectrum transmissions. The legal limits are one watt of transmitter output power and four watts of effective radiated power (ERP). Four watts of ERP are equivalent to 1 watt with an antenna system that has 6-dB gain, or 500 milliwatts with an antenna of 9-dB gain, etc.* The transmitters and antennas in PC Cards are obviously well within those limits—and you're not getting close even if you use a commercial antenna. But it is possible to cover larger areas by using an external amplifier and a higher-gain antenna. There's no fundamental problem with doing this, but you must make sure that you stay within the FCC's power regulations.

Types of spread spectrum

The radio-based physical layers in 802.11 use three different spread-spectrum techniques:

Frequency hopping (FH or FHSS)
> Frequency-hopping systems jump from one frequency to another in a random pattern, transmitting a short burst at each subchannel. The 2-Mbps FH PHY is specified in clause 14.

Direct sequence (DS or DSSS)
> Direct-sequence systems spread the power out over a wider frequency band using mathematical coding functions. Two direct-sequence layers were specified. The initial specification in clause 15 standardized a 2-Mbps PHY, and 802.11b added clause 18 for the HR/DSSS PHY.

Orthogonal Frequency Division Multiplexing (OFDM)
> OFDM divides an available channel into several subchannels and encodes a portion of the signal across each subchannel in parallel. The technique is similar to the Discrete Multi-Tone (DMT) technique used by some DSL modems. Clause 17, added with 802.11a, specifies the OFDM PHY.

---

* Remember that the transmission line is part of the antenna system, and the system gain includes transmission line losses. So an antenna with 7.5-dB gain and a transmission line with 1.5-dB loss has an overal system gain of 6 dB. It's worth noting that transmission line losses at UHF freqencies are often very high; as a result, you should keep your amplifier as close to the antenna as possible.

The Unlikely Invention of Spread Spectrum

Spread spectrum was patented in the early 1940s by Austrian-born actress Hedy Lamarr. She was certainly better known for other reasons: appearing in the first nude scene on film in the Czech film *Ecstasy*, her later billing as "the most beautiful woman in the world" by Hollywood magnate Louis Mayer, and as the model for Catwoman in the Batman comics.

Before fleeing the advance of Nazi Germany, she was married to an Austrian arms merchant. While occupying the only socially acceptable role available to her as a hostess and entertainer of her husband's business clients, she learned that radio remote control of torpedoes was a major area of research for armaments vendors. Unfortunately, narrowband radio communications were subject to jamming, which neutralized the advantage of radio-guided weapons. From these discussions, she first hit on the idea of using a complex but predetermined hopping pattern to move the frequency of the control signal around. Even if short bursts on a single frequency could be jammed, they would move around quickly enough to prevent total blockage. Lamarr worked out everything except how to precisely control the frequency hops.

After arriving in the United States, she met George Antheil, an avant-garde American composer known as the "bad boy of music" for his dissonant style. His famous *Ballet mécanique* used (among many outrageous noisemakers) 16 player pianos controlled from a single location. Performing the piece required precisely controlled timing between distributed elements, which was Lamarr's only remaining challenge in controlling the hopping pattern. Together, they were granted U.S. patent number 2,292,387 in 1942. The patent expired in 1959 without earning a cent for either of them, and Lamarr's contributions went unacknowledged for many years because the name on the patent was Hedy Kiesler Markey, her married name at the time. The emerging wireless LAN market in the late 1990s led to the rediscovery of her invention and widespread recognition for the pioneering work that laid the foundation for modern telecommunications.

Frequency-hopping techniques were first used by U.S. ships blockading Cuba during the Cuban Missile Crisis. It took many years for the electronics underpinning spread-spectrum technology to become commercially viable. Now that they have, spread-spectrum technologies are used in cordless and mobile phones, high-bandwidth wireless LAN equipment, and every device that operates in the unlicensed ISM bands. Unfortunately, Hedy Lamarr died in early 2000, just as the wireless LAN market was gaining mainstream attention.

Frequency-hopping systems are the cheapest to make. Precise timing is needed to control the frequency hops, but sophisticated signal processing is not required to extract the bit stream from the radio signal. Direct-sequence systems require more sophisticated signal processing, which translates into more specialized hardware and higher electrical power consumption. Direct-sequence techniques also allow a higher data rate than frequency-hopping systems.

RF and 802.11

802.11 has been adopted at a stunning rate. Many network engineers accustomed to signals flowing along well-defined cable paths are now faced with a LAN that runs over a noisy, error-prone, quirky radio link. In data networking, the success of 802.11 has inexorably linked it with RF engineering. A true introduction to RF engineering requires at least one book, and probably several. For the limited purposes I have in mind, the massive topic of RF engineering can be divided into two parts: how to make radio waves and how radio waves move.

RF Components

RF systems complement wired networks by extending them. Different components may be used depending on the frequency and the distance that signals are required to reach, but all systems are fundamentally the same and made from a relatively small number of distinct pieces. Two RF components are of particular interest to 802.11 users: antennas and amplifiers. Antennas are of general interest since they are the most tangible feature of an RF system. Amplifiers complement antennas by allowing them to pump out more power, which may be of interest depending on the type of 802.11 network you are building.

Antennas

Antennas are the most critical component of any RF system because they convert electrical signals on wires into radio waves and vice versa. In block diagrams, antennas are usually represented by a triangular shape, as shown in Figure 9-2.

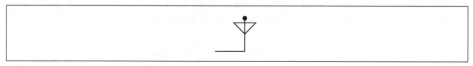

Figure 9-2. Antenna representations in diagrams

To function at all, an antenna must be made of conducting material. Radio waves hitting an antenna cause electrons to flow in the conductor and create a current. Likewise, applying a current to an antenna creates an electric field around the antenna. As the current to the antenna changes, so does the electric field. A changing electric field causes a magnetic field, and the wave is off.

The size of the antenna you need depends on the frequency: the higher the frequency, the smaller the antenna. The shortest simple antenna you can make at any frequency is 1/2 wavelength long (though antenna engineers can play tricks to reduce antenna size further). This rule of thumb accounts for the huge size of radio broadcast antennas and the small size of mobile phones. An AM station broadcasting at 830 kHz has a wavelength of about 360 meters and a correspondingly large antenna, but an 802.11b network interface operating in the 2.4-GHz band has a wavelength of just 12.5 centimeters. With some engineering tricks, an antenna can be incorporated into a PC Card, and a more effective external antenna can easily be carried in a backpack.

Antennas can also be designed with directional preference. Many antennas are omnidirectional, which means they send and receive signals from any direction. Some applications may benefit from directional antennas, which radiate and receive on a narrower portion of the field. Figure 9-3 compares the radiated power of omnidirectional and directional antennas.

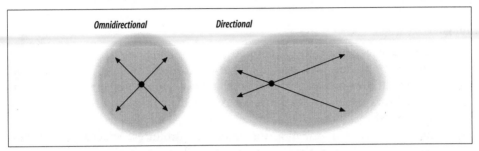

Figure 9-3. Radiated power for omnidirectional and directional antennas

For a given amount of input power, a directional antenna can reach farther with a clearer signal. They also have much higher sensitivity to radio signals in the dominant direction. When wireless links are used to replace wireline networks, directional antennas are often used. Mobile telephone network operators also use directional antennas when cells are subdivided. 802.11 networks typically use omnidirectional antennas for both ends of the connection, though there are exceptions—particularly if you want the network to span a longer distance. Also, keep in mind that there is no such thing as a truly omnidirectional antenna. We're accustomed to thinking of vertically mounted antennas as omnidirectional because the signal doesn't vary significantly as you travel around the antenna in a horizontal plane. But if you look at the signal radiated vertically (i.e., up or down) from the antenna, you'll find that it's a different story. And that part of the story can become important if you're building a network for a college or corporate campus and want to locate antennas on the top floors of your buildings.

Of all the components presented in this section, antennas are the most likely to be separated from the rest of the electronics. In this case, you need a transmission line (some kind of cable) between the antenna and the transceiver. Transmission lines usually have an impedance of 50 ohms.

In terms of practical antennas for 802.11 devices in the 2.4-GHz band, the typical wireless PC Card has an antenna built in. As you can probably guess, that antenna will do the job, but it's mediocre. Most vendors, if not all, sell an optional external antenna that plugs into the card. These antennas are decent but not great, and they will significantly increase the range of a roaming laptop. You can usually buy some cable to separate the antenna from the PC Card, which can be useful for a base station. However, be careful—coaxial cable (especially small coaxial cable) is very lossy at these frequencies, so it's easy to imagine that anything you gain by better antenna placement will be lost in the cable. People have experimented with building high-gain antennas, some for portable use, some for base station use. And commercial antennas are available—some designed for 802.11 service, some adaptable if you know what you're doing.

Amplifiers

Amplifiers make signals bigger. Signal boost, or *gain*, is measured in decibels (dB). Amplifiers can be broadly classified into three categories: low-noise, high-power, and everything else. Low-noise amplifiers (LNAs) are usually connected to an antenna to boost the received signal to a level that is recognizable by the electronics the RF system is connected to. LNAs are also rated for *noise factor*, which is the measure of how much extraneous information the amplifier introduces. Smaller noise factors allow the receiver to hear smaller signals and thus allow for a greater range.

High-power amplifiers (HPAs) are used to boost a signal to the maximum power possible before transmission. Output power is measured in dBm, which are related to watts (see the sidebar). Amplifiers are subject to the laws of thermodynamics, so they give off heat in addition to amplifying the signal. The transmitter in an 802.11 PC Card is necessarily low-power because it needs to run off a battery if it's installed in a laptop, but it's possible to install an external amplifier at fixed access points, which can be connected to the power grid where power is more plentiful.

This is where things can get tricky with respect to compliance with regulations. 802.11 devices are limited to one watt of power output and four watts effective radiated power (ERP). ERP multiplies the transmitter's power output by the gain of the antenna minus the loss in the transmission line. So if you have a 1-watt amplifier, an antenna that gives you 8 dB of gain, and 2 dB of transmission line loss, you have an ERP of 4 watts; the total system gain is 6 dB, which multiplies the transmitter's power by a factor of 4.

RF Propagation

In fixed networks, signals are confined to wire pathways, so network engineers do not need to know anything about the physics of electrical signal propagation. Instead, there are a few rules used to calculate maximum segment length, and as long as the rules are obeyed, problems are rare. RF propagation is not anywhere near as simple.

Decibels and Signal Strength

Amplifiers may boost signals by orders of magnitude. Rather than keep track of all those zeroes, amplifier power is measured in decibels (dB).

dB = 10 × log10 (power out/power in)

Decibel ratings are positive when the output is larger than the input and negative when the output is smaller than the input. Each 10-dB change corresponds to a factor of 10, and 3-dB changes are a factor of 2. Thus, a 33-dB change corresponds to a factor of 2000:

33 dB = 10 dB + 10 dB + 10 dB + 3 dB = 10 × 10 × 10 × 2 = 2000

Power is sometimes measured in dBm, which stands for dB above one milliwatt. To find the dBm ratio, simply use 1 mW as the input power in the first equation.

It's helpful to remember that doubling the power is a 3-dB increase. A 1-dB increase is roughly equivalent to a power increase of 1.25. With these numbers in mind, you can quickly perform most gain calculations in your head.

Multipath interference

One of the major problems that plague radio networks is multipath fading. Waves are added by superposition. When multiple waves converge on a point, the total wave is simply the sum of any component waves. Figure 9-4 shows a few examples of superposition.

In Figure 9-4c, the two waves are almost exactly the opposite of each other, so the net result is almost nothing. Unfortunately, this result is more common than you might expect in wireless networks. Most 802.11 equipment uses omnidirectional antennas, so RF energy is radiated in every direction. Waves spread outward from the transmitting antenna in all directions and are reflected by surfaces in the area. Figure 9-5 shows a highly simplified example of two stations in a rectangular area with no obstructions.

This figure shows three paths from the transmitter to the receiver. The wave at the receiver is the sum of all the different components. It is certainly possible that the paths shown in Figure 9-5 will all combine to give a net wave of 0, in which case the receiver will not understand the transmission because there is no transmission to be received.

Because the interference is a delayed copy of the same transmission on a different path, the phenomenon is called multipath fading or multipath interference. In many cases, multipath interference can be resolved by changing the orientation or position of the receiver.

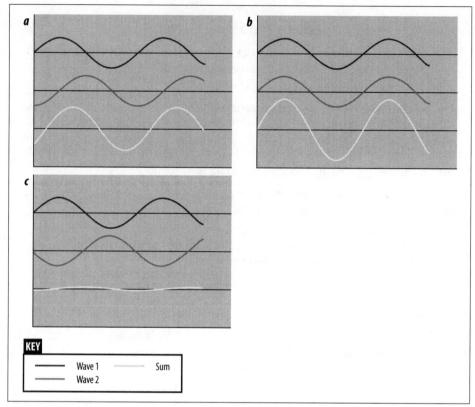

Figure 9-4. Wave combination by superposition

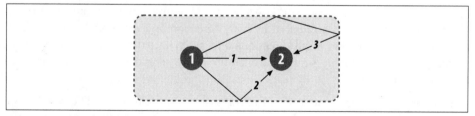

Figure 9-5. Multiple paths

Inter-symbol interference (ISI)

Multipath fading is a special case of inter-symbol interference. Waves that take different paths from the transmitter to the receiver will travel different distances and be delayed with respect to each other, as in Figure 9-6. Once again, the two waves combine by superposition, but the effect is that the total waveform is garbled. In real-world situations, wavefronts from multiple paths may be added. The time between the arrival of the first wavefront and the last multipath echo is called the *delay spread*. Longer delay spreads require more conservative coding mechanisms. 802.11b networks can handle delay spreads of up to 500 ns, but performance is much better when the delay spread is lower. When the delay spread is large, many cards will reduce the transmission rate; several vendors claim that a 65-ns delay spread is required for full-speed 11-Mbps performance at a reasonable frame error rate. A few wireless LAN analysis tools can directly measure delay spread.

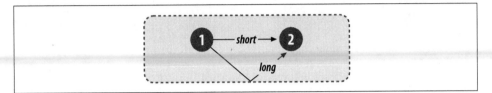

Figure 9-6. Inter-symbol interference

CHAPTER 10
The ISM PHYs: FH, DS, and HR/DS

This chapter goes into detail about the physical layers specified by the 802.11 standards for use in the microwave ISM band at 2.4 GHz. As such, it is one of the most difficult, most interesting, and least useful chapters in the book. Feel free to skip it—everything you're likely to need to know about the physical layer is covered in Chapter 9. But if you want a challenge, or if you find the internals of wireless networks fascinating, read on.

The current version of the 802.11 standard specifies three physical layers in the 2.4-GHz ISM band:

FH PHY
> A low-rate, frequency-hopping layer

DS PHY
> A low-rate, direct-sequence layer

HR/DSSS PHY
> A high-rate, direct-sequence layer added by 802.11b

The last of these is probably the only one you'll see in use, particularly if you don't have a lot of older equipment. But if you're taking the trouble to dive through this chapter, you might as well see how the technology developed. There is one additional physical layer, a very high-speed layer standardized in 802.11a; it is discussed in Chapter 11. Standardization work has begun on a fourth physical layer for the 2.4-GHz ISM band that promises speeds of up to 54 Mbps.

802.11 FH PHY

Of all the physical layers standardized in the first draft of 802.11 in 1997, the frequency-hopping, spread-spectrum (FH or FHSS) layer was the first layer to see widespread deployment. The electronics used to support frequency-hopping modulation are relatively cheap and do not have high power requirements. Initially, the main advantage to using frequency-hopping networks was that a greater number of networks could coexist, and the aggregate throughput of all the networks in a given area was high. With the advent of higher-rate, direct-sequence systems, the aggregate throughput advantage of frequency-hopping has been demolished.

This chapter describes the basic concepts and modulation techniques used by the FH PHY. It also shows how the physical layer convergence procedure prepares frames for transmission on the radio link and touches briefly on a few details about the physical medium itself. At this point, the FH PHY is largely a footnote in the history of 802.11, so you may want to skip this section and move ahead to the next section on the DS PHY. However, understanding how 802.11 technology developed will give you a better feeling for how all the pieces fit together.

Frequency-Hopping Transmission

Frequency hopping depends on rapidly changing the transmission frequency in a predetermined, pseudorandom pattern, as illustrated in Figure 10-1. The vertical axis of the graph divides the available frequency into a number of slots. Likewise, time is divided into a series of slots. A hopping pattern controls how the slots are used. In the figure, the hopping pattern is {2,8,4,7}. Timing the hops accurately is the key to success; both the transmitter and receiver must be synchronized so the receiver is always listening on the transmitter's frequency.

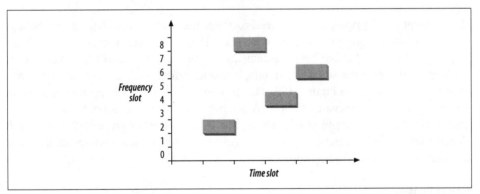

Figure 10-1. Frequency hopping

Frequency hopping is similar to frequency division multiple access (FDMA) but with an important twist. In FDMA systems, each device is allocated a fixed frequency. Multiple devices share the available radio spectrum by using different frequencies. In frequency-hopping systems, the frequency is time-dependent rather than fixed. Each frequency is used for a small amount of time, called the *dwell time*.

Among other things, frequency hopping allows devices to avoid interfering with primary users assigned to the same frequency band. It works because primary users are assigned narrow frequency bands and the right to transmit at a power high enough to override the wireless LAN. Any interference caused by the secondary user that affects the primary user is transient because the hopping sequence spreads the energy out over a wide band.* Likewise, the primary user only knocks out one of the spread-spectrum device's slots and looks like transient noise. Figure 10-2 shows the result when frequency slot 7 is given to a primary user. Although the transmission in the fourth time slot is corrupted, the first three transmissions succeed.

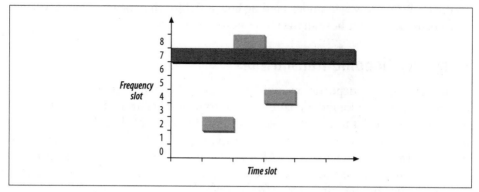

Figure 10-2. Avoiding interference with frequency hopping

If two frequency-hopping systems need to share the same band, they can be configured with different hopping sequences so they do not interfere with each other. During each time slot, the two hopping sequences must be on different frequency slots. As long as the systems stay on different frequency slots, they do not interfere with each other, as shown in Figure 10-3. The gray rectangles have a hopping sequence of {2,8,4,7}, as in the previous figures. A second system with a hopping sequence of {6,3,7,2} is added. Hopping sequences that do not overlap are called *orthogonal*. When multiple 802.11 networks are configured in a single area, orthogonal hopping sequences maximizes throughput.

802.11 FH details

802.11 divides the microwave ISM band into a series of 1-MHz channels. Approximately 99% of the radio energy is confined to the channel. The modulation method used by 802.11 encodes data bits as shifts in the transmission frequency from the channel center. Channels are defined by their center frequencies, which begin at 2.400 GHz for channel 0. Successive channels are derived by adding 1-MHz steps: channel 1

---

* If the primary user of a frequency band notices interference from secondary users, regulators can (and will) step in to shut down the secondary user, hence the low power used by spread-spectrum modulation techniques.

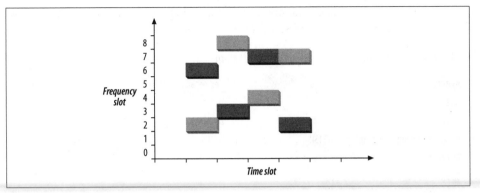

Figure 10-3. Orthogonal hopping sequences

has a center frequency of 2.401 GHz, channel 2 has a center frequency of 2.402 GHz, and so on up to channel 95 at 2.495 GHz. Different regulatory authorities allow use of different parts of the ISM band; the major regulatory domains and the available channels are shown in Table 10-1.

Table 10-1. Channels used in different regulatory domains

Regulatory domain	Allowed channels
US (FCC)	2 to 79 (2.402–2.479 GHz)
Canada (IC)	2 to 79 (2.402–2.479 GHz)
Europe (excluding France and Spain) (ETSI)	2 to 79 (2.402–2.479 GHz)
France	48 to 82 (2.448–2.482 GHz)
Spain	47 to 73 (2.447–2.473 GHz)
Japan (MKK)	73 to 95 (2.473–2.495 GHz)

The dwell time used by 802.11 FH systems is 390 time units, which is almost 0.4 seconds. When an 802.11 FH PHY hops between channels, the hopping process can take no longer than 224 microseconds. The frequency hops themselves are subject to extensive regulation, both in terms of the size of each hop and the rate at which hops must occur.

802.11 hop sequences

Mathematical functions for deriving hop sets are part of the FH PHY specification and are found in clause 14.6.8 of the 802.11 specification. As an example, hopping sequence 1 for North America and most of Europe begins with the sequence {3, 26, 65, 11, 46, 19, 74, 50, 22, ...}. 802.11 further divides hopping sequences into non-overlapping sets, and any two members of a set are orthogonal hopping sequences. In Europe and North America, each set contains 26 members. Regulatory authorities in other areas have restricted the number of hopped channels, and therefore each set has a smaller number of members. Table 10-2 has details.

Table 10-2. Size of hop sets in each regulatory domain

Regulatory domain	Hop set size
US (FCC)	26
Canada (IC)	26
Europe (excluding France and Spain) (ETSI)	26
France	27
Spain	35
Japan (MKK)	23

Joining an 802.11 frequency-hopping network

Joining a frequency-hopping network is made possible by the standardization of hop sequences. Beacon frames on FH networks include a timestamp and the FH Parameter Set element. The FH Parameter Set element includes the hop pattern number and a hop index. By receiving a Beacon frame, a station knows everything it needs to synchronize its hopping pattern.

Based on the hop sequence number, the station knows the channel-hopping order. As an example, say that a station has received a Beacon frame that indicates that the BSS is using the North America/Europe hop sequence number 1 and is at hop index 2. By looking up the hop sequence, the station can determine that the next channel is 65. Hop times are also well-defined. Each Beacon frame includes a Timestamp field, and the hop occurs when the timestamp modulo dwell time included in the Beacon is 0.

ISM emission rules and maximum throughput

Spectrum allocation policies are the limiting factor of frequency-hopping 802.11 systems. As an example, consider the three major rules imposed by the FCC in the U.S.:[*]

1. There must be at least 75 hopping channels in the band, which is 83.5-MHz wide.

2. Hopping channels can be no wider than 1 MHz.

3. Devices must use all available channels equally. In a 30-second period, no more than 0.4 seconds may be spent using any one channel.

Of these rules, the most important is the second one. No matter what fancy encoding schemes are available, only 1 MHz of bandwidth is available at any time. The frequency

---

[*] These rules are in rule 247 of part 15 of the FCC rules (47 CFR 15.247).

at which it is available shifts continuously because of the other two rules, but the second rule limits the number of signal transitions that can be used to encode data.

With a straightforward, two-level encoding, each cycle can encode one bit. At 1 bit per cycle, 1 MHz yields a data rate of 1 Mbps. More sophisticated modulation and demodulation schemes can improve the data rate. Four-level coding can pack 2 bits into a cycle, and 2 Mbps can be squeezed from the 1-MHz bandwidth.

The European Telecommunications Standards Institute (ETSI) also has a set of rules for spread-spectrum devices in the ISM band, published in European Telecommunications Standard (ETS) 300-328. The ETSI rules allow far fewer hopping channels; only 20 are required. Radiated power, however, is controlled much more strictly. In practice, to meet both the FCC and ETSI requirements, devices use the high number of hopping channels required by the FCC with the low radiated power requirements of ETSI.

Effect of interference

802.11 is a secondary use of the 2.4-GHz ISM band and must accept any interference from a higher-priority transmission. Catastrophic interference on a channel may prevent that channel from being used but leave other channels unaffected. With approximately 80 usable channels in the U.S. and Europe, interference on one channel reduces the raw bit rate of the medium by approximately 1.25%. (The cost at the IP layer will be somewhat higher because of the interframe gaps, 802.11 acknowledgments, and framing and physical-layer covergence headers.) As more channels are affected by interference, the throughput continues to drop. See Figure 10-4.

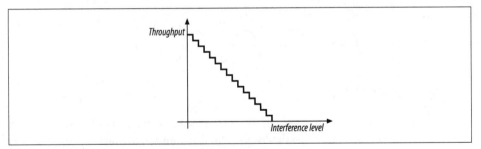

Figure 10-4. Throughput response to interference in FHSS systems

Gaussian Frequency Shift Keying (GFSK)

The FH PHY uses Gaussian frequency shift keying (GFSK).[*] Frequency shift keying encodes data as a series of frequency changes in a carrier. One advantage of using

---

[*] The term *keying* is a vestige of telegraphy. Transmission of data across telegraph lines required the use of a key. Sending data through a modern digital system employs modulation techniques instead, but the word keying persists.

frequency to encode data is that noise usually changes the amplitude of a signal; modulation systems that ignore amplitude (broadcast FM radio, for example) tend to be relatively immune to noise. The *Gaussian* in GFSK refers to the shape of radio pulses; GFSK confines emissions to a relatively narrow spectral band and is thus appropriate for secondary uses. Signal processing techniques that prevent wide-spread leakage of RF energy are a good thing, particularly for secondary users of a frequency band. By reducing the potential for interference, GFSK makes it more likely that 802.11 wireless LANs can be built in an area where another user has priority.

2-Level GFSK

The most basic GFSK implementation is called 2-level GFSK (2GFSK). Two differ-ent frequencies are used, depending on whether the data that will be transmitted is a 1 or a 0. To transmit a 1, the carrier frequency is increased by a certain deviation. Zero is encoded by decreasing the frequency by the same deviation. Figure 10-5 illus-trates the general procedure. In real-world systems, the frequency deviations from the carrier are much smaller; the figure is deliberately exaggerated to show how the encoding works.

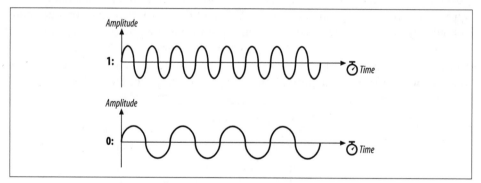

Figure 10-5. 2-level GFSK

The rate at which data is sent through the system is called the *symbol rate*. Because it takes several cycles to determine the frequency of the underlying carrier and whether 1 or 0 was transmitted, the symbol rate is a very small fraction of the carrier fre-quency. Although the carrier frequency is roughly 2.4 GHz, the symbol rate is only 1 or 2 million symbols per second.

Frequency changes with GFSK are not sharp changes. Instantaneous frequency changes require more expensive electronic components and higher power. Gradual frequency changes allow lower-cost equipment with lower RF leakage. Figure 10-6 shows how frequency varies as a result of encoding the letter M (1001101 binary) using 2GFSK. Note that the vertical axis is the frequency of the transmission. When a 1 is transmitted, the frequency rises to the center frequency plus an offset, and when a 0 is transmitted, the frequency drops by the same offset. The horizontal axis, which represents time, is divided into symbol periods. Around the middle of each period, the receiver measures the frequency of the transmission and translates that frequency into a symbol. (In 802.11 frequency-hopping systems, the higher-level data is scrambled before transmission, so the bit sequence transmitted to the peer station is not the same as the bit sequence over the air. The figure illustrates how the principles of 2GFSK work and doesn't step through an actual encoding.)

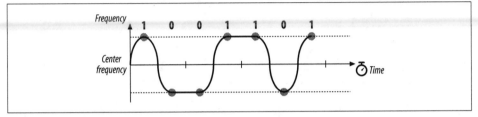

Figure 10-6. 2GFSK encoding of the letter M

4-Level GFSK

Using a scheme such as this, there are two ways to send more data: use a higher symbol rate or encode more bits of information into each symbol. 4-level GFSK (4GFSK) uses the same basic approach as 2GFSK but with four symbols instead of two. The four symbols (00, 01, 10, and 11) each correspond to a discrete frequency, and therefore 4GFSK transmits twice as much data at the same symbol rate. Obviously, this increase comes at a cost: 4GFSK requires more complex transmitters and receivers. Mapping of the four symbols onto bits is shown in Figure 10-7.

With its more sophisticated signal processing, 4GFSK packs multiple bits into a single symbol. Figure 10-8 shows how the letter M might be encoded. Once again, the vertical axis is frequency, and the horizontal axis is divided into symbol times. The frequency changes to transmit the symbols; the frequencies for each symbol are shown by the dashed lines. The figure also hints at the problem with extending GFSK-based methods to higher bit rates. Distinguishing between two levels is fairly easy. Four is harder. Each doubling of the bit rate requires that twice as many levels be present, and the RF components distinguish between ever smaller frequency changes. These limitations practically limit the FH PHY to 2 Mbps.

FH PHY Convergence Procedure (PLCP)

Before any frames can be modulated onto the RF carrier, the frames from the MAC must be prepared by the Physical Layer Convergence Procedure (PLCP). Different

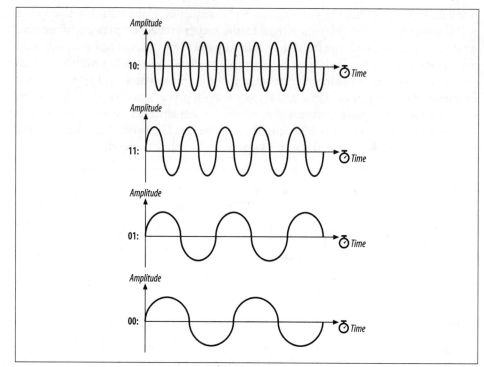

Figure 10-7. Mapping of symbols to frequencies in 4GFSK

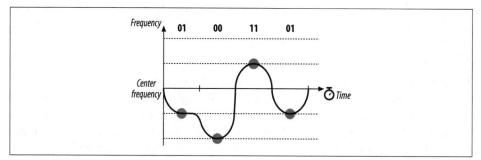

Figure 10-8. 4GFSK encoding of the letter M

underlying physical layers may have different requirements, so 802.11 allows each physical layer some latitude in preparing MAC frames for transmission over the air.

Framing and whitening

The PLCP for the FH PHY adds a five-field header to the frame it receives from the MAC. The PLCP is a relay between the MAC and the physical medium dependent (PMD) radio interface. In keeping with ISO reference model terminology, frames passed from the MAC are PLCP service data units (PSDUs). The PLCP framing is shown in Figure 10-9.

Preamble
As in a wired Ethernet, the preamble synchronizes the transmitter and receiver and derives common timing relationships. In the 802.11 FH PHY, the Preamble is composed of the Sync field and the Start Frame Delimiter field.

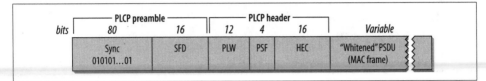

Figure 10-9. PLCP framing in the FH PHY

Sync
The sync field is 80 bits in length and is composed of an alternating zero-one sequence (010101...01). Stations search for the sync pattern to prepare to receive data. In addition to synchronizing the sender and receiver, the Sync field serves three purposes. Presence of a sync signal indicates that a frame is imminent. Second, stations that have multiple antennas to combat multipath fading or other environmental reception problems can select the antenna with the strongest signal. Finally, the receiver can measure the frequency of the incoming signal relative to its nominal values and perform any corrections needed to the received signal.

Start Frame Delimiter (SFD)
As in Ethernet, the SFD signals the end of the preamble and marks the beginning of the frame. The FH PHY uses a 16-bit SFD: 0000 1100 1011 1101.

Header
The PLCP header follows the preamble. The header has PHY-specific parameters used by the PLCP. Three fields comprise the header: a length field, a speed field, and a frame check sequence.

PSDU Length Word (PLW)
The first field in the PLCP header is the PLW. The payload of the PLCP frame is a MAC frame that may be up to 4,095 bytes long. The 12-bit length field informs the receiver of the length of the MAC frame that follows the PLCP header.

PLCP Signaling (PSF)
Bit 0, the first bit transmitted, is reserved and set to 0. Bits 1–3 encode the speed at which the payload MAC frame is transmitted. Several speeds are available, so this field allows the receiver to adjust to the appropriate demodulation scheme. Although the standard allows for data rates in increments of 500 kbps from 1.0

Mbps to 4.5 Mbps, the modulation scheme has been defined only for 1.0 Mbps and 2.0 Mbps.* See Table 10-3.

Table 10-3. PSF meaning

Bits (1-2-3)	Data rate
000	1.0 Mbps
001	1.5 Mbps
010	2.0 Mbps
011	2.5 Mbps
100	3.0 Mbps
101	3.5 Mbps
110	4.0 Mbps
111	4.5 Mbps

Header Error Check (HEC)

To protect against errors in the PLCP header, a 16-bit CRC is calculated over the contents of the header and placed in this field. The header does not protect against errors in other parts of the frame.

No restrictions are placed on the content of the Data field. Arbitrary data may contain long strings of consecutive 0s or 1s, which makes the data much less random. To make the transmitted data more like random white noise, the FH PHYs apply a *whitening* algorithm to the MAC frame. This algorithm scrambles the data before radio transmission. Receivers invert the process to recover the data.

Frequency-Hopping PMD Sublayer

Although the PLCP header has a field for the speed at which the MAC frame is transmitted, only two of these rates have corresponding standardized PMD layers. Several features are shared between both PMDs: antenna diversity support, allowances for the ramp up and ramp down of the power amplifiers in the antennas, and the use of a Gaussian pulse shaper to keep as much RF power as possible in the narrow frequency-hopping band. Figure 10-10 shows the general design of the transceiver used in 802.11 frequency-hopping networks.

PMD for 1.0-Mbps FH PHY

The basic frequency-hopping PMD enables data transmission at 1.0 Mbps. Frames from the MAC have the PLCP header appended, and the resulting sequence of bits is

---

* It is unlikely that significant further work will be done on high-rate, frequency-hopping systems. For high data rates, direct sequence is a more cost-effective choice.

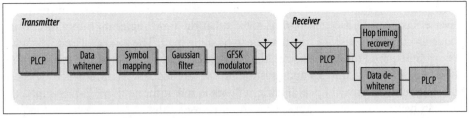

Figure 10-10. Frequency-hopping transceiver

transmitted out of the radio interface. In keeping with the common regulatory restriction of a 1-MHz bandwidth, 1 million symbols are transmitted per second. 2GFSK is used as the modulation scheme, so each symbol can be used to encode a single bit. 802.11 specifies a minimum power of 10 milliwatts (mW) and requires the use of a power control function to cap the radiated power at 100 mW, if necessary.

PMD for 2.0-Mbps FH PHY

A second, higher-speed PMD is available for the FH PHY. As with the 1.0-Mbps PMD, the PLCP header is appended and is transmitted at 1.0 Mbps using 2GFSK. In the PLCP header, the PSF field indicates the speed at which the frame body is transmitted. At the higher data rate, the frame body is transmitted using a different encoding method than the physical-layer header. Regulatory requirements restrict all PMDs to a symbol rate of 1 MHz, so 4GFSK must be used for the frame body. Two bits per symbol yields a rate of 2.0 Mbps at 1 million symbols per second. Firmware that supports the 2.0-Mbps PMD can fall back to the 1.0-Mbps PMD if signal quality is too poor to sustain the higher rate.

Carrier sense/clear channel assessment (CS/CCA)

To implement the CSMA/CA foundation of 802.11, the PCLP includes a function to determine whether the wireless medium is currently in use. The MAC uses both a virtual carrier-sense mechanism and a physical carrier-sense mechanism; the physical layer implements the physical carrier sense. 802.11 does not specify how to determine whether a signal is present; vendors are free to innovate within the required performance constraints of the standard. 802.11 requires that 802.11-compliant signals with certain power levels must be detected with a corresponding minimum probability.

Characteristics of the FH PHY

Table 10-4 shows the values of a number of parameters in the FH PHY. In addition to the parameters in the table, which are standardized, the FH PHY has a number of parameters that can be adjusted to balance delays through various parts of an 802.11 frequency-hopping system. It includes variables for the latency through the MAC, the

PLCP, and the transceiver, as well as variables to account for variations in the transceiver electronics. One other item of note is that the total aggregate throughput of all frequency-hopping networks in an area can be quite high. The total aggregate throughput is a function of the hop set size. All sequences in a hop set are orthogonal and non-interfering. In North America and most of Europe, 26 frequency-hopping networks can be deployed in an area at once. If each network is run at the optional 2-Mbps rate, the area can have a total of 52-Mbps throughput provided that the ISM band is relatively free of interference.

Table 10-4. FH PHY parameters

Parameter	Value	Notes
Slot time	50 µs	
SIFS time	28 µs	The SIFS is used to derive the value of the other interframe spaces (DIFS, PIFS, and EIFS).
Contention window size	15–1,023 slots	
Preamble duration	96 µs	Preamble symbols are transmitted at 1 MHz, so a symbol takes 1 s to transmit; 96 bits require 96 symbol times.
PLCP header duration	32 µs	The PLCP header is 32 bits, so it requires 32 symbol times.
Maximum MAC frame	4,095 bytes	802.11 recommends a maximum of 400 symbols (400 bytes at 1 Mbps, 800 bytes at 2 Mbps) to retain performance across different types of environments.

802.11 DS PHY

Direct-sequence modulation has been the most successful modulation technique used with 802.11. The initial 802.11 specification described a physical layer based on low-speed, direct-sequence spread spectrum (DS or DSSS). Direct-sequence equipment requires more power to achieve the same throughput as a frequency-hopping system. 2-Mbps direct-sequence interfaces will drain battery power more quickly than 2-Mbps frequency-hopping interfaces. The real advantage to direct-sequence transmission is that the technique is readily adaptable to much higher data rates than frequency-hopping networks.

This section describes the basic concepts and modulation techniques used by the initial DS PHY. It also shows how the PLCP prepares frames for transmission on the radio link and touches briefly on a few details of the physical medium itself.

Direct-Sequence Transmission

Direct-sequence transmission is an alternative spread-spectrum technique that can be used to transmit a signal over a much wider frequency band. The basic approach of direct-sequence techniques is to smear the RF energy over a wide band in a carefully controlled way. Changes in the radio carrier are present across a wide band, and receivers can perform correlation processes to look for changes. The basic high-level approach is shown in Figure 10-11.

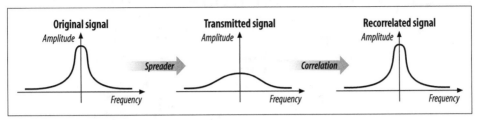

Figure 10-11. Basic DSSS technique

At the left is a traditional narrowband radio signal. It is processed by a *spreader*, which applies a mathematical transform to take a narrowband input and flatten the amplitude across a relatively wide frequency band. To a narrowband receiver, the transmitted signal looks like low-level noise because its RF energy is spread across a very wide band. The key to direct-sequence transmission is that any modulation of the RF carrier is also spread across the frequency band. Receivers can monitor a wide frequency band and look for changes that occur across the entire band. The original signal can be recovered with a *correlator*, which inverts the spreading process.

At a high level, a correlator simply looks for changes to the RF signal that occur across the entire frequency band. Correlation gives direct-sequence transmissions a great deal of protection against interference. Noise tends to take the form of relatively narrow pulses that, by definition, do not produce coherent effects across the entire frequency band. Therefore, the correlation function spreads out noise across the band, and the correlated signal shines through, as illustrated in Figure 10-12.

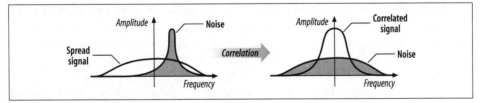

Figure 10-12. Spreading of noise by the correlation process

Direct-sequence modulation works by applying a chipping sequence to the data stream. A *chip* is a binary digit used by the spreading process. Bits are higher-level data, while chips are binary numbers used in the encoding process. There's no mathematical difference between a bit and a chip, but spread-spectrum developers have adopted this terminology to indicate that chips are only a part of the encoding and transmission process and do not carry any data. Chipping streams, which are also called pseudorandom noise codes (PN codes), must run at a much higher rate than the underlying data. Figure 10-13 illustrates how chipping sequences are used in the transmission of data using direct-sequence modulation. Several chips are used to encode a single bit into a series of chips. The high-frequency chipped signal is transmitted on an RF carrier. At the other end, a correlator compares the received signal to the same PN sequence to determine if the encoded bit was a 0 or a 1.

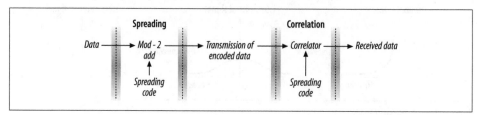

Figure 10-13. Chipping

The process of encoding a low bit rate signal at a high chip rate has the side effect of spreading the signal's power over a much wider bandwidth. One of the most important quantities in a direct-sequence system is its *spreading ratio*, which is the number of chips used to transmit a single bit.[*] Higher spreading ratios improve the ability to recover the transmitted signal but require a higher chipping rate and a larger frequency band. Doubling the spreading ratio requires doubling the chipping rate and doubles the required bandwidth as well. There are two costs to increased chipping ratios. One is the direct cost of more expensive RF components operating at the higher frequency, and the other is an indirect cost in the amount of bandwidth required. Therefore, in designing direct-sequence systems for the real world, the spreading ratio should be as low as possible to meet design requirements and to avoid wasting bandwidth.

Direct-sequence modulation trades bandwidth for throughput. Compared to traditional narrowband transmission, direct-sequence modulation requires significantly more radio spectrum and is much slower. However, it can often coexist with other interference sources because the receiver's correlation function effectively ignores narrowband noise. It is easier to achieve high throughput using direct-sequence techniques than with frequency hopping. Regulatory authorities do not impose a limit on the amount of spectrum that can be used; they generally set a minimum lower bound on the processing gain. Higher rates can be achieved with a wider band, though wider bands require a higher chip rate.

802.11 direct-sequence details

For the PN code, 802.11 adopted an 11-bit Barker word. Each bit is encoded using the entire Barker word as a chipping sequence. Detailed discussion of Barker words and their properties are well beyond the scope of this book. The key attribute for

---

[*] The spreading ratio is related to a figure known as the *processing gain*. The two are sometimes used interchangeably, but the processing gain is slightly lower because it takes into account the effects of using real-world systems as opposed to perfect ideal systems with no losses.

802.11 networks is that Barker words have good *autocorrelation* properties, which means that the correlation function at the receiver operates as expected in a wide range of environments and is relatively tolerant to multipath delay spreads.

Regulatory authorities require a 10-dB processing gain. Using an 11-bit spreading code for each bit allows 802.11 to meet the regulatory requirements with some margin of safety, but it is small enough to allow as many overlapping networks as possible. Longer spreading codes allow higher processing gains but require wider frequency channels.

Encoding in 802.11 direct-sequence networks

802.11 uses the Barker sequence {+1, −1, +1, +1, −1, +1, +1, +1, −1, −1, −1}. As used in 802.11, +1 becomes 1, and −1 becomes 0, so the Barker sequence becomes 10110111000. It is applied to each bit in the data stream by a modulo-2 adder.[*] When a 1 is encoded, all the bits in the spreading code change; for 0, they stay the same. Figure 10-14 shows the encoding process.

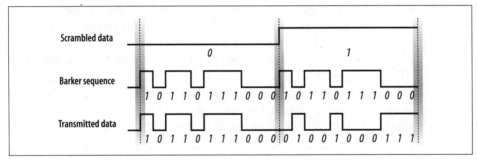

Figure 10-14. Encoding with the Barker word

Receivers can look at the number of 1s in a received bit time. The Barker sequence has six 1s and five 0s. An 11-bit sequence with six 1s must therefore correspond to a transmitted 0, and an 11-bit sequence with six 0s must correspond to a transmitted 1. In addition to counting the numbers of 1s and 0s, the receiver can analyze the pattern of received bits to infer the value of the transmitted bit.

Operating channels

Channels for the DS PHY are much larger than the channels for the FH PHY. The DS PHY has 14 channels in the 2.4-GHz band, each 5 MHz wide. Channel 1 is placed at

---

[*] Encoding with the Barker sequence is similar to a number of other techniques. Some cellular systems, most notably in North America, use code division multiple access (CDMA) to allow several stations to access the radio medium. CDMA exploits some extremely complex mathematics to ensure that transmissions from each mobile phone look like random noise to every other mobile phone in the cell. The underlying mathematics are far more complicated than a simple fixed pseudo-random noise code.

2.412 GHz, channel 2 at 2.417 GHz, and so on up to channel 14 at 2.484 GHz. Table 10-5 shows which channels are allowed by each regulatory authority. Channel 10 is available throughout North America and Europe, which is why most products use channel 10 as the default operating channel.

Table 10-5. Channels used in different regulatory domains

Regulatory domain	Allowed channels
US (FCC)/Canada (IC)	1 to 11 (2.412–2.462 GHz)
Europe, excluding France and Spain (ETSI)	1 to 13 (2.412–2.472 GHz)
France	10 to 13 (2.457–2.472 GHz)
Spain	10 to 11 (2.457–2.462 GHz)
Japan (MKK)	14 (2.484 GHz)

Channel energy spread

Within a channel, most of the energy is spread across a 22-MHz band. Because the DS PHY uses an 11-MHz chip clock, energy spreads out from the channel center in multiples of 11 MHz, as shown in Figure 10-15. To prevent interference to adjacent channels, the first side lobe is filtered to 30 dB below the power at the channel center frequency, and additional lobes are filtered to 50 dB below the power at the channel center. This corresponds to reducing the power by a factor of 1,000 and 100,000, respectively. These limits are noted in Figure 10-15 by the use of dBr, which means dB relative to the power at the channel center. Figure 10-15 is not to scale: –30 dBr is only one thousandth, and –50 dBr is one hundred thousandth.

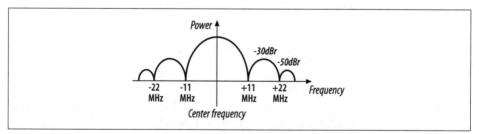

Figure 10-15. Energy spread in a single 802.11 DS transmission channel

With the transmit filters in place, RF power is confined mostly to 22-MHz frequency bands. European regulators cap the maximum radiated power at 100 mW; the FCC in the U.S. allows a substantially higher radiated power of 1,000 mW, but most products fall far below this in practice.

To prevent interference from networks operating on adjacent channels, 802.11 direct-sequence equipment must be separated by a frequency band of at least 22 MHz between channel center frequencies. With a channel spacing of 5 MHz, networks must be separated by five channel numbers to prevent interference, as illustrated in

Figure 10-16. If directly adjacent channels were selected, there would be a great deal of overlap in the center lobes.

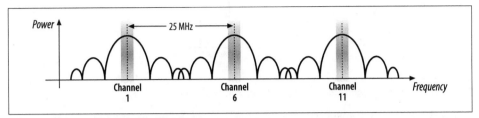

Figure 10-16. Channel separation in 802.11 DS networks

Maximum theoretical throughput

If the signal processing techniques used by the DS PHY are used, then the maximum throughput would be a function of the frequency space used. Roughly speaking, the ISM band is 80-MHz wide. Using the same spreading factor of 11 would lead to a maximum bit rate of slightly more than 7 Mbps. However, only one channel would be available, and products would need to have an oscillator running at 77 MHz to generate the chipping sequence. High-frequency devices are a tremendous drain on batteries, and the hypothetical high-rate encoding that uses the entire band makes terrible use of the available spectrum. To achieve higher throughput, more sophisticated techniques must be used. 802.11b increases the symbol rate slightly, but it gets far more mileage from more sophisticated encoding techniques.

Interference response

Direct-sequence–modulated signals are more resistant to interference than frequency-hopping signals. The correlation process enables direct-sequence systems to work around narrowband interference much more effectively. With 11 chips per bit, several chips can be lost or damaged before a single data bit is lost. The disadvantage is that the response of direct-sequence systems to noise is not incremental. Up to a certain level, the correlator can remove noise, but once interference obscures a certain amount of the frequency band, nothing can be recovered. Figure 10-17 shows how direct-sequence systems degrade in response to noise.

Direct-sequence systems also avoid interfering with a primary user more effectively than frequency-hopping systems. After direct-sequence processing, signals are much wider and have lower amplitudes, so they appear to be random background noise to traditional narrowband receivers. Two direct-sequence users in the same area can cause problems for each other quite easily if the two direct-sequence channels are not

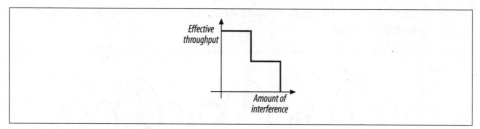

Figure 10-17. Throughput response to interference in DSSS systems

separated by an adequate amount. Generally speaking, interference between two direct-sequence devices is a problem long before a primary band user notices anything.

Differential Phase Shift Keying (DPSK)

Differential phase shift keying (DPSK) is the basis for all 802.11 direct-sequence systems. As the name implies, phase shift keying (PSK) encodes data in phase changes of the transmitted signal. The absolute phase of a waveform is not relevant in PSK; only changes in the phase encode data. Like frequency shift keying, PSK resists interference because most interference causes changes in amplitude. Figure 10-18 shows two identical sine waves shifted by a small amount along the time axis. The offset between the same point on two waves is the phase difference.

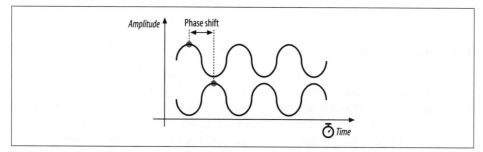

Figure 10-18. Phase difference between two sine waves

Differential binary phase shift keying (DBPSK)

The simplest form of PSK uses two carrier waves, shifted by a half cycle relative to each other. One wave, the reference wave, is used to encode a 0; the half-cycle shifted wave is used to encode a 1. Table 10-6 summarizes the phase shifts, and Figure 10-19 illustrates the encoding as a phase difference from a preceding sine wave.

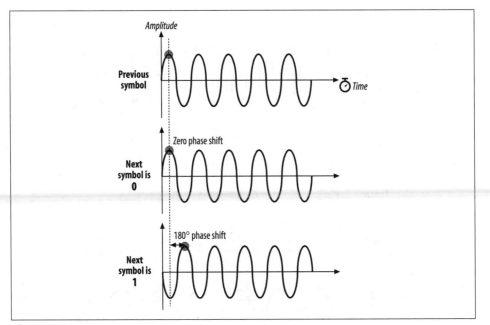

Figure 10-19. DBPSK encoding

Table 10-6. DBPSK phase shifts

Symbol	Phase shift
0	0
1	180° (π radians)

To stick with the same example, encoding the letter M (1001101 in binary) is a matter of dividing up the time into seven symbol times then transmitting the wave with appropriate phase shift at each symbol boundary. Figure 10-20 illustrates the encoding. Time is divided into a series of symbol periods, each of which is several times the period of the carrier wave. When the symbol is a 0, there is no change from the phase of the previous symbol, and when the symbol is a 1, there is a change of half a cycle. These changes result in "pinches" of the carrier when 1 is transmitted and a smooth transition across the symbol time boundary for 0.

Differential quadrature phase shift keying (DQPSK)

Like 2GFSK, DBPSK is limited to one bit per symbol. More advanced receivers and transmitters can encode multiple bits per symbol using a technique called differential quadrature phase shift yeying (DQPSK). Rather than a fundamental wave and a half-cycle shifted wave, DQPSK uses a fundamental wave and three additional waves, each shifted by a quarter cycle, as shown in Figure 10-21. Table 10-7 summarizes the phase shifts.

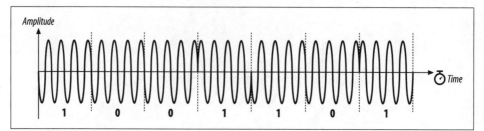

Figure 10-20. The letter M encoded in DBPSK

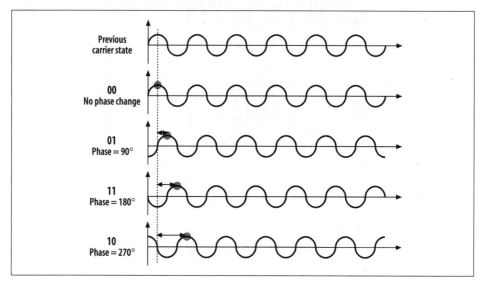

Figure 10-21. DQPSK encoding

Table 10-7. DQPSK phase shifts

Symbol	Phase shift
00	0
01	90° (π/2 radians)
11	180° (π radians)
10	270° (3π/2 or –π/2 radians)

Now encode M in DQPSK (Figure 10-22). In the UTF-8 character set, M is represented by the binary string 01001101 or, as the sequence of four two-bit symbols, 01-00-11-01. In the first symbol period, there is a phase shift of 90 degrees; for clarity, the figure shows the phase shift from a pure sine wave. The second symbol results in no phase shift, so the wave continues without a change. The third symbol causes a phase shift of 180 degrees, as shown by the sharp change from the highest amplitude to the lowest amplitude. The final symbol causes a phase shift of 90 degrees.

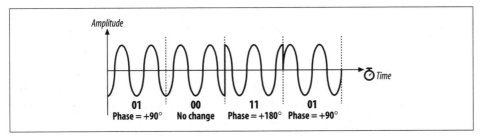

Figure 10-22. The letter M encoded in DQPSK

The obvious advantage of DQPSK relative to DBPSK is that the four-level encoding mechanism can have a higher throughput. The cost of using DQPSK is that it cannot be used in some environments because of severe multipath interference. Multipath interference occurs when the signal takes several paths from the transmitter to the receiver. Each path has a different length; therefore, the received signal from each path has a different delay relative to the other paths. This delay is the enemy of an encoding scheme based on phase shifts. Wavefronts are not labeled or painted different colors, so a wavefront could arrive later than expected because of a long path or it could simply have been transmitted late and phase shifted. In environments where multipath interference is severe, DQPSK will break down much quicker than DBPSK.

DS Physical-Layer Convergence (PLCP)

As in the FH PHY, frames must be processed by the PLCP before being transmitted into the air.

Framing and scrambling

The PLCP for the DS PHY adds a six-field header to the frames it receives from the MAC. In keeping with ISO reference model terminology, frames passed from the MAC are PLCP service data units (PSDUs). The PLCP framing is shown in Figure 10-23.

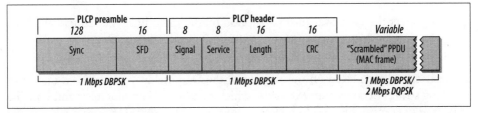

Figure 10-23. DS PLCP framing

The FH PHY uses a data whitener to randomize the data before transmission, but the data whitener applies only to the MAC frame trailing the PLCP header. The DS PHY has a similar function called the *scrambler*, but the scrambler is applied to the entirety of the direct-sequence frame, including the PLCP header and preamble.

Preamble

The Preamble synchronizes the transmitter and receiver and allows them to derive common timing relationships. It is composed of the Sync field and the Start Frame Delimiter field. Before transmission, the preamble is scrambled using the direct-sequence scrambling function.

Sync

The Sync field is a 128-bit field composed entirely of 1s. Unlike the FH PHY, the Sync field is scrambled before transmission.

Start Frame Delimiter (SFD)

The SFD allows the receiver to find the start of the frame, even if some of the sync bits were lost in transit. This field is set to 0000 0101 1100 1111, which is different from the SFD used by the FH PHY.

Header

The PLCP header follows the preamble. The header has PHY-specific parameters used by the PLCP. Five fields comprise the header: a signaling field, a service identification field, a Length field, a Signal field used to encode the speed, and a frame check sequence.

Signal

The Signal field is used by the receiver to identify the transmission rate of the encapsulated MAC frame. It is set to either 0000 1010 (0x0A) for 1-Mbps operation or 0001 0100 (0x14) for 2-Mbps operation.

Service

This field is reserved for future use and must be set to all 0s.

Length

This field is set to the number of microseconds required to transmit the frame as an unsigned 16-bit integer, transmitted least significant bit to most significant bit.

CRC

To protect the header against corruption on the radio link, the sender calculates a 16-bit CRC over the contents of the four header fields. Receivers verify the CRC before further frame processing.

No restrictions are placed on the content of the Data field. Arbitrary data may contain long strings of consecutive 0s or 1s, which makes the data much less random. To make the data more like random background noise, the DS PHY uses a polynomial scrambling mechanism to remove long strings of 1s or 0s from the transmitted data stream.

DS Physical Medium Dependent Sublayer

Unlike the FH PHY, the DS PHY uses a single PMD specification. This is a complex and lengthy specification that incorporates provisions for two data rates (1.0 and 2.0 Mbps). Figure 10-24 shows the general design of a transceiver for 802.11 direct-sequence networks.

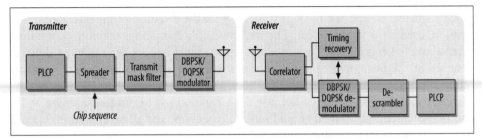

Figure 10-24. Direct-sequence transceiver

Transmission at 1.0 Mbps

At the low data rate, the direct-sequence PMD enables data transmission at 1.0 Mbps. The PLCP header is appended to frames arriving from the MAC, and the entire unit is scrambled. The resulting sequence of bits is transmitted from the physical interface using DBPSK at a rate of 1 million symbols per second. The resulting throughput is 1.0 Mbps because one bit is encoded per symbol. Like the FH PMD, the DS PMD has a minimum power requirement and can cap the power at 100 mW if necessary to meet regulatory requirements.

Transmission at 2.0 Mbps

Like the FH PHY, transmission at 2.0 Mbps uses two encoding schemes. The PLCP preamble and header are transmitted at 1.0 Mbps using DBPSK. Although using a slower method for the header transmission reduces the effective throughput, DBPSK is far more tolerant of noise and multipath interference. After the preamble and header are finished, the PMD switches to DQPSK modulation to provide 2.0-Mbps service. As with the FH PHY, most products that implement the 2.0-Mbps rate can detect interference and fall back to lower-speed 1.0-Mbps service.

CS/CCA for the DS PHY

802.11 allows the CS/CCA function to operate in one of three modes:

Mode 1
> When the energy exceeds the energy detection (ED) threshold, it reports that the medium is busy. The ED threshold depends on the transmit power.

Mode 2

Implementations using Mode 2 must look for an actual DSSS signal and report the channel busy when one is detected, even if the signal is below the ED threshold.

Mode 3

Mode 3 combines Mode 1 and Mode 2. A signal must be detected with sufficient energy before the channel is reported busy to higher layers.

Once a channel is reported busy, it stays busy for the duration of the intended transmission, even if the signal is lost. The transmission's duration is taken from the time interval in the Length field. Busy medium reports must be very fast. When a signal is detected at the beginning of a contention window slot, the CCA mechanism must report a busy medium by the time the slot has ended. This relatively high performance requirement must be set because once a station has begun transmission at the end of its contention delay, it should seize the medium, and all other stations should defer access until its frame has concluded.

Characteristics of the DS PHY

Table 10-8 shows the values of a number of parameters in the DS PHY. In addition to the parameters in the table, which are standardized, the DS PHY has a number of parameters that can be adjusted to balance delays through various parts of an 802.11 direct-sequence system. It includes variables for the latency through the MAC, the PLCP, and the transceiver, as well as variables to account for variations in the transceiver electronics. One other item of note is that the total aggregate throughput of all direct-sequence networks in an area is much lower than the total aggregate throughput of all nonoverlapping frequency-hopping networks in an area. The total aggregate throughput is a function of the number of nonoverlapping channels. In North America and most of Europe, three direct-sequence networks can be deployed in an area at once. If each network is run at the optional 2-Mbps rate, the area can have a total of 6-Mbps throughput, which is dramatically less than the frequency-hopping total aggregate throughput.

Table 10-8. DS PHY parameters

Parameter	Value	Notes
Slot time	20 µs	
SIFS time	10 µs	The SIFS is used to derive the value of the other interframe spaces (DIFS, PIFS, and EIFS).
Contention window size	31 to 1,023 slots	
Preamble duration	144 µs	Preamble symbols are transmitted at 1 MHz, so a symbol takes 1 s to transmit; 144 bits require 144 symbol times.
PLCP header duration	48 µs	The PLCP header is 48 bits, so it requires 48 symbol times.
Maximum MAC frame	4–8,191 bytes	

Like the FH PHY, the DS PHY has a number of attributes that can be adjusted by a vendor to balance delays in various parts of the system. It includes variables for the latency through the MAC, the PLCP, and the transceiver, as well as variables to account for variations in the transceiver electronics.

802.11b: HR/DSSS PHY

When the initial version of 802.11 was ratified in 1997, the real work was only just beginning. The initial version of the standard defined FH and DS PHYs, but they were only capable of data rates up to 2 Mbps. 2 Mbps is barely useful, especially when the transmission capacity must be shared among all the users in an area. In 1999, the 802.11 working group released its second extension to the basic 802.11 specification. In keeping with the IEEE numbering convention, the second extension was labeled 802.11b.

802.11b adds another physical layer into the mix. It uses the same MAC as all the other physical layers and is based on direct-sequence modulation. However, it enables transmission at up to 11 Mbps, which is adequate for modern networks. Higher data rates led to a stunning commercial success. 802.11b has blazed new trails where other wireless technologies failed to make an impact. The 802.11b PHY is also known as the high-rate, direct-sequence PHY, abbreviated HR/DS or HR/DSSS. Even though the modulation is different, the operating channels are exactly the same as the channels used by the original low-rate direct sequence.

Complementary Code Keying

802.11 direct-sequence systems use a rate of 11 million chips per second. The original DS PHYs divided the chip stream up into a series of 11-bit Barker words and transmitted 1 million Barker words per second. Each word encoded either one bit or two bits for a corresponding data rate of 1.0 Mbps or 2.0 Mbps, respectively. Achieving higher data rates and commercial utility requires that each code symbol carry more information than a bit or two.

Straight phase shift encoding cannot hope to carry more than a few bits per code word. DQPSK requires that receivers distinguish quarter-cycle phase differences. Further increasing the number of bits per symbol would require processing even finer phase shifts, such as an eighth-cycle or sixteenth-cycle shift. Detecting smaller phase shifts is more difficult in the presence of multipath interference and requires more sophisticated (and thus expensive) electronics.

Instead of continuing with straight phase-shift keying, the IEEE 802.11 working group turned to an alternate encoding method. Complementary code keying (CCK) divides the chip stream into a series of 8-bit code symbols, so the underlying transmission is based on a series of 1.375 million code symbols per second. CCK is based on sophisticated mathematical transforms that allow the use of a few 8-bit sequences to encode 4 or even 8 bits per code word, for a data throughput of 5.5 Mbps or 11 Mbps. In addition, the mathematics underlying CCK transforms allow receivers to distinguish between different codes easily, even in the presence of interference and multipath fading. Figure 10-25 illustrates the use of code symbols in CCK. It is quite similar to the chipping process used by the slower direct-sequence layers; the difference is that the code words are derived partially from the data. A static repeating code word such as the Barker word is not used.

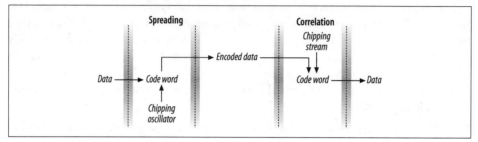

Figure 10-25. Code symbols in CCK

Barker spreading, as used in the lower-rate, direct-sequence layers, uses a static code to spread the signal over the available frequency band. CCK uses the code word to carry information, as well as simply to spread the signal. Several phase angles are used to prepare a complex code word of eight bits.

High-Rate, Direct-Sequence PLCP

Like the other physical layers, the HR/DSSS PHY is split into two parts. As with the other physical layers, the PLCP adds additional framing information.

Framing and scrambling

Unlike the other physical layers, two options exist for the PLCP framing. Both are shown in Figure 10-26. The "long" frame format is identical to the classic DS PLCP format and must be supported. For efficiency and improved throughput, stations may also support the optional "short" PLCP format.

Naturally, the optional short format may be used only if all stations support it. To prevent networks configured for the short format from disappearing, 802.11b requires that stations answering Probe Requests from an active scan return a response using the same PLCP header that was received. If a station that supports only the long PLCP header sends a Probe Response, an access point returns a response using the long header, even if the BSS is configured for the short header.

Preamble
> Frames begin with the preamble, which is composed of the Sync field and the SFD field. The preamble is transmitted at 1.0 Mbps using DBPSK.

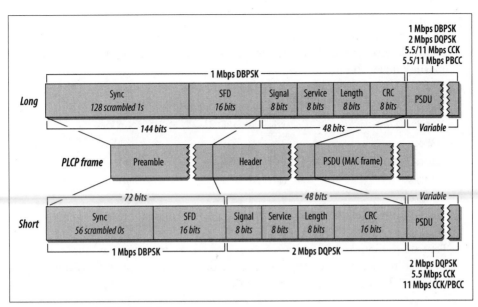

Figure 10-26. HR/DSSS PLCP framing

Long Sync

The Long Sync field is composed of 128 1 bits. It is processed by the scrambler before transmission, though, so the data content varies. High-rate systems use a specified seed for the scrambling function but support backwards compatibility with older systems that do not specify a seed.

Short Sync

The Short Sync field is composed of 56 0 bits. Like the Long Sync, it is also processed by the scrambler.

Long SFD

To indicate the end of the Sync field, the long preamble concludes with a Start of Frame Delimiter (SFD). In the long PLCP, the SFD is the sequence 1111 0011 1010 0000. As with all IEEE specifications, the order of transmission from the physical interface is least-significant bit first, so the string is transmitted right to left.

Short SFD

To avoid confusion with the Long SFD, the Short SFD is the reverse value, 0000 0101 1100 1111.

The PLCP header follows the preamble. It is composed of the Signal, Service, Length, and CRC fields. The long header is transmitted at 1.0 Mbps using DBPSK. However, the short header's purpose is to reduce the time required for overhead transmission so it is transmitted at 2.0 Mbps using DQPSK.

Long Signal

The Long Signal field indicates the speed and transmission method of the enclosed MAC frame. Four values for the 8-bit code are currently defined and are shown in Table 10-9.

Table 10-9. Signal field values

Speed	Value (msb to lsb)	Hex value
1 Mbps	0000 1010	0x0A
2 Mbps	0001 0100	0x14
5.5 Mbps	0011 0111	0x37
11 Mbps	0110 1110	0x6E

Short Signal

The Short Signal field indicates the speed and transmission method of the enclosed frame, but only three values are defined. Short preambles can be used only with 2 Mbps, 5.5 Mbps, and 11 Mbps networks.

Service

The Service field, which is shown in Figure 10-27, was reserved for future use by the first version of 802.11, and bits were promptly used for the high-rate extensions in 802.11b. First of all, the Length field describes the amount of time used for the enclosed frame in microseconds. Above 8 Mbps, the value becomes ambiguous. Therefore, the eighth bit of the service field is used to extend the Length field to 17 bits. The third bit indicates whether the 802.11b implementation uses locked clocks; clock locking means that transmit frequency and symbol clock use the same oscillator. The fourth bit indicates the type of coding used for the packet, which is either 0 for CCK or 1 for PBCC. All reserved bits must be set to 0. The Service field is transmitted from left to right (b0 to b7), which is the same in both the short and long PLCP frame formats.

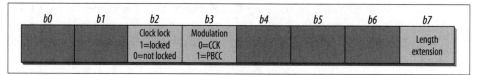

Figure 10-27. Service field in the HR/DSSS PLCP header

Length

The Length field is the same in both the short and long PLCP frame formats and is the number of microseconds required to transmit the enclosed MAC frame. Approximately two pages of the 802.11b standard are devoted to calculating the value of the Length frame, but the details are beyond the scope of this book.

CRC

The CRC field is the same in both the short and the long PLCP frames. Senders calculate a CRC checksum using the Signal, Service, and Length fields. Receivers can use the CRC value to ensure that the header was received intact and was not damaged during transmission. CRC calculations take place before data scrambling.

The data scrambling procedure for the HR/DSSS PHY is nearly identical to the data scrambling procedure used with the original DS PHY. The only difference is that the scrambling function is seeded to specified values in the HR/DSSS PHY. Different seeds are used for short and long PLCP frames.

HR/DSSS PMD

Unlike the FH PHY, the DS PHY uses a single PMD specification. The general transceiver design is shown in Figure 10-28.

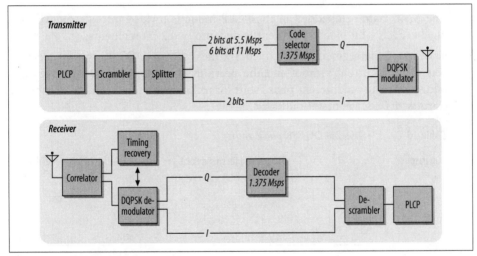

Figure 10-28. HR/DSSS transceiver

Transmission at 1.0 Mbps or 2.0 Mbps

To ensure backwards compatibility with the installed base of 802.11-based, direct-sequence hardware, the HR/DSSS PHY can transmit and receive at 1.0 Mbps or 2.0 Mbps. Slower transmissions are supported in the same manner as the lower-rate, direct-sequence layers described in Chapter 9.

Transmission at 5.5 Mbps with CCK

Higher-rate transmission is accomplished by building on the DQPSK-based phase shift keying techniques. DQPSK transmits two bits per symbol period, encoded as one of four different phase shifts. By using CCK, the symbol words themselves carry additional information. 5.5-Mbps transmission encodes four data bits into a symbol. Two are carried using conventional DQPSK, and the other two are carried through the content of the code words. Figure 10-29 illustrates the overall process.

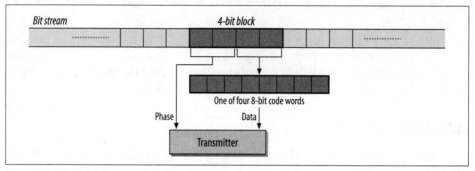

Figure 10-29. 802.11b transmission at 5.5 Mbps

1. The MAC frame embedded in the PCLP frame is divided into a string of 4-bit blocks. Each 4-bit block is further divided into two 2-bit segments.

2. The first 2-bit segment is encoded by means of a DQPSK-type phase shift between the current symbol and the previous symbol (Table 10-10). Even and odd symbols use a different phase shift for technical reasons. Symbol numbering starts with 0 for the first 4-bit block.

Table 10-10. Inter-symbol DQPSK phase shifts

Bit pattern	Phase angle (even symbols)	Phase angle (odd symbols)
00	0	π
01	$\pi/2$	$3\pi/2$
11	π	0
10	$3\pi/2$	$\pi/2$

3. The second 2-bit segment is used to select one of four code words for the current symbol (Table 10-11). The four code words can be derived using the mathematics laid out in clause 18.4.6.5 of the 802.11 standard.

Table 10-11. Mbps code words

Bit sequence	Code word
00	i,1,i,−1,i,1,−i,1
01	−i,−1,−i,1,1,1,−i,1
10	−i,1,−i,−1,−i,1,i,1
11	i,−1,i,1,−i,1,i,1

Transmission at 11 Mbps with CCK

To move to a full 11 Mbps, 8 bits must be encoded with each symbol. As with other techniques, the first two bits are encoded by the phase shift of the transmitted symbol relative to the previous symbol. Six bits are encoded using CCK. Figure 10-30 illustrates the process.

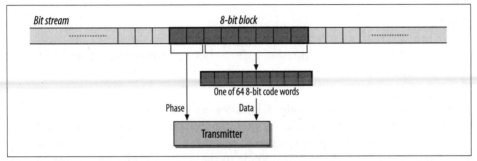

Figure 10-30. 802.11b transmission at 11 Mbps

1. The MAC frame embedded in the PCLP frame is divided into a string of 8-bit blocks. Each 8-bit block is further divided into four 2-bit segments.

2. The first 2-bit segment is encoded by means of a DQPSK-type phase shift between the current symbol and the previous symbol. As with the 5.5-Mbps rate, even and odd symbols use a different phase shift for technical reasons. Symbol numbering starts with 0 for the first 8-bit block. The phase shifts are identical to the phase shifts used in 5.5-Mbps transmission.

3. The remaining six bits are grouped into three successive pairs. Each pair is associated with the phase angle in Table 10-12 and is used to derive a code word.

Table 10-12. Phase angle encoding for 11-Mbps transmission

Bit pattern	Phase angle
00	0
01	$\pi/2$
10	π
11	$3\pi/2$

As an example, consider the conversion of the bit sequence 0100 1101 into a complex code for transmission on an 802.11b network. The first two bits, 01, encode a phase shift from the previous symbol. If the symbol is an even symbol in the MAC frame, the phase shift is $\pi/2$; otherwise, the shift is $3\pi/2$. (Symbols in the MAC frame are numbered starting from 0, so the first symbol in a frame is even.) The last six bits are divided into three 2-bit groups: 00, 11, and 01. Each of these is used to encode an angle in the code word equation. The next step in transmission is to convert the phase angles into the complex code word for transmission.

Clear channel assessment

Like the original DS PHY, high-rate implementers have three choices for the CS/CCA operation mode. All the direct-sequence CCA modes are considered to be part of the same list. Mode 1 is identical to the DS PHY's CCA Mode 1, and Modes 2 and 3 are used exclusively by the original DS PHY. Modes 4 and 5 are the HR/DSSS-specific CCA modes.

Mode 1

> When the energy exceeds the energy detection (ED) threshold, the medium is reported busy. The ED threshold depends on the transmit power used. This mode is also available for classic direct-sequence systems.

Mode 4

> Implementations using Mode 4 look for an actual signal. When triggered, a Mode 4 CCA implementation starts a 3.65 ms timer and begins counting down. If no valid HR/DSSS signal is received by the expiration of the timer, the medium is reported idle. 3.65 ms corresponds to the transmission time required for the largest possible frame at 5.5 Mbps.

Mode 5

> Mode 5 combines Mode 1 and Mode 4. A signal must be detected with sufficient energy before the channel is reported busy to higher layers.

Once a channel is reported busy, it stays busy for the duration of the intended transmission, even if the signal is lost. The channel is considered busy until the time interval in the Length field has elapsed. Implementations that look for a valid signal may override this requirement if a second PLCP header is detected.

Optional Features of the 802.11b PHY

802.11b includes two optional physical-layer features.

Packet Binary Convolutional Coding (PBCC)

PBCC is an optional coding method that has not been widely implemented. Proposals for further revisions to wireless LAN technology in the ISM band specified PBCC, but those proposals were rejected in the summer of 2001.

Channel agility

To avoid interfering with existing 802.11 networks based on frequency-hopping technology, 802.11b includes the *channel agility* option. When employing the channel agility option, 802.11b networks periodically hop to a different channel. Three direct-sequence channels are used for nonoverlapping networks; the hop sequences and dwell times are designed to avoid interfering with a frequency-hopping network deployed in the same area.

Characteristics of the HR/DSSS PHY

Table 10-13 shows the values of a number of parameters in the HR/DSSS PHY. Like the DS PHY, the HR/DSSS PHY has a number of parameters that can be adjusted to compensate for delays in any part of a real system.

Table 10-13. HR/DSSS PHY parameters

Parameter	Value	Notes
Maximum MAC frame length	4,095 bytes	
Slot time	20 µs	
SIFS time	10 µs	The SIFS is used to derive the value of the other interframe spaces (DIFS, PIFS, and EIFS).
Contention window size	31 to 1,023 slots	
Preamble duration	144 µs	Preamble symbols are transmitted at 1 MHz, so a symbol takes 1 s to transmit; 96 bits require 96 symbol times.
PLCP header duration	48 bits	The PLCP header transmission time depends on whether the short preamble is used.

One other item of note is that the total aggregate throughput of all HR/DSSS networks in an area is still lower than the total aggregate throughput of all nonoverlapping frequency-hopping networks in an area. The total aggregate throughput is a function of the number of nonoverlapping channels. In North America and most of Europe, three HR/DSSS networks can be deployed in an area at once. If each network is run at the optional 11-Mbps rate, the area can have a total of 33-Mbps throughput, which is less than the frequency-hopping total aggregate throughput.

CHAPTER 11

802.11a: 5-GHz OFDM PHY

Many of the wireless devices that are currently on the market use the 2.4-GHz ISM band, which is rapidly becoming crowded. In an attempt to attain higher data rates and avoid overcrowding, the 802.11 working group is looking at the unlicensed bands around 5 GHz. In the U.S., the 5-GHz bands that are reserved for unlicensed use are designated as the Unlicensed National Information Infrastructure (U-NII). The U-NII bands provide more spectrum space than the 2.4-GHz bands and are much less heavily used; there are very few devices on the market that operate in these bands. The 802.11a working group is responsible for developing physical layers for high-rate wireless service on the 5-GHz bands.

802.11a hardware hit the market in late 2001. There are three main chipset vendors: Intersil, the developer of the widely used PRISM chipsets for the 2.4-GHz ISM band; the ever acquisitive Cisco, through its acquisition of chip-maker Radiata in late 2000; and Atheros Communications, a start-up founded by several notable Stanford researchers. 802.11a products hit the market about the time this book went to press, so I have not evaluated any vendor claims about increased range, throughput, or performance. Most of the products on the market look very much like the current 802.11b products: many are PC Cards and have similar configuration and installation routines.

In spite of its many advantages, 802.11a does not look like a sure-fire commercial success. Higher frequencies have higher path losses; some observers estimate that access points will have to be deployed much more densely than in an 802.11b network; some observers have estimated that one and a half times as many (or more) access points may be required. Most of the testing on 802.11a has been conducted by vendors in offices dominated by cubicles. How 11a systems will fare in other environments can be answered only by more deployment and testing. Higher-frequency RF systems require higher power, which may mean that 802.11a cards are not well-suited for mobile battery-powered systems. Many of the questions swirling around 802.11a can be answered only by the delivery of commercial products to the marketplace in volume. The 802.11a standard as it currently stands is only for the U.S., but a task group is working on extending the standard to other regulatory domains.

This chapter begins with a qualitative introduction to the basis of OFDM. When all the mathematical formalism is stripped away, OFDM is a method for chopping a large frequency channel into a number of subchannels. The subchannels are then used in parallel for higher throughput. I anticipate that many readers will skip the first section, either because they are already familiar with OFDM or are interested only in how the frequency bands are used and how the PCLP wraps up frames for transmission.

Orthogonal Frequency Division Multiplexing (OFDM)

802.11a is based on *orthogonal frequency division multiplexing* (OFDM). OFDM is not a new technique. Most of the fundamental work was done in the late 1960s, and U.S. patent number 3,488,445 was issued in January 1970. Recent DSL work (HDSL, VDSL, and ADSL) and wireless data applications have rekindled interest in OFDM, especially now that better signal-processing techniques make it more practical.[*] OFDM does, however, differ from other emerging encoding techniques such as code division multiple access (CDMA) in its approach. CDMA uses complex mathematical transforms to put multiple transmissions onto a single carrier; OFDM encodes a single transmission into multiple subcarriers. The mathematics underlying the code division in CDMA is far more complicated than in OFDM.

OFDM devices use one wide frequency channel by breaking it up into several component subchannels. Each subchannel is used to transmit data. All the "slow" subchannels are then multiplexed into one "fast" combined channel.

Carrier Multiplexing

When network managers solicit user input on network build-outs, one of the most common demands is for more speed. The hunger for increased data transmissions has driven a host of technologies to increase speed. OFDM takes a qualitatively similar approach to Multilink PPP: when one link isn't enough, use several in parallel.

OFDM is closely related to plain old frequency division multiplexing (FDM). Both divide the available bandwidth into slices called *carriers* or *subcarriers* and make those carriers available as distinct channels for data transmission. OFDM boosts

---

[*] The lack of interest in OFDM means that references on it are sparse. Readers interested in the mathematical background that is omitted in this chapter should consult *OFDM for Wireless Multimedia Applications* by Richard van Nee and Ramjee Prasad (Artech House, 2000).

throughput by using several subcarriers in parallel and multiplexing data over the set of subcarriers.

Traditional FDM was widely used by first-generation mobile telephones as a method for radio channel allocation. Each user was given an exclusive channel, and guard bands were used to ensure that spectral leakage from one user did not cause problems for users of adjacent channels. Figure 11-1 illustrates the traditional FDM approach.

Figure 11-1. Traditional FDM

The trouble with traditional FDM is that the guard bands waste bandwidth and thus reduce capacity. To wasting transmission capacity with unused guard bands, OFDM selects channels that overlap but do not interfere with each other. Figure 11-2 illustrates the contrast between traditional FDM and OFDM.

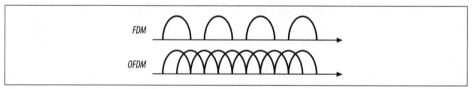

Figure 11-2. FDM versus OFDM

Overlapping carriers are allowed because the subcarriers are defined so that they are easily distinguished from one another. The ability to separate the subcarriers hinges on a complex mathematical relationship called *orthogonality*.

Orthogonality Explained (Without Calculus)

Orthogonal is a mathematical term derived from the Greek word *orthos*, meaning straight, right, or true. In mathematics, the word "orthogonal" is used to describe independent items. Orthogonality is best seen in the frequency domain, looking at a spectral breakdown of a signal. OFDM works because the frequencies of the subcarriers are selected so that at each subcarrier frequency, all other subcarriers do not contribute to the overall waveform. One common way of looking at orthogonality is shown in Figure 11-3. The signal has been divided into its three subcarriers. The peak of each subcarrier, shown by the heavy dot at the top, encodes data. The subcarrier set is carefully designed to be orthogonal; note that at the peak of each of the subcarriers, the other two subcarriers have zero amplitude.

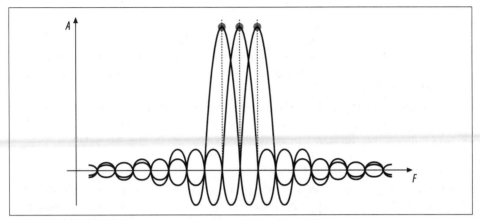

Figure 11-3. Orthogonality in the frequency domain

OFDM takes the coded signal for each subchannel and uses the inverse fast Fourier transform (IFFT) to create a composite waveform from the strength of each subchannel. OFDM receivers can then apply the FFT to a received waveform to extract the amplitude of each component subcarrier.

Guard Time

With the physical layers discussed in Chapter 10, the main problem for receivers was inter-symbol interference (ISI) (Figure 11-4). ISI occurs when the delay spread between different paths is large and causes a delayed copy of the transmitted bits to shift onto a previously arrived copy.

With OFDM, inter-symbol interference does not pose the same kind of problem. The Fourier transform used by OFDM distills the received waveform into the strengths of the subcarriers, so time shifts do not cause dramatic problems. In Figure 11-4, there would be a strong peak for the fundamental low-frequency carrier, and the late-arriving high-frequency component could be ignored.

As with all benefits, however, there is a price to pay. OFDM systems use multiple subcarriers of different frequencies. The subcarriers are packed tightly into an operating channel, and small shifts in subcarrier frequencies may cause interference between carriers, a phenomenon called *inter-carrier interference* (ICI). Frequency shifts may occur because of the Doppler effect or because there is a slight difference between the transmitter and receiver clock frequencies.

To address both ISI and ICI, OFDM transceivers reserve the beginning portion of the symbol time as the *guard time* and perform the Fourier transform only on the

Fourier Analysis, the Fourier Transform, and Signal Processing

The Fourier transform is often called "the Swiss Army knife of signal processing." Signal processing often defines actions in terms of frequency components. Receivers, however, process a time-varying signal amplitude. The *Fourier transform* is a mathematical operation that divides a waveform into its component parts. Fourier analysis takes a time-varying signal and converts it to the set of frequency-domain components that make up the signal.

Signal-processing applications often need to perform the reverse operation as well. Given a set of frequency components, these applications use them like a recipe to build the composite waveform with these frequency components. The mathematical operation used to build the composite waveform from the known ingredients in the frequency domain is the *inverse Fourier transform*.

Strictly speaking, Fourier analysis is applied to smooth curves of the sort found in physics textbooks. To work with a set of discrete data points, a relative of Fourier transform called the *discrete Fourier transform* (DFT) must be used. Like the Fourier transform, the DFT has its inverted partner, the inverse DFT (IDFT).

The DFT is a computationally intensive process of order N^2, which means that its running time is proportional to the square of the size of the number of data points. If the number of data points is an even power of two, however, several computational shortcuts can be taken to cut the complexity to order $N \log N$. On large data sets, the reduced complexity boosts the speed of the algorithm. As a result, the "short" DFT applied to 2^n data points is called the fast Fourier transform (FFT). It also has an inverted relative, the inverse fast Fourier transform (IFFT).

Fast Fourier transforms used to be the domain of supercomputers or special-purpose, signal-processing hardware. But with the microprocessor speeds available today, sophisticated signal processing is well within the capabilities of a PC. Specialized digital signal processors (DSPs) are now cheap enough to be used in almost anything—including the chip sets on commodity 802.11 cards.

non–guard time portion of the symbol time. The non–guard time portion of the symbol is often called the *FFT integration time* because the Fourier transform is performed only on that portion of the symbol.

Delays shorter than the guard time do not cause ICI because they do not allow frequency components to leak into successive symbol times. Selecting the guard time is a major task for designers of OFDM systems. The guard time obviously reduces the overall throughput of the system because it reduces the time during which data transmission is allowed. A guard time that is too short does not prevent interference but does reduce throughput, and a guard time that is too long reduces throughput unnecessarily.

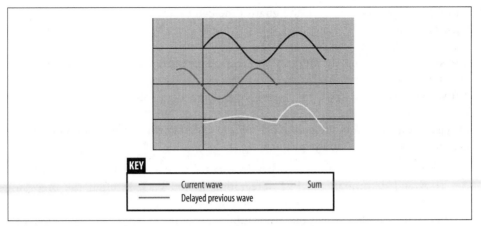

Figure 11-4. ISI reviewed

Cyclic Extensions (Cyclic Prefixes)

The most straightforward method of implementing the guard time would be simply to transmit nothing during the guard time, as shown in Figure 11-5.

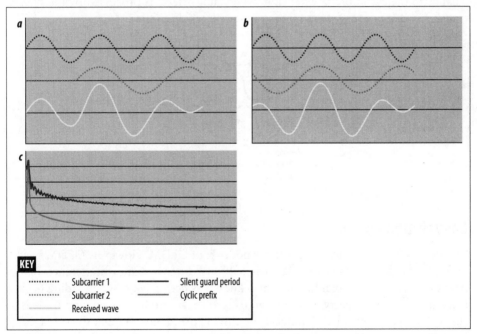

Figure 11-5. Naive implementation of guard time (do not do this!)

Simplistic implementations of the guard time can destroy orthogonality in the presence of common delay spreads. OFDM depends on having an integer number of wavelengths between each of the carriers. When the guard time is perfectly quiet, it is easy to see how a delay can destroy this necessary precondition, as in Figure 11-5. When the two subcarriers are added together, the spectral analysis shows subcarrier 1 (two cycles/symbol) as a strong presence and a relatively smaller amount of subcarrier 2 (three cycles/symbol). In addition, the spectral analysis shows a large number of high-frequency components, muddying the waters further. These components are the consequence of suddenly turning a signal "on."

Solving the problems associated with a quiet guard time is quite simple. Each subcarrier is extended through the FFT integration period back through the preceding guard time. Extending each subcarrier (and hence the entire OFDM symbol) yields a Fourier transform that shows only the amplitudes of the subcarrier frequencies. This technique is commonly called *cyclic extension*, and it may be referred to as the "cyclic prefix extension." The guard time with the extended prefix is called the *cyclic prefix*.

In Figure 11-6, the cyclic prefix preserves the spectral analysis. Subcarrier 1 was not shifted and is not a problem. Subcarrier 2 is delayed, but the previous symbol appears only in the guard time and is not processed by the Fourier transform. Thanks to the cyclic prefix extension, when subcarrier 2 is processed by the Fourier transform, it is a pure wave at three cycles per integration time.

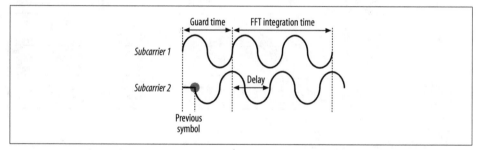

Figure 11-6. Cyclic prefix extension

Convolution Coding

Strictly speaking, convolution coding is not part of OFDM. However, OFDM is used in applications for which the signal is subject to narrowband interference or frequency-specific narrowband fading, also known as *deep fading*. When fading occurs, a channel's ability to carry data may go to zero because the received amplitude is so small. To keep a few faded channels from driving the bit error rate to the sky, OFDM implementations often apply an error correction code across all the subchannels. Implementations that use an error correction code in conjunction with OFDM are sometimes called *coded OFDM* (COFDM).

One common technique applied by OFDM transceivers is *convolution coding*, which is a specialized form of a forward error-correcting code. Full details of convolution coding are beyond the scope of this book. One important point is that the convolution code is described by a rate (R) that specifies the number of data bits transmitted per code bit. A convolution code with R=1/2 transmits one data bit for every two code bits. As the code rate decreases, more code bits are available to correct errors, and the code becomes more robust. However, the price of robustness is decreased throughput. 802.11a uses convolution codes extensively. The most conservative data rates use codes with a rate of 1/2, and the aggressive codes used for the highest data rates use a coding rate of 3/4.

Windowing

One further enhancement helps OFDM transceivers cope with real-world effects. Transitions can be abrupt at symbol boundaries, causing a large number of high-frequency components (noise). To make OFDM transmitters good radio citizens, it is common to add padding bits at the beginning and end of transmissions to allow transmitters to "ramp up" and "ramp down" from full power. Padding bits are frequently needed when error correction coding is used. Some documentation may refer to the padding as "training sequences."

Windowing is a technique used to bring the signal for a new symbol gradually up to full strength while allowing the old symbol to fade away. Figure 11-7 shows a common windowing function based on a cosine curve. At the start of the symbol period, the new function is brought up to full strength according to the cosine function. When the symbol ends, the cosine curve is used to fade out the bits at the end of the symbol.

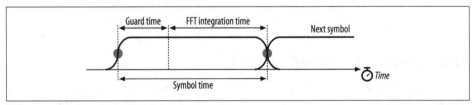

Figure 11-7. Cosine windowing technique

OFDM as Applied by 802.11a

802.11a is not a radical application of OFDM. The task group responsible for standardizing OFDM took the middle ground to apply OFDM to wireless LAN.

OFDM Parameter Choice for 802.11a

When choosing OFDM parameters, there are usually three given items of information. Bandwidth is fixed, often by regulatory authorities. Delay is determined by the environment in which the OFDM system will operate; most office buildings generally show a delay spread of 40–70 ns, though in some environments, the delay spread can approach 200 ns. Finally, the bit rate is usually a design goal, though the goal is usually "make the bit rate as high as possible, given the constraints of the other parameters."

One common guideline is that the guard time should be two to four times the average delay spread. As a result, the 802.11a designers selected a guard time of 800 ns. Symbol duration should be much larger than the guard time, but within reason. Larger symbol times mean that more subcarriers can fit within the symbol time. More subcarriers increase the signal-processing load at both the sender and receiver, increasing the cost and complexity of the resulting device. A practical choice is to select a symbol time at least five times the guard time; 802.11a matches the 800-ns guard time with a 4-μs symbol time. Subcarrier spacing is inversely related to the FFT integration time. 802.11a has a 3.2-μs integration time and a subcarrier spacing of 0.3125 MHz (1/3.2 μs).

Operating channels in 802.11a are specified as 20 MHz wide. The bandwidth of an operating channel is a design decision. Wider operating channels have higher throughput, but fewer operating channels fit into the assigned frequency spectrum. The use of a 20-MHz operating channel allows for reasonable speeds on each channel (up to 54 Mbps), as well as a reasonable number of operating channels in the assigned spectrum. 802.11a offers a wide variety of choices in modulation and coding to allow for a trade-off between robust modulation and conservative coding, which yields low, reliable throughput and finer-grained modulation and aggressive coding, resulting in higher, yet somewhat more fragile, throughput.

Structure of an Operating Channel

Like the DS PHYs, the OFDM physical layer organizes the spectrum into operating channels. Each 20-MHz channel is composed of 52 subcarriers. Four of the subcarriers are used as *pilot carriers* for monitoring path shifts and ICI, while the other 48 subcarriers are used to transmit data. Subcarriers are spaced 0.3125 MHz apart. As shown in Figure 11-8, channels are numbered from −26 to 26. Subcarrier 0 is not used for signal-processing reasons.

Pilot subcarriers are assigned to subcarriers −21, −7, 7, and 21. To avoid strong spectral lines in the Fourier transform, the pilot subcarriers transmit a fixed bit sequence specified in 802.11a using a conservative modulation technique.

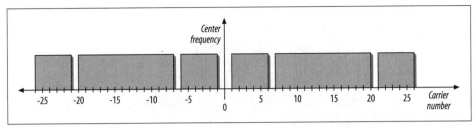

Figure 11-8. Structure of an OFDM channel

Operating Channels

In the U.S., the channels in the 5-GHz band are numbered starting every 5 MHz according to the following formula:

center frequency (MHz) = 5,000 + 5 × n, n=0,1,2, .. 200

Obviously, each 20-MHz 802.11a channel occupies four channels in the U-NII bands. The recommended channel use is given in Table 11-1.

Table 11-1. United States channels for 802.11a

Band	Allowed power[a]	Channel numbers	Center frequency (GHz)
U-NII lower band	40 mW	36	5.180
(5.15–5.25 GHz)	(2.5 mW/MHz)	40	5.200
		44	5.220
		48	5.240
U-NII mid-band	200 mW	52	5.260
(5.25–5.35 GHz)	(12.5 mW/MHz)	56	5.280
		60	5.300
		64	5.320
U-NII upper band	800 mW	149	5.745
(5.725–5.825 GHz)	(50 mW/MHz)	153	5.765
		157	5.785
		161	5.805

[a] The allowed power is the maximum output power using a 6-dBi antenna gain.

There is one other feature of note about the operating bands. As with the DS PHYs, a transmit mask limits power leakage into the side bands. The mask is shown in Figure 11-9.

Figure 11-10 gives an overall view of the 802.11a channels available in the U.S. Four channels are available in each of the U-NII bands in the U.S. In the two lower U-NII

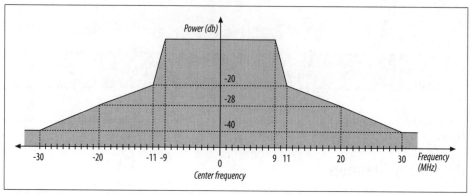

Figure 11-9. Transmit spectrum mask for 802.11a

bands, channels are allowed to overlap, and a 30-MHz guard band is present at both the lower end of the low U-NII band and the upper end of the mid U-NII band.

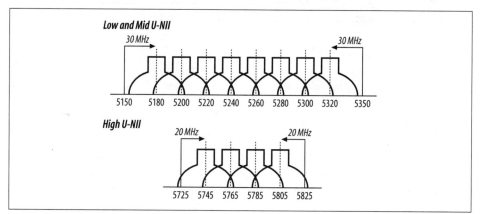

Figure 11-10. Operating bands from Table 11-1

OFDM PLCP

Like all the other physical layers, the OFDM PHY includes its own PLCP, which adds physical layer–specific framing parameters.

Framing

The OFDM PHY adds a preamble and a PLCP header. It also adds trailing bits to assist the encoding schemes used. This section divides the PLCP frame logically, but some components span different fields in the protocol unit. Figure 11-11 is the jumping-off point for discussion of the OFDM frame.

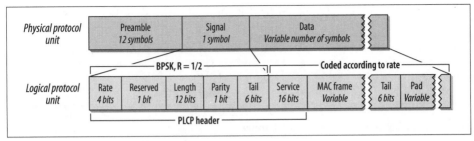

Figure 11-11. OFDM PLCP framing format

Figure 11-12 shows the start of a frame, but includes the guard intervals and windowing used by the transmitter. The preamble lasts 16 μs, which is evenly divided between short and long training sequences; the difference between the two is described in the next section. After the preamble, one OFDM symbol carries the Signal field, then a variable number of data symbols carry the end of the PLCP header, the MAC payload, and the trailer. All symbols use a modified cosine window to ensure smooth transitions. After the short preamble, which is used to synchronize frequencies, a guard time protects against multipath fading.

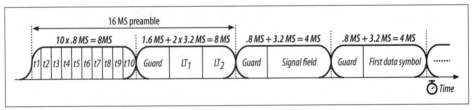

Figure 11-12. Preamble and frame start

Preamble

As with all other common IEEE 802 networks, and certainly all 802.11 physical layers, the OFDM physical protocol unit begins with a preamble. It is composed of 12 OFDM symbols that synchronize various timers between the transmitter and the receiver. The first 10 symbols are a *short training sequence*, which the receiver uses to lock on to the signal, select an appropriate antenna if the receiver is using multiple antennas, and synchronize the large-scale timing relationships required to begin decoding the following symbols. The short training sequences are transmitted without a guard period. Two *long training sequences* follow the short training sequences. Long training sequences fine-tune the timing acquisition and are protected by a guard interval.

Header

The PLCP header is transmitted in the Signal field of the physical protocol unit; it incorporates the Service field from the Data field of the physical protocol unit. As shown in Figure 11-13, the Signal field incorporates the Rate field, a Length field, and a Tail field.

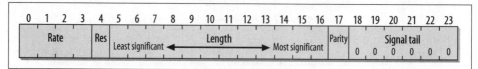

Figure 11-13. Signal field of OFDM PLCP frame

Rate (4 bits)

Four bits encode the data rate. Table 11-2 shows the bits used to encode each of the data rates. See the section "OFDM PMD" for details on the encoding and modulation scheme used for each data rate.

Table 11-2. Rate bits

Data rate (Mbps)	Bits (transmission order)
6	1101
9	1111
12	0101
18	0111
24	1001
36	1011
48	0001
54	0011

Length (12 bits)

Twelve bits encode the number of bytes in the embedded MAC frame. Like most fields, it is transmitted least-significant bit to most-significant bit. The length is processed by a convolution code to protect against bit errors.

Parity (1 bit) and Reserved (1 bit)

Bit 4 is reserved for future use and must be set to 0. Bit 17 is an even parity bit for the first 16 Signal bits to protect against data corruption.

Tail (6 bits)

The Signal field ends with six 0 tail bits used to unwind the convolution code. As such, they must by definition be processed by the convolution code.

Service (16 bits)

The final field in the PLCP header is the 16-bit Service field. Unlike the other components of the PLCP header, it is transmitted in the Data field of the physical protocol unit at the data rate of the embedded MAC frame. The first eight bits are set to 0. As with the other physical layers, MAC frames are scrambled before transmission; the first six bits are set to 0 to initialize the scrambler. The remaining nine bits are reserved and must set to 0 until they are adopted for future use.

Data

The encoding scheme used for the data depends on the data rate. Before transmission, data is scrambled, as it is with the other physical layers. The Service field of the header is included in the Data field of the physical protocol unit because it initializes the scrambler.

Trailer

The Data field of the physical protocol unit ends with a trailer. (The 802.11a specification does not call the ending fields a trailer, but it is a descriptive term.) It is composed of two fields:

Tail (6 bits)
> Like the tail bits in the PLCP header, the tail bits appended to the end of the MAC frame bring the convolution code smoothly to an end.

Pad (variable)
> As used by 802.11a, OFDM requires that fixed-size blocks of data bits be transferred. The Data field is padded so that its length is an integer multiple of the block size. The block size depends on the modulation and coding used by the data rate; it is discussed in the next section.

OFDM PMD

The OFDM PHY uses a cocktail of different modulation schemes to achieve data rates ranging from 6 Mbps to 54 Mbps. In all cases, the physical layer uses a symbol rate of 250,000 symbols per second across 48 subchannels; the number of data bits per symbol varies. An OFDM symbol spans all 48 subchannels.

There are four rate tiers with the OFDM PHY: 6 and 9 Mbps, 12 and 18 Mbps, 24 and 36 Mbps, and 48 and 54 Mbps. Support is required for 6, 12, and 24 Mbps, which are lowest speeds in each of the first three tiers, and therefore the most robust in the presence of interference. The lowest tier uses binary phase shift keying (BPSK) to encode 1 bit per subchannel, or 48 bits per symbol. The convolution coding means that either half or one quarter of the bits are redundant bits used for error correction, so there are only 24 or 36 data bits per symbol. The next tier uses quadrature phase shift keying (QPSK) to encode 2 bits per subchannel, for a total of 96 bits per symbol. After subtracting overhead from the convolution code, the receiver is left with 48 or 72 data bits. The third and fourth tiers use generalized forms of BPSK and QPSK known as quadrature amplitude modulation (QAM). 16-QAM encodes 4 bits using 16 symbols, and 64-QAM encodes 6 bits using 64 symbols. The third tier uses 16-QAM along with the standard R=1/2 and R=3/4 convolution codes. To achieve higher rates with 64-QAM, however, the convolution codes use R=2/3 and R=3/4. Table 11-3 summarizes the coding methods used by each data rate in the OFDM PHY.

Table 11-3. Encoding details for different OFDM data rates

Speed (Mbps)	Modulation and coding rate (R)	Coded bits per carrier[a]	Coded bits per symbol	Data bits per symbol[b]
6	BPSK, R=1/2	1	48	24
9	BPSK, R=3/4	1	48	36
12	QPSK, R=1/2	2	96	48
18	QPSK, R=3/4	2	96	72
24	16-QAM, R=1/2	4	192	96
36	16-QAM, R=3/4	4	192	144
48	64-QAM, R=2/3	6	288	192
54	64-QAM, R=3/4	6	288	216

[a]Coded bits per subchannel is a function of the modulation (BPSK, QPSK, 16-QAM, or 64-QAM).
[b]The data bits per symbol is a function of the rate of the convolution code.

Clear Channel Assessment

The OFDM PHY specification leaves implementers a great deal of latitude in selecting techniques for noting a busy channel. Received signal strength thresholds determine whether the channel is in use, but the main guideline for 802.11a equipment is that it must meet certain performance standards. Implementations are free to use the Packet Length field from the PLCP header to augment clear channel assessment, but this is not required.

An Example of OFDM Encoding

OFDM encoding, as you can no doubt see by now, is an intense, multistep process. One of the additions that 802.11a made to the original specification was Annex G, an encoding of Schiller's *Ode to Joy* for transmission over an 802.11a network.* Shortly after 802.11a was published, the IEEE 802.11 working group discovered several errors in the example and published a correction. If you are interested in learning about OFDM encoding in detail, you can refer to this example.

Characteristics of the OFDM PHY

Parameters specific to the OFDM PHY are listed in Table 11-4. Like the physical layers presented in Chapter 10, the OFDM PHY also incorporates a number of parameters to

---

* Well, an English translation, anyway...

adjust for the delay in various processing stages in the electronics. As a final note, the extra radio bandwidth provided by the U-NII bands offers a great deal of throughput. There are eight overlapping channels available for the OFDM PHY, so it can offer up to 432 Mbps in an area where all eight channels are co-located.

Table 11-4. OFDM PHY parameters

Parameter	Value	Notes
Maximum MAC frame length	4,095 bytes	
Slot time	9 μs	
SIFS time	16 μs	The SIFS is used to derive the value of the other interframe spaces (DIFS, PIFS, and EIFS).
Contention window size	15 to 1,023 slots	
Preamble duration	20 μs	
PLCP header duration	4 μs	

Like the other physical layers, the OFDM PHY has a number of attributes that can be adjusted by a vendor to balance delays in various parts of the system. It includes variables for the latency through the MAC, the PLCP, and the transceiver, as well as variables to account for variations in the transceiver electronics.

CHAPTER 12
Using 802.11 on Windows

Whether you've made it to this point by skipping Chapters 3–11, or whether you've read all the theory, we're now going to get our hands dirty and start installing equipment.

From the standpoint of practical system and network administration, working with 802.11 is similar to working with Ethernet. Installing 802.11 drivers is nearly identical to installing Ethernet drivers, and the network interfaces behave almost exactly like Ethernet interfaces. 802.11 interfaces cause an ARP cache to be brought into existence, and other software may even perceive the wireless interface as an Ethernet interface. Unlike many Ethernet drivers, however, 802.11 drivers can have a number of advanced knobs and features that reflect the additional management features presented in Chapter 7.

This chapter is not intended to be a definitive guide to Windows drivers for 802.11 network cards. There are two major development lines in Windows (9x versus NT and progeny), and adding additional software such as a VPN client can further complicate matters. (My advice is to install the wireless LAN card before any VPN client software.) There are a number of vendors, and, as you'd expect, the driver software varies from one vendor to the next. The examples show how to install a driver on Windows and explain the non-Ethernet driver features in some detail. I selected two 802.11 cards as examples: the Nokia C110/C111 and the Lucent ORiNOCO. While not particularly common, the Nokia card is interesting because it has a number of advanced features and exposes a number of the network parameters that were discussed in Chapters 2–10. The Lucent card (which is sold under a number of different labels) probably has the lion's share of the market, and it hides most of the exotic configuration parameters from the user. Most cards that are available fall somewhere between these two extremes.

Nokia C110/C111

Nokia's 802.11b solution comes in two similar form factors. The C110 is a Type 2 PC Card with an integrated antenna; the C111 is basically the same, but with two external antenna connectors. The card ships with a CD to enable basic installation, and updated drivers are available from *http://forum.nokia.com/* after registering.

Installation

Driver installation begins before inserting the card, so start by inserting the CD-ROM into the CD-ROM drive. After a splash screen, an installation program begins. Its main screen is shown in Figure 12-1. Select Installing Nokia C110/C111 to launch the installer.

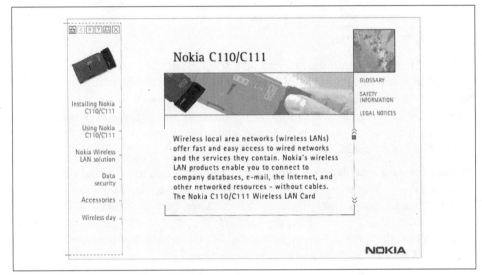

Figure 12-1. Installation screen

The next steps are very familiar. Selecting the install option launches InstallShield and brings up an admonition to close all other programs. Like all commercial software, the Nokia driver is licensed. Accept the license agreement to proceed. Next, the driver asks for the country in which the card is being used. This information is used to set the regulatory domain, which affects the radio channels that can be used. See Figure 12-2.

The setup program then asks where it should put the files that it installs. The default location is *C:\Program Files\Nokia C110*. Next, the driver asks which components should be installed. The software package is composed of three major components: drivers, help files, and administrator components. Typical users install only the first

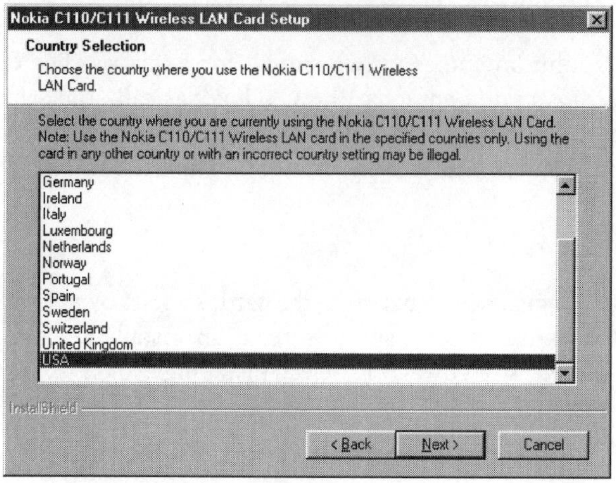

Figure 12-2. Country selection

two, but network administrators can use features in the software to streamline installation procedures for large numbers of users. A Typical installation consists of only the first two, and an Administrator installation uses all three. For good measure, a Custom installation allows any subset of the three components to be installed. In a Custom installation, the administrator component is not installed by default and must be selected explicitly.

At this point, the installation program has collected all the information necessary to install the driver. It copies files that were unpacked during the installation and makes registry changes to activate the new driver. After that completes, a dialog box appears and prompts you to insert the card into the computer to complete the installation. When the card is inserted into the PC Card slot, the message shown in Figure 12-3 appears, and the installation is complete.

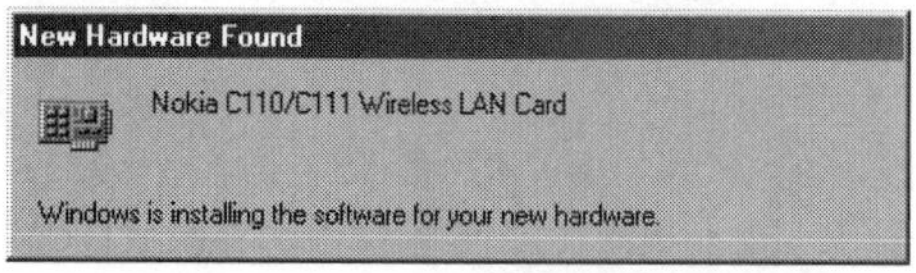

Figure 12-3. Driver installation prompt

The installer prompts you for the creation of a network profile before restarting the computer. Profiles are one of the card's advanced features; they are optional, but they make card management much simpler. It will be interesting to see whether other vendors pick up on this idea.

Network Profiles

The Nokia card groups settings into *profiles*, which allow users to switch easily between networks. Immediately after installing the driver, the user is prompted to create a profile if none exists. Administrators may create customized driver installation disks or smart cards to distribute settings more easily. In addition to the run-of-the-mill network settings, the Nokia driver can control whether the system attempts to log in to a domain and a Microsoft workgroup. Profiles can also contain WEP keys as well as a number of 802.11 parameters. Figure 12-4 shows the initial Profile Wizard screen. Profiles are assigned text names; the name need not have anything to do with the SSIDs in use.

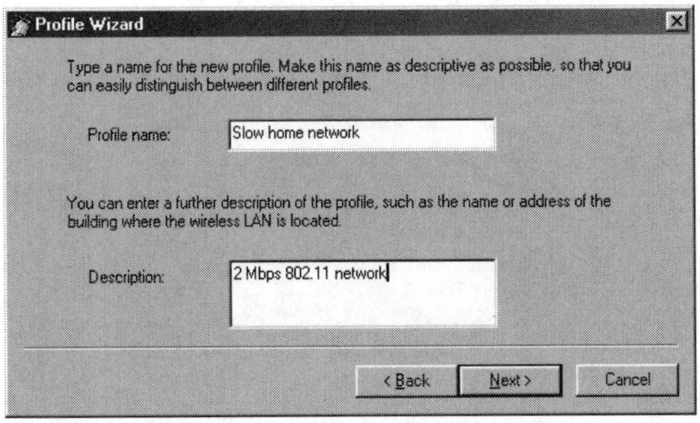

Figure 12-4. Initial Profile Wizard screen

After naming the profile and entering a detailed description, the user must then select the type of network in use. Infrastructure networks use access points, and ad hoc networks are independent BSSs.[*] After selecting the network operating mode, the user proceeds to a network selection window (Figure 12-5). Networks are distinguished by their service set IDs, which are called names for simplicity.

This window allows you to enter channel information. Unless you have an overwhelming reason to set the channel explicitly, leave the channel set to automatic, which means that the driver scans all channels when it is initialized. There are two ways to select the network name. One is to type the SSID for which the driver should search. To make it easier for basic users, the small unobtrusive button to the right of the network name field pops up a list of networks currently in range (Figure 12-6). This window is a nice touch; it shows you data rates and signal strengths to help you make an intelligent choice.

---

[*] Earlier Nokia products also had an operating mode called Instawave, which allowed direct station-to-station communication simultaneously with station-to-access point communication. Instawave was nonstandard and never found extensive use in production networks.

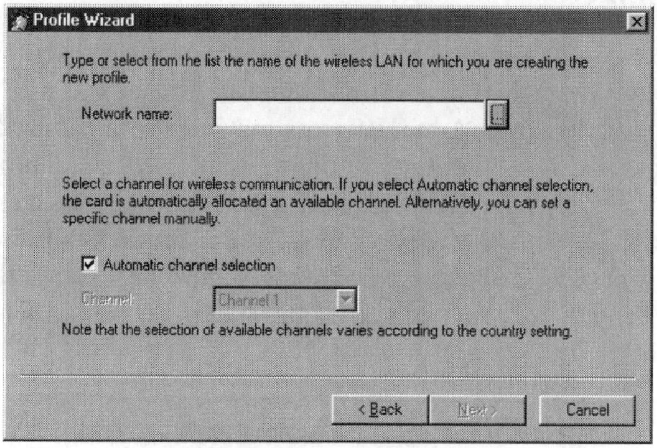

Figure 12-5. Network parameter dialog box

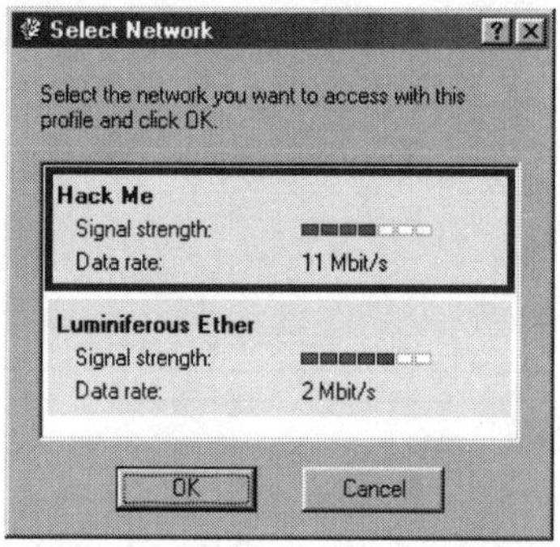

Figure 12-6. Network selection box

After selecting a network, the user is presented with the final screen for selecting basic network parameters (Figure 12-7). Most 802.11 networks use DHCP to assign IP addresses. If not, the profile can be modified later to specify an address explicitly. You can also specify Windows domain and workgroup names.

At this point, a network profile has been created. It appears on the main screen, as shown in Figure 12-8.

To select a profile, highlight it and click Apply. The selected profile gets a big green check mark to show that it has been selected. As part of choosing a profile, the driver maintains network configuration settings. These settings can be updated as the user changes profiles. When a new profile is selected, the dialog box in Figure 12-9 appears. My experience has been that you usually need to restart the system when you apply a new profile.

When the system comes back up, there will be a small default monitoring window, in addition to a taskbar icon. The small window, shown in Figure 12-10, displays the

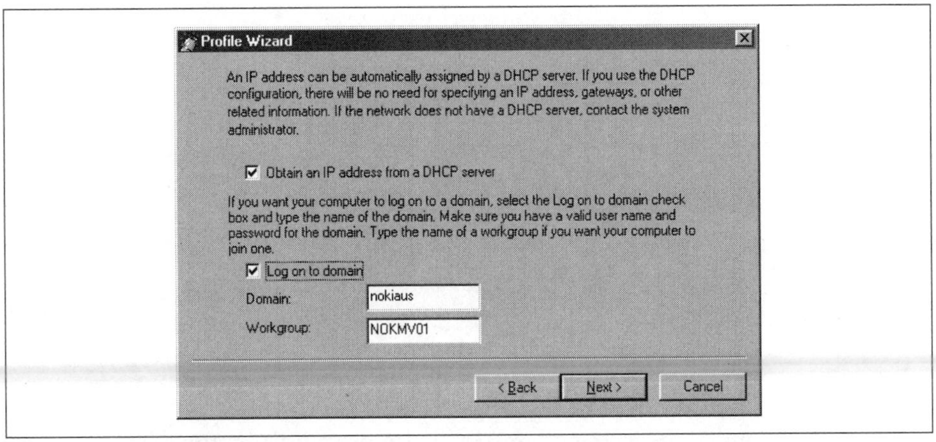

Figure 12-7. Addressing and login options

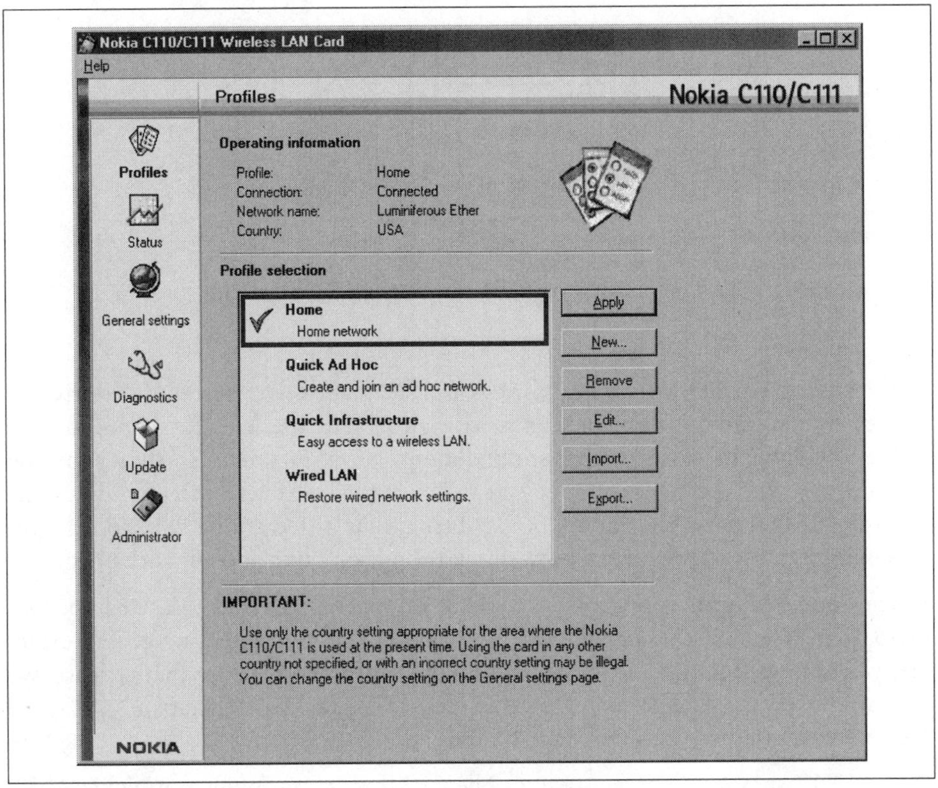

Figure 12-8. Profile selection screen

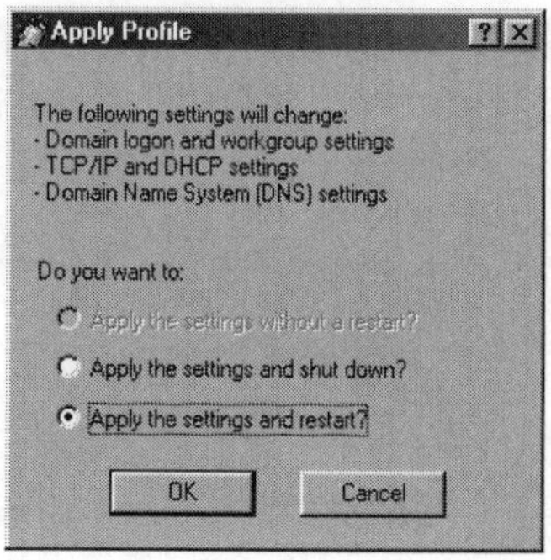

Figure 12-9. Options when changing profiles

network profile and a signal strength meter. It also provides a button next to the profile name for gaining access to the detailed configuration window.

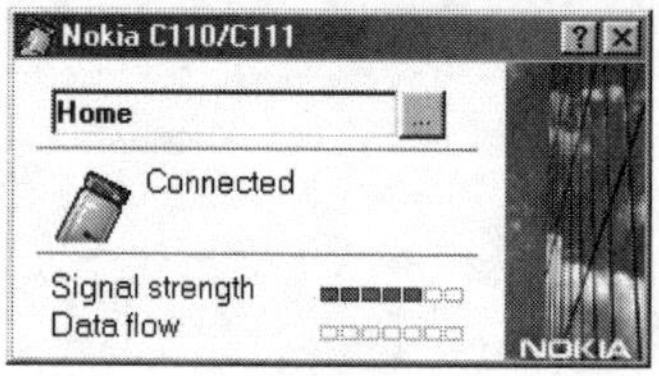

Figure 12-10. Default monitoring window

Using the Driver

Clicking on the small gray button brings up the main driver screen. The driver is divided into six broad categories, each with an icon at the left. Categories may be further divided into tabs for more specific information. Figure 12-11 shows the Status category, with the General tab selected. The Status → General screen shows a signal strength meter and the amount of data being transmitted on the BSS. Both graphs are continually updated and can be useful in troubleshooting and network planning.

When troubleshooting connectivity problems or expanding a network, it can be useful to run a card as a scanner, simply to see the access points within range. For example, you can walk around a building with your laptop and ensure that at least two access points are reachable in high-traffic areas. Like the general statistics page, the access point listing is reached as a tab off the status page.

Figure 12-12 shows two access points. The 11-Mbps access point is a Nokia A032, which is capable of transmitting its IP address and workload. The mechanism used to accomplish this will be discussed in more detail in Chapter 16.

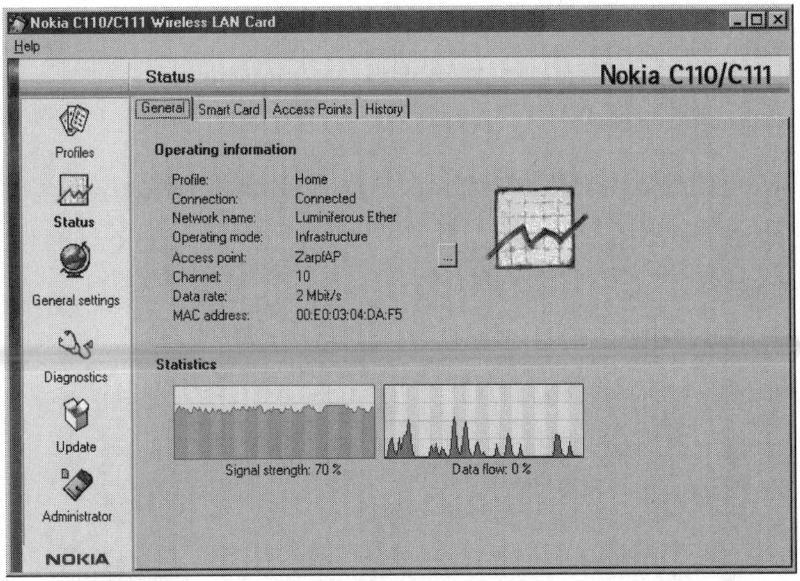

Figure 12-11. Status → General driver screen

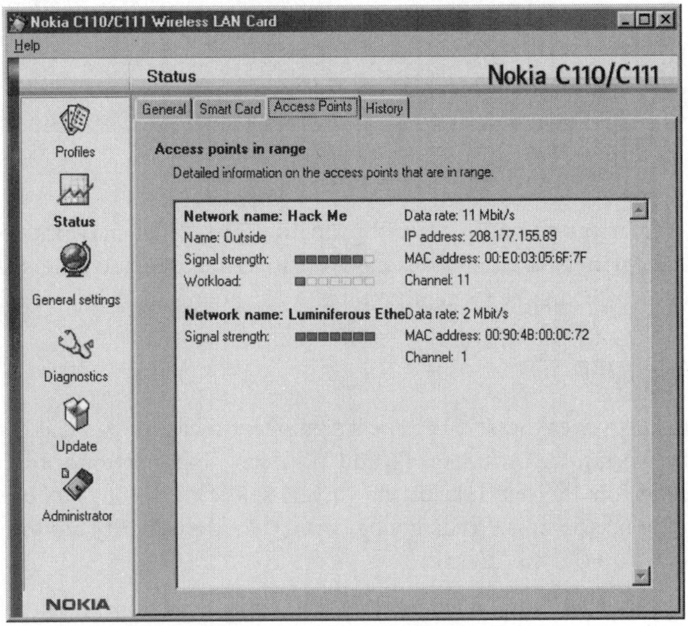

Figure 12-12. General → Access point tab

Global driver configuration options

The General settings button can be used to gain access to the general driver settings used on a global basis. Figure 12-13 shows the General settings → General tab, which allows you to select the regulatory domain and enable low-power operation.

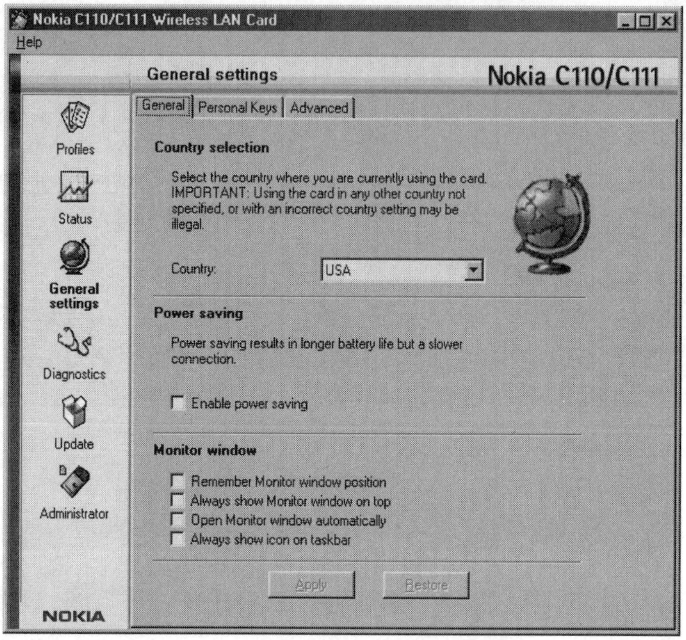

Figure 12-13. The General settings → General tab

By default, the driver manages TCP/IP properties and other network configuration and treats 802.11 network names as case-sensitive network identifiers. All of these can be changed by using the General settings → Advanced tab (Figure 12-14).

Configuring WEP

Despite its security weaknesses, WEP is a significant measure you can take to secure an 802.11 network from intruders. To add WEP keys to a network profile, go to the profile category on the left side of the driver, select the profile to use, and click **Edit...** to bring up the Edit Profile dialog box. Select the Security tab to bring up the WEP configuration (Figure 12-15).

Keys may be imported from an external text file using the Import... button or may be added from scratch using the Add... button. Figure 12-16 shows the dialog box used to edit a shared WEP key.

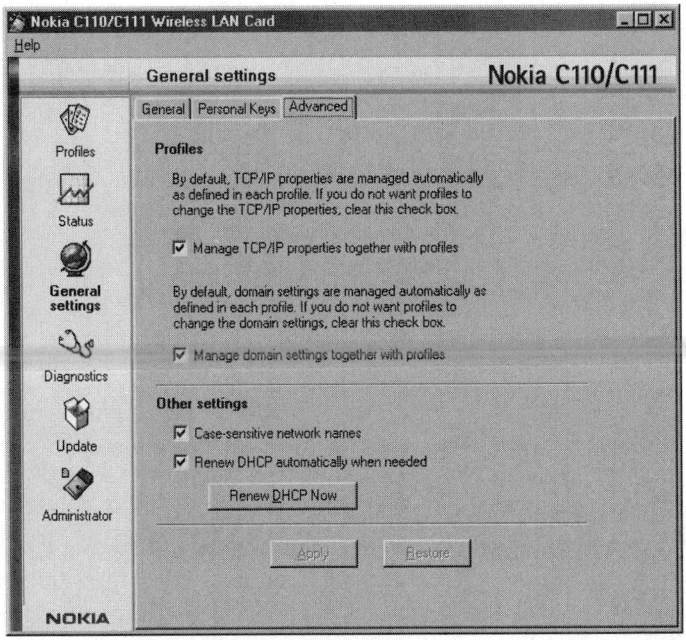

Figure 12-14. General settings → Advanced tab

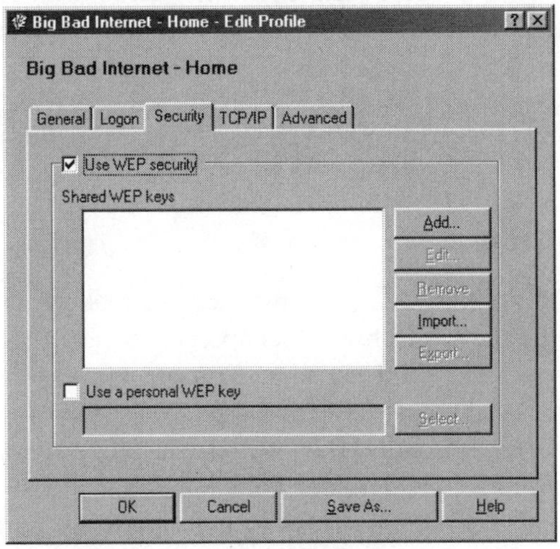

Figure 12-15. WEP configuration

802.11 permits four shared keys per SSID. Not all drivers support using all four, but Nokia's driver does. At the top of the dialog box there are fields for selecting the

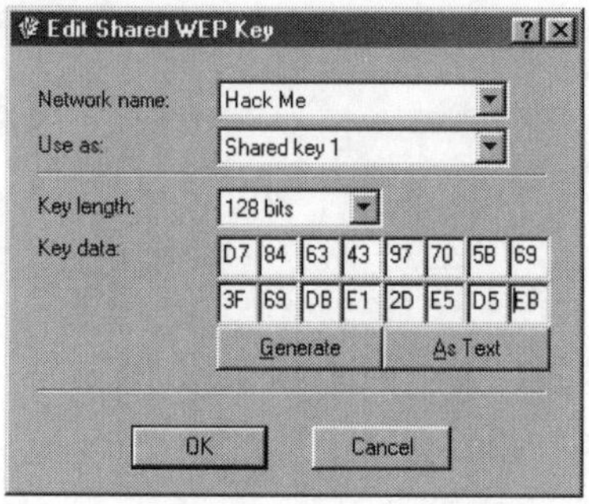

Figure 12-16. Editing a shared WEP key

SSID (network name) and the key number to which the key applies. The bottom part of the screen shows the key length and the key itself. Note that this screen specifies key length in terms of the actual number of secret bits; a 40-bit key corresponds to the standardized 64-bit RC4 key described in Chapter 5; most other vendors would refer to this as a 64-bit key. No other key lengths are standardized; Nokia also supports a 128-bit WEP key, which requires a 152-bit RC4 key. Most other vendors also support a 128-bit key but don't interpret key lengths the same way; for most vendors, 128 bits means a 128-bit RC4 key with 104 secret bits. The result is that Nokia cards won't interoperate with other vendors' products at the 128-bit key length.

For the first station on a network, the Generate button may be used to generate a random key. The As Text button allows you to cut and paste a hexadecimal string to use as the key.

When WEP is configured for a network, the wireless LAN card icon in the monitor window appears with a padlock. The padlock shows that WEP is in use.

Advanced Properties

The Nokia driver allows network administrators to make detailed changes to the 802.11 parameters discussed in previous chapters. To get to the advanced settings, go to the main configuration window, select a profile, and choose **Edit...**, which displays the main profile editing page. On this page, select the Advanced tab to display the advanced properties. Normally, the "advanced" properties are configured automatically. If you want to set the parameters by hand, uncheck the Automatic configuration checkbox. Clicking on the Advanced Properties... button takes you to a window that lets you modify several of the basic 802.11 properties (Figure 12-17). Table 12-1 describes the available options and their defaults.

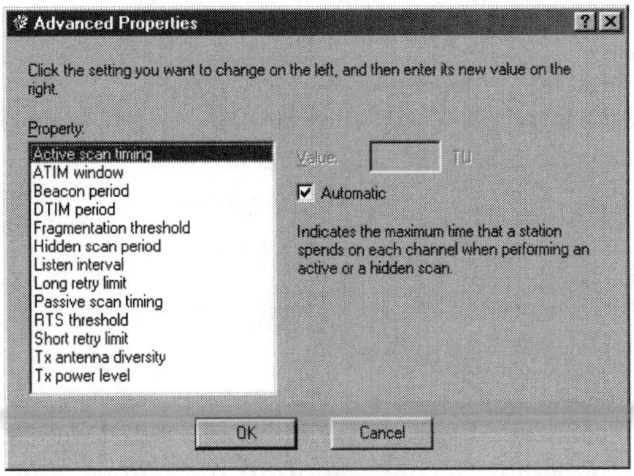

Figure 12-17. Advanced Properties configuration screen

Table 12-1. Parameter defaults used by the Nokia driver

Property	Default ("automatic") value	Measurement units	Description	Reference
Active scan timing	30	TU	Number of time units spent monitoring each channel during an active scan.	Chapter 7; 802.11 clause 11.1.3
ATIM window	0	TU	Amount of time that stations in an ad hoc network must remain awake after a beacon.	Chapter 7; 802.11 clause 11.2.2
Beacon period	100	TU	Amount of time between target beacon transmissions for an ad hoc BSS .	Chapter 7; 802.11 clause 11.1.2
DTIM period	10	beacon periods	Number of beacon periods between DTIM messages.	Chapter 7; 802.11 clause 11.2.1.3
Fragmentation threshold	2,346	bytes	Packets larger than the threshold are fragmented at the MAC layer for transmission.	Chapter 3; 802.11 clause 9.4
Hidden scan period	30	seconds		
Listen interval	10	beacon periods	Number of beacon periods between station waking up to listen to DTIMs for buffered traffic delivery.	Chapter 7; 802.11 clause 11.2
Long retry limit	4	attempts	Maximum number of attempts to transmit a frame bigger than the RTS threshold.	Chapter 3; 802.11 clause 9.5.2.3
Passive scan timing	250	TU	Amount of time spent listening for traffic on each radio channel during a passive scan.	Chapter 7; 802.11 clause 11.1
RTS threshold	0	bytes	Packets larger than the RTS are preceded by an RTS/CTS handshake.	Chapter 3; 802.11 clause 9.2
Short retry limit	7	attempts	Maximum number of attempts to transmit a frame shorter than the RTS threshold.	Chapter 3; 802.11 clause 9.5.2.3

Table 12-1. Parameter defaults used by the Nokia driver (continued)

Property	Default ("automatic") value	Measurement units	Description	Reference
Tx antenna diversity	1	N/A	0–enabled 1–discabled	
Tx power level	1	N/A	1–high power 2–low power	

Smart Cards

When 802.11 networks initially gained prominence, one of the biggest concerns was how to distribute configuration information to the mobile computers on the network. One of the more novel solutions was Nokia's smart cards. The C11x cards have an integrated smart-card reader. Administrators can write profiles out to smart cards using the Administrator menu in the main configuration screen and distribute smart cards to users. Smart cards can store the entire profile, including WEP keys and TCP/IP configuration, which reduces the possibility of user error—users don't have to type network parameters or keys correctly. Smart cards also present a tamper-resistant barrier to sensitive information (such as WEP keys) that might otherwise be stored in a file on the hard disk.

Unlocking the smart card

Users with a smart card are presented with a challenge to unlock the card when the wireless card is placed in a PC Card slot. First, the dialog box of Figure 12-18 appears as the smart card is opened.

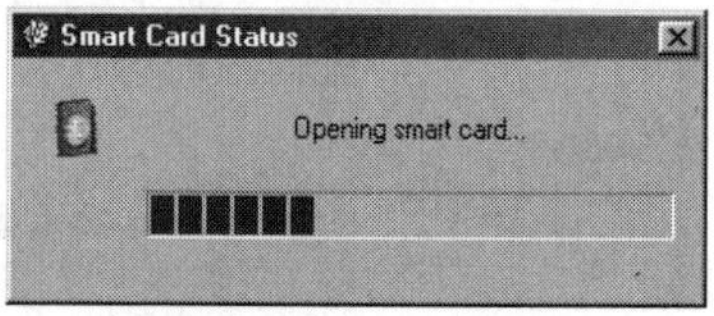

Figure 12-18. Smart-card opening screen

When the smart-card initialization completes, the user enters the PIN for the smart card, using the window in Figure 12-19.

After three unsuccessful attempts to open the smart card, it locks up and cannot be unlocked even by the correct PIN. Only the PIN Unlocking Key (PUK) distributed with the smart card, can be used to unlock the smart card after it locks. When the smart card is unlocked, any profiles that it stores can be used by the driver. Smart-card profiles cannot be edited directly and are identified with a special icon on the main configuration screen (Figure 12-20).

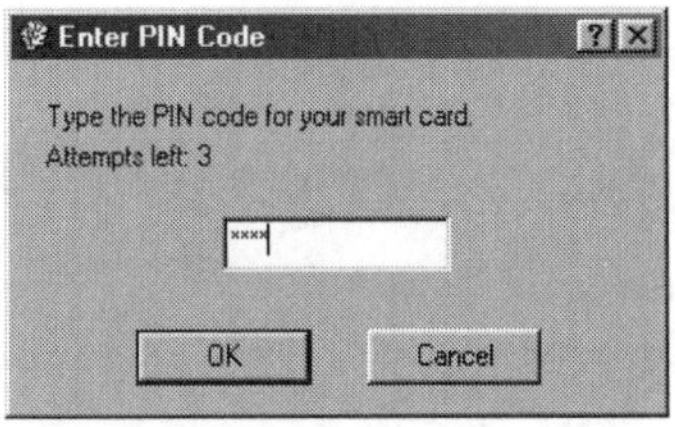

Figure 12-19. Smart-card PIN entry

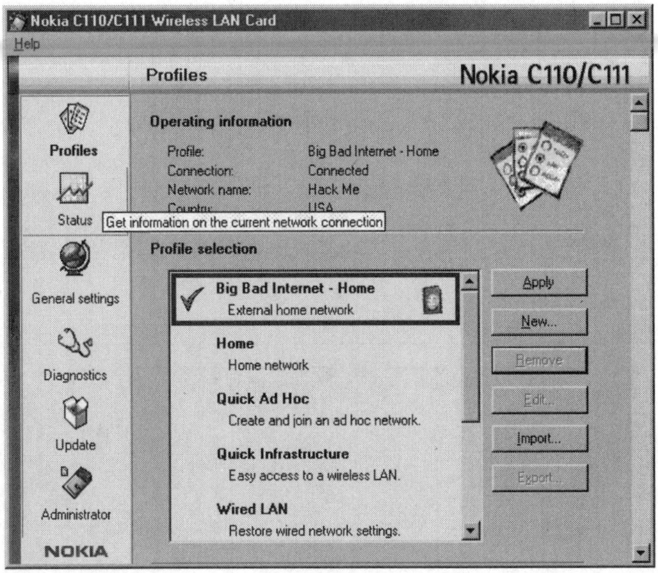

Figure 12-20. Smart-card profile

Locking the smart card and changing the PIN

If desired, the smart card can be locked from the driver configuration panel. Select Status, then choose the Smart Card tab, and click on the **Lock...** button shown in Figure 12-21. You can also use this screen to change the PIN by clicking the Change **PIN Code...** button at the bottom.

Moving profiles onto the smart card

Only driver installations that include the administrator routines can create or modify the data stored on a smart card. The **Administrator** button on the lefthand banner accesses administrative functions. Two main administrator functions are available: one to move profiles to smart cards and one to create installation disks with profiles readily available. See Figure 12-22.

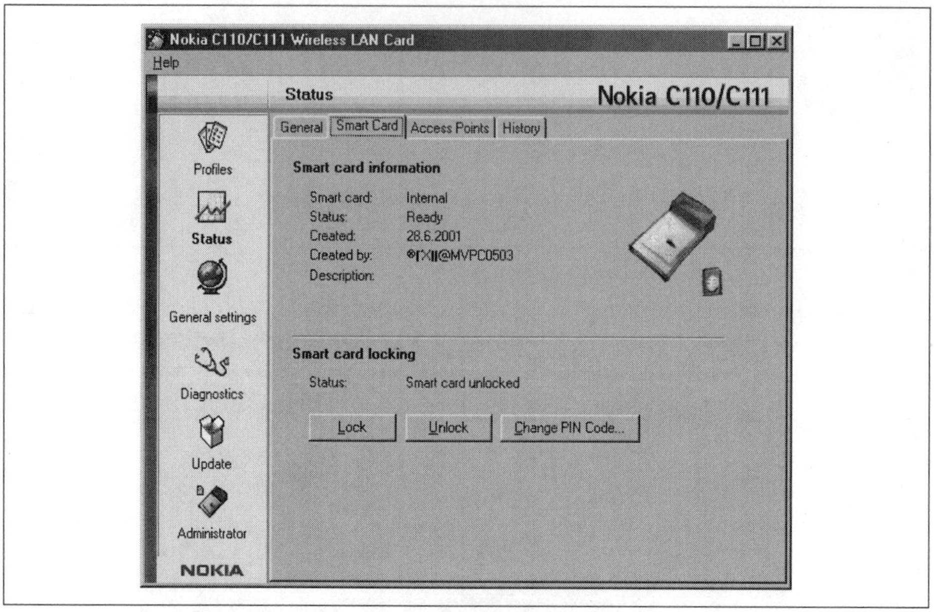

Figure 12-21. Smart-card management tab

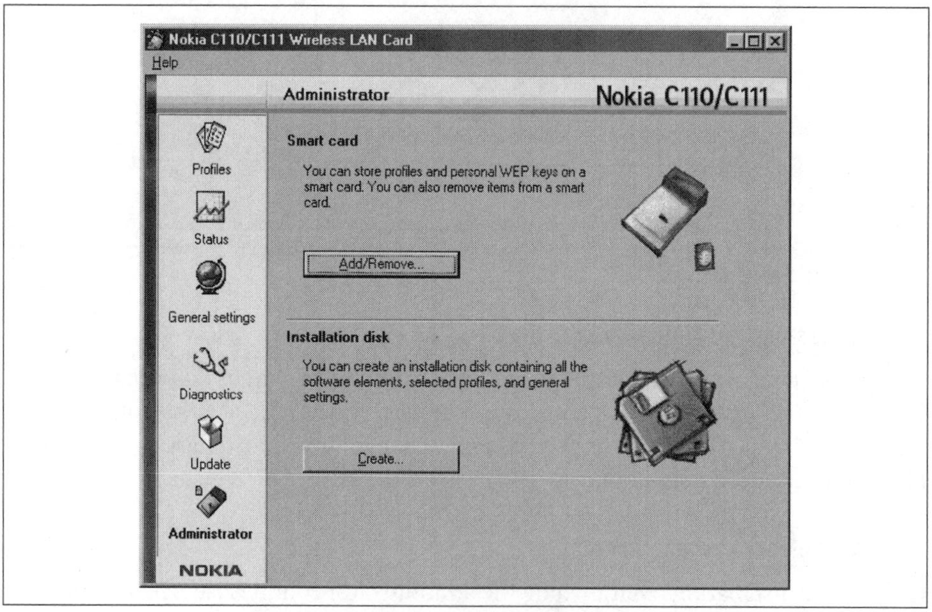

Figure 12-22. Administrator functions of the C11x driver

To access the smart-card functions, click on the **Add/Remove...** button at the top of the page. This brings you to Figure 12-23, which allows you to erase the smart card and move profiles from disk to smart card and vice versa.

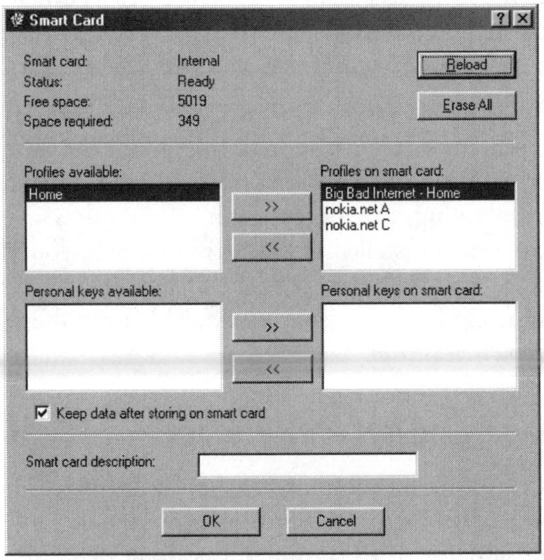

Figure 12-23. Smart card profile management

Lucent ORiNOCO

With the acquisition of WaveLAN, Lucent Technologies became an overnight leader in the wireless LAN market space. WaveLAN has been involved in wireless LAN development since the early 1990s. Naturally, standardized products were not available until the late 1990s with the adoption of the initial 802.11 standard. After experiencing financial trouble throughout much of 2001, Lucent's reorganization efforts have split the company into several pieces. As this book was written, the reorganization had yet to affect the physical appearance of the product—the card I ordered still had Lucent branding.

Lucent sells two flavors of the card. The cards are identical, except for the size of the WEP key supported. ORiNOCO Silver cards support WEP keys with 40 secret bits (marketed as 64-bit cards), and ORiNOCO Gold cards support WEP keys with 104 secret bits (marketed as 128-bit cards).

Installation

Lucent's card installation is more conventional. Begin by putting the card in an available PC Card slot and have the CD handy. When the card is inserted, Windows may identify it as a WaveLAN/IEEE card. Once 802.11 was ratified and products were brought to market, Lucent distinguished between the earlier proprietary cards and the 802.11-compliant cards by adding "IEEE" to the product name.

Drivers for the ORiNOCO cards are bundled with a CD-ROM. Windows 2000 ships with Lucent drivers, but the bundled drivers have caused problems in a number of installations. Fetch an update from *http://www.orinocowireless.com* before inserting the card for the first time.

Allow Windows to search for the drivers and then point the installation program at the CD-ROM drive. Different versions of Windows have different drivers, so select the directory corresponding to your version of Windows (e.g., *D:\DRIVERS\ WIN98*). Once the driver is installed in the network stack, you must install the Client Manager, which is the user frontend to the driver. The client manager is distributed on a CD with the card, and updates are available from the ORiNOCO web site at *http://www.orinocowireless.com*.

The Client Manager and Network Profiles

Like drivers for other cards on the market, the Lucent driver holds configuration information in profiles. Versions of the driver distributed in early 2001 were limited to four profiles, but fall 2001 revisions lifted that limit. This section covers the fall 2001 driver. After the driver and client manager are installed, you can create profiles to hold information about networks in the area. To get to the configuration, start the Client Manager. Figure 12-24 shows the main Client Manager screen.

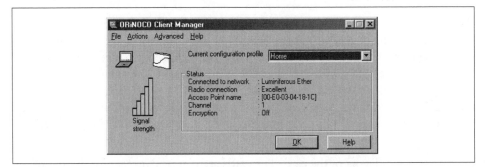

Figure 12-24. Client Manager main screen

Go to the **Actions** menu and select **Add/Edit Configuration Profile**. This brings up the main profile window, shown in Figure 12-25. Click on the **Add** button to begin creating the profile. The dialog box shown in Figure 12-26 appears. Name the profile on the lefthand side of the box and select the network type on the right. Access Point networks and Residential Gateways are infrastructure networks, and Peer-to-Peer networks are infrastructure networks.

Next, identify the network. As with other products, the network name is the SSID of the network. You can either type it into the network name field or use the Scan button to pull up a list of networks whose Beacons are currently being received.

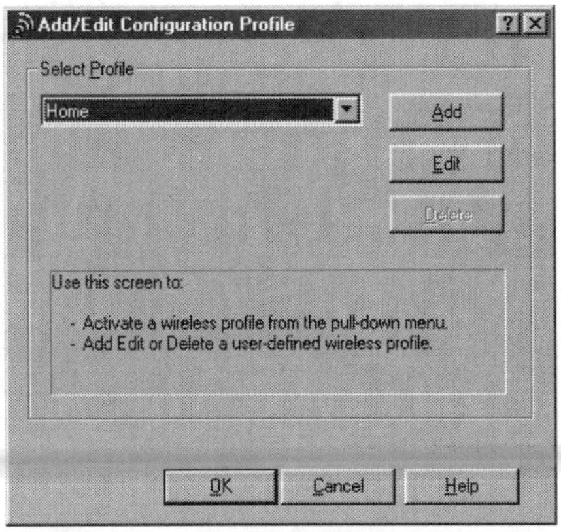

Figure 12-25. Add/Edit Configuration Profile window

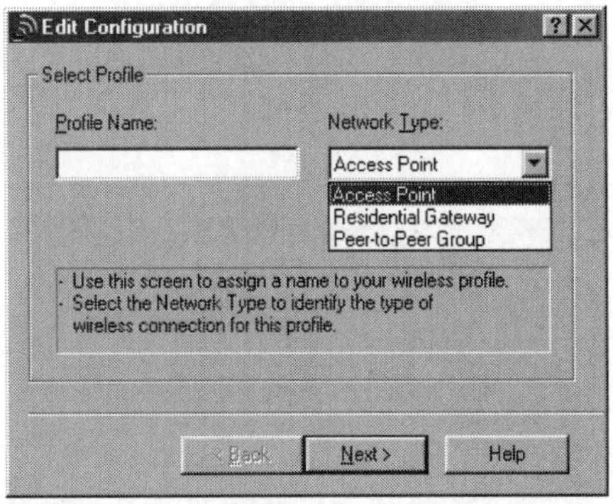

Figure 12-26. Profile creation

Figure 12-27 shows the network name configuration box, and Figure 12-28 shows the scan result box. Unfortunately, the scan result box gives no indication of signal strength.

Next, the user can configure WEP keys using the dialog box in Figure 12-29. Keys can be entered as alphanumeric strings and hashed into a bit string used as a key, or they can be entered directly. The algorithm used to generate a key from an alphanumeric string is not documented, which might lead to security questions. Much of the security of WEP resides in the key, and a simple key generator might compromise security by allowing dictionary attacks on the key.

Power management is controlled on a network-by-network basis and is configured after WEP using the dialog box in Figure 12-30.

The final item contained in a profile controls TCP/IP behavior and is set using the dialog box in Figure 12-31. The only option available with the Lucent driver is

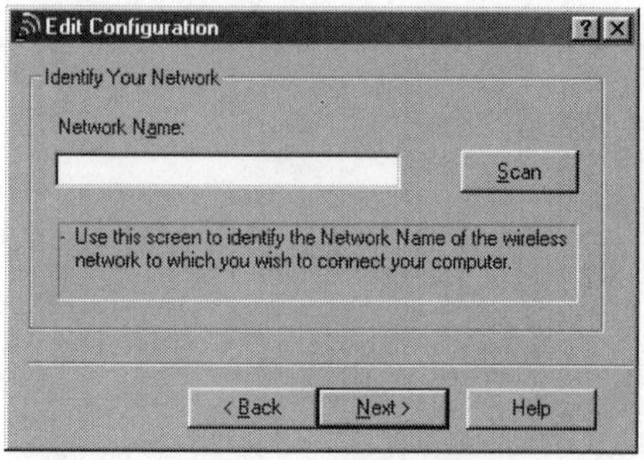

Figure 12-27. Network name configuration

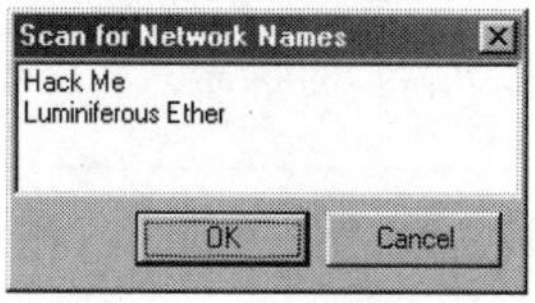

Figure 12-28. Scan result dialog box

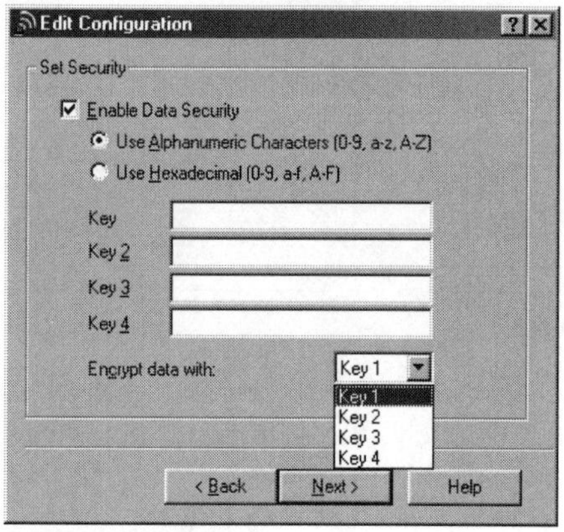

Figure 12-29. WEP configuration

whether a DHCP renewal will be issued when changing between profiles. No provisions are available for controlling Windows networking configuration.

Using the Driver

Miscellaneous system administration tasks are performed through the Client Manager. The radio can be disabled, even when the card is active, by going to the File menu and choosing Disable Radio.

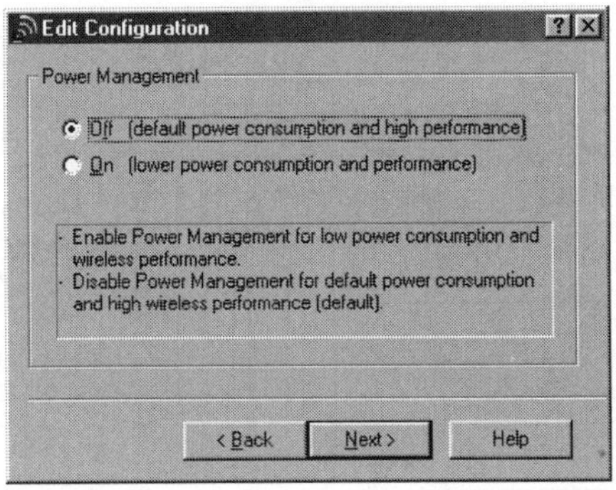

Figure 12-30. Power management configuration

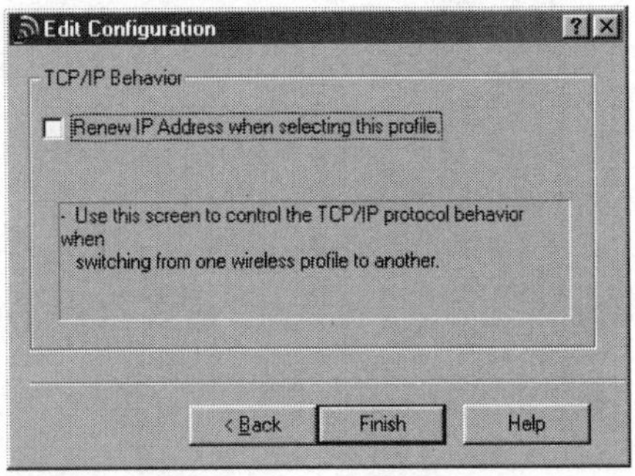

Figure 12-31. Network control

Changing between profiles

One of the most common configuration tasks is changing between profiles. The operating profile can be changed through the drop-down box on the right side of the Client Manager or through the Action menu. Changing profiles does not require a system reboot, even if the new profile requires an IP address renewal. See Figure 12-32.

Version information

Choosing Version Info from the Help menu brings up the version information. A version information window is shown in Figure 12-33. The driver and related software are implemented by several independent software pieces, all of which have their own version number. Most importantly, the driver for the card and the Client Manager user interface are separate and must be upgraded separately.

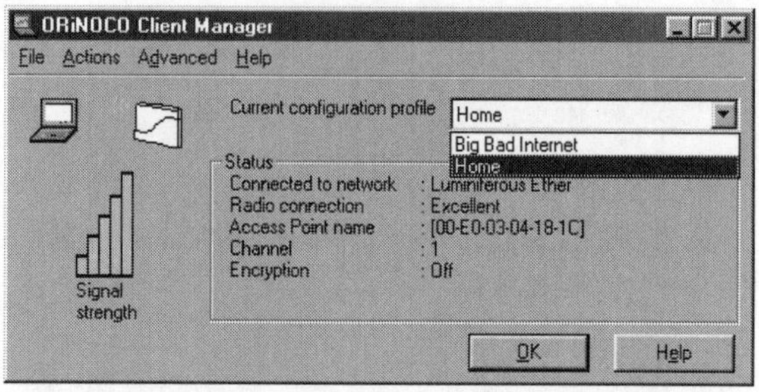

Figure 12-32. Changing profiles

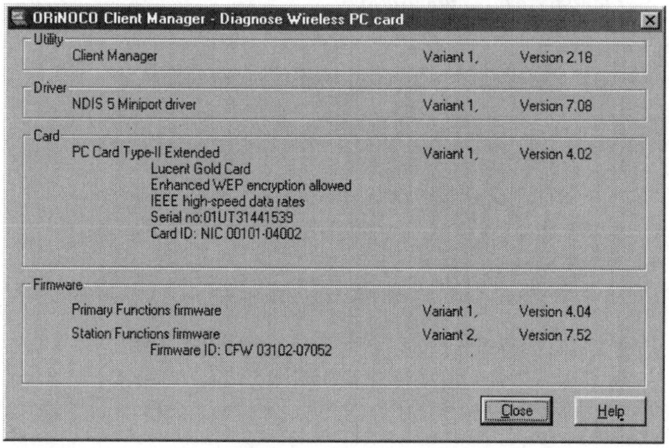

Figure 12-33. Version information

Site Monitor

The Site Monitor can be accessed by going to the Advanced Menu and choosing Site Monitor, which displays network information for open networks in the area. Networks that require WEP authentication are left off the list, which limits the use of Site Monitor to older networks not using WEP or networks with intentionally loose security, such as neighborhood or community networks.

If you are currently associated with an open network, the Site Monitor begins by displaying the AP list, which is shown in Figure 12-34. By default, the AP list shows only the signal-to-noise ratio (SNR), but it can be set to display the signal and noise figures themselves. One field not shown in the figure is the AP name, which is available only when the access point is also a Lucent access point.

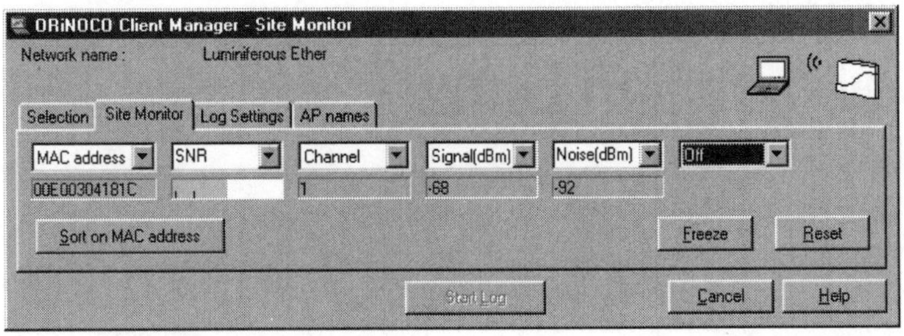

Figure 12-34. Network details

CHAPTER 13
Using 802.11 on Linux

Of the operating systems currently in wide use and active development, Unix environments offer the flexibility and stability required by power users and network administrators. When new hardware hits the market, the technical staff responsible for making purchase recommendations often asks about Linux support because of the additional functionality that can frequently be gained from the environment.

By now, though, the successful 802.11 hardware vendors have come to understand that Linux support increases sales and customer satisfaction without imposing significant additional costs. Linux friendliness among vendors was not always the case. One common strategy in past years was to release a fully featured driver as a binary module and a limited-functionality open source driver. What this strategy failed to take into account was the wide diversity of Linux hardware platforms and the difficulty in compiling and troubleshooting a closed-source binary driver without low-level documentation. Binary-only drivers are usually painful to install and troubleshoot, while open source counterparts are developed rapidly and are well-supported by the user community. Vendors that tried the two-driver approach often watched in shock as the open source driver quickly evolved to match the functionality of the closed-source driver, thanks to the magic of rapid collaborative development. Linux users have rejected the closed-source approach for a variety of reasons, and the marketplace has rejected products that do not have open source drivers available. This could be just a coincidence, but that is unlikely.

In recognition of the pain of installing a binary driver, this chapter describes only the open source solutions for 802.11 networking on Linux. Installing and troubleshooting open source drivers is possible on a wide variety of supported hardware, and it is a well-known procedure that many people use each day. Linux drivers for Lucent-based cards are now part of the standard Personal Computer Memory Card Industry Association (PCMCIA) distribution, and I expect that *linux-wlan* will eventually become part of the standard operating-system distribution. As with Windows drivers, installing wireless cards on Linux creates Ethernet interfaces. Many Linux drivers expose an Ethernet interface through the kernel. (Frequently, wireless interfaces even have the *eth* prefix!) Programs can use the Ethernet interface to send and receive data at the link layer, and the driver handles Ethernet-to-802.11 conversions. Many of the things you would expect to see with an Ethernet interface remain the same. ARP works identically, and the IP configuration is done with the same utilities provided by the operating-system distribution. *ifconfig* can even be used to monitor the interface status and see the data sent and received.

A Few Words on 802.11 Hardware

As with other devices running under Linux, the more you know about the hardware, the better off you are. Only a handful of 802.11 chipset manufacturers exist. Most vendors use chipsets produced by Intersil (*http://www.intersil.com*, formerly known as Harris Semiconductor). Intersil's industry-leading position is the result of the success of its PRISM chipset. The initial PRISM, whose name is an acronym for Programmable Radio in the ISM band, was a common solution for vendors seeking a 2-Mbps DSSS 802.11 solution. When 802.11b was standardized in 1999, Intersil brought out the PRISM-2 chipset, which supported the 5.5-Mbps and 11-Mbps data rates.

Intersil's chipsets are used by Linksys, Nortel/Netgear, D-Link, and SMC for interface cards. Several new laptops with integrated 802.11 support are hitting the market, and many of these wireless-enabled laptops are powered by Intersil chipsets. Choosing between the supported Intersil-based cards is a personal trade-off between price, performance, range, and other factors.

Lucent's Hermes chipset is the major competitor to Intersil's PRISM. Unlike Intersil, Lucent also produces interface cards for the end user. Lucent's cards were first to market, so they are quite common. Several vendors seeking to bring a wireless solution to market chose OEM Lucent gear; the most notable example is Apple's AirPort, which is based on Lucent technology. OEM and rebranding relationships are quite common. Table 13-1 divides the major industry vendors by the radio chipset used in each vendor's cards, which should help you in choosing which driver to use. (In some cases, the OEM relationship is little more than a new sticker. Vendor B simply takes Vendor A's equipment and slaps a new logo on it.)

Table 13-1. The silicon behind the brand

Lucent chipset-based cards	Intersil PRISM-based cards
Lucent Wavelan/IEEE and Orinoco	Linksys
Cabletron/Enterasys RoamAbout	SMC
Apple AirPort	Compaq (WL100 and WL200)
Compaq (WL110, WL210, and WL215)	D-Link
IBM High Rate Wireless LAN	Nokia
HP 802.11b Wireless LAN	Cisco (Aironet)
Dell TrueMobile 1150 (earlier versions were OEM Aironet cards)	

In addition to the radio chipset, cards must have a MAC controller. Most cards on the market use an Intersil MAC controller. Several first-generation cards used an AMD Am930 MAC controller but have switched to the integrated MAC controller in the PRISM-2 chipset. Cisco's Aironet product line uses an Aironet-developed MAC controller with a PRISM-2 radio chipset.

The PC Card form factor is the dominant form factor, though it is not used exclusively. PC Cards can be used directly in portable computers and can be plugged into PCMCIA interfaces for other purposes. Many, but by no means all, access points use PC Card slots instead of fixed radio interfaces, which, conveniently, also allows for upgrades by swapping out the radio interface. Even PCI-based 802.11 solutions use PC Cards. Typically, a PCI solution consists of a PC Card plus a PCI carrier card with a PC Card interface.

PCMCIA Support on Linux

Most add-on 802.11 solutions for laptop computers are based on the PCMCIA form factor. Adding 802.11 support to Linux requires an understanding of how the PCMCIA subsystem in Linux is put together and how it works to enable drivers for PCMCIA cards.

PCMCIA Card Services Overview

Card Services grew out of an attempt to simplify system configuration. Rather than dedicating system resources to individual devices, the host system maintained a pool of resources for PC Cards and allocated resources as necessary. Figure 13-1 shows the procedure by which cards are configured on Linux.

When a card is inserted, the *cardmgr* process orchestrates the configuration of the device, as shown in Figure 13-1. The orchestration pulls together system resources, kernel components, and kernel driver modules through the configuration files stored in */etc/pcmcia*. Roughly speaking, the host takes the following steps:

1. A card is inserted into an empty PC Card socket, and *cardmgr* is notified of this event. In addition to any hardware operations (such as supplying power to the socket), *cardmgr* queries the *card information structure* (CIS) to determine the type of card inserted and the resources it needs. For more information on the CIS, see the sidebar "Card Information Structure."

2. *cardmgr* consults the card database stored in */etc/pcmcia/config* to determine which card was inserted. Part of the configuration is to associate cards with a *class*. For the purposes of configuring network cards, the important point to note is that items in the *network* class have additional network configuration operations performed on them later. The card is identified by the CIS data from step 1, and the class setting is set in the main system configuration file. At this point,

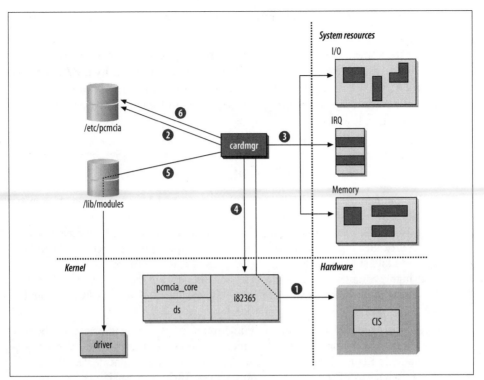

Figure 13-1. Linux PCMCIA configuration system

cardmgr beeps once. Successful identification results in a high-pitched beep; unsuccessful identifications are indicated by a beep of lower pitch.

3. *cardmgr* determines which resources are available to allocate to the card. Blocks of system resources are reserved for PCMCIA card use in the main configuration file, and *cardmgr* doles out resources as needed to cards. The number of I/O ports and the size of the memory window are obtained from the CIS.

4. Resources allocated by *cardmgr* are programmed into the PCMCIA controller, which is depicted in Figure 13-1 as interaction with the device driver. PCMCIA controllers implement *resource steering* to map resources required by the card onto available system resources. A card may ask for an interrupt, but the actual assigned interrupt is irrelevant. In operation, the card simply asks the PCMCIA controller to raise an interrupt, and the controller is responsible for looking up the interrupt assigned to the socket and firing the correct interrupt line.

5. Part of the configuration information obtained from the lookup in step 2 is the name of the device driver that should be loaded to use the newly inserted card. Drivers for PCMCIA cards are implemented as kernel modules. As part of the insertion process, the driver is informed of resources allocated in step 4. With

proper module dependencies, module stacking can be used to load multiple modules.

6. Further user-space configuration is performed based on the class of the device. Network cards, for example, have further configuration done by the */etc/pcmcia/network* script, which is configured by editing */etc/pcmcia/network.opts*. Successful configuration in this step generates a second high beep, and failure is reported with a low beep.

Card Information Structure

To enable automatic configuration, every PC Card has a blob of data that enables the card to describe itself to the host system. The blob is called the *card information structure* (CIS) and takes a relatively straightforward link-list format. The building blocks of the CIS are called *tuples* because they have three components: a type code to identify the type of tuple, a length field, and a series of data bytes. Tuple formats range from trivial to highly complex, which is why this book does not attempt to classify them any further. Brave, stout-hearted readers can order the specification from the PCMCIA and use the *dump_cis* tool on Linux to read the CIS of inserted cards.

The CIS assists the host in automatic configuration by reporting information about itself to the host operating system. For example, network interface cards identify themselves as such, and the CIS enables the Card Services software to allocate the appropriate resources such as I/O ports and interrupt request (IRQ) lines. On Linux, the system administrator uses configuration files to match the CIS data to the driver.

PCMCIA Card Services Installation

Installation of Card Services is documented in the PCMCIA-HOWTO. Both the software and documentation are available from *http://pcmcia-cs.sourceforge.net/*. Begin by unpacking the software and configuring it with *make config*.

Card Services asks for the current kernel source tree and picks relevant options out of it. In addition, it asks four questions. *Trusting* versions of the utilities allow operations by nonroot users, and are therefore set to no by default. *CardBus support* is included for newer cards, though no PRISM-2 cards currently use the CardBus interface. *PnP resource checking* is not required unless the computer hardware has plug-and-play hardware. Enabling this option can cause problems on computers that do not have PnP hardware and on several laptops. Finally, you must specify a module install directory. By default, modules are installed in */lib/modules/<version>/modules*, in which *<version>* is the version of the kernel source tree.

```
[root@bloodhound pcmcia-cs-3.1.28]# make config

-------- Linux PCMCIA Configuration Script --------
```

```
The default responses for each question are correct for most users.
Consult the PCMCIA-HOWTO for additional info about each option.

Linux source directory [/usr/src/linux]:

The kernel source tree is version 2.2.19.
The current kernel build date is Sat Aug 25 07:11:52 2001.

Build 'trusting' versions of card utilities (y/n) [n]:
Include 32-bit (CardBus) card support (y/n) [y]:
Include PnP BIOS resource checking (y/n) [n]:
Module install directory [/lib/modules/2.2.19]:

Kernel configuration options:
     Symmetric multiprocessing support is disabled.
     PCI BIOS support is enabled.
     Power management (APM) support is enabled.
     SCSI support is disabled.
     IEEE 1394 (FireWire) support is disabled.
     Networking support is enabled.
      Radio network interface support is enabled.
      Token Ring device support is disabled.
      Fast switching is disabled.
      Frame Diverter is disabled.
     Module version checking is enabled.
     Kernel debugging support is disabled.
     /proc filesystem support is enabled.
     Maximum physical memory: 1GB

It looks like you have a System V init file setup.

X Windows include files found.
Forms library not installed.
     If you wish to build the 'cardinfo' control panel, you need the Forms
     library and the X Windows include files.  See the HOWTO for details.

Configuration successful.
```

After configuration, the installation can be accomplished with *make install*. Most configuration information is automatically detected from the environment without difficulty, though you need to set the PCIC environment variable to the correct type of PCMCIA controller. Two major types of controller are supported: the Databook TCIC-2 and compatibles, and the Intel i82365SL and compatibles. On RedHat and derived distributions, the variable is set in */etc/sysconfig/pcmcia*. Nearly all systems should set it to *i82365*.

Troubleshooting Resource Conflicts

One of the revolutionary developments hyped by PCMCIA card vendors was that users were no longer directly responsible for maintaining low-level hardware configurations on IBM-compatible hardware. In many respects, this hype was drastically overblown because users are still responsible for maintaining the resource pools used by PCMCIA Card Services to draw from for automatic configuration, and therefore they must still be familiar with the hardware configuration. Three major resources are managed by Card Services for users: IRQ lines, I/O ports, and direct memory access (DMA) channels. DMA channels are not required by network cards, however, and are not discussed in this section.

IRQs

IRQs are used by devices that must use of the CPU periodically. Interfaces use IRQs so that when a buffer fills, the system CPU can be notified and drain the buffer. One limitation of the PC architecture is that it has only 15 available IRQs, and many are occupied by standard hardware. Table 13-2 shows common IRQ usage, which may help you determine which IRQs are available for PCMCIA cards. Disabling any extra components frees the IRQ. Table 13-2 also shows common IRQ settings on PC hardware. As a rule of thumb, IRQs 3, 5, and 10 are readily available on most machines.

Table 13-2. Common IRQ settings

IRQ number	Common usage	Purpose
0	System timer	Fires 18 times per second to maintain coarse clocking.
1	Keyboard	Allows operating system to monitor keyboard strokes by user.
2	Cascade	Two interrupt controller chips are used; the second controls IRQs 8–15 and is wired into IRQ 2 on the primary.
3	Second serial port	The second and fourth serial ports (COM2 and COM4 under Windows) both use IRQ 3. If only one serial port is present, IRQ 3 may be used by expansion devices.
4	First/third serial port	The first and third serial ports (COM1 and COM3 under Windows) both use IRQ 4. Generally, it is not a good idea to use IRQ 4 for expansion devices because loss of the serial port also means that terminal-emulation software cannot be used.
5	Second parallel port	Most systems have only one parallel port, but IRQ 5 is also commonly used for sound cards.
6	Floppy controller	All systems have floppy disks, which can be especially important on portable computers.
7	First parallel port	The first parallel port can frequently be disabled on laptops without an issue, unless the parallel port is used extensively for printing.
8	RTC	The Real-Time Clock maintains finer-grained timers
9	Video (older systems)	Older systems required an IRQ for the video controller, and it was typically assigned to IRQ 9. Most video controllers are now on the PCI bus and do not require a dedicated IRQ.
10		Usually available for expansion devices.
11	Usually PCI bus or SCSI controller	Generally not available for expansion devices.
12	Usually PS/2 mouse port	Generally not available.

Table 13-2. Common IRQ settings (continued)

IRQ number	Common usage	Purpose
13	FPU	The floating-point unit IRQ is used by the math coprocessor, even on systems with a CPU with an integrated math coprocessor such as the Pentium series.
14	Primary IDE	The first IDE channel is used by the main system hard disk, and thus IRQ 14 is almost never available on a portable system.
15	Secondary IDE	Portable systems typically place the CD-ROM on IRQ 15, making this IRQ unavailable for use.

I/O ports

I/O addresses are used for bidirectional communication between the system and a peripheral device. They tend to be somewhat poorly organized, and many devices have overlapping defaults. Each I/O port can be used to transfer a byte between the peripheral device and the CPU. Most devices require the ability to transfer multiple bytes at a time, so a block of ports is assigned to the device. The lowest port number is also called the base I/O address. A second parameter describes the size of the I/O window. Table 13-3 lists some of the common port assignments. Refer to your hardware vendor's documentation for details on additional devices such as IR ports, USB controllers, the PCMCIA controller, and any resources that may be required by motherboard components.

Table 13-3. Common I/O ports

Device name	I/O range (size)
Communication ports	
First parallel port	0x3bc–0x3bf (4)
First serial port	0x3f8–0x3ff (8)
Second serial port	0x2f8–0x2ff (8)
Disk drives	
Primary IDE	master: 0x1f0–0x1f7 (8)
	slave: 0x3f6–0x3f7 (2)
Secondary IDE	master: 0x170–0x177 (8)
	slave: 0x376 (1)
Floppy controller	0x3f0–0x3f5 (6)
Input devices	
Keyboard	0x060 (1)
	0x064 (1)
Multimedia/gaming	
Sound card	0x220–0x22f (16)
	FM Synth: 0x388–0x38b (4)
	MIDI: 0x330–0x331 (2)

Table 13-3. Common I/O ports (continued)

Device name	I/O range (size)
Joystick/Game port	0x200–0x207 (8)
System devices	
Interrupt controllers	0x020–0x021 (2)
	0x0a0–0x0a1 (2)
DMA controllers	DMA channels 0-3: 0x000–0x00f (16)
	Page registers: 0x080–0x08f (16)
	DMA channels 4-7: 0x0c0–0x0df
CMOS/real time clock	0x070–0x073 (4)
Speaker	0x061
Math coprocessor	0x0f0–0x0ff (16)

linux-wlan-ng for Intersil-Based Cards

The most commonly used driver for PRISM-based cards is the *linux-wlan* open source driver developed by Absolute Value Systems. In a shining example for other vendors, Intersil has actively supported the *linux-wlan* project. Two subprojects exist. The original *linux-wlan* code supports cards based on the original PRISM chipset, which generally run at 2 Mbps, and the newer *linux-wlan-ng* codebase supports cards based on the PRISM-2 chipset running at 11 Mbps. *linux-wlan-ng* supports most cards based on the PRISM-2 chipset.* The examples in this section were written with a Linksys WPC11 as the example card, largely because of its affordability relative to other PRISM-2 cards.

At this point, most users will be interested in 11-Mbps cards supported by *linux-wlan-ng*. Both projects aim toward developing a complete 802.11 layer for Linux. Currently, both projects support simple encapsulation of 802.11 frames and RFC 1042 encapsulation. In practice, this poses a problem only with strange access points that support only 802.1h translation.

Prerequisites

Before starting the installation of *linux-wlan-ng*, there are some housekeeping tasks to take care of. Compile-time configuration is taken care of in part by pulling some configuration information out of the kernel configuration and the PCMCIA utility configuration. Most distributions include the option of installing source code but do

---

* Nokia's C11x cards are based on the PRISM-2, but the addition of the smart-card reader changed the programming interface enough so that the C11x is not supported by *linux-wlan-ng*.

not include the configuration used to build the kernel or any of the additional software packages.

Officially, *linux-wlan* is developed against kernels later than 2.0.36 and PCMCIA Card Services (*pcmcia-cs*) later than 3.0.9, but *linux-wlan-ng* was largely developed against kernel 2.2 and PCMCIA services 3.1. Compiling *linux-wlan-ng* requires configured source trees for both the kernel and PCMCIA, so during the preinstallation process, it is a good idea to update both components to the latest versions available. Refer to the documentation bundled with *linux-wlan-ng* to get an idea of the software environments it has been tested against and upgrade to current versions. Kernel configuration and compilation has been extensively documented elsewhere; refer to the documentation for your distribution. Card Services software is now hosted at *http://pcmcia-cs.sourceforge.net*, and documentation is bundled with the source package. The examples in this section were written using kernel 2.2.19 and *pcmcia-cs* 3.1.28, though there is nothing specific about them.

Kernel compilation

Because the configuration in the kernel source tree is used by the subsequent configuration of both PCMCIA Card Services and *linux-wlan*, it must match the currently running kernel. Many problems can be avoided, and countless hours can be saved if you begin the process by downloading clean kernel source and configuring from scratch. *linux-wlan* does not require any specific options for support other than general network support, but it is useful for other reasons to enable certain options. The ISC Dynamic Host Configuration Protocol (DHCP) client, for example, requires that both the packet socket (*CONFIG_PACKET*) and socket filtering (*CONFIG_FILTER*) be enabled. Some applications of the driver also are enabled by the kernel/user network link driver (*CONFIG_NETLINK*). Kernel configuration and compilation is extensively documented in both online and offline resources and may have been installed with your documentation. Kernel source code is available from *ftp://ftp.kernel.org* and countless mirror sites worldwide.

Compiling and Installing linux-wlan-ng

The first step is to get the software from *http://www.linux-wlan.org*. Version numbering follows the Linux kernel convention, with odd minor numbers used for development versions and even minor numbers used for stable production versions. The software can be obtained by FTP from *ftp://ftp.linux-wlan.org/pub/linux-wlan-ng/*; the latest version as this book was written was 0.1.8-pre13.

Compile-time configuration

Run *make config* to configure the software. A configuration script is run, and you need to supply the location of your configured kernel source and PCMCIA Card Services source trees. A few minor questions follow; these guidelines may help you answer those questions:

- Building with debugging information compiled in is a good idea when you're troubleshooting. Debugging can be disabled easily, and the code is a minuscule performance hit when compiled in and not used.
- Kernel PCMCIA is the PCMCIA software included with the 2.4 kernel series. Users of kernel Version 2.4 need to choose whether to use Kernel PCMCIA or PCMCIA Card Services; users of earlier kernels must use PCMCIA Card Services.
- PLX-based adapters are PCI wireless adapters. Most users will use PCMCIA cards and can disable PLX support.
- Card Services drivers support PCMCIA cards and should be enabled.

A sample configuration looks something like this:

```
[gast@bloodhound linux-wlan-ng-0.1.8-pre13]$ make config
-------------- Linux WLAN Configuration Script -------------
The default responses are correct for most users.
Linux source directory [/usr/src/linux]:
The kernel source tree is version 2.2.19.
The current kernel build date is Sat Aug 25 07:11:52 2001.
pcmcia-cs source dir [/usr/src/pcmcia-cs-3.1.28]:
Alternate target install root directory on host []:
  Module install directory [/lib/modules/2.2.19]:
PCMCIA script directory [/etc/pcmcia]:
It looks like you have a System V init file setup.
Target Architecture? (i386, ppc, or alpha) [i386]:
Prefix for build host compiler? (rarely needed) []:
Compiling with a cross compiler? (y/n) [n]:
Build for debugging (see doc/config.debug) (y/n) [n]: y
Build for Kernel PCMCIA? (y/n) [n]:
Build PLX???? based PCI (_plx) adapter drivers? (y/n) [n]:
Build PCMCIA Card Services (_cs) drivers? (y/n) [y]:
Configuration successful.
```

Building the software

Run *make all* to build the software. After some compilation messages, four main components are compiled:

wlanctl-ng
> The general administrative utility used to control the current running configuration and change the state of the hardware.

wlancfg
> Used to change values in the management information base and alter the configuration.

p80211.o

A generic 802.11 utility layer for Linux, implemented as a kernel module. It includes data structures required to handle buffers, build frames, translate between the supported frame types (RFC 1042-encapsulated, 802.1h, vanilla encapsulated, and the raw packet buffers used by the kernel), interact with the network devices in the kernel, and perform the functions placed in the MAC Layer Management Entity (MLME).

prism2_cs.o

The kernel module driver for PRISM-2–based cards. It implements the hardware interface to the Intersil HFA384x chipset used in supported cards, implements hardware interrupt service, allows user-space utilities to gather statistics and counters data from the hardware, and enables the management operations discussed in Chapter 7, such as scanning, joining, authentication, and association.

Installing the software

After compilation, become *root* and run *make install* to install the software. By default, the two administration programs (*wlanctl-ng* and *wlancfg*) are placed in */sbin*, and the two modules are installed in the module directory tree that corresponds to your current kernel version. On kernel Version 2.2.19, for example, *p80211.o* would be installed in */lib/modules/2.2.19/net* and *prism2_cs.o* would be placed in */lib/modules/2.2.19/pcmcia*.

The installation also places some configuration files in the main PCMCIA Card Services directory, which is */etc/pcmcia* by default. *wlan-ng.conf* contains card definitions for hardware known to work with *linux-wlan-ng*. It is copied to the Card Services directory, and a directive is put at the end of the main card definition file, */etc/pcmcia/config*, to include the PRISM-2 card definitions. The configuration script for wireless interfaces, *wlan-ng*, is also placed in */etc/pcmcia*. *wlan-ng* pulls in configuration options from an auxiliary option file, *wlan-ng.opts*. If either *wlan-ng* or *wlan-ng.opts* exists, the older versions will be backed up and will receive the suffix *.O*.

Administration of the 802.11 Interface

The main administrative tool in *linux-wlan-ng* is *wlanctl-ng*, a tool to control the internal state of the driver through *ioctl()* commands. As an example, consider the *wlanctl-ng* command used to join a network:

```
[root@bloodhound]# /sbin/wlanctl-ng wlan0 lnxreq_autojoin ssid="Luminferous Ether" \
authtype=opensystem
message=lnxreq_autojoin
  ssid=Luminferous Ether
  authtype=opensystem
  resultcode=success
```

Commands operate on an interface, which is supplied as the first argument. The command to perform is the second argument. In the join command, two additional arguments are required. One is the SSID, so the kernel driver can identify the Beacon frames corresponding to the desired network. SSIDs with spaces can be used, provided that quotation marks are used to delimit the SSID. The other argument is the authentication type. Shared-key authentication is required if the WEP key is set.

wlanctl-ng commands fall into three broad classes. Commands that begin with *dot11req_*, such as *dot11req_mibset*, work with data structures specified in 802.11. The second class of commands, which begin with *p2req_*, work with the PRISM-2 chipset. A third class, prefaced with *lnxreq_*, are commands specific to the Linux driver.

WEP keys are set by writing the MIB variables corresponding to the default key on the interface the key must be set for:

```
[root@bloodhound]# wlanctl-ng wlan0 dot11req_mibset \
mibattribute=dot11WEPDefaultKey3=01:02:03:04:05
message=dot11req_mibset
    mibattribute=dot11WEPDefaultKey3=01:02:03:04:05
    resultcode=success
```

Some commands are not implemented and return a result code of *not implemented*. One such command is *dot11req_scan*, which should run a generalized active scan.

One command that network administrators are likely to find near and dear is the command that enables promiscuous mode packet capture.* The driver command is *lnxreq_wlansniff*, and it takes two additional arguments. One is the channel to sniff on, and the final argument is the enable flag, which can be used to enable and disable the sniffing functionality.

```
[root@bloodhound]# wlanctl-ng wlan0 lnxreq_wlansniff channel=1 enable=true
message=lnxreq_wlansniff
    enable=true
    channel=1
    resultcode=success
```

For convenience, I have written shell functions around the *lnxreq_wlansniff* command to cut down on typing. Both shell functions take two arguments: the interface name and the channel. Some users may not use multiple 802.11 cards and may choose to have the shell function take just one argument instead. In any case, here are the functions I use, which you are free to customize:

```
wlan-promisc ()
{
    /sbin/wlanctl-ng $1 lnxreq_wlansniff channel=$2 enable=true
}
```

---

* Promiscuous mode packet capture was disabled in *linux-wlan*-0.1.7 and later, but patches to enable the functionality are available. See Chapter 16 for details.

```
wlan-normal ()
{
    /sbin/wlanctl-ng $1 lnxreq_wlansniff channel=$2 enable=false
}
```

To activate promiscuous packet capture on channel 5, I run *wlan-promisc wlan0 5*. When promiscuous capture is activated, it is not possible to use the network for communication. To restore network connectivity, simply run *wlan-normal wlan0 5*. With only one wireless interface, the shell functions can be simplified even further by hardcoding *wlan0* as the interface used by the function and taking only the channel number as an argument.

IP addresing

Setting IP addresses is distribution-specific. On RedHat and derivative distributions, including Mandrake, configuration is stored in */etc/sysconfig/network-scripts*, with data for each interface shown in *ifcfg-interface*. *linux-wlan-ng* interfaces begin with *wlan*: *wlan0*, *wlan1*, and so forth. An example static IP configuration for the first wireless LAN interface would hold IP address and netmask information just as with any other interface:

```
[root@bloodhound network-scripts]# cat ifcfg-wlan0
DEVICE=wlan0
BOOTPROTO=static
IPADDR=192.168.200.125
NETMASK=255.255.255.0
NETWORK=192.168.200.0
BROADCAST=192.168.200.255
ONBOOT=no
```

Bringing up the interface is a matter of running *ifup* with the interface name as an argument as *root*. Most Linux kernels are built without bridging support and cannot by default be configured with two interfaces on the same logical IP subnet. This is often a danger for stations with wireless LAN interfaces because the wireless interface is sometimes used to replace an existing wired interface.

```
[root@bloodhound network-scripts]# ifup wlan0
```

Dynamic IP configuration with DHCP is allowed; refer to your distribution's documentation for details on enabling dynamic boot protocols. DHCP configuration depends on forming a successful association with an access point. If the association fails, the DHCP discovery packets result in "not associated" error messages in the log.

Configuring linux-wlan-ng

Card definitions are stored in */etc/pcmcia/config*. At the end of the file, there is a line that reads *source ./*.conf*. This line enables additional PCMCIA driver packages to add card definitions. *linux-wlan-ng* adds the file *wlan-ng.conf*, which is a series of driver associations. As an example, consider the definition of the Linksys WPC11 card:

```
card "Linksys WPC11 11Mbps 802.11b WLAN Card"
    version "Instant Wireless ", " Network PC CARD", "Version 01.02"
    bind "prism2_cs"
```

The first line is a text string used to identify the card to the human user, and the *bind* directive specifies which driver will be loaded to support the card. The *version* strings are used to match the CIS of the card, which can be viewed using the *dump_cis* utility:

```
[root@bloodhound]# dump_cis
Socket 0:
  dev_info
    NULL Ons, 512b
  attr_dev_info
    SRAM 500ns, 1kb
  vers_1 5.0, "Instant Wireless ", " Network PC CARD", "Version 01.02",
    ""
  manfid 0x0156, 0x002
  funcid network_adapter
  lan_technology wireless
  lan_speed 1 mb/sec
  lan_speed 2 mb/sec
  lan_speed 5 mb/sec
  lan_speed 11 mb/sec
  lan_media 2.4_GHz
  lan_node_id 00 04 5a 0d 0c 70
  lan_connector Closed connector standard
  config base 0x03e0 mask 0x0001 last_index 0x01
  cftable_entry 0x01 [default]
    Vcc Vmin 4750mV Vmax 5250mV Iavg 300mA Ipeak 300mA
    Idown 10mA
    io 0x0000-0x003f [lines=6] [16bit]
    irq mask 0xffff [level] [pulse]

Socket 1:
  no CIS present
```

Note that the CIS specifies how large an I/O window is necessary. In this case, 64 (0x3F) bytes of I/O space are required by the card. When the card is inserted, the kernel configuration prints out the resources assigned to the driver in */var/log/kernel/info*:

```
Oct 26 21:03:38 bloodhound kernel: prism2_cs: index 0x01: Vcc 5.0, irq 10, io
0x0100-0x13f
```

In addition to the card associations in *wlan-ng.conf*, the configuration script *wlan-ng* and its option file *wlan-ng.opts* are installed in */etc/pcmcia*. *wlan-ng* is called whenever a PRISM-2 wireless card is inserted. It identifies the card, associates with an access point or starts an independent BSS if desired, and initializes the network interface using whatever hooks are provided by the Linux distribution. *wlan-ng.opts* is used to configure the desired SSID and WEP keys.

Selecting a network to join

To configure the network to join, some parameters in *wlan-ng.opts* must be changed. One section of the script is labeled "STA START" and contains the network parameters AuthType and DesiredSSID:

```
#========STA START=====================================
AuthType="opensystem"
DesiredSSID="linux-wlan"
```

AuthType can be set to *opensystem* for a network not employing access control, and *sharedkey* for networks that use the shared-key authentication mechanism of WEP. The *DesiredSSID* parameter must be set to the SSID announced by the Beacon frames for the network that the station will join.

Configuring WEP

Stations that use WEP must also configure WEP-related parameters in *wlan-ng.opts*:

```
#========WEP===========================================
dot11PrivacyInvoked=true
dot11WEPDefaultKeyID=2

dot11WEPDefaultKey0=01:02:03:04:05
dot11WEPDefaultKey1=01:02:03:04:05:06:07:08:09:0a:0b:0c:0d
dot11WEPDefaultKey2=
dot11WEPDefaultKey3=
```

Several settings matter only for access points; the settings that matter for stations are:

dot11PrivacyInvoked
: This must be set to true to enable WEP. If it is set to false, WEP is disabled.

dot11WEPDefaultKeyID
: This is set to 0, 1, 2, or 3, depending on which of the WEP keys are used on the network.

Four dot11WEPDefaultKeyXs (in which X is 0, 1, 2, or 3)
: These are used to program the WEP keys themselves. Keys are entered like MAC addresses, in which each byte is entered as a two-character hexadecimal number, and the bytes are separated by colons.

Enabling debugging output

If the *linux-wlan-ng* module was built with debugging code enabled, the PCMCIA Card Services system can be set up to pass configuration options to the driver. Module options are configured in */etc/pcmcia/config.opts*, using the *opts* parameter to the *module* directive, like this:

```
module "prism2_cs" opts "prism2_debug=3"
```

Debugging can be enabled for both the protocol module (*p80211*) and the PRISM-2 hardware driver (*prism2_cs*). Debugging of the protocol module is enabled with the *wlan_debug* option, and debugging of the driver is enabled with the *prism2_debug* option. Five debugging levels are defined, with higher levels increasing the log output; Table 13-4 describes them in detail. Debugging levels are cumulative, so level 3 includes all messages from level 2 plus additional information.

Table 13-4. linux-wlan-ng debug levels

Level	Meaning
1	Error messages for rare exceptions.
2	More exceptions are logged.
3	Basic status output.
4	Additional status output.
5	Function entry and exit.

After making changes to *config.opts*, the card manager must be restarted so that the options are passed to the driver when the card is inserted. The easiest way to restart *cardmgr* is to send it the HUP signal:

```
kill -HUP `ps aux | grep cardmgr | grep -v grep | awk '{ print $2 }'`
```

Using linux-wlan-ng

Using wireless LAN interfaces driven by *linux-wlan-ng* is no different from using regular wired Ethernet interfaces. Configuration is identical to wired interfaces, and operations are similar. System administrators can, for the most part, treat 802.11 interfaces like Ethernet interfaces, but with higher latency. The higher latency is due partly to the lower bit rate of the wireless medium and partly to the requirement for fully acknowledged frame exchanges.

Common Problems

Most common problems are really resource conflicts, but resource conflicts may manifest themselves as a variety of error messages. Tracking down resource conflicts is a large task described in more detail in the section "Troubleshooting Resource Conflicts." Resource conflict tracking is often a tedious process of listing out the resources commonly used by a system and attempting to identify the conflict. It can be particularly annoying on laptop hardware because of the number of built-in devices that may be sucking up resources without extensive notification. This section describes the common problems that users may face before the next section delves into the hairy business of resolving resource conflicts.

Compilation difficulties

Most compilation difficulties can be traced to relying on an improper source tree for a dependent package. The most reliable way to install *linux-wlan-ng* is to first build both a new kernel and new PCMCIA package from a clean source before attempting to build *linux-wlan-ng*. Although this takes time, it does guarantee that the compile-time configuration stored in the source tree matches the running version, and it will, therefore, eliminate most compilation problems.

Cards are identified as "anonymous memory card"

Card Services on Linux attempts to identify cards based on configuration information stored on the card itself in the CIS on the PCMCIA card. If Card Services is unable to identify a card, as a last resort, it identifies a card as an anonymous memory card. This error message almost always means that there is a resource conflict; as a result of the conflict, Card Services software is unable to communicate with the card to read the identifying data structures on the card. Vary the resource exclusion ranges to resolve the conflict; see "Troubleshooting Resource Conflicts" earlier in this chapter.

"Tx attempt prior to association, frame dropped" error message

This message is quite self-explanatory: a frame was queued for transmission before the station successfully associated with an access point. Several things might cause this error:

- If the desired SSID is not found, no association is made.
- Authentication is a precondition of association. If the authentication type is mismatched or the WEP key used for authentication is incorrect, the association fails.
- Resource conflicts can interfere with the sending and receiving of frames, which may cause transmissions (and therefore authentication or associations) to fail. Reconsider resource allocations and PCMCIA Card Services configuration.

Odd behavior from the lights on the card

linux-wlan-ng does not try to control the lights on the card in a consistent way between different card vendors. Generally speaking, one light becomes solid when the station associates with an access point, and a second light blinks to indicate traffic. If your card behaves differently, don't panic. Check at the access point for an association; if an association exists, then the card is functioning normally but uses the lights in a different manner. Naturally, the truly brave may attempt to rewrite the driver, but for most of the world, it is easier simply to note the behavior of the lights.

Dropped sessions

Associations may be dropped for a variety of reasons, many of which are not the fault of the client wireless LAN card. One frequent cause of this behavior is access points that conserve resources by timing out idle associations. Nokia access points are notable for this behavior.

The original *linux-wlan* package for PRISM-1–based cards did not reassociate. *linux-wlan-ng* attempts to reassociate when an association times out, but it may not always be successful. If timeouts must always be avoided, run a script on the wireless station to send traffic periodically to prevent the association from timing out.

"MAC initialization failure, result=xxx"

The first major task for the PRISM-2 driver is to initialize the MAC controller chip on the card. The error code is one major clue. Positive result codes indicate that the firmware is at fault, and negative error codes are due to driver faults. Frequently, the error is due to a timeout period expiring; retry the operation to ensure that the error is caused by the system and not by a timeout expiration. Firmware problems are rare and generally seen only when the firmware loaded on the card was bad or the firmware load was incomplete. Driver problems are usually due to resource conflicts, especially with I/O ports. In some cases, a laptop with 5-volt PCMCIA slots may experience problems with a 3-volt card, though the failure usually happens later in the initialization process. I saw this message on an IBM ThinkPad T21 when the card was inserted, and the system was on battery power. If the T21 was plugged into AC power, however, the driver would load and configure without a hitch.

Agere (Lucent) Orinoco

Wireless networking is far older than the 802.11 standard. The first commercial wireless network hardware was manufactured by the WaveLAN division of AT&T and gained market acceptance in the early 1990s. When Lucent was spun off from AT&T in the late 1990s, the WaveLAN division, like most communications product manufacturing at AT&T, was made a part of Lucent.

Early WaveLAN hardware was a completely proprietary system. After 802.11 was finally standardized in 1997, new hardware that complied with the standard was sold under the WaveLAN brand. To distinguish the standards-compliant cards from the proprietary cards, the former were called "WaveLAN IEEE" cards, while the latter were simply "WaveLAN" cards.

As the market for 802.11 hardware continued to develop, Lucent decided to rename the WaveLAN division under another brand name. The new name, Orinoco, comes from the third largest river system in the world. During the rainy season in South America, the Orinoco swells with fresh rainfall flowing in from over 200 tributaries. At its peak, the river grows to over 10 miles wide and more than 300 feet deep. Nearly 1,000 miles of the Orinoco's 1,300 miles are navigable; it is no wonder that the river's name is derived from the native words for "a place to paddle."

Lucent's initial strategy for support on open source platforms was to offer a choice of drivers. Two drivers were available. A closed-source proprietary binary driver, *wavelan2_cs*, provided full functionality largely equivalent to the drivers available for other platforms. A second, less functional open source driver, *wvlan_cs*, was made available under the GPL. For a variety of reasons, the proprietary driver was shunned in favor of the open source driver, and a devoted group of programmers enhanced the open source driver until it was equivalent to the proprietary driver.

Two open source drivers are now available for Lucent cards on Linux, depending on the kernel version employed. Kernel Versions 2.0 and 2.2 use the older *wvlan_cs* driver bundled with the *pcmcia-cs* package; kernel Version 2.4 uses the *orinoco_cs* driver in the kernel. The older *wvlan_cs* driver was based on a low-level library provided by Lucent, which was difficult to maintain and was a recurring source of bugs. Rather than continuing along an evolutionary dead-end, the maintainers of *wvlan_cs* learned from the *wlan-ng* driver and rewrote the lower layers of *wvlan_cs*. The result was *orinoco_cs*, a much more stable and robust driver. (*orinoco_cs* was originally known as *dldwd_cs*, which stood for David's Less Dodgy WaveLAN Driver!) *wvlan_cs* is no longer being maintained, and new installations should use *orinoco_cs* instead. Some Linux distributions may even ship with *orinoco_cs*.

Kernel 2.0/2.2: wvlan_cs

In kernel Version 2.2 and earlier, support for WaveLAN adapters is provided by the *wvlan_cs* driver bundled with PCMCIA Card Services for Linux.

Compiling and installing

Some wireless LAN support code is activated in the kernel by enabling the Wireless LAN extensions (*CONFIG_NET_RADIO*) kernel configuration option. *CONFIG_NET_RADIO*-enabled kernels collect wireless statistics and expose additional data structures used by the WaveLAN driver.

The driver for PCMCIA WaveLAN cards is part of the PCMCIA Card Services package. Previous sections of this chapter described how to compile and install the PCMCIA Card Services package and how PCMCIA cards are dynamically configured on Linux systems. After building a kernel with the wireless LAN extensions, you must rebuild the PCMCIA utilities as well.

The standard wireless tools are also required. They can be downloaded from *http:// www.hpl.hp.com/personal/Jean_Tourrilhes/Linux/Tools.html*. Building the wireless tools is a straightforward task. After unzipping the file into a temporary directory, just run *make* in the root directory of the software distribution, and it will build the wireless tools.

PCMCIA configuration

Although the Orinoco card is rebadged on the outside, the CIS still identifies the card as a Lucent WaveLAN/IEEE, and the software is the same as it has always been for the WaveLAN/IEEE:

```
[root@bloodhound]# dump_cis
Socket 0:
  dev_info
    NULL 0ns, 512b
  attr_dev_info
    SRAM 500ns, 1kb
  vers_1 5.0, "Lucent Technologies", "WaveLAN/IEEE", "Version 01.01", ""
  manfid 0x0156, 0x002
  funcid network_adapter
  lan_technology wireless
  lan_speed 1 mb/sec
  lan_speed 2 mb/sec
  lan_speed 5 mb/sec
  lan_speed 11 mb/sec
  lan_media 2.4_GHz
  lan_node_id 00 02 2d 38 82 e4
  lan_connector Closed connector standard
  config base 0x03e0 mask 0x0001 last_index 0x01
  cftable_entry 0x01 [default]
    Vcc Vmin 4750mV Vmax 5250mV Iavg 300mA Ipeak 300mA
    Idown 10mA
    io 0x0000-0x003f [lines=6] [16bit]
    irq mask 0xffff [level] [pulse]

Socket 1:
  no CIS present
```

When the card is inserted, the */etc/pcmcia/wireless* script is run, using the configuration options in */etc/pcmcia/wireless.opts*. The wireless script is a frontend to the *iwconfig* program. Editing fields in *wireless.opts* sets the arguments to *iwconfig*. Therefore, knowing how *iwconfig* works allows you to set the appropriate fields in *wireless.opts*.

iwconfig

The main command-line tool for managing a WaveLAN wireless interface is *iwconfig*. When run with no parameters other than the interface name, *iwconfig* displays extended information about the radio interface, provided the kernel was built with radio extensions:

```
[root@bloodhound]# iwconfig wvlan0
wvlan0    IEEE 802.11-DS  ESSID:"Luminiferous Ether"  Nickname:"HERMES I"
          Mode:Managed  Frequency:2.457GHz  Access Point:00:E0:03:04:18:1C
          Bit Rate:2Mb/s  Tx-Power=15 dBm  Sensitivity:1/3
          RTS thr:off  Fragment thr:off
          Encryption key:off
          Power Management:off
```

```
Link Quality:46/92 Signal level:-51 dBm  Noise level:-94 dBm
Rx invalid nwid:0  invalid crypt:0  invalid misc:0
```

The nickname is an internal name used by the driver. By default, it is set to "HER-MES I" after the name of the Lucent chipset used in Lucent's wireless LAN cards.

Setting the network name

The basic task required to join a network is to select the appropriate network name, or SSID. *iwconfig* uses the *essid** parameter to set the desired network name. If the network name includes a space, it must be enclosed in quotation marks:

```
[root@bloodhound]# iwconfig wvlan0 essid "Luminiferous Ether"
```

Setting the network channel

The network-operating frequency can be selected in two ways. The *freq* parameter can take an operating frequency directly, or the *channel* parameter can be used with the appropriate channel number, and the driver will derive the frequency from the channel number. The following two commands are equivalent:

```
[root@bloodhound]# iwconfig wvlan0 freq 2.432G
[root@bloodhound]# iwconfig wvlan0 channel 4
```

Setting the network mode and associating with an access point

Most 802.11 stations are in either ad hoc networks or infrastructure networks. The *iwconfig* nomenclature for these two modes is *Ad-hoc* and *Managed*. Select between them by using the *mode* parameter:

```
[root@bloodhound]# iwconfig wvlan0 mode Ad-hoc
[root@bloodhound]# iwconfig wvlan0 mode Managed
```

For stations in an infrastructure network, the *ap* parameter may be used to request an association with the specified MAC address. However, the station is not required to remain associated with the specified access point and may choose to roam to a different access point if the signal strength drops too much:

```
[root@bloodhound]# iwconfig wvlan0 ap 01:02:03:04:05:06
```

Setting the data rate

Most cards support multiple bit rates. *iwconfig* allows the administrator to choose between them by using the *rate* parameter. Bit rates can be specified after the *rate* parameter, or the keyword *auto* can be used to specify that the card should fall back

---

* I use the term SSID in this book to refer to a network name. Some drivers, including the WaveLAN drivers, use ESSID instead. The distinction is that an ESSID is a network name assigned to an extended service set, not any old service set.

to lower bit rates on poor-quality channels. If *auto* is combined with a bit rate, the driver may use any rate lower than the specified rate:

```
[root@bloodhound]# iwconfig wvlan0 rate 11M auto
```

Configuring WEP

The key parameter controls the WEP function of the driver. Keys can be entered as hexadecimal strings as in the PRISM driver. Enter the string four digits at a time with dashes between the two-byte groups. (Although it is not mentioned in the documentation, I can enter keys in the colon-separated MAC address format as well.)

```
[root@bloodhound]# iwconfig wvlan0 key 0123-4567-89
[root@bloodhound]# iwconfig wvlan0 key 01:23:45:67:89
```

Multiple keys can be entered using a bracketed index number:

```
[root@bloodhound]# iwconfig wvlan0 key 0123-4567-89
[root@bloodhound]# iwconfig wvlan0 key 9876-5432-01 [2]
[root@bloodhound]# iwconfig wvlan0 key 5432-1678-90 [3]
```

Longer keys can be entered simply by using more bytes. If the key length is longer than 40 bits, the key is assumed to be a 104-bit key.

```
[root@bloodhound]# iwconfig wvlan0 key 0011-2233-4455-6677-8899-0011-22 [4]
```

Once multiple keys have been entered, select one by entering the index number without a key value:

```
[root@bloodhound]# iwconfig wvlan0 key [2]
```

Activate WEP processing using key on and disable WEP using key off. These can be combined with an index number to select a new WEP key:

```
[root@bloodhound]# iwconfig wvlan0 key [3] on
[root@bloodhound]# iwconfig wvlan0 key off
```

Finally, two types of WEP processing can be done. An *open* system accepts data frames sent in the clear, and a *restricted* system discards cleartext data frames. Both of these parameters can be combined with an index number:

```
[root@bloodhound]# iwconfig wvlan0 key [4] open
[root@bloodhound]# iwconfig wvlan0 key [3] restricted
```

The *key* parameter may also be accessed with the *encryption* parameter, which may be abbreviated as *enc*.

Tuning 802.11 parameters

iwconfig allows you to tune the RTS and fragmentation thresholds. The RTS threshold in the *wvlan_cs* driver is 2,347, which effectively disables RTS clearing. In an environment likely to have hidden nodes, it can be set using the *rts_threshold* parameter with *iwconfig*. *rts_threshold* can be abbreviated as *rts*.

```
[root@bloodhound]# iwconfig wvlan0 rts 500
```

The default value of the fragmentation threshold is 2,346. In noisy environments, it may be worth lowering the fragmentation threshold to reduce the amount of data, which must be retransmitted when frames are lost to corruption on the wireless medium. Set the parameter by using the *fragmentation_threshold* argument to *iwconfig*. It may be set anywhere from 256 to 2,356, but it may take on only even values. *fragmentation_threshold* may be abbreviated as *frag*.

```
[root@bloodhound]# iwconfig wvlan0 frag 500
```

802.11 stations maintain several retry counters. When frames are retransmitted "too many" times or wait for transmission for "too long," they are discarded. Two retry counters are maintained. The long retry counter, set by the *retry* parameter, is the number of times transmission is attempted for a frame longer than the RTS threshold. The short retry counter, set by the *retry min* parameter, is the number of times transmission will be attempted for a frame shorter than the RTS threshold. Unlike many drivers, *iwconfig* also allows for configuration of the maximum frame lifetime with the *retry lifetime* parameter. To specify a value in milliseconds or microseconds, append "m" or "u" to the value:

```
[root@bloodhound]# iwconfig wvlan0 retry 4
[root@bloodhound]# iwconfig wvlan0 retry min 7
[root@bloodhound]# iwconfig wvlan0 retry lifetime 400m
```

wvlan_cs driver parameters

Several options can be passed to the *wvlan_cs* module by *cardmgr* when it is loaded into the kernel. These options are most easily set in */etc/pcmcia/config.opts*. See Table 13-5.

Table 13-5. wvlan_cs driver parameters

Parameter	Value type	Description
irq_list	Comma-separated integer list	Specifies interrupts that may be used by driver.
port_type	integer, range 1–3	Sets network type to infrastructure (1), wireless distribution system (2), or ad hoc network (3).
station_name	string	Sets station name; defaults to card setting.
network_name	string	Configures name for ad hoc network or name of target infrastructure network.
channel	integer, range 0–14	Channel number/operating frequency for ad-hoc networks; not used for infrastructure networks. Default is 3.
ap_density	integer, range 1–3	Sets threshold for roaming based on a low-density (1), medium-density (2), or high-density (3) installation. The default is a low-density installation, which minimizes roaming activity.
medium_reservation	integer, range 0–2,347	Sets RTS/CTS threshold. Default is 2,347.
frag_threshold	even integer, range 256–2,346	Sets fragmentation threshold. Default is 2,346.
transmit_rate	integer, range 1–7	Each integer has a meaning; default is *auto select high speed* (3), which allows for fallback to lower speed.

Table 13-5. wvlan_cs driver parameters (continued)

Parameter	Value type	Description
eth	integer, range 0–1	If set to 1, all devices are *ethN*. If set to 0, all devices are *wvlanN*. By default, this is set to 1, so all devices are *ethN*.
mtu	integer, range 256–2,296	Maximum transfer unit; default is 1,500.

Troubleshooting

Naturally, all the PCMCIA troubleshooting notes from the previous section apply.

Kernel 2.4: orinoco_cs

In addition to the WaveLAN cards and any OEM versions of WaveLAN cards, *orinoco_cs* contains basic support for some PRISM-2–based cards and Symbol cards that use the same MAC chipset. *orinoco_cs* has been part of the Linux kernel distribution since kernel Version 2.4.3.

Compiling and installing

Some wireless LAN support code is activated in the kernel by enabling the Wireless LAN extensions (*CONFIG_NET_RADIO*) kernel configuration option. *CONFIG_NET_RADIO*-enabled kernels collect wireless statistics and expose additional data structures used by the *orinoco_cs* driver. To compile the *orinoco_cs* driver itself, recompile the kernel with Hermes support (controlled by the *CONFIG_PCMCIA_HERMES* variable).

The standard wireless tools are also required. They can be downloaded from *http://www.hpl.hp.com/personal/Jean_Tourrilhes/Linux/Tools.html*. As with the previous driver, installation is a straightforward matter of running *make* in the right spot.

PCMCIA configuration

Most distributions ship with the *wvlan_cs* driver still enabled. To change the driver used by the distribution, it is sufficient to change the module binding the PCMCIA configuration. The author of *orinoco_cs* supplies a file, *hermes.conf*, which contains card definitions for the cards supported by *orinoco_cs*. Because *hermes.conf* ends in *.conf*, it is sourced by the line at the end of */etc/pcmcia/config* that reads all *.conf* files. However, to avoid binding conflicts, you must comment out all the lines that bind the older *wvlan_cs* driver to newly inserted cards. Alternatively, it is sufficient to edit the definition of your wireless card to bind the *orinoco_cs* driver after grabbing identification information from the output of *dump_cis*:

```
# in hermes.conf
#
card "Lucent Technologies Wavelan/IEEE"
    version "Lucent Technologies", "WaveLAN/IEEE"
    bind "orinoco_cs"
```

```
# from standard /etc/pcmcia/config
#
# card "Lucent Technologies WaveLAN/IEEE"
#    version "Lucent Technologies", "WaveLAN/IEEE"
#    bind "wvlan_cs"
```

Configuring the orinoco_cs interface

Configuration of *orinoco_cs* is identical to the configuration of *wvlan_cs*. When the card is inserted, the */etc/pcmcia/wireless* script is run, using the configuration options in */etc/pcmcia/wireless.opts*. The wireless script is a frontend to the *iwconfig* program. Editing fields in *wireless.opts* sets the arguments to *iwconfig*. For details on configuring the options to *iwconfig*, see the previous section on the *wvlan_cs* driver.

## CHAPTER 14

Using 802.11 Access Points

In even the simplest 802.11 network, proper configuration of the access points is essential. Without properly configured network interfaces, no traffic will be bridged on to the wired network.

Access points can be divided into two groups. Home gateways and small office products are targeted at price-conscious users and do not offer much in the way of functionality beyond simple connectivity. Business-grade products are more expensive, but they possess functionality that is key to working with larger networks containing multiple access points. This chapter takes a look at two access points targeted at the high-end commercial user: the ORiNOCO AP-1000 and the Nokia A032. Extrapolating low-end product administration from the basic set of tasks is straightforward.

The major tasks facing a network administrator are to connect the access point to the wired network, configure the network interfaces, enable security features, and perform any configuration adjustments necessary to tune the wireless network to the area in which it is deployed. This chapter assumes that power and wired network connections are straightforward and have been taken care of.

General Functions of an Access Point

All access points provide a similar set of features to network users because the standard feature set is specified by 802.11. Configuration of these features, of course, is vendor-specific, but the products are fairly similar to each other.

Access points are bridges between the wireless world and the wired world. As bridges, then, all access points have features that one would expect to see on a network bridge. They have at least two network interfaces: a wireless interface that understands the details of 802.11 and a second interface to connect to wired networks. To take advantage of the installed base and expertise, the wired interface is almost always an Ethernet port. Many products also have a WAN port. Sometimes the WAN port is a serial port that can be connected to a modem for use with a dial-up ISP account. It is also common to find DSL interfaces in access points. Still, other access points add a second Ethernet port for connection to a DSL modem or cable modem. Some access points have multiple wireless interfaces so network managers can increase hot-spot capacity by using two interfaces on nonoverlapping channels. Many access points also offer the option of using external antennas to further boost range and allow for fine-tuning of antenna placement. Bridges have some buffer memory to hold frames as they are transferred between the two interfaces, and they store MAC address associations for each port in a set of internal tables.

Bridging tables are, of course, highly implementation-specific, and there is no guarantee of similarities across the industry. Generally speaking, though, inexpensive consumer devices are fundamentally designed with the assumption that they will be the sole access point for a network, while the more expensive commercial devices include more advanced features to make large deployments and rollouts easier. Commercial-grade devices are also designed to work cooperatively; the most common feature is a vendor-proprietary Inter-Access Point Protocol (IAPP). An IAPP allows wireless stations to move from access point to access point without interrupting link-layer connectivity. At this point, no standard for an IAPP exists, though the 802.11 working group is addressing this shortcoming. (Some cheaper products may support an IAPP, however.) Network management is generally much more sophisticated on commercial-grade products to enable network engineers to manage the tens or hundreds of devices used to create a large-scale coverage area.

All but the cheapest access points have a TCP/IP network interface. TCP/IP interfaces are intended for remote management and typically accept only basic configurations; anything beyond an IP address, netmask, and a single static default route is atypical. Depending on the level of sophistication of the hardware and software, varying levels of low-level interface configuration are possible. Naturally, all products allow the configuration of the network name. Other low-level parameters, however, may or may not be configurable. For access points that use PCMCIA network interfaces, the configuration of the wireless interface may depend on the firmware present on the PCMCIA interface card.

Depending on the market for which an access point is developed, it may offer services to its wireless clients. The most popular service is DHCP; wireless stations may be assigned addresses automatically upon association. Many access points can also perform network address translation (NAT), especially the "home gateway"–type products that can connect to a modem and dial up an ISP.

Security has been a sore point for wireless network managers since before the advent of 802.11's success. Access points have a privileged position with respect to security concerns because they are the gateways to the wired network and are ideally positioned to implement security policies. As detailed elsewhere in this book, the tools that access points provide to enforce security polices are sorely lacking. Naturally, WEP implementations are fully configurable with new keys and can be set to either open-system or shared-key authentication, but few other standardized access control tools exist. (Naturally, several vendors have implemented proprietary approaches.) The major access control method implemented by access points is *MAC address filtering*. With address filtering, network administrators can give each access point a list of the MAC addresses of clients that should be allowed to access the network. Many products that offer remote network management provide some tools to filter management access, but few of the filters are based on anything other than easily forged source IP addresses.

Management interfaces often leave something to be desired. Configuration of access points tends to be challenging because access points must be manufactured cheaply, and low-cost devices tend not to have the processing power to run an easy-to-use configuration engine. Most vendors use lightweight operating systems running on low-powered hardware, but one of the trade-offs of using a lightweight operating system is that it does not provide the programming environment necessary to build rich functionality. Early access points offered both a cryptic command-line interface and a web-based management interface. This is still a common model. It is not unheard of for a vendor to supply proprietary management software for just one operating-system platform. (Most offenders in this category are management applications confined to run on Microsoft Windows.) Typically, host software connects over a serial port, either RS-232 or USB, and runs a proprietary management protocol to change configuration variables. Moreover, it is only recently that vendors have even begun to address seriously the concerns of large-scale access point management.

Debugging and troubleshooting tools are as advanced as management tools, which unfortunately means that they often leave network administrators mired in inconclusive or irrelevant information. Ideally, products should maintain detailed logs of activities, but it is common to find vague logs of results that give very little insight into failures. Counters can be helpful, but only if the right counters are accurately maintained. Tools such as *ping* and *traceroute* are common, but network analyzers and packet capture tools are not.

Types of Access Points

Broadly speaking, there are two classes of access points in the marketplace. A low-cost tier is sold widely through retail channels directly to the end user. These low-cost devices are specialized computing platforms with only limited memory and storage. The higher-cost tier incorporates additional features required to support large deployments; frequently, these devices have additional memory and storage and resemble small general-purpose computing platforms in their design.

For the home: residential gateways

The low-cost tier is composed of devices often called *residential gateways*. Residential gateways are designed to be as low-cost as possible, so only the basic features

---

required for the typical small or home office are included. Residential gateways generally share the following characteristics:

- Most devices include a DHCP server to make plug-and-play configuration easier.
- They are often deployed by users with one routable IP address, so NAT implementations are common.
- Depending on the type of customer the residential gateway is aimed at, the WAN interface is a modem, a serial port, or even DSL. (Some residential gateway products may use an Ethernet port as the "WAN" connection to a cable modem or DSL modem.)
- They are often built as a single integrated unit, complete with a built-in antenna. If suitable coverage cannot be found, it is necessary to relocate the entire unit.
- Many products now claim to have an *IPSec pass-through* feature to allow the use of IPSec through NAT, which works with varying degrees of success depending on the IPSec VPN solution chosen.
- Configuration of residential gateways often relies on a Windows program that is installed and uses a proprietary protocol over serial or USB to configure the device.
- They are often sold directly to the end user and are designed to be aesthetically pleasing. Unfortunately for many end users, the improved visual design prevents the stacking of residential gateways with other network equipment.

As this book was written, residential gateways typically cost $150 to $300. Examples of the residential gateway class of device are the 3Com Home Wireless Gateway, the Apple AirPort, the D-Link DWL-1000AP access point, the Intel Wireless Gateway, the Linksys WAP11, and the the Orinoco RG-1100.

For the office: enterprise (corporate) gateways

Enterprise gateways, which often go by many other names that imply the buyer values features over cost, provide everything residential gateways do, plus additional features useful for larger-scale environments. Enterprise gateways generally share the following characteristics:

- The area over which mobility is required is much larger and requires several access points working in concert. Enterprise products support an IAPP so that a group of access points can be used to provide mobility through large areas. All IAPPs are proprietary at the time this book was written, but efforts to standardize the IAPP and enable roaming with devices from different vendors are underway.
- Upgrades are much easier with enterprise products. The wireless interfaces themselves are often PCMCIA cards, which makes the upgrade path much easier. As an example, many enterprise gateways do not require "forklift" upgrades to move to 802.11a. Instead, the wireless interface can be replaced

with an 802.11a-compatible interface, and a software upgrade provides a driver for the new card and the software features necessary for 802.11a.

- Enterprise-class products are designed to make deployment as easy as possible. Many high-end products can draw power over the unused pins in the Ethernet cable by complying with draft versions of the IEEE 802.3af standard.

- Frequently, site survey tools come bundled with enterprise-class products so network managers can plan large deployments by directly assessing coverage quality.

- Wireless interfaces on enterprise gateways usually allow for the possibility of using external antennas, and a wide selection of antennas is available to provide coverage in specific types of areas. External antennas may come standard with some enterprise products. Transmission power can be adjusted on many devices to enlarge or shrink the coverage area.

- Security developments appear on high-end products first. Enterprise gateways were the first to implement address filtering, and they are the test-bed for new security features implemented in software. Some vendors have enhanced the association process with proprietary key exchanges. 802.1x is beginning to appear in these products as well.

- Reflecting the administrative demands, configuration of enterprise-class devices is done with easily scripted command-line interfaces or SNMP, and monitoring and management capabilities are far more extensive than in residential gateways.

Naturally, these additional capabilities do not come without a price. As this book was written, enterprise gateways typically cost $800 to $1,100. Prices for enterprise-class products are not subject to the same downward pressure as residential gateways. Generally, enterprise-class products are made with much more generic hardware than residential gateways. Software upgrades are more common and can continue to add value through the life of the product. Examples of the enterprise gateway class of device are the 3Com AirConnect, the Cisco Aironet 350 Series Access Point, the Intel PRO/Wireless LAN Access Point, the Nokia A032, the Orinoco AP-1000 and AP-2000, and the Proxim RangeLAN2. This chapter describes the management of the Nokia A032 and Orinoco AP-1000 as examples. As you'll see, the mechanisms for configuring and managing these access points are different, but the information you need to supply and the configuration parameters that you can control are fundamentally similar. Even if you don't use Orinoco (a.k.a. Lucent, a.k.a. WaveLAN, a.k.a. Agere) or Nokia products, this chapter will show you what you need to do to configure any commercial access point.

Selecting Access Points

When choosing an access point, you should take a number of factors into account. With the emergence of 802.11 as the main vendor-neutral standard, standards compliance is generally not a big factor. Most 802.11 equipment has gone through compatibility testing with the Wireless Ethernet Compatibility Alliance (WECA); equipment that has received WECA's "Wi-Fi" (short for "wireless fidelity") certification has proven successful interoperability and standards compliance. Originally, the Wi-Fi program was only for 802.11b equipment, though a successor certification program called Wi-Fi5 is in development for 802.11a gear. Wi-Fi certification is almost certainly something to look for because it is practically a guarantee of interoperability.

802.11 is a complex standard, however, with several optional features. External antennas are often useful for creating a dense coverage blanket over an area. Not all access points can connect to external antennas; it may be an extra-cost option. Even if an access point has an external antenna connector, there is no guarantee that you'll be able to find a wide range of antennas available for use. 802.11 only requires that any connectors for external antennas have a standard impedance of 50 ohms. The actual physical connector may be proprietary to the vendor. If external antennas are important for your deployment plans, make sure that a wide range of antennas is available, whether through the 802.11 vendor or another source.

Security has been an area of notable innovation. The standard specifies one method, WEP, with a short key length. Some vendors offer longer key length versions of WEP, which are nonstandard but generally interoperable. Longer key length WEP implementations may add cost, however. More importantly, though, WEP has been conclusively demonstrated to be severely flawed. Some attempts at fixing WEP have been made by vendors, but they are fundamentally constrained by the design. As a result, there are a number of proprietary prestandard security mechanisms based on 802.1x (which also appears to be flawed). Some products have even begun to support 802.1x, with a few enhancements for wireless use. Before you commit to an evolutionary dead end, ensure that any solution can be easily upgraded to incorporate the standard security framework being developed by the 802.11i task group.

If roaming is important, a single-vendor solution is mandatory. Most vendors ship products with a protocol that enables roaming between access points, but products from different vendors are not guaranteed to interoperate. In the absence of a standard, there cannot be compliance testing. While this is being addressed within the 802.11 working group, until a standard is finalized, only a single-vendor solution can provide roaming between access points.[*] Until a standardized protocol hits the market, you may want to investigate the situations in which the vendor claims to enable roaming. Can stations move between access points even when WEP is enabled? How quickly can stations move between access points? It may also be worthwhile to

---

[*] While this is generally true, there are some exceptions due to OEM relationships. The Apple AirPort has been reported as allowing roaming connections to and from Lucent access points, but the AirPort is essentially a rebadged Lucent access point with a far superior aesthetic appearance.

obtain a guarantee from the vendor that any access points you purchase now can be easily upgraded to the forthcoming standard.

802.11 includes a number of power-saving functions in the standard. Most are optional. If your deployment is based heavily on battery-powered devices, it may be worth evaluating which power-saving features are included with particular devices. It may also be worth experimenting with devices to see just how much longer batteries last with the power-saving functions enabled.

In some deployments, getting power to the access points can be a major headache. To blanket an area with the coverage required for a large implementation, access points often need to be placed in an area where power is not easily accessible. Long antenna runs can degrade signal quality unacceptably, so it is much better to bring power to the location. Installing new electrical conduits is often quite expensive. Work must be performed by licensed electricians, and building codes may impose additional restrictions. Some products can supply power over the unused pins in the Ethernet cable. Network wire is not subject to the same restrictions as electrical cable and can be installed by network administrators.

Device management is an important consideration. Wireless networks are a new service, and network staff will need to plan, evaluate, purchase, deploy, and maintain the additional hardware. Large deployments may have tens or hundreds of access points, which can easily make network management a headache without good tools. Does the vendor offer an access point manager to configure large numbers of devices in parallel? Can management of the access points be incorporated into your existing network management infrastructure using tools that you already have deployed? Are the management tools secure enough? Many products can be managed only with clear-text protocols, which may be just an annoyance or a major violation of a security policy. Experience with other network devices has shown that software upgrades are a frequent occurrence. How is the software upgraded, and how much functionality can upgrades add? Can new protocol features be added with firmware updates?

Depending on the size of the deployment, it may be possible to evaluate equipment before buying. See if you can get a feel for the range of each access point and test with a variety of common cards. Capacity on an 802.11 network is ultimately limited by the radio link, but you will want to make sure that there are no other capacity restrictions. Does the access point provide the processing power to run the wireless side at maximum capacity with WEP enabled? Some products incorporate cryptographic processors to help with the load of WEP, but many do not. Products that depend on a central processor to run WEP may run out of capacity if they are upgraded to the faster 802.11a standard. Products upgraded to 802.11a will also suffer if they do not have Fast Ethernet ports. Try to set up a test network and get a feel for the configuration required to integrate the access points with the rest of your network gear.

As with many other purchasing decisions, of course, there are a number of "soft" factors that may not be easily quantifiable. Warranties, a relationship with the vendor, and the quality of the technical support may all influence the purchasing decision. Soft factors are not technical nor easily quantifiable, however, so I will not discuss them.

Are Access Points Really Necessary?

Access points are not required for a wireless network. Wireless stations can be used in independent networks, which do not require an access point. Building a Unix box that routes between an Ethernet network and a wireless network is not difficult, and hardware can often be reused from the scrap pile. Why, then, would anybody use an access point?

Now that residential gateways have fallen well below the $200 mark, building a Unix router is no longer a cost-effective option for single–access point networks. Once you consider what staff time is worth, building a Unix router is a pretty silly use of staff time. Access point hardware has some advantages over redeployed general-purpose platforms, too. Access points are small devices with no moving parts. As a result, they do not consume a great deal of electrical power and do not generate much heat. There is one notable exception to this rule, though. Apple offers a "software base station" that transforms any desktop machine into a bridging access point. With a few mouse clicks and very little effort, a desktop computer can become a base station.

Unix-based routers have never been effective in larger deployments because of the lack of mobility support. Effective roaming requires transparent *bridged* access, not routed access, to the link layer at different physical locations. However, roaming with 802.11 is possible only when access points can communicate with each other to track the movement of a wireless station. In the future, it is likely that an open source Unix distribution will have the features necessary for an access point: low-level access to fundamental 802.11 parameters on the card, Ethernet bridging, and an IAPP. Until then, though, there is no substitute for commercial products.

ORiNOCO (Lucent) AP-1000 Access Point

The AP-1000 is the mid-range Orinoco product. The low end of the product line consists of products for the home market; the high-end products (for example, the AP-2000) has features such as enhanced security and upgrade ability to 802.11a.

In addition to purchasing the AP-1000 base unit, you must purchase wireless interfaces separately. Unlike many other products, the AP-1000 has two slots for PCM-CIA wireless interface cards. (A less expensive version of the AP-1000, the AP-500, has only a single slot.)

Unix-Based Access Points

One of the most basic preconditions for making a Unix-based access point is enabling access point functions in the wireless interface card. One of the major hurdles is rewriting the 802.11 headers. All traffic in an infrastructure network flows through the access point. Access points must rewrite the transmitter and receiver addresses in the 802.11 headers. Other management functions may be required as well. For example, 802.11 includes a number of power-saving mechanisms for infrastructure networks in the specification, but they can be used only on networks with access points that implement them.

There is also a nontechnical hurdle. Many vendors have actively supported the development of open source Unix drivers for their cards. After all, vendors make money selling hardware, and it is a good thing for them to sell cards for all client systems, even those that run open source Unix. Access points are a different story, however. Vendors have not been as forthcoming with the interface used to put cards into the access point mode. Access points are quite lucrative, and providing a driver interface in the access point mode in the card could potentially cannibalize access point sales.

At one point, the only way to get an Intersil-based card to act as an access point interface was to purchase the reference design from Intersil. (The reference design shipped with firmware that had access point functionality, and that firmware was not sold separately.) Intersil's shipping station firmware does, however, include something called a "Host AP Mode." In the Host AP Mode, the PRISM-2 chipset automatically takes care of "menial" tasks, such as transmitting Beacon frames and acknowledging incoming transmissions. Jouni Malinen has developed a driver to use the Host AP Mode with Linux kernel 2.4. In conjunction with the Ethernet bridging implementation in the kernel, this driver can be used to build an access point. It is available from *http://www.epitest.fi/Prism2/*.

With the present state of driver software, it is possible to build a Unix-based router. (I mean "router" pedantically, as "layer 3 network device.") One interface would connect to a wired network as it always has, and a second wireless interface could be run in IBSS mode. Ross Finlayson has established a community network at a coffee house in Mountain View, California using a FreeBSD-based router. The project's home page is at *http://www.live.com/danastreet/*, and there is a page devoted specifically to the router itself at *http://www.live.com/wireless/unix-base-station.html*.

The Lucent access points in this class do not include an internal DHCP server, but they are compatible with external DHCP servers. This is a reasonable assumption—if you are adding wireless capability to an existing network, it's almost certain that you already have a DHCP server on your network. Lucent's products for home use incorporate a DHCP server.

The Management Interface

The AP-1000 is managed almost exclusively with SNMP through a Windows-based SNMP tool designed specifically for the AP-1000. Command-line support was added in the Fall 2001 software release (Version 3.83). Only basic configuration can be done over the serial port. Three main items may be configured with the serial port: the IP network interface (address, mask, and router, or the use of DHCP), the wireless interface (network name, channel, and WEP settings), and the SNMP "password" (community string). The use of SNMP as a management protocol is a strange choice. A great deal of the configuration information on the AP-1000 should remain secret, but SNMP does not provide any facilities for protecting new settings as they travel across the wire. Even worse, the community string is easily recovered with a packet sniffer. Once the community string is recovered, a malicious attacker could change the settings on your access point.

The default configuration is to boot with the DHCP client enabled, so any DHCP server on the network can assign it an address. If you like, you can set up your DHCP server to assign a fixed address to the access point by associating the desired address with the Ethernet address printed on the AP-1000.

Introduction to the Orinoco AP Manager

The AP Manager software runs only on Windows (95/98/ME/NT/2000/XP). It is essentially a frontend to SNMP software, so you can build your own frontend on any SNMP-capable workstation.

The main AP Manager window is shown in Figure 14-1. When the software starts, it sends UDP probes to port 192 on the local network to locate existing access points. After an AP boots, it answers the requests, and the AP Manager displays a list organized by IP address:

```
[gast@bloodhound]$ tcpdump ip host 192.168.200.222
tcpdump: listening on eth0
19:33:18.190921 192.168.200.222.2159 > 255.255.255.255.192: udp 116
19:33:18.191196 192.168.200.100.192 > 192.168.200.222.2159: udp 116 (DF)
```

After locating access points, the AP Manager software monitors each AP it finds for reachability using ICMP echo requests.

Applying configuration changes

Many configuration changes require a restart. First, the changes are saved to the access point using SNMP Version 1 *SET* requests. Then the access point is restarted so it can reboot with the new configuration. Any change to the access point typically requires a reboot.

The access point's operating system is based on software from KarlNet, so it is not a surprise that the SNMP protocol operations direct the access point to set a large

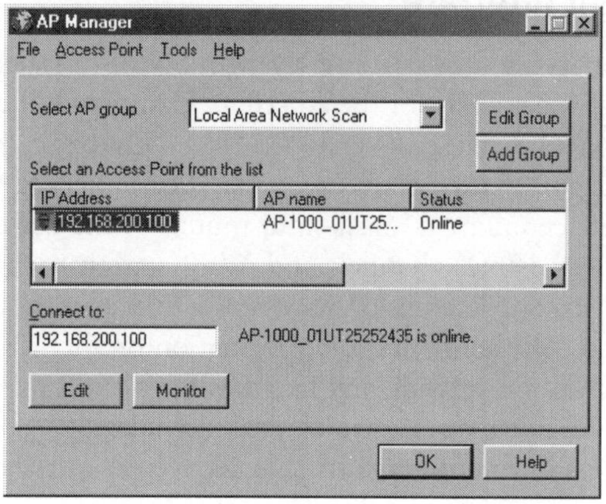

Figure 14-1. AP list

number of variables using KarlNet's SNMP enterprise number (762). Decoding the SNMP traffic and understanding it are two different matters, however. Just because it is easy to find where objects in the SNMP MIB are being set does not make it easy to find out what they do.

Basic Management Tasks

Running the access point is simple. Straight out of the box, the AP-1000 uses DHCP to obtain the address for the management interface.

Viewing the network configuration

Edit the access point from the main window and select the Access Point IP tab. Specify an IP address, network mask, and default gateway. Somewhat unusually, the AP-1000 also allows you to set the default TTL. See Figure 14-2.

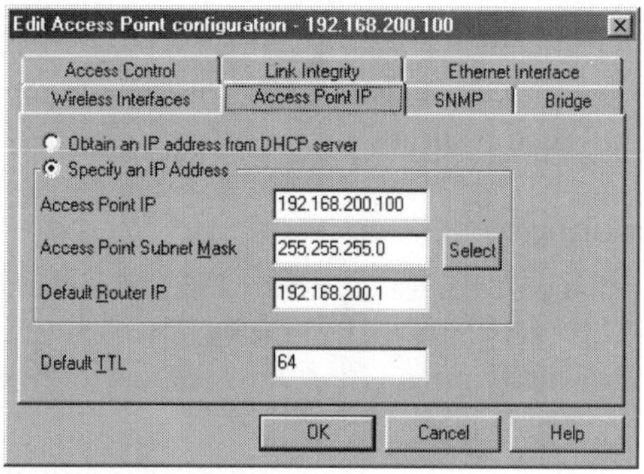

Figure 14-2. Access point IP interface

One nice thing about the AP Manager is that assigning the subnet mask is especially easy. The Select button raises a subnet mask panel that shows the mask in dotted decimal, hexadecimal, and mask-length notations. See Figure 14-3.

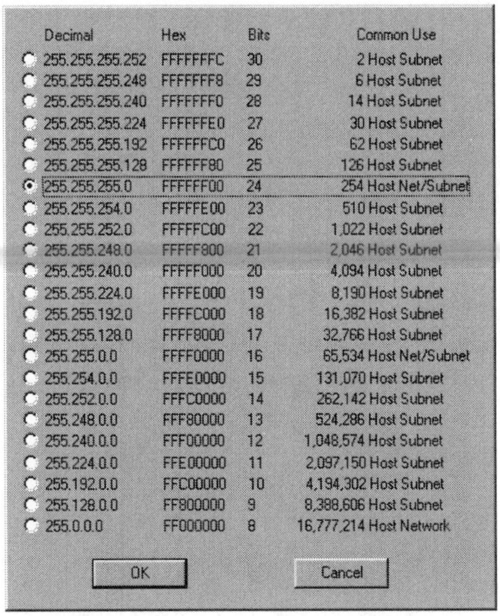

Decimal	Hex	Bits	Common Use
255.255.255.252	FFFFFFFC	30	2 Host Subnet
255.255.255.248	FFFFFFF8	29	6 Host Subnet
255.255.255.240	FFFFFFF0	28	14 Host Subnet
255.255.255.224	FFFFFFE0	27	30 Host Subnet
255.255.255.192	FFFFFFC0	26	62 Host Subnet
255.255.255.128	FFFFFF80	25	126 Host Subnet
255.255.255.0	FFFFFF00	24	254 Host Net/Subnet
255.255.254.0	FFFFFE00	23	510 Host Subnet
255.255.252.0	FFFFFC00	22	1,022 Host Subnet
255.255.248.0	FFFFF800	21	2,046 Host Subnet
255.255.240.0	FFFFF000	20	4,094 Host Subnet
255.255.224.0	FFFFE000	19	8,190 Host Subnet
255.255.192.0	FFFFC000	18	16,382 Host Subnet
255.255.128.0	FFFF8000	17	32,766 Host Subnet
255.255.0.0	FFFF0000	16	65,534 Host Net/Subnet
255.254.0.0	FFFE0000	15	131,070 Host Subnet
255.252.0.0	FFFC0000	14	262,142 Host Subnet
255.248.0.0	FFF80000	13	524,286 Host Subnet
255.240.0.0	FFF00000	12	1,048,574 Host Subnet
255.224.0.0	FFE00000	11	2,097,150 Host Subnet
255.192.0.0	FFC00000	10	4,194,302 Host Subnet
255.128.0.0	FF800000	9	8,388,606 Host Subnet
255.0.0.0	FF000000	8	16,777,214 Host Network

OK   Cancel

Figure 14-3. Selecting a subnet mask

Configuring the radio network

Configuration of the radio network is done on the Wireless Interfaces tab, shown in Figure 14-4. Each PCMCIA slot may have a wireless interface. Two configuration buttons are present for each interface. The Security button configures WEP, and the Advanced button configures the channel and radio parameters. The only parameter set on the main page is the network name (referred to in the specification as the ESSID).

The Advanced wireless interface configuration dialog box is shown in Figure 14-5. The channel, which is displayed both as a channel number and as a channel frequency, can be changed in the top dialog box. When you select the operating channel, you must be aware of any regulatory restrictions in your location.

Settings for the DTIM interval and RTS/CTS thresholds should be left as their default values unless they need to be changed to address a performance problem. Chapter 17 addresses changing 802.11 parameters in response to problems.

The multicast data rate is set with its own button in the advanced setup. Multicast messages are transmitted to all stations simultaneously, so it is vital that any multicast transmissions are made at a rate intelligible to all associated wireless stations.

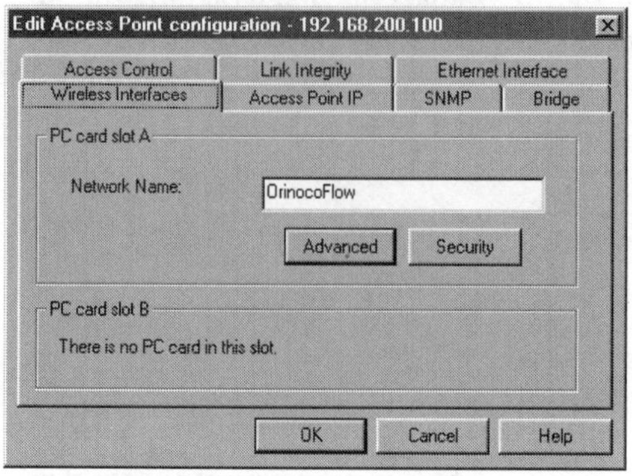

Figure 14-4. Wireless Interfaces tab

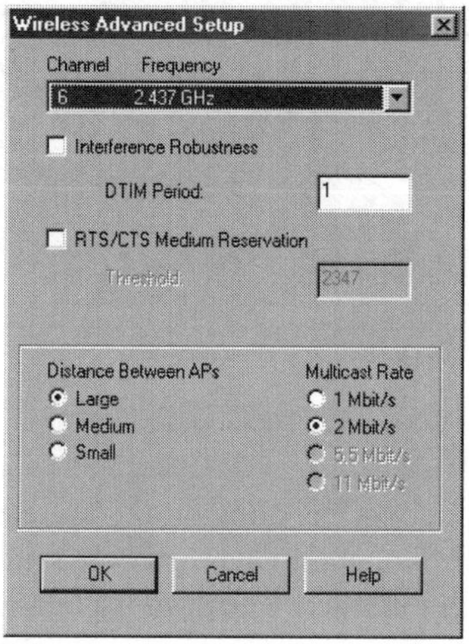

Figure 14-5. Advanced wireless interface configuration

The default value for the multicast rate is 2 Mbps because all commercial 802.11 direct-sequence cards are capable of 2-Mbps operation. You may change this to a higher rate, but you must ensure that network coverage is good and all stations are equipped with 802.11b cards compatible with the higher data rates.

The vendor cautions that the Interference Robustness setting should be used rarely with specific directions from an expert. There is a further warning that if the setting is needlessly enabled, connectivity and roaming may suffer. The documentation suggests that the Interference Robustness setting is used to work around interference close to the base station or in the path from the client to the base station. Based on their description, in many cases, it would be easier to redesign the wireless network than to suffer through what appears to be a nonstandard option.

The Distance Between APs option claims to tune the access point configurations to match the deployment. "Large" networks have very little overlap between BSSs and stations close to the edge of the BSS coverage area. "Medium" networks have 20% overlap, and "small" networks have an overlap area of 50% or more. It is not clear, however, which parameters are changed in response to setting this option.

Configuring the wired network

Configuring the wired network is done with the Ethernet Interface tab, shown in Figure 14-6. The interface is an RJ-45 jack, and the Ethernet transceiver is capable of full-duplex operation if it is connected to an Ethernet switch. By default, the port is set to automagically negotiate speed and duplex. Not all autonegotiation implementations are created equal, though, so you may need to pick a setting for compatible operation. One way to tell if the Ethernet interface is not negotiating properly is to monitor the number of collisions, especially late collisions, on the switch port. Late collisions are abnormal at any level and are a common indicator of mismatched duplex settings.

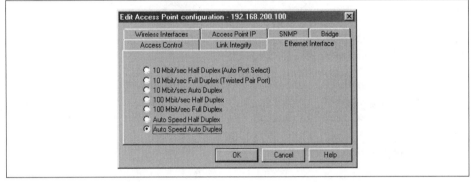

Figure 14-6. Ethernet interface configuration

Security Configuration

As with most 802.11 access points, security configuration is limited to configuring WEP, MAC address filtering, and limiting management access based on source IP address.

Configuring WEP

To enter WEP keys, click the Security button on the Wireless Interfaces tab of the main access point configuration screen. The security configuration is essentially WEP configuration; clicking the Security button brings up the WEP configuration dialog box shown in Figure 14-7. The AP-1000 supports both "64-bit WEP" (40 secret bits) and "128-bit WEP" (104 secret bits), depending on the wireless interface card used. "Silver" Orinoco cards support only the shorter length, and "Gold" cards support both. Keys can be entered either as alphanumeric strings or hexadecimal strings. Figure 14-7 shows a key being entered with a leading *0x* to denote that the key is being entered as a hexadecimal number.

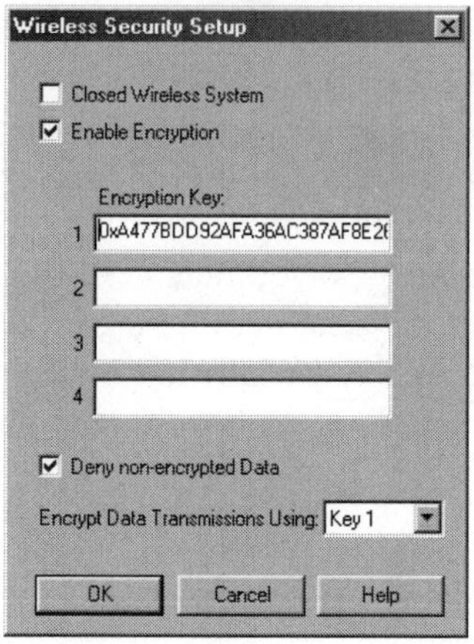

Figure 14-7. WEP configuration dialog box

Closed Wireless System is a Lucent proprietary extension to 802.11 that drops any frames from stations with a wildcard network name. It is compatible only with Orinoco cards and will drop traffic from cards manufactured by other vendors.

Filtering management connections

Management is done over SNMP and is controlled through the SNMP tab on the main access point configuration screen. The SNMP configuration box is shown in Figure 14-8. Read Password and Read/Write Password are community strings; both are set to public as the default. Traps are sent to the specified trap host; a setting of 0.0.0.0 disables traps.

Management access can be restricted using the SNMP IP Access List, which may contain up to five entries. (It's also based on source IP address filtering, which is a common but dubious security mechanism.) To add an entry to the list, click on the Add button to the right of the access list display. Doing so brings up the entry creation and edit screen, shown in Figure 14-9. Each entry is composed of an IP address and mask, and any source IP address matching one of the entries is permitted to access SNMP data. You can use the final field to restrict the interface on which SNMP processing takes place; 1 is used for the Ethernet interface, 2 and 3 for the two wireless interfaces, and X for any interface.

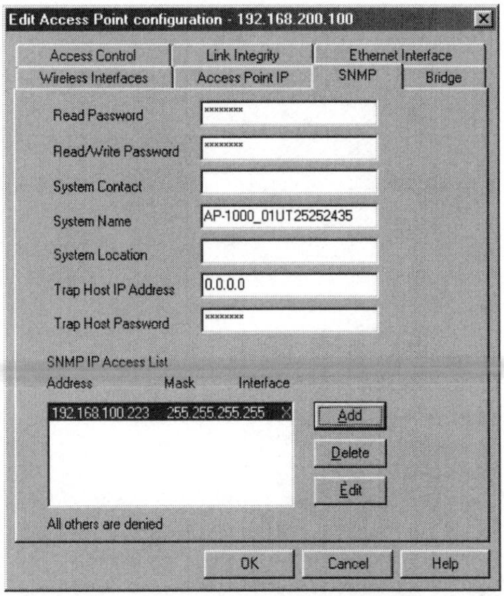

Figure 14-8. SNMP tab

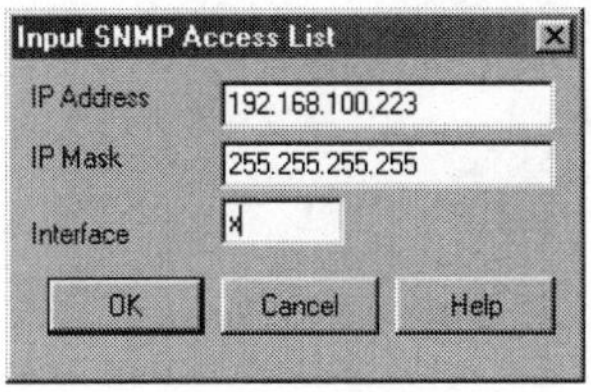

Figure 14-9. SNMP access filter dialog box

Restricting associations

Address filtering is configured under the Access Control tab, shown in Figure 14-10. AP Authentication is a local table stored inside the access point of MAC addresses that are allowed to connect. MAC addresses can also be stored in a RADIUS server. Adding addresses to the list of AP-authenticated addresses requires a system restart.

Monitoring Wireless Stations

Monitoring can also be performed using the AP Manager. Instead of editing the access point, monitor it. The main monitoring window is shown in Figure 14-11. By clicking on the various tabs across the top, you can see the bridge table, ARP table, various network statistics, and the list of associated stations.

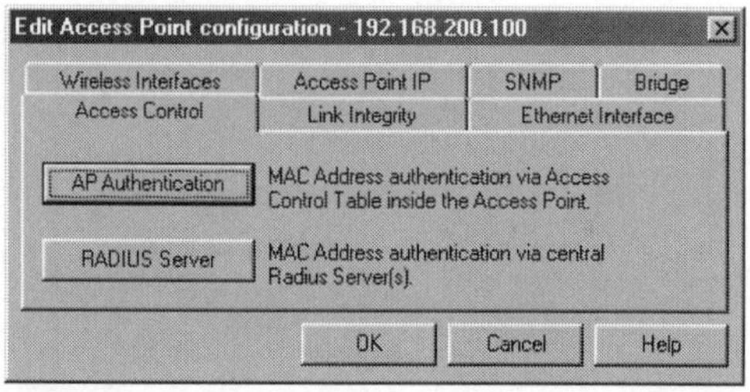

Figure 14-10. Access control tab

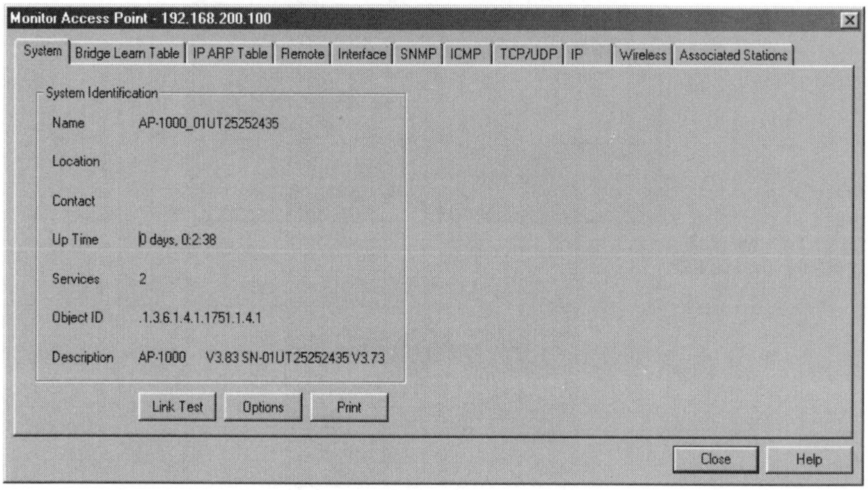

Figure 14-11. Access point monitoring

Monitoring associated stations

A common management task is to show the list of associated stations. Obtaining the list in the AP Manager is straightforward. Simply click on the Associated Stations tab at the top of the monitoring window, and the list of stations is displayed, as in Figure 14-12.

Naturally, associated stations must be given entries in the system bridge table. To view the bridging table, click on the Bridge Learn Table tab at the top. Figure 14-13 shows a simple example. Interface numbers have the same meaning as they do for SNMP access list purposes. Only one of the stations shown in Figure 14-13 is a wireless station. Beneath the display of this window is an implementation of the bridge group MIB.

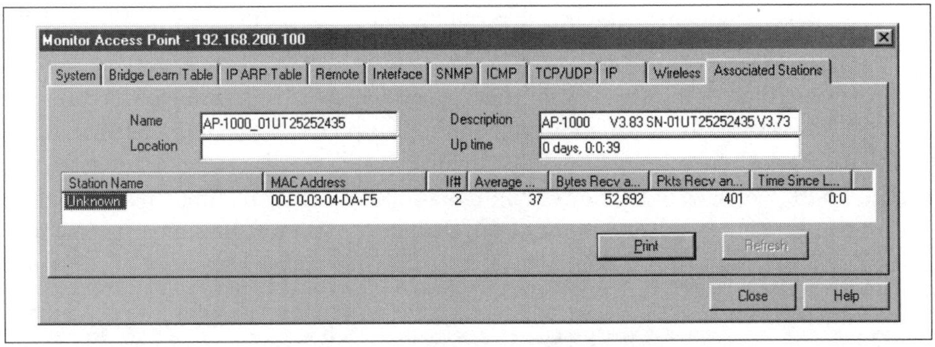

Figure 14-12. Associated stations

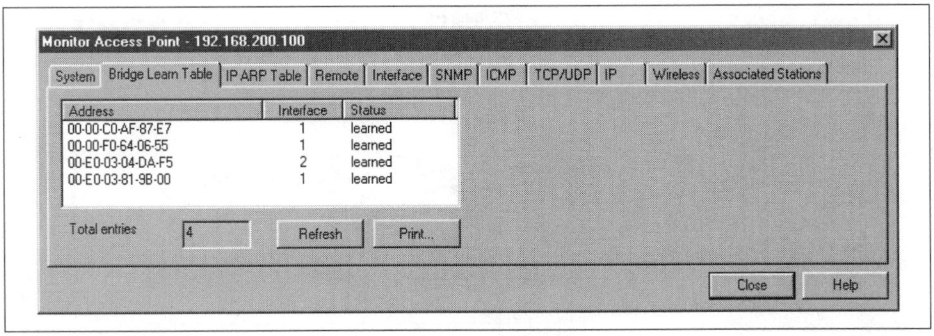

Figure 14-13. Bridge table

Nokia A032 Access Point

The A032 access point is the only access point in Nokia's current product line. It replaces the A020 and A021 access points. Unlike some products on the market, it comes with an interface card in the box and even ships with an external omnidirectional antenna. I found the external antenna to be problematic. Shortly after I started using it, the interface card stopped working, and I was unable to get a replacement.

A Tale of Two Management Interfaces

Like many network devices, the A032 has a console port that can be accessed using a null-modem cable. Configure the terminal emulator to the standard settings (9,600 bps, no parity, 8 data bits, and 1 stop bit) to access the console port. If a network address has already been configured, you can telnet to the device to gain access to the command-line interface.

The command-line interface lacks a great deal of the sophistication of the command line on more powerful devices. It has only limited help and does not assist with command completion. Configuration is based on assigning values to parameters with the *set* command; its general format is set *parameter value*.

Alternatively, there is a web interface that can be accessed by pointing a web browser at the device's IP address. After clicking on the Setup link in the upper left-hand corner and entering the administration password, you'll see the basic setup screen in Figure 14-14. Changes to the device configuration frequently require a restart. Before the system is restarted, as in Figure 14-14, the edited data will be shown on the web screen.

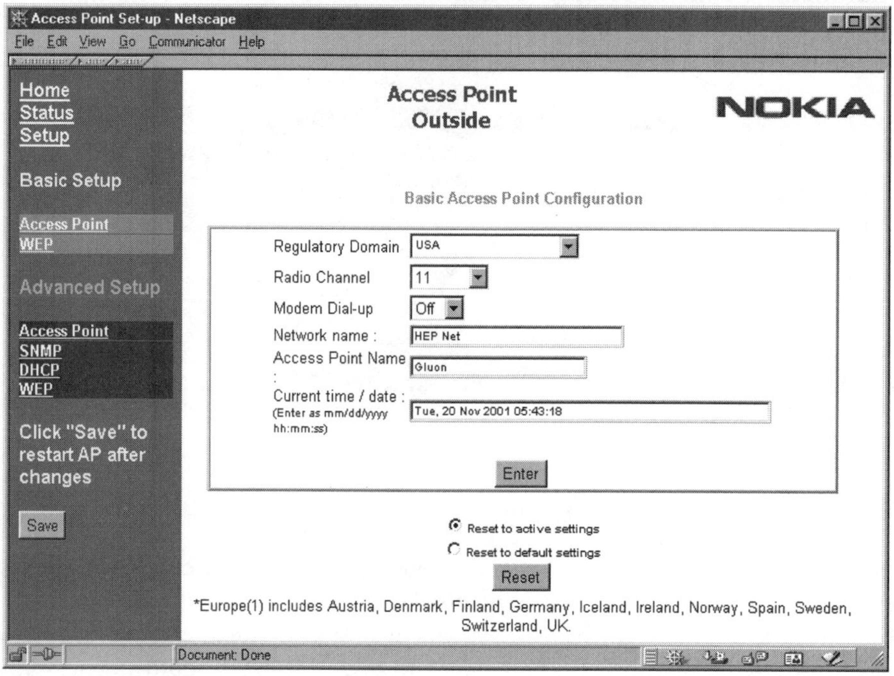

Figure 14-14. Web-based management interface

Web management is not for those concerned about security. Due to the limited computational power and storage space of the A032, it does not implement a secure web server, so the password is transmitted in the clear over the link layer. Of course, the link layer may be protected using WEP, but that is hardly reassuring.

Basic Management Tasks

To enable remote management and run the access point in the most basic way, you should configure the IP network interface for remote access and configure the wireless network interface with the necessary parameters. Bridging is implicitly enabled and needs no explicit configuration.

Viewing the network configuration

The current configuration can be displayed by typing the *config* command at the command line:

```
CMD:config
=========Current Configuration =========
net_name: Photon        AP_name: Outside
channel:   5   domain: USA      lan: 10baseT
IP_address: 192.168.155.90  subnet_mask: 255.255.255.0
gateway: 192.168.155.1
RTS_threshold: 2301     Frag_threshold: 2346
short_retry: 15  long_retry: 15
sifs_time: default    protocols: all
telnet: On:23  web: On:80
lock: off
manager: Specific      admission: All
basic rates: 1000 2000 kbits/s
wep-key range: min 128 max 128
community_get: public   community_set: private
Specific Managers (manager_IP):
    192.168.155.91 <accept requests> <no traps>
    <empty>
    <empty>
    <empty>
Radio NID: 00E003056F7F  Management NID: 00E003802F88
```

Configuring the radio network

The most basic parameter for the radio network is the channel to be used. Several channels are defined by the standard, but not all are allowed in each geographical area where 802.11 equipment is sold. To ensure that a legal channel is selected, the A032 also includes a way to set the regulatory domain, which prevents inappropriate radio channels from being selected. This information can be set in the web interface from the basic setup screen shown in Figure 14-14.

The ESSID, or network name, is configured with the *net_name* parameter on the command line. Spaces are allowed if the network name is enclosed in quotation marks. The network name must be shared by every access point within the BSS..

```
CMD:set domain usa
Configuration has been updated
CMD:set channel 11
Configuration will be updated on next restart
CMD:set net_name "HEP Net"
Configuration will be updated on next restart
CMD:set ap_name Gluon
Configuration will be updated on next restart
```

Older Nokia access points had two modes of operation. One mode was in accord with 802.11 standards, and the second was a proprietary mode that has been eliminated in current shipping versions.

Several 802.11 parameters can be set only at the command line:

Short retry counter (short_retry)
> By default, the short retry is set to 15, though it can be set as high as 31.

Long retry counter (long_retry)
> By default, the long retry is also set to 15, though it can also be set as high as 31.

RTS threshold (rts_threshold)
> By default, the RTS threshold is set to 2,301 bytes. It can be set as low as 1 byte or as high as 2,500 bytes.

Fragmentation threshold (frag_threshold)
> By default, the fragmentation threshold is 2,346 bytes as prescribed by the 802.11 standard. It may be set as low as 257 or as high as 2,346.

```
CMD:set short_retry 29
Configuration will be updated on next restart
CMD:set long_retry 7
Configuration will be updated on next restart
CMD:set rts_threshold 512
Configuration will be updated on next restart
CMD:set frag_threshold 1024
Configuration will be updated on next restart
```

The A032 also allows adjustment of the SIFS time, though this should not be necessary in practice because the interface is set to comply with the 802.11 standard.

Configuring the wired network, bridging, and management parameters

The predecessor to the A032 had both a 10baseT (twisted-pair RJ-45) and a 10base2 ("Thinnet") interface. In recognition of the dominance of twisted-pair physical connections, the A032 comes with only an RJ-45 port.

For management purposes, an IP address and default route can be assigned to the A032. The address may be used as a default gateway by associated wireless stations, but in practice, it often makes more sense to use the IP address simply for device management purposes. The IP interface is configured with the *ip_address*, *subnet_mask*, and *gateway* parameters:

```
CMD:set ip_address 10.1.2.100
Configuration will be updated on next restart
CMD:set subnet_mask 255.255.255.0
Configuration will be updated on next restart
CMD:set gateway 10.1.2.1
Configuration will be updated on next restart
```

One additional setting can be applied to the wired network. The A032 can be configured to bridge only TCP/IP frames. Many other link-layer protocols rely heavily on multicast frames, and if the A032 is connected to such a network, the available transmission time on the wireless network will dwindle as the multicasts are forwarded:

```
CMD:set protocols tcpip
Configuration will be updated on next restart
```

The command-line interface is normally accessible over Telnet connections on port 23, and the web interface is available on port 80. Both of these services can be run on arbitrary ports or disabled to prevent management. To disable a service, simply use the value off with the appropriate parameter:

```
CMD:set telnet 23
Configuration will be updated on next restart
CMD:set web off
Configuration will be updated on next restart
```

All of these parameters can be configured through the web interface by using the advanced access point setup link on the lefthand bar. The advanced access point page is shown in Figure 14-15.

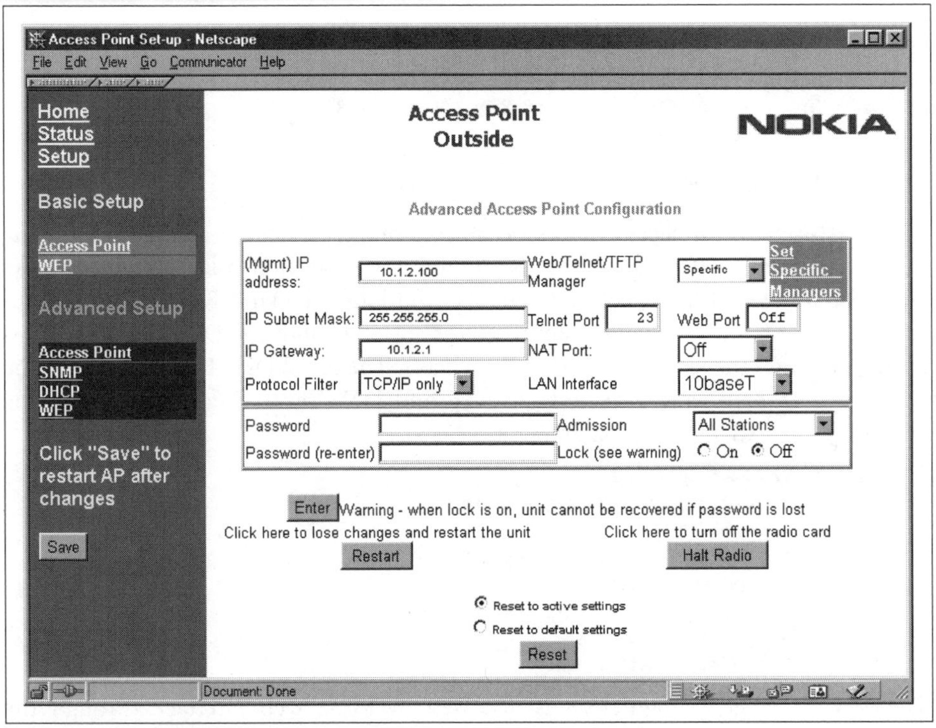

Figure 14-15. Network interface configuration

Viewing the next restart configuration

Configuration changes to the A032 do not take effect immediately. When the system starts up, it reads the configuration from nonvolatile memory. Many configuration commands can be used with + appended to show the settings that will be effective on the next restart. For example, *config+* can be used to show the network settings that will be effective on the next restart:

```
CMD:config+
=====Next Configuration (effective after restart)======
```

```
net_name: HEP Net      AP_name: Gluon
channel:  11   domain: USA       lan: 10baseT
IP_address: 10.1.2.100  subnet_mask: 255.255.255.0
gateway: 10.1.2.1
RTS_threshold: 512     Frag_threshold: 1024
short_retry: 29  long_retry: 7
sifs_time: default    protocols: TCPIP
telnet: On:23  web: Off
lock: off
manager: Specific       admission: All
basic rates: 1000 2000 kbits/s
wep-key range: min 128 max 128
community_get: public   community_set: private
Specific Managers (manager_IP):
    <empty>
    <empty>
    <empty>
    <empty>
Radio NID: 00E003056F7F  Management NID: 00E003802F88
```

Configuring DHCP

DHCP is useful with access points because it minimizes client configuration. The A032 includes a DHCP server that is suitable for small networks; larger networks may wish to take advantage of more generic solutions. The DHCP server can be allocated a pool of addresses. The administrator specifies both the DHCP base address (*dhcp_base*) and the size of the pool (*dhcp_pool*). The A032 DHCP server can also be configured to hand out a default gateway and DNS server information with the *dhcp_gateway* and *dhcp_dns* parameters:

```
CMD:set dhcp_base 10.1.2.200
Configuration will be set at next restart
CMD:set dhcp_pool 50
Configuration will be set at next restart
CMD:set dhcp_gateway 10.1.2.1
Configuration will be set at next restart
CMD:set dhcp_dns 192.168.100.5
Configuration will be set at next restart
```

The DHCP server configuration is accessed over the web interface through the DHCP link in the advanced setup section. The parameters that can be set over the web interface should be evident from Figure 14-16.

Security Configuration

The A032 supplies three main security tools for the network administrator. All are based on 802.11 and therefore inherit all the security limitations of 802.11. The three tools are WEP, filtering of management connections, and filtering of associated stations.

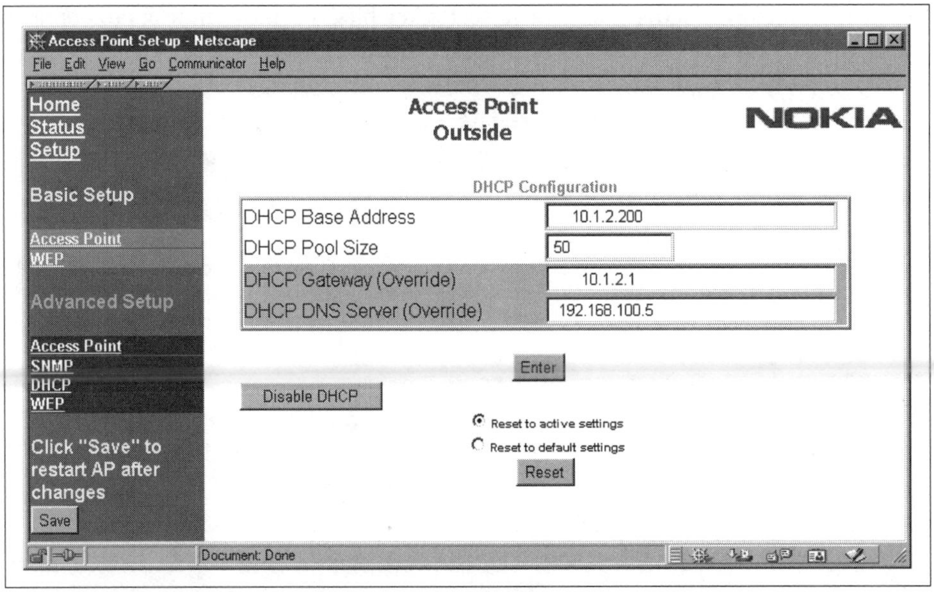

Figure 14-16. DHCP configuration

Configuring WEP

WEP keys can be stored locally on the A032 or fetched from a RADIUS server. Local keys are entered by the administrator and stored on the device. They are configured by setting the *wep_key* parameter to *set*. Unlike many other parameters, *wep_key* takes two values: the key number and its value. To erase a key, the value *n* can be used. As mandated by the specification, four keys can be entered; one must be set active by using the *wep_key_active* parameter:

```
CMD:set wep_key 1 BF8D2E9D0D6F669F4A36DA254FA651AC
Configuration will be set at next restart
CMD:set wep_key 2 n
Configuration will be set at next restart
CMD:set wep_key_active 1
Configuration will be set at next restart
```

The A032 provides two WEP-related settings to help control associations. One is the *WEP mode*. Normally, the WEP mode is set to *wep*, which means that stations can use either a shared WEP key or a key from RADIUS to authenticate the station to the access point. The mode can also be set to *open*, for no authentication, *personal*, to require a key from RADIUS, or *wifi*, for compatibility with equipment that attempts open authentication but transmits using a shared key for encryption.

```
CMD:set wep_mode wep
Configuration will be updated on next restart
```

Additionally, the administrator can specify a required key length so only longer keys are permitted. The *wep_key_range* parameter takes two arguments, the minimum and maximum key lengths, specified in secret key bits. To allow all users to connect, allow anything from a 40-bit key up to a 128-bit secret key:

```
CMD:set wep_key_range 40 128
Configuration will be set at next restart
```

Alternatively, the key range can be set to *normal* to allow only 40-secret-bit keys or *high* to allow only 128-secret-bit keys:

```
CMD:set wep_key_range high
Configuration will be set at next restartAs noted in Chapter 5, Nokia quotes all WEP
key lengths as the length of the secret key. Nokia's 128-bit keys have 128 secret
bits and are not compatible with most other vendors' implementations.
```

 As with all other command-line work, the settings described in this section can be made through the Advanced WEP configuration page. Figure 14-7 shows this page, set to use the local (device) key database. RADIUS keys are discussed in the next section.

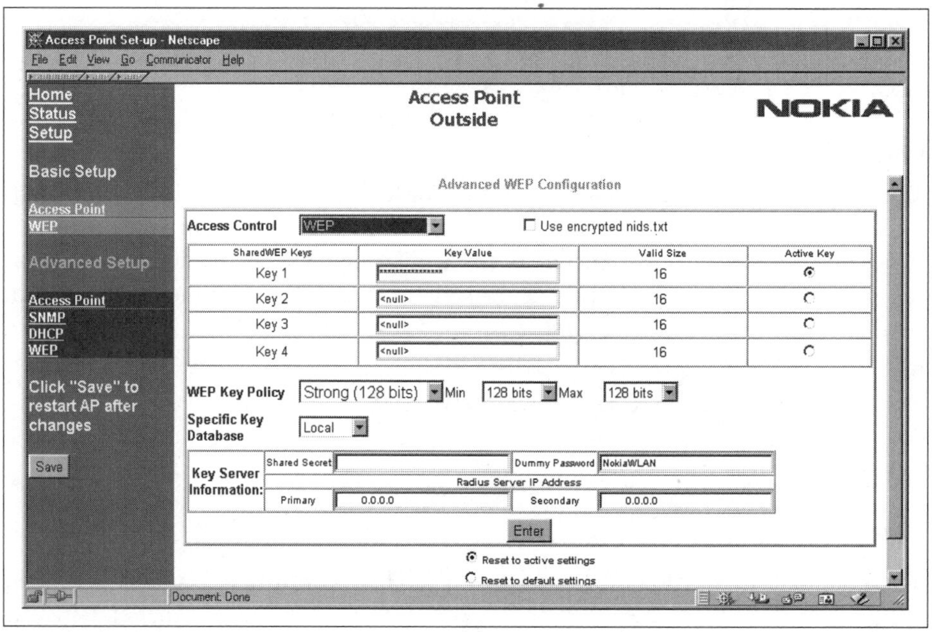

Figure 14-17. Advanced WEP configuration

Personal WEP and RADIUS

Personal WEP is something of a misnomer because it does not map keys to users. It maps keys to MAC addresses. Each MAC address must be configured as a user account on the specified RADIUS server. When the A032 receives an association request from a station, it queries the RADIUS server for the WEP key stored in the

RADIUS database for the MAC address in the association request. After receiving the WEP key, the association proceeds normally.

Keys are stored in the RADIUS server under the MAC addresses that are allowed. A RADIUS "account" for each card must be created. When the A032 receives an association request, it sends an authentication request to the server consisting of the client's MAC address and the dummy password in Figure 14-17. The RADIUS server returns an acceptance message if there is an "account" for the MAC address that includes the client's WEP key in its response.

Filtering management connections

It is conceivable that an access point may need to be configured to allow management connections only from selected stations. If access is restricted using the *set manager specific* command, the A032 checks each incoming management connection against the list and validates its access privileges. Stations can be added to the list using the *set manager_ip* command, which takes three arguments. The first is the IP address of the manager. The second and third arguments are for accepting requests and sending SNMP traps; a setting of 1 is used to enable the function, and a setting of 0 is used to disable it. To allow management connections from 10.1.2.88, use the following commands:

```
CMD:set manager_ip 1 10.1.2.88 1 0
Configuration will be set at next restart
CMD:set manager specific
Configuration will be updated on next restart
```

Specific manager configurations can be updated from the "Set Specific Managers" link in the Advanced Access Point Set-up, as shown in Figure 14-18.

Naming allowed stations

For ease of management of a number of features on the A032, MAC addresses can be associated with text entries called *network identifiers* (NIDs). Naming stations is done only at the command line using the *nid* command, which takes one of three arguments, all of which are self-explanatory:

```
CMD:nid add 00005e000145 Matthew
CMD:nid list
----NID----- ------Name------ M
00005e000145 Matthew         ,NH
CMD:nid delete 00005e000145 Matthew
CMD:nid list
<list empty>
```

NID mappings can be retrieved from or sent to the access point using TFTP. Simply fetch or send the file named *nids.txt* from the access point's IP address. If management filtering is on, the TFTP client must be on the manager list. In the file itself, the last column in the NID list is used to note whether the entry is a station (N) or a

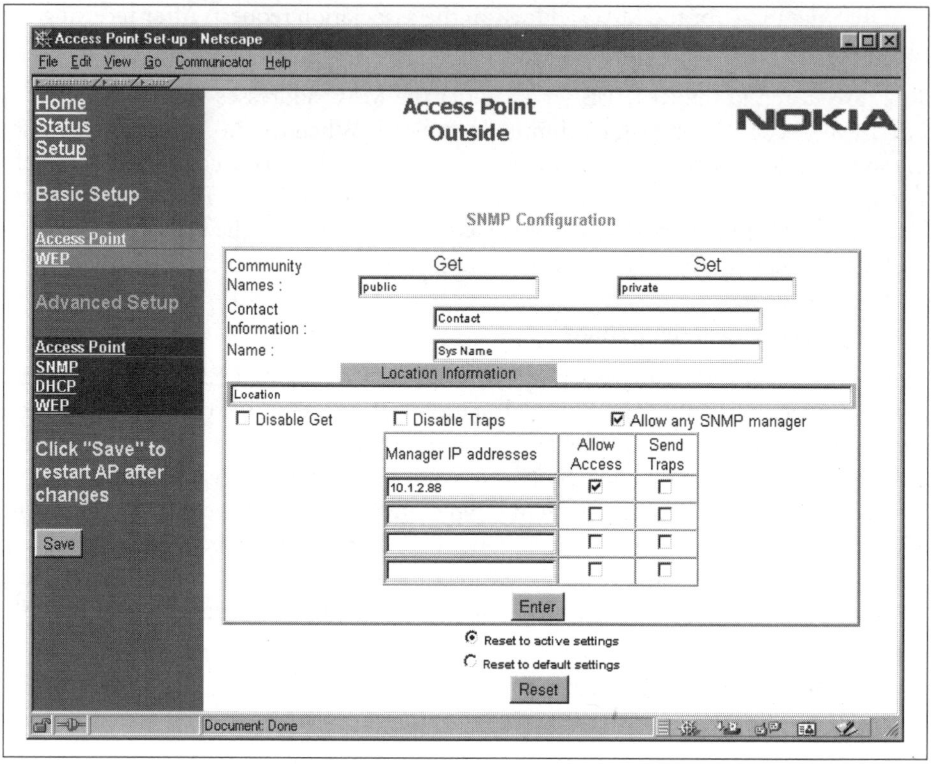

Figure 14-18. Setting specific managers

bridge (B). Bridge entries are relevant only when the A032 is deployed as a wireless bridge.

```
[gast@bloodhound]$ tftp a032
tftp> get nids.txt
Received 140 bytes in 0.0 seconds
tftp> quit
[gast@bloodhound]$ cat nids.txt
/ NID/Bridge list for AP(Outside) on Sat, 24 Nov 2001 23:12:39
49f7e6ca2f478073a1dcdf2cfeba08cc
00005e000145 Matthew          ,NH,
```

Up to 200 name/MAC pairs can be stored. No facility is provided by Nokia to synchronize the lists. System administrators must develop scripts to keep a single copy of *nids.txt* up to date and push it out to access points using TFTP.

Restricting associations

MAC address filtering is performed using the NIDs. Associations can be restricted to "named" stations. If a station does not have an entry in the NID list, it is not allowed to associate:

```
CMD:set admission named
Configuration will be updated on next restart
```

Address filtering is enabled with the web interface by restricting admission to named stations, as shown in Figure 14-19.

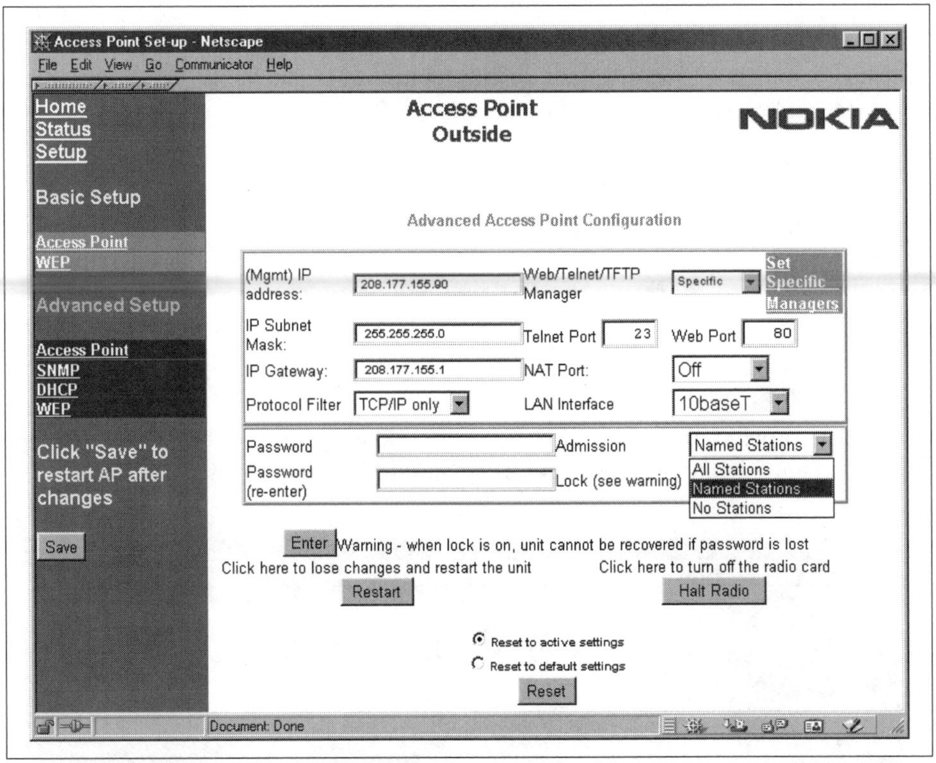

Figure 14-19. Enabling address filtering for associations

Monitoring Wireless Stations

802.11 is a link-layer protocol, and monitoring the link-layer associations is important to troubleshooting. The status menu in the web interface allows the administrator to see all the associated wireless stations, all the known wireless stations, and all the known MAC addresses.

All the currently associated stations are listed with *show a*. Stations with a name-to-MAC mapping are displayed by name:

```
CMD:show a
Total bridge entries      :6
Number Wireless Stations :1
   MAC Address    State       Channel Power IP Address
   c110           Associated   11      On    10.1.2.91
```

The difference between "all associated stations" and "all wireless stations" is that the latter includes any wireless stations learned about from another access point. All wireless stations are displayed with *show s*.

All known stations are printed with *show g*. Stations connected to the Ethernet port are shown as "LAN" stations, and wireless stations are shown as "AIR" stations. A few MAC addresses are reserved for internal use.

```
CMD:show g
Total bridge entries    :6
Number Wireless Stations :1
    Net ID          Interface  IP Address
  0000C06F37EE        LAN      208.177.155.88
  001067003F86        LAN      208.177.155.1
  c110                AIR      208.177.155.91
  00E003056F7F     Internal
  00E003000000     Internal
  00E003802F88     Internal   208.177.155.90
```

show g also provides the content for the "Network Summary" in the web interface, as shown in Figure 14-20. Internal stations are not displayed in the web interface.

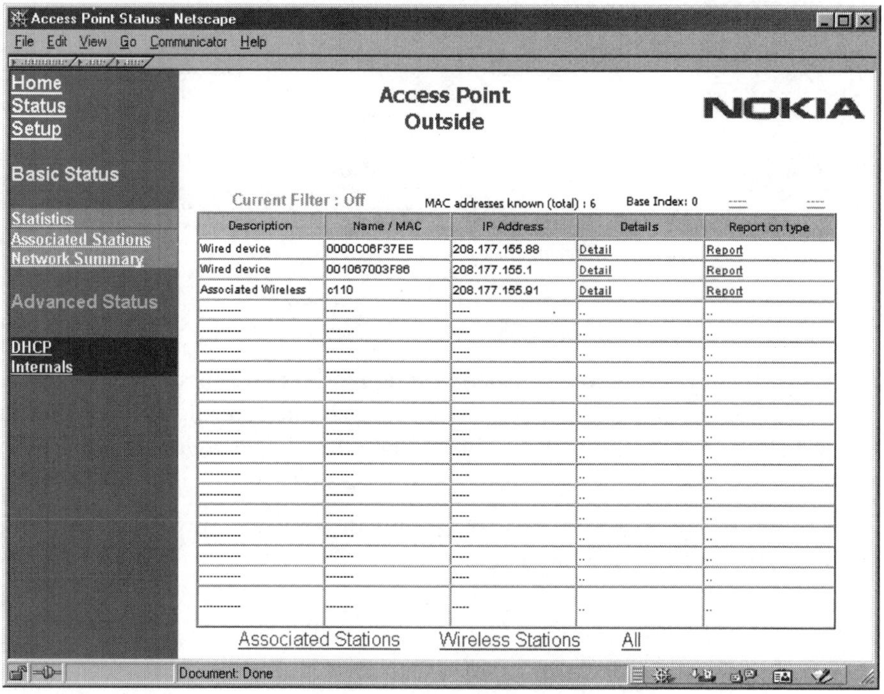

Figure 14-20. Network summary page

Monitoring System Resources and Load

Counters can be monitored at the command line using the *stats* command. Statistics for both the wired and wireless interfaces are maintained, and they can be viewed by using *stats lan* and *stats air*:

```
CMD:stats lan
Stats last cleared : Sat, 24 Nov 2001 23:56:18
Accumulation time (secs) :     661

LAN Statistics:        Last 10s  Cumulative
tx lan frames    :       4358      23747
tx data bytes    :     371680    2039080
rx lan frames(all):     5952      36074
rx frames accepted:     5948      30980
rx data bytes    :     513936    2717364
rx discard frames :        0        311
CMD:stats air
Stats last cleared : Sat, 24 Nov 2001 23:56:18
Accumulation time (secs) :     663

Air Statistics:        Last 10s  Cumulative
tx frames :             5972      31657
tx bytes :             630273    3529370
tx fail  :                 0         62
rx frames(all) :        4360      23882
rx frames(mgmnt):          0          3
rx frames(data):        4360      23879
rx data bytes  :       441773    2433732
discard frames :           0        116
```

Software versions and basic system information are shown on the "Advanced Internals" status page in the web interface, reproduced in Figure 14-21. The bar graph at the bottom gives some indication of the system load. The buffer load shows the percentage of buffer memory used. Under normal situations, it should be 60% or less. System loading is the processor utilization. Radio usage is self-evident. Obviously, the access point shown in Figure 14-21 is under a heavy load.

Troubleshooting Tools

Troubleshooting is not the A032's strong point. The only network troubleshooting tool supplied with the A032 firmware is the lowly *ping*, and it works as expected. *traceroute* is not included.

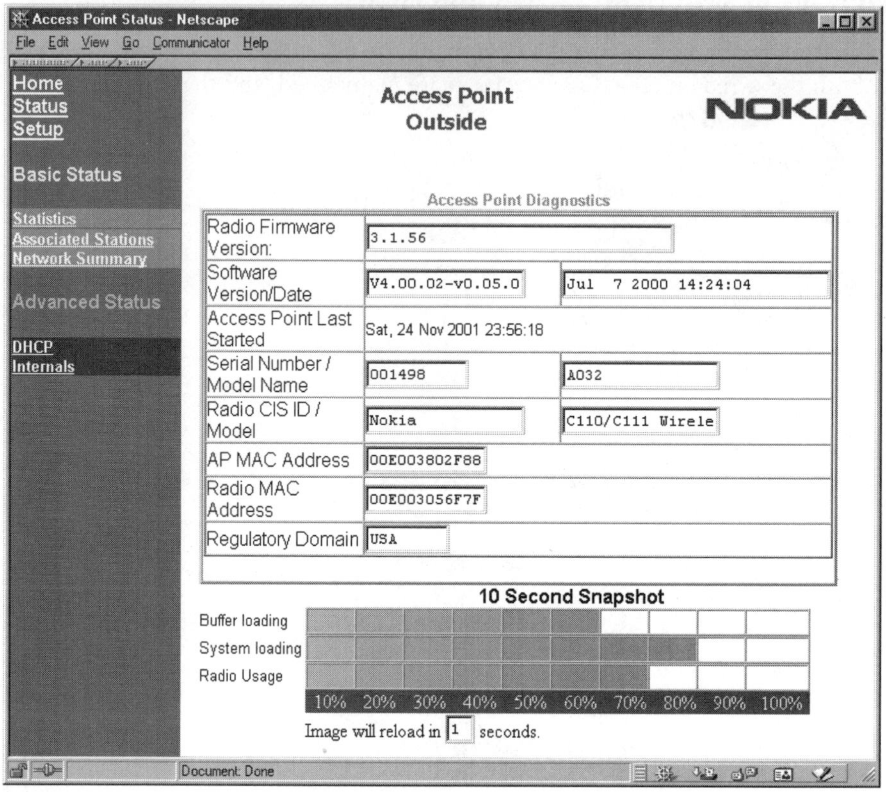

Figure 14-21. Advanced Internals status page

## CHAPTER 15

802.11 Network Deployment

Deploying a wireless LAN is a considerable undertaking. Significant planning is required before you can even touch the hardware. Deploying a wireless network is not simply a matter of identifying user locations and connecting them to the backbone. Wireless LANs provide mobility through roaming capabilities, but this feature comes with a price. Wireless LANs are much more susceptible to eavesdropping and unauthorized access. Working to mitigate the security problems while offering high levels of service makes large wireless LAN deployments topologically more complex, especially because solving security problems means that a great deal of integration work may be required to get all the different pieces of the solution working in concert.

Wireless networks require far more deployment planning because of the nature of the radio link. Every building has its own personality with respect to radio transmissions, and unexpected interference can pop up nearly everywhere because of microwave ovens, electrical conduits, or severe multipath interference. As a result, each wireless LAN deployment is unique in many respects, and careful planning and a meticulous site survey are required before removing any equipment from the box.

Beyond considerations due to the physical environment, wireless networks often extend an existing wired infrastructure. The wired infrastructure may be quite complex to begin with, especially if it spans several buildings in a campus setting. Wireless networks depend on having a solid, stable, well-designed wired network in place. If the existing network is not stable, chances are the wireless extension is doomed to instability as well.

This chapter is about deployment considerations for wireless LANs, written from a technical perspective. How do the features of wireless LANs influence network topology? Besides the 802.11 equipment, what do you need to deploy a network? How should the logical network be constructed for maximum mobility? What do you need to look for in a site survey to make a deployment successful?

The Topology Archetype

Figure 15-1 shows how many wireless LAN deployments evolve. This figure serves as the road map for this chapter. The guiding principle of Figure 15-1 is that mobility must be limited to the link layer, because network-layer mobility is not generally available on IP networks. The other design decisions help augment the access control of the wireless device and lower management overhead by taking advantage of existing services, each of which will be considered in turn.

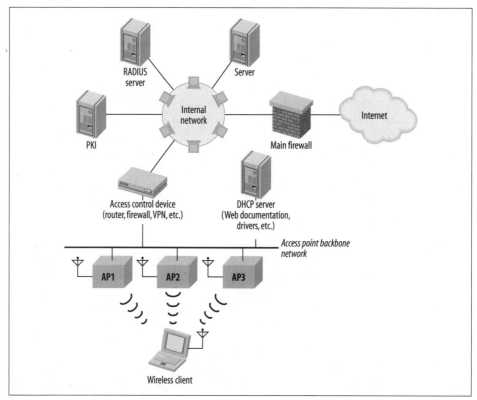

Figure 15-1. Standard wireless LAN deployment topology

Some deployments may look like multiple instances of Figure 15-1. The topology shown in the figure provides seamless mobility between the access points connected to the access point backbone network. In very large deployments, such as a campuswide deployment across a large number of buildings, it may be desirable to limit the coverage areas in which seamless roaming is provided. One common strategy is to provide seamless mobility within individual buildings, but not provide roaming between buildings. Each building would have a wireless LAN that looked something like Figure 15-1, and all the access point backbone networks would ultimately connect to a campus backbone.

Roaming and Mobility

In Figure 15-1, the network linking all the access points, which I call the *access point backbone*, is a single IP subnet. To allow users to roam between access points, the network should be a single IP subnet, even if it spans multiple locations, because IP does not generally allow for network-layer mobility. To understand this design restriction, it is important first to appreciate the difference between true *mobility* and mere *portability*.*

Portability certainly results in a net productivity gain because users can access information resources wherever it is convenient to do so. At the core, however, portability removes only the physical barriers to connectivity. It is easy to carry a laptop between several locations, so people do. But portability does not change the ritual of connecting to networks at each new location. It is still necessary to physically connect to the network and reestablish network connections, and network connections cannot be used while the device is being moved.

Mobility, on the other hand, is a far more powerful concept: it removes further barriers, most of which are based on the logical network architecture. Network connections stay active even while the device is in motion. This is critical for tasks requiring persistent, long-lived connections, which may be found in database applications. Support personnel frequently access a tracking database that logs questions, problems, and resolutions. The same argument can be made for a number of tracking applications in a health care setting. Accessing the database through a wireless network can boost productivity because it allows people to add small amounts of information from different locations without needing to reconnect to the database each time. Inventory applications are another example and one of the reasons why retail and logistics are two of the markets that have been quicker to adopt 802.11. When taking inventory, it makes far more sense to count boxes or products where they sit and relay data over a wireless network than to record data on paper and collate the data at the end of the process.

Traditional wired Ethernet connections provide portability. I can take my laptop computer anywhere on the campus at work and plug in. (If I'm willing to tolerate slow speeds, I can even make a phone call and access my corporate network from anywhere in the world.) Each time I access the network, though, I'm starting from scratch. I have to reestablish connections, even if I only moved a few feet. What I'd really like is to walk into the conference room and connect to the corporate network without doing anything.

---

* The exception to this general rule is, of course, a network in which Mobile IP is deployed. I am enthusiastic about Mobile IP, especially on wireless networks, but it is far from ubiquitous as I write this book. Most network engineers are, therefore, designing networks without the benefit of network-layer mobility.

And therein lies the rub. 802.11 is implemented at the link layer and provides link-layer mobility. IP affords the network designer no such luxury. 802.11 hosts can move within the last network freely, but IP, as it is currently deployed, provides no way to move across subnet boundaries. To the IP-based hosts of the outside world, the VPN/access control boxes of Figure 15-1 are the last-hop routers. To get to an 802.11 wireless station with an IP address on the wireless network, simply go through the IP router to that network. It doesn't matter whether a wireless station is connected to the first or third access point because it is reachable through the last-hop router. As far as the outside world can tell, the wireless station might as well be a workstation connected to an Ethernet.

A second requirement for mobility is that the IP address does not change when connecting to any of the access points. New IP addresses interrupt open connections. If a wireless station connects to the first access point, it must keep the same address when it connects to the third access point.

A corollary to the second requirement is that all the wireless stations must be on the same IP subnet. As long as a station stays on the same IP subnet, it does not need to reinitialize its networking stack and can keep its TCP connections open. If it leaves the subnet, though, it needs to get a IP new address and reestablish any open connections. The purpose of the design in Figure 15-1 is to assign a single IP subnet to the wireless stations and allow them to move freely between access points. Multiple subnets are not forbidden, but if you have different IP subnets, seamless mobility between subnets is not possible.

The "single IP subnet backbone" restriction of the design in Figure 15-1 is a reflection on the technology deployed within most organizations. Mobile IP was standardized in late 1996 in RFC 2002, but it has yet to see widespread deployment. (See the sidebar for a description of how Mobile IP allows stations to change IP addresses without interrupting connections.) Until Mobile IP can be deployed, network designers must live within the limitations of IP and design networks based on fixed locations for IP addresses. In Figure 15-1, the backbone network may be physically large, but it is fundamentally constrained by the requirement that all access points connect directly to the backbone router (and each other) at the link layer.

Spanning multiple locations with an 802.11 network

Access points that cooperate in providing mobility need to be connected to each other at layer 2. One method of doing this, shown in Figure 15-2a, builds the wireless infrastructure of Figure 15-1 in parallel to the existing wired infrastructure. Access points are supported by a separate set of switches, cables, and uplinks in the core network. Virtual LANs (VLANs) can be employed to cut down on the required physical infrastructure, as in Figure 15-2b. Rather than acting as a simple layer-2 repeater, the switch in Figure 15-2b can logically divide its ports into multiple layer-2 networks. The access points can be placed on a separate VLAN from the existing wired stations, and the "wireless VLAN" can be given its own IP subnet. Frames leaving the switch for the network core are tagged with the VLAN number to keep them logically distinct and may be sent to different destinations based on the tag. Multiple subnets can be run over the same uplink because the VLAN tag allows frames to be logically separated. Incoming frames for the wired networks are tagged with one VLAN identifier, and frames for the wireless VLAN are tagged with a different VLAN identifier. Frames are sent only to ports on the switch that are part of the same VLAN, so incoming frames tagged with the wireless VLAN are delivered only to the access points.

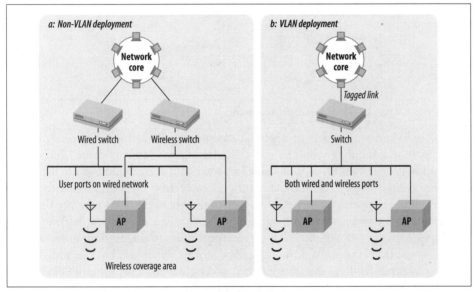

Figure 15-2. Physical topologies for 802.11 network deployment

Even better, VLANs can easily span long distances. VLAN-aware switches can be connected to each other, and the tagged link can be used to join multiple physical locations into a single logical network. In Figure 15-3, two switches are connected by a tagged link, and all four access points are assigned to the same VLAN. The four access points can be put on the same IP subnet and will act as if they are connected to a single hub. The tagged link allows the two switches to be separated, and the distance can depend on the technology. By using fiber-optic links, VLANs can be made to go between buildings, so a single IP subnet can be extended across as many buildings as necessary.

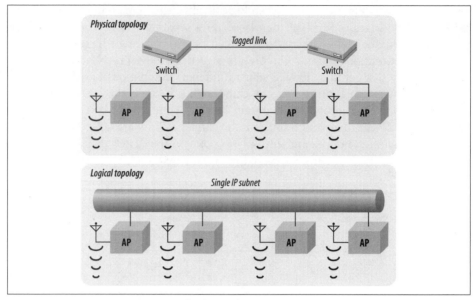

Figure 15-3. Using VLANs to span multiple switches

Tagged links can vary widely in cost and complexity. To connect different physical locations in one building, you can use a regular copper Ethernet cable. To connect two buildings together, fiber-optic cable is a must. Different buildings are usually at different voltage levels relative to each other. Connecting two buildings with a conductor such as copper would enable current to flow between (and possibly through) the two Ethernet switches, resulting in expensive damage. Fiber-optic cable does not conduct electricity and will not pick up electrical noise in the outdoor environment, which is a particular concern during electrical storms. Fiber also has the added benefit of high speeds for long-distance transmissions. If several Fast Ethernet devices are connected to a switch, the uplink will be a bottleneck if it is only a Fast Ethernet interface. For best results on larger networks, uplinks are typically Gigabit Ethernet.

For very large organizations with very large budgets, uplinks do not need to be Ethernet. One company I have worked with uses a metro-area ATM cloud to connect buildings throughout a city at the link layer. With appropriate translations between Ethernet and ATM, such a service can be used as a trunk between switches. Computer trade shows such as Comdex and Interop regularly use metro-area networks to showcase both the metro-area services and the equipment used to access those services.

Limits on mobility

The access point backbone network must be a single IP subnet and a single layer-2 connection throughout an area over which continuous coverage is provided. It may span multiple locations using VLANs. Large campuses may be forced to break up the access point backbone network into several smaller networks, each of which resembles Figure 15-1.

802.11 allows an ESS to extend across subnet boundaries, as in Figure 15-4a. Users can roam throughout each "island" of connectivity, but network connections will be interrupted when moving between islands. One solution is to teach users one SSID and let them know that mobility is restricted; another alternative is to name each SSID separately. Both solutions have advantages. In the first case, there is only one SSID and no user confusion, but there may be complaints if the coverage areas do not provide mobility in the right ways. In the second case, mobility is always provided within an SSID, but there are several SSIDs and more opportunity for user confusion.

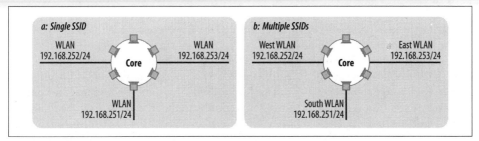

Figure 15-4. Noncontiguous deployments

When a campus is broken into several disjointed coverage areas as in Figure 15-4, be sure to preserve the mobility most important to the users. In most cases, mobility within a building will be the most important, so each building's wireless network can be its own IP subnet. In some environments, mobility may be restricted to groups of several buildings each, so the islands in Figure 15-4 may consist of multiple buildings.

Address assignment through DHCP

Multiple independent data sets that must be synchronized are an accident waiting to happen in any field. With respect to wireless LANs, they present a particular problem for DHCP service. To make life as easy as possible for users, it would be best if stations automatically configured themselves with IP network information. DHCP is the best way to do this. Access points frequently include DHCP servers, but it would be folly to activate the DHCP server on every access point. Multiple independent DHCP lease databases are the network equivalent of a tanker-truck pile-up waiting to happen. To avoid the "multiple independent database" problem, have a single source for IP addressing information. Furthermore, some access points may reclaim addresses if an association lapses, regardless of whether the lease has expired. For these reasons, I recommend using an existing DHCP server or installing a new server specifically to support wireless clients. Depending on the importance of the wireless infrastructure, it may be worth considering a backup server as well.

Mobile IP and Roaming

802.11 performs a sleight-of-hand trick with MAC addresses: stations communicate with a MAC address as if it were fixed in place, just like any other Ethernet station. Instead of being fixed in a set location, however, access points note when the mobile station is nearby and relay frames from the wired network to it over the airwaves. It does not matter which access point the mobile station associates with because the appropriate access point performs the relay function. The station on the wired network can communicate with the mobile station as if it were directly attached to the wire.

Mobile IP performs a similar trick with IP addresses. The outside world uses a single IP address that appears to remain in a fixed location, called the *home location*. Rather than being serviced by a user's system, however, the IP address at the home location (the *home address*) is serviced by what is called the *home agent*. Like the access point, the home agent is responsible for keeping track of the current location of the mobile node. When the mobile node is "at home," packets can simply be delivered directly to it. If the mobile node attaches to a different network (called a *foreign network* or *visited network*), it *registers* its so-called foreign location with the home agent so that the home agent can redirect all traffic from the home address to the mobile node on the foreign network.

Consider an example in which two wireless LANs are built on different IP subnets. On its home subnet, a wireless station can send and receive traffic "normally," since it is on its home network.

When the wireless station moves from its home subnet to the second subnet, it attaches to the network using the normal procedure. It associates with an access point and probably requests an IP address using DHCP. On a wireless station that is unable to use Mobile IP, connections are interrupted at this point because the IP address changes suddenly, invalidating the state of all open TCP connections.

Wireless stations equipped with Mobile IP software, however, can preserve connection state by registering with the home agent. The home agent can accept packets for the mobile station, check its registration tables, and then send the packets to the mobile station at its current location. The mobile station has, in effect, two addresses. It has its home address, and it can continue to use this address for connections that were established using the home address. It may also use the address it has been assigned on the foreign network. No TCP state is invalidated because the mobile station never stopped using its home address.

—continued—

Naturally, this sidebar has omitted a great deal of the detail of the protocol operations. Designing a protocol to allow a station to attach anywhere in the world and use an address from its home network is a significant engineering endeavor. Several security problems are evident, most notably the authentication of protocol operations and the security of the redirected packets from the home network to the mobile station's current location. Maintaining accurate routing information, both the traditional forwarding tables at Internet gateways and the Mobile IP agents, is a major challenge. And, of course, the protocol must work with both IPv4 and IPv6. For a far more detailed treatment of Mobile IP, I highly recommend *Mobile IP: Design Principles and Practices* by Charles Perkins (Prentice Hall).

Within the context of Figure 15-1, there are two places to put a DHCP server. One is on the access point backbone subnet itself. A standalone DHCP server would be responsible for the addresses available for wireless stations on the wireless subnet. Each subnet would require a DHCP server as part of the rollout. Alternatively, most devices capable of routing also include DHCP relay. The security device shown in Figure 15-1 includes routing capabilities, and many firewalls and VPN devices include DHCP relay. With DHCP relay, requests from the wireless network are bridged to the access point backbone by the access point and then further relayed by the access controller to the main corporate DHCP server. If your organization centralizes address assignment with DHCP, take advantage of the established, reliable DHCP service by using DHCP relay. One drawback to DHCP relay is that the relay process requires additional time and not all clients will wait patiently, so DHCP relay may not be an option.

Static addressing is acceptable, of course. The drawback to static addressing is that more addresses are required because all users, active or not, are using an address. To minimize end user configuration, it is worth considering using DHCP to assign fixed addresses to MAC addresses.

As a final point, there may be an interaction between address assignment and security. If VPN solutions are deployed, it is possible to use RFC 1918 (private) address space for the infrastructure. DHCP servers could hand out private addresses that enable nodes to reach the VPN servers, and the VPN servers hand out routable addresses once VPN authentication succeeds.

Use a single DHCP server per access point backbone or DHCP relay at the access point network router to assign addresses to wireless stations. Static addressing or fixed addressing through DHCP is also acceptable.

Security

Informally, data security is defined in terms of three attributes, all of which must be maintained to ensure security:*

Integrity
> Broadly speaking, integrity is compromised when data is modified by unauthorized users. ("Has somebody improperly changed the data?")

Secrecy
> Of the three items, secrecy is perhaps the easiest to understand. We all have secrets and can easily understand the effect of a leak. ("Has the data been improperly disclosed?")

Availability
> Data is only as good as your ability to use it. Denial-of-service attacks are the most common threat to availability. ("Can I read my data when I want to?")

Wireless LAN technology has taken a fair number of knocks for its failures in all three areas. Most notably, though, wireless LANs have two major failings with respect to the informal definition of security. First, secrecy is difficult on a wireless network. Wireless networks do not have firm physical boundaries, and frames are transmitted throughout a general area. Attackers can passively listen for frames and analyze data. To defeat attacks against secrecy, network security engineers must employ cryptographic protocols to ensure the confidentiality of data as it travels across the wireless medium. WEP has been a failure in this respect, but other protocols and standards may be employed instead of or in addition to WEP.

Second, integrity may be compromised by wireless hosts. Quick wireless LAN deployments are often connected directly to a supposedly secure internal network, allowing attackers to bypass the firewall. In many institutions, internal stations are afforded higher levels of access privileges. Physical security may have made some additional privileges rational or inevitable, but wireless stations may not necessarily be trusted hosts run by internal users. Attacks against integrity may frequently be defeated by strong access control.

Vendors often tout WEP as a security solution, but the proven flaws in the design of WEP should give even the most freewheeling security administrators cause for concern. WEP is, in the words of one industry observer, "unsafe at any key length."† Future approaches based on 802.1x and EAP may improve the picture, but current deployments must depend on solutions that are available now. Although products

---

* My definitions here are not meant to be formal. In this section, I'm trying to take a fundamental approach to security by showing how wireless LAN security fails and how some of the failures can be solved by applying solutions the industry has already developed.

† Or, in the words of one reviewer, "WEP is trash that just gets in the way."

claiming to support 802.1x are currently appearing on the market, they have yet to establish a track record with respect to either security or interoperabilty.

Access control and authentication

Connecting to wireless networks is designed to be easy. In fact, the ease of connection is one of the major advantages to many newer wireless technologies. 802.11 networks announce themselves to anybody willing to listen for the Beacon frames, and access control is limited by the primitive tools supplied by 802.11 itself. To protect networks against the threat of unauthorized access, strong access control should be applied. A helpful rule of thumb is to treat wireless access points like open network drops in the building lobby. 802.11 networks can benefit from access control at two points:

- Before associating with an access point, wireless stations must first authenticate. At present, this process is either nonexistent or based on WEP.

- After association with the access point, the wireless station is attached to the wireless network. However, strong authentication can be applied to any wireless stations to ensure that only authorized users are connecting to protected resources. This form of access control is no different from the access control widely enforced by firewalls today.

At the present time, the initial authentication during the association process is pitifully weak. Current deployments must depend on two methods, one of which was never specified by the standard but is widely used.

One approach is to allow only a specified set of wireless LAN interface MAC addresses to connect to access points. Maintaining the list is its own administrative headache. Distributing the list to access points may be even worse. In a network with access points from multiple vendors, the script may need to massage the list into different file formats to cope with what different products require. Frequently, the list of allowed devices must be distributed by TFTP. Even if the distribution is automated by administrative scripts, TFTP comes with its own security woes. Furthermore, like wired Ethernet cards, 802.11 cards may change the transmitter MAC address, which totally undermines the use of the MAC address as an access control token. Attackers equipped with packet sniffers can easily monitor successful associations to acquire a list of allowed MAC addresses.

A second approach is to allow connections from stations that possess a valid WEP key. Stations that pass the WEP challenge are associated, and stations that fail are not. As noted in Chapter 5, this method is not very strong because WEP is based on RC4, and it is possible to fake a legitimate response to a WEP challenge without any knowledge of the WEP key. In spite of its limitations, WEP makes a useful speed bump for attackers to jump over. Use it, but be aware of its limitations. Or disable it, but be cognizant of the fact that association is unrestricted.

In some products, these methods may be combined. However, both are easily defeated. Maintaining strong security over a wireless LAN requires solutions outside the scope of 802.11, in large part to augment the relatively weak access control supplied by 802.11.

Many networks deploy firewalls to protect against unauthorized access and use of systems by outsiders. In many respects, wireless stations should be considered untrusted until they prove otherwise, simply because of the lack of control over the physical connection. In the network topology shown in Figure 15-1, an access control device is used to protect the internal network from wireless stations. This access control device could be one of several things: a firewall, a VPN termination device, or a custom solution tailored to the requirements of 802.11 networks.

At the time this book was written, many security-conscious organizations opted to use existing firewalls or VPN devices or build systems to meet their own internal requirements. Firewalls are well-known for providing a number of strong authentication mechanisms, and they have a proven ability to integrate with one-time password systems such as RSA's SecurID tokens. New releases of IPSec VPN devices also increasingly have this capability. Initial versions of the IPSec specification allowed authentication only through digital certificates. Certificates work well for site-to-site VPNs, but the idea of rolling out a public-key infrastructure (PKI) to support remote access was frightening for most users. As a result, several new approaches allow for traditional ("legacy") user authentication mechanisms by passing VPN user authentication requests to a RADIUS server. Several mechanisms were in draft form as this book was written: Extended Authentication (XAUTH), Hybrid Mode IKE, and CRACK (Challenge/Response for Authenticated Control Keys).

Several wireless LAN vendors have also stepped up to the plate to offer specialized "wireless access controller" devices, which typically combine packet filtering, authentication, authorization, and accounting services (AAA), and a DHCP server; many devices also include a DNS server and VPN termination. AAA features are typically provided by an interface to an existing corporate infrastructure such as RADIUS, which frequently has already been configured for remote access purposes. Some products may also include dynamic DNS so that a domain name is assigned to a user, but the IP number can be assigned with DHCP.

Several vendors have access controller solutions. Cisco offers an external access control server for the Aironet product line. Lucent's ORiNOCO AS-2000 access server has an integrated RADIUS server. Nokia's P020 Public Access Zone Controller is an integrated network appliance with a RADIUS client and DHCP server, and the companion P030 Mobility Services Manager offers the RADIUS server and billing functions.

 Recognize the limitations of WEP. Treat wireless stations as you would treat untrusted external hosts. Isolate wireless LAN segments with firewalls, and use strong authentication for access control. Consider using existing user databases as part of the authentication roll-out.

Confidentiality: WEP, IPSec, or something else?

Confidentiality is the second major goal in wireless LAN deployments. Traffic is left unprotected by default, and this is an inappropriate security posture for most organizations. Users can choose among three options:

- Use WEP.
- Use a proven cryptographic product based on open protocols.
- Use a proprietary protocol.

Option three locks you into a single vendor and leaves you at their mercy for upgrades and bug fixes. Proprietary cryptographic protocols also have a poor track record at ensuring security. In the end, the choice really comes down to whether WEP is good enough. Given the insecurity of WEP, there are two questions to ask:

"Does the data on this network need to stay secret for more than a week?" WEP is not strong encryption by any stretch of the imagination, and you should assume that a sufficiently motivated attacker could easily capture traffic from the wireless network, recover the WEP key, and decrypt any data.

"Do users need to be protected from each other?" In most WEP deployments, keys are distributed to every authorized station. When all users have access to the key, the data is protected from outsiders only. WEP does not protect an authorized user with the key from recovering the data transmitted by another authorized user. If users need to be protected from each other, which is a common requirement in many computing environments, then additional security precautions are required.

Choosing a cryptographic protocol or product is subject to a few basic ground rules, conveniently summarized in the Cryptographic Snake Oil FAQ.* While looking for signs of snake oil is not sure protection, it should filter out the most egregious duds. Cryptography is like a fine wine—it gets better with age. If a protocol or algorithm has withstood extensive public analysis, it is probably better than something just invented.

There are only a few non–snake oil solutions that are worth considering. To provide confidentiality at the network layer, there is only one standard: IPSec. Unfortunately, IPSec is not without its drawbacks. It is a complex system to understand and use, so you must be prepared for a learning curve for network administrators. The complexity of IPSec contributes to a relatively high management overhead, at least at the beginning of deployment. IPSec solutions require the installation of client software on wireless stations to protect outbound traffic, and desktop software management is

---

* The full document title is "Snake Oil Warning Signs: Encryption Software to Avoid." Get your very own copy from *http://www.interhack.net/people/cmcurtin/snake-oil-faq.html*, among many other places. Bruce Schneier wrote a nice summary of the Snake Oil FAQ in the February 15, 1999, Crypto-Gram newsletter, available from *http://www.counterpane.com/crypto-gram-9902.html*.

always unpleasant at best. Perhaps the most frustrating attribute of IPSec is the difficulty in configuring two different systems to be interoperable. Extensive testing of IPSec interoperability can be a huge burden, one that should not be taken lightly.

An alternative is to allow only applications with strong built-in cryptographic systems. Web-based systems can be secured with the secure socket layer (SSL). Host logins can be secured with SSH. SSH can also be used to secure many types of TCP-based network traffic, though the port-forwarding configuration may be too complex for many users. Some environments may have already deployed a framework such as Kerberos for application layer security, in which case, it can probably be extended to wireless stations without great difficulty.

 Consider the wireless network to be transmitting data in the clear if you are not using strong, proven cryptographic solutions such as IPSec or SSH.

Availability through redundancy

Nothing in Figure 15-1 requires single points of failure. Clustered solutions for all the major components exist, so availability is not necessarily compromised by the failure of any of the security components. Clusters are composed of several independent devices that get together and share state information among multiple machines. When any member of the cluster fails, survivors pick up the workload with no interruption. If you elect to use either firewalls or VPNs, consider using a clustered product. Clustering is particularly important for VPN access because you own the infrastructure, and users are far less forgiving of internal problems than flaky Internet connectivity.

One item to watch for in this area is redundancy for DHCP servers. No standard exists for synchronizing the data held by DHCP servers. However, the Network Working Group of the IETF is working towards a standardized DHCP failover protocol, which will increase the reliability of the address allocation service.

Summary and Analysis of Archetypal Topology

Several points about the archetypal topology of Figure 15-1 are important and bear repeating:

1. 802.11 provides for mobility only within an extended service set, and Inter-Access Point Protocols (IAPPs) cooperate only when directly connected at the link layer. Until a standard is developed, proprietary IAPPs are not guaranteed to interoperate; you need to select a single access point vendor for each area of continuous coverage. Each extended service set (ESS) should therefore be a single IP subnet. It is acceptable to use VLANs and other bridging technologies to achieve this goal.

2. Address assignment is best done as dynamic addressing to minimize end user configuration. Only one DHCP server should be responsible for handing out addresses to wireless stations because it is important to prevent accidental readdressing. That server may be placed on the access point backbone. DHCP relay can also be used to take advantage of DHCP servers that are already deployed.

3. Consider the use of WEP. In many cases, it is not recommended because it does not significantly bolster security, but it may complicate roaming, and it is just another configuration item to get wrong. Some vendors charge more for cards that implement the "strong" 128-bit WEP, too.

4. Consider the security policy and goals for your wireless network. WEP is problematic, but it may be better than running open access points. In many environments, though, WEP should be disabled. With large numbers of users, WEP is just another configuration item to get wrong. Deploying WEP may also complicate roaming between access points.

5. Carefully consider the limitations of WEP and deploy additional solutions to enhance:

   Authentication
   > WEP does not provide strong user authentication, so treat any wireless stations as you would untrusted external hosts. Your security policy may offer guidance here—how do you protect against threats from existing mobile users, such as telecommuters and road warriors? Isolate wireless LAN segments with firewalls and use strong authentication for access control. Existing user databases such as RADIUS servers can probably be used as part of the access control deployment.

   Confidentiality
   > If you do not want to broadcast data to the world, use strong, proven cryptographic solutions to protect data as it traverses the airwaves. IPSec is the best standardized solution, especially since it now provides strong user authentication with existing token-based systems.

6. To maintain availability and increase uptime, use clustered solutions whenever possible and cost-effective.

Project Planning

Site survey work is the heart of installing a wireless LAN. To successfully run a site survey, though, preparation is very important.

Gathering Requirements

Before "breaking cable" on a network expansion, gather end user requirements and information to find out which expectations are important. Use the following checklist to flesh out the customer requirements; each point is detailed further in a subsequent section:

Throughput considerations

How much throughput is required? This is partly dependent on the type of device that will be used on the wireless LAN, though if it is a PC-like device with the ability to display large and complex graphics, you will want your wireless LAN to be as fast as possible. In most cases, this will lead to choosing 802.11b-based networks to use the 11-Mbps physical layer. If you like leading-edge technology, you may want to consider 802.11a products, several of which appeared just as this book went to press.

Coverage area

Where should coverage be provided, and what is the density of users in particular areas?

Mobility

How much movement between coverage is needed? Does it need to be full mobility, with continuous connections as the wireless station moves around the network? Or can the network simply enable effective portability by facilitating automatic reconfiguration when the mobile station moves between coverage areas?

User population

How many people will use the wireless network, and what quality of service do they expect? As always, be sure to allow for growth!

Physical network planning

Will new network cabling be needed to supply the wireless LAN backbone, or can you make do with existing cabling? Are an adequate number of outlets available in the correct locations? Can the access points and antennas be installed in the open or must they be confined to wiring closets or other hidden locations?

Logical network planning

How many IP addresses will be set aside for wireless users? Is a large enough address block available, or will the existing network need to be renumbered to accommodate the wireless network? If the necessary IP address space is not available, it may mean cutting back on the level of seamless mobility on the wireless LAN.

Application characteristics

Can address translation be used to save IP address space? Are any applications sensitive to high or variable delays? Do any applications provide time-critical data? If so, consider looking for products that support the point coordination function and contention-free delivery, but be aware that many products do not support the PCF.

Security requirements

Wireless LANs have been subject to a number of security concerns. The two main goals of wireless LAN security planning are ensuring adequate access control and preserving the confidentiality of data as it traverses the wireless network. Security requirements may be dictated by legal requirements or the legal threat of unauthorized data disclosure.

Authentication has long been a weak point of 802.11 networks. The two main options provided by 802.11 are to filter on the MAC addresses of wireless stations allowed to connect or use shared WEP keys for stronger authentication. In practice, MAC address filtering is too cumbersome and error-prone, so the choices are to use WEP authentication or depend on external solutions.

Data confidentiality is provided by encryption services. One option is the WEP standard, though higher-security sites may opt for additional VPN technology on top of the 802.11 layer.

Site environmental considerations

A number of factors can affect radio propagation and signal quality. Building materials, construction, and floor plan all affect how well radio waves can move throughout the building. Interference is a fact of life, but it is more pronounced in some buildings than in others. Temperature and humidity have minor effects. Early site visits can assist in anticipating several factors, and a detailed site survey can spot any real problems before installation begins in earnest.

Purchasing wireless LAN hardware and software

At some point, wireless LAN hardware and software must be purchased. Many vendors exist, and the decision can be based on a number of criteria. (Selecting an access point vendor was discussed in Chapter 14.) Selecting cards may depend on your institution's policies. Some organizations may choose to purchase all cards centrally from a single vendor. Others may choose to select a small set of officially "supported" vendors but allow users to select alternative hardware if they are willing to forego official support from the network staff. At least one wireless network analyzer should be part of the budget. Depending on the size of the wireless LAN and the number of network administrators, you may wish to budget for more than one.

Project management

As with many other projects, drawing up a schedule and budget is a necessary component. This chapter does not provide any guidance on nontechnical factors because they are often organization-specific.

Network performance requirements

Depending on the applications used on the wireless network, different requirements are imposed. One of the most important items, and the one that is least under the control of the network architect, is the characteristics of the application. Most applications can now be run over TCP/IP, but they may require widely varying throughput, delay, or timing characteristics. More importantly, though, is how an application reacts to network address translation (NAT)—translating its IP addresses with intermediate devices.

Single TCP connections, such as those used by HTTP and SSH, are easily translated with no side effects. Other network protocols, most notably those in the Microsoft Networking family, embed the source IP address in the data portion of the packet and cannot be used in conjunction with address translation without great difficulty.* NAT also causes problems for most videoconferencing applications. At the time this book was written, standardized IPSec also did not work when the IPSec packet was passed through an address translator because IPSec authenticates the source IP address of the packet. Translating the source IP address caused the integrity check to fail.

The remaining three factors are under direct control of the end user. A coverage area must be defined, and a form of mobility between the coverage areas is a likely companion requirement. (Mobility imposes its own requirements on the IP addressing architecture, which was discussed previously.)

Finally, end users will have a target throughput requirement. Any throughput goals must be carefully considered because wireless LANs are a shared medium, but one without an upgrade path similar to dropping in an Ethernet switch.

Table 15-1 shows the number of users that can be served on 11-Mbps 802.11b networks, with different sustained loads per user. Wireless LAN bit rates are low, and the extra management features limit throughput to a relatively low fraction of the available bit rate. As you can see from the table, though, 11-Mbps networks are likely to be practical for office environments, which are mainly email, web browsing, and intermittent file access. It is likely that 20–30 users per access point is a reasonable estimate for capacity planning.

Table 15-1. Network capacity compared to sustained throughput per user

Connection method and speed	Effective number of simultaneous users on 11-Mbps networks (6 Mbps data throughput)
Cellular modem, 9.6 kbps	625
Modem, 50 kbps	120
Single ISDN B channel, 64 kbps	93
Dual ISDN, 128 kbps	46
100 kbps sustained LAN usage	60
150 kbps sustained LAN usage	40

* NAT devices can block logon traffic and the inter-domain controller chatter used by NT-based networks. See articles Q172227 and Q186340 in the Microsoft Knowledge Base.

Table 15-1. Network capacity compared to sustained throughput per user (continued)

Connection method and speed	Effective number of simultaneous users on 11-Mbps networks (6 Mbps data throughput)
200 kbps sustained LAN usage	30
300 kbps sustained LAN usage	20

Realistic throughput expectations for 802.11b networks

In terms of throughput, the performance of 802.11 LANs is similar to shared Ethernet. As more users are added, the available capacity per user is divided up. A practical rule of thumb is that the highest throughput that can be attained using the DCF is 75% of the nominal bit rate. The 75% figure is a theoretical result derived from the protocol itself; it includes overhead such as the preamble, interframe spaces, and framing headers. However, throughput rates as low as 50% may be observed. A target of 65% of the nominal bit rate is commonly observed.

For 2-Mbps networks, this translates to a top speed of 1.5 Mbps, though rates as low as 1.3 Mbps are common. Applying similar percentages to 11-Mbps networks yields a practical throughput range of 6 to 8 Mbps.

For networks under the operation of the PCF, throughput is higher because it uses shorter interframe spaces and more efficient acknowledgments. Implementation of the PCF is not required by the standard, so implementations are quite uncommon.

Security

The security trade-offs were discussed in the previous "Security" section. In many cases, an IPSec-based VPN is the logical choice. IPSec was designed for precisely the environment that wireless LANs typify. Intruders can easily capture traffic and perform extensive offline attacks with stored data. Now that IPSec is evolving to support remote clients connecting to central sites, it can also be used to provide strong authentication without a difficult PKI rollout. Many products now support one of the various standards to allow an IPSec termination device to perform user authentication through RADIUS, which allows administrators to take advantage of existing authentication databases. The new 802.1x standard incorporates RADIUS; unless there's a critical problem in 802.1x (as there was in WEP), future wireless security is likely to be based on the 1x standard.

Coverage and physical installation restrictions

Part of the end user requirement is a desired coverage area, and possibly some physical restrictions to go along with it. Physical restrictions, such as a lack of available electrical power and network connections, can be mundane. Some institutions may also require that access points and antennas are hidden; this may be to maintain the physical security of the network infrastructure, or it may be simply to preserve the aesthetic appeal of the building.

11a, 11b, 11g, and more?

Where do you go past 11 Mbps? That's the question people have been asking with increasing frequency over the past year. Right now, the leading standard for higher wireless data rates is 802.11a; it provides 54 Mbps in the 5-GHz band. 802.11a products are on the market now, though it's really too early to say anything substantial about them. Some vendors are announcing that their access points can be upgraded to 802.11a by purchasing a new card and installing new firmware. Software upgrades may be helpful, but only if the hardware is ready for 802.11a. Some vendors have boasted about the easy software upgrade to the 54-Mbps performance of 802.11a, but the access point in question had only a 10-Mbps Ethernet port. Any access points you consider software upgrades for should have Fast Ethernet ports. 802.11a is somewhat more expensive than 11b, though prices should begin to drop soon.

Because 802.11a uses the same MAC layer as 802.11b, with the OFDM PHY layer discussed in Chapter 12, I expect the installation and administration of products to be essentially the same as it is for 802.11b products. In short, just about everything discussed in this book still applies. I am guessing that the range should be similar; OFDM looks like a superior modulation technique, but at the higher frequency, there should be greater problems with path loss, multipath fading, reflections, etc. One estimation was that the radius of 802.11a access points would be 20–25% shorter. Because the 5GHz band is much larger than the ISM band and isn't already occupied by microwave ovens and other devices, there should be fewer problems with interference.

Another standard waiting in the wings is 802.11g. 11g is a 2.4-GHz standard, like 11b, but it uses the OFDM modulation technique of 11a. It also operates at 54 Mbps. The standard isn't finalized yet, and it's hard to imagine products appearing before the end of 2002. The upgrade path from 11b to 11g might be easier than that from 11b to 11a; because both standards use the same frequency band, you should be able to upgrade your access points without worrying about changing their coverage. (For better or worse, the RF characteristics of your site will be different at 2.4 and 5 GHz, so you may find you need to move or add access points if you migrate to the higher-frequency band.) 802.11g also promises to be less expensive than 11a, though in practice this probably means only that the existence of 11g will drive down the price of 11a products.

Some organizations may want to provide coverage outdoors as well, though this is confined to mild climates. Any equipment placed outdoors should be sturdy enough to work there, which is largely a matter of waterproofing and weather resistance. One solution is to install access points inside and run antennas to outdoor locations, but external antenna cables that are long enough are not always available. Outdoor network extensions can be difficult because most 802.11 equipment is not suited to outdoor use, and even if it was, power and Ethernet connections are not readily available outdoors. The best approach to providing outdoor coverage is to keep the access points inside and use external weatherproof antennas on the roof.

The Building

It is a great help to get blueprints or floor plans and take a tour of the installation site as early as possible in the process. Based on a walk-through with the floor plans, you can note where coverage must be provided, nearby network and power drops, and any relevant environmental factors. Most importantly, you can correct the blueprints based on any changes made to the structure since the blueprints were drawn. Many minor changes will not be reflected on the blueprints.

Different materials have different effects on the radio link. Signal power is most affected by metal, so elevator shafts and air ducts cause significant disruption of communications. Tinted or coated windows frequently cause severe disruption of radio signals. Some buildings may have metal-coated ceilings or significant amounts of metal in the floor. Wood and most glass panes have only small effects, though bullet-proof glass can be quite bad. Brick and concrete have effects somewhere between metal and plain untreated glass. To a large extent, though, the expected drop in signal quality due to building construction is a judgment call that improves with experience.

During a pre-survey walk-though, also note any potential sources of interference. The 2.4-GHz ISM band is unlicensed, so many types of devices using the band can be deployed without central coordination. Newer cordless phones operate in the 2.4-GHz band, as well as Bluetooth-based devices and a number of other unlicensed radio devices. Depending on the quality and amount of shielding, microwave ovens may also emit enough radiation to disrupt 802.11 communications. If you anticipate a large amount of interference, testing tools called *spectrum analyzers* can identify the amount of radiation in the wireless LAN frequency band. If your organization does RF testing, it may be necessary to shield any labs where testing is done to avoid interference with the wireless LAN. As a rule of thumb, keep access points at least 25 feet away from any strong interference sources. End user devices also suffer if they are located too close to sources of interference, but only end user communications are interrupted in that case.

The Network

There are two components to network planning. The first, physical planning, is largely legwork. In addition to the building map, it helps to obtain a physical network map, if one exists. It is much easier to install wireless LAN hardware when no expensive and time-consuming wiring needs to be done. Knowing the location and contents of all the wiring closets is an important first step.

The second component of network planning is the plan for changes to the logical network. How will mobile stations be addressed? How will access points be reconnected to their firewall or router?

Network addressing

802.11 provides mobility between access points as long as both access points are part of the same ESS. Roaming works only when mobile stations can transfer from one access point to another and keep the same IP address. All access points of the same ESS must therefore be connected to the same IP subnet so that wireless stations can keep addresses as they associate with different access points.

To get the IP space allocated, you will probably need to work with a network administrator. The administrator will want to know how many addresses you need and why. In addition to the planned number of wireless stations, be sure to include an address for each access point and any servers and security devices on the wireless subnet.

After tentatively locating access points on a blueprint or sketch of the area, work with the physical network map to plug the access points into the nearest wiring closet. If the access device is a switch with VLAN capability, the access point can probably be placed on the access point backbone VLAN. If not, it may be necessary to patch the access point back to a switch capable of VLAN connections or replace the access device with a small multi-VLAN switch.

Preliminary Plan

Based on the floor plans, use the map to come up with a preliminary plan. The preliminary plan is based on the coverage area required and the typical coverage radius from an access point. At this point, detailed radio channel use planning is not yet necessary. The main use of the preliminary plan is to come up with trial access point locations to begin signal quality measurements as part of the detailed site survey. Table 15-2 is based on the best-case coverage radius from a typical omnidirectional antenna.

Table 15-2. "Rule-of-thumb" coverage radius for different types of space

Type of space	Maximum coverage radius
Closed office	up to 50–60 feet
Open office (cubicles)	up to 90 feet
Hallways and other large rooms	up to 150 feet
Outdoors	up to 300 feet

The Site Survey

After coming up with the preliminary plan, it is time to move on to the heart of the deployment routine: the site survey. Several options exist for performing a site survey. Vendors may provide site surveys to early adopters who agree to be reference accounts. Value-added resellers may also have the skills to perform detailed site surveys; resellers may sell site survey consulting services or use site surveys as a way of coming up with a wireless LAN deployment bid. Some companies that specialize in technical education also offer classes on performing site surveys.

Refining the preliminary design is the purpose of the site survey. Radio transmission is complicated, and some things must be done by experiment. All sites will require adjustments to the preliminary design as part of the site survey. In many cases, use of site survey tools can help eliminate access points from a network design and result in substantial cost savings. The major goal of a site survey is to discover any unforeseen interference and redesign the network accordingly. In most cases, interference problems can be repaired by relocating an access point or using a different antenna.

The site survey should assess the following:

- The actual coverage of the access points and the optimum location of access points in the final network

- Actual bit rates and error rates in different locations, especially locations with a large number of users

- Whether the number of access points is sufficient—more or fewer may be required, depending on the characteristics of the building with respect to radio waves

- The performance characteristics of customer applications on the wireless LAN

Tools

Site survey work consists mostly of seemingly endless signal quality measurements. Depending on the tool used, the signal quality measurements may be any of the following:

Packet Error Rate (PER)
> The fraction of frames received in error, without regard to retransmissions. A common rule of thumb is that the PER should be less than 8% for acceptable performance.

Received Signal Strength Indication (RSSI)
> A value derived from the underlying mathematics. Higher values correspond to stronger (and presumably better) signals.

Multipath time dispersion
> Some software or instruments may be able to measure the degree to which a signal is spread out in time by path differences. Higher delay spreads make the correlation of the wideband signals more difficult. Devices need to accept either a higher error rate at high delay spreads or fall back to a more conservative coding method. Either way, throughput goes down. The higher the delay spread, the more throughput suffers.

Signal quality measurements can be carried out by a dedicated hardware device or a software program running on a laptop with the card vendor's site survey tool. Several wireless LAN vendors, such as Intel, Proxim, and 3Com, bundle site survey tools with their access points. Handheld site survey tools designed specifically for 802.11 networks also exist.

Patience and comfortable shoes are among the most important items to bring to a site survey. Measuring signal quality in an area is a painstaking process, requiring many measurements, often taken after making minor changes to the antenna or access point configuration. You will spend a lot of time walking, so wear shoes that you can walk all day in.

Particularly stubborn interference may require the use of a *spectrum analyzer* to locate the source of interference from a non-802.11 network. Devices that can scan a wide frequency band to locate transmissions are not cheap. Expect to pay several thousand dollars, or you can hire a consultant. In either case, a spectrum analyzer is the tool of last resort, necessary for only the most stubborn problems.

Antenna Types

Wireless cards all have built-in antennas, but these antennas are, at best, minimally adequate. If you were planning to cover an office—or an even larger area, such as a campus—you will almost certainly want to use external antennas for your access points. When considering specialized antennas, there are only a few specifications that you need to pay attention to:

Antenna type
> The antenna type determines its radiation pattern—is it omnidirectional, bidirectional, or unidirectional? Omnidirectional antennas are good for covering large areas; bidirectional antennas are particularly good at covering corridors; unidirectional antennas are best at setting up point-to-point links between buildings, or even different sites.

Gain
> The gain of the antenna is the extent to which it enhances the signal in its preferred direction. Antenna gain is measured in dBi, which stands for decibels relative to an isotropic radiator. An isotropic radiator is a theoretical beast that radiates equally in all directions. To put some stakes in the ground: I've never seen a specification for the gain of the built-in antenna on a wireless card, but I would guess that it's negative (i.e., worse than an isotropic radiator). Simple external antennas typically have gains of 3 to 7 dBi. Directional antennas can have gains as high as 24 dBi.*

Half-power beam width
> This is the width of the antenna's radiation pattern, measured in terms of the points at which the antenna's radiation drops to half of its peak value. Understanding the half-power beam width is important to understanding your

---

* If you want one more stake, the radio telescope at Arecibo has a gain in excess of 80 dBi.

antenna's effective coverage area. For a very high-gain antenna, the half-power beam width may be only a couple of degrees. Once you get outside the half-power beam width, the signal typically drops off fairly quickly, though that depends on the antenna's design. Don't be fooled into thinking that the half-power beam width is irrelevant for an omnidirectional antenna. A typical omni-directional (vertical) antenna is only omnidirectional in the horizontal plane. As you go above or below the plane on which the antenna is mounted, the signal decreases.

We've discussed antennas entirely in terms of their properties for transmitting, largely because most people find that easier to understand. Fortunately, an antenna's receiving properties are identical to its transmitting properties—an antenna enhances a received signal to the same extent that it enhances the transmitted signal. This result is probably what you would expect, but proving it is beyond the scope of this book.

Now, let's talk about some of the antenna types that are available; Figure 15-5 shows a number of different antenna types:

Vertical

This is a garden variety omnidirectional antenna. Most vendors sell several different types of vertical antenna, differing primarily in their gain; you might see a vertical antenna with a published gain as high as 10 dBi or as low as 3 dBi. How does an omnidirectional antenna generate gain? Remember that a vertical antenna is omnidirectional only in the horizontal plane. In three dimensions, its radiation pattern looks something like a donut. A higher gain means that the donut is squashed. It also means that the antenna is larger and more expensive, though no antennas for 802.11 service are particularly large.

If you want to cover a confined outdoor area—for example, a courtyard between several buildings of a corporate campus—note that the half-power beam width means that a roof-mounted vertical antenna might be less than ideal, particularly if the building is tall. Vertical antennas are good at radiating out horizontally; they're not good at radiating down. In a situation like this, you would be better off mounting the antenna outside a first- or second-story window.

Dipole

A dipole antenna has a figure eight radiation pattern, which means it's ideal for covering a hallway or some other long, thin area. Physically, it won't look much different from a vertical—in fact, some vertical antennas are simply vertically mounted dipoles.

Yagi

A Yagi antenna is a moderately high-gain unidirectional antenna. It looks somewhat like a classic TV antenna. There are a number of parallel metal elements at right angles to a boom. However, you are not likely to see the elements on a Yagi for 802.11 service; the commercially made Yagis that I have seen are all enclosed

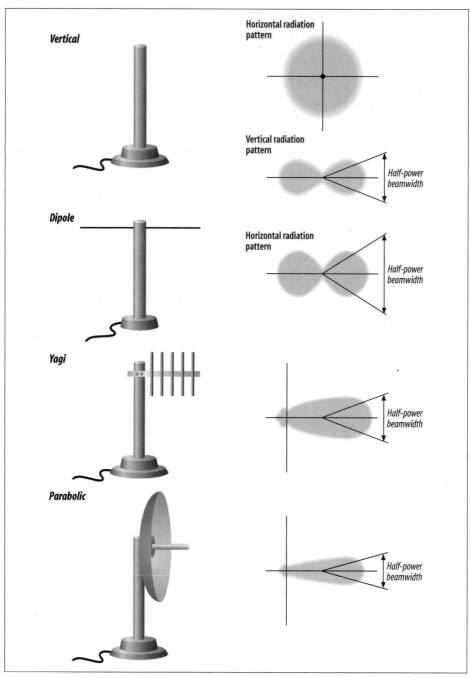

Figure 15-5. Antenna types

in a *radome*, which is a plastic shell that protects the antenna from the elements in outdoor deployments. Yagi antennas for 802.11 service have gains between 12 and 18 dBi; aiming them is not as difficult as aiming a parabolic antenna, though it can be tricky.

Parabolic

This is a very high-gain antenna. Because parabolic antennas have very high gains (up to 24 dBi for commercially made 802.11 antennas), they also have very narrow beam widths. You would probably use a parabolic antenna only for a link between buildings; because of the narrow beam width, they are not very useful for providing services to end users. Vendors publish ranges of up to 20 miles for their parabolic antennas. Presumably, both ends of the link are using a similar antenna. Do not underestimate the difficulty of aiming a parabolic antenna properly—one commercial product has a published beam width of only 6.5 degrees. If you decide to install a parabolic antenna, make sure that you have it mounted firmly. You do not want a bad storm to nudge it a bit and take down your connection.

Some vendors make an issue of the distinction between "mesh" or "grid" parabolas (in which the antenna's reflector looks like a bent barbecue grill) and solid parabolas. Don't sweat it—if the antenna is well-designed, the difference in performance between a mesh and a solid reflector is not worth worrying about. A mesh does have an advantage, though, in areas subject to high winds.

Parabolic and Yagi antennas are useful primarily for links between buildings. The biggest problem is aiming them properly. If the two sites are visible to each other, you can play some tricks with gunsights—though if you can see one site from the other, you probably don't need such a sophisticated antenna system. Otherwise, buy a good compass and a topographical map from the U.S. Geological Survey, and compute the heading from one site to the other. Remember to correct for magnetic north. If you can spend some extra money, you might be able to simplify the setup by installing a high-gain vertical antenna at one site; then you need to aim only one antenna. If the signal is marginal, replace the vertical with a parabolic antenna once you have the first antenna aimed correctly.

High-gain antennas can become a regulatory problem, particularly in Europe (where power limits are lower than in the U.S.). Lucent notes that their high-gain parabolic antenna cannot be used legally on channels 1, 2, 10, and 11 in the U.S., though it can be used on channels 3 through 9. But that limitation probably assumes that you're using a Lucent wireless card, and Lucent's transceiver produces less output power than the Intersil chip set used by most other vendors. If you connect the Lucent parabolic antenna to a Nokia wireless card, you'll be be way beyond the maximum legal effective radiated power.

Cabling

Having put so much effort into thinking about antennas, we have to spend some time thinking about how to connect the antennas to the access points or wireless cards. Most vendors sell two kinds of cable: relatively inexpensive thin cable (typically 0.1 inch in diameter) and "low-loss cable" that's substantially thicker (typically 0.4 inch) and much more expensive. The thin cable is usually available only in lengths of a couple of feet, and that's as it should be: it is very lossy, and more than a few feet can easily eat up your entire signal. It's intended for connecting a wireless card in a laptop to a portable antenna on your desktop, and that's all. To put numbers behind this: one vendor specifies a loss of 2.5 dB for a 2-meter cable. That means that close to half of your signal strength is disappearing in just two meters of cable. One cable vendor, for a cable that would typically be used in this application, specifies a loss of 75 dB per 100 feet at 2.4 GHz. That means that your signal strength will drop by a factor of 2^{25} (roughly 33 million), clearly not something you want to contemplate. I know of one vendor that recommends using RG58 cable with medium-gain antennas. RG58 is better than the really thin cable intended for portable use, but not much better (35 dB per 100 feet); if you use RG58 cable, keep the cable run as short as possible. Better yet, ditch the RG58 and see if you can replace it with LMR-200 (a high-quality equivalent with half the loss).

What does the picture look like when you're using a *real* low-loss cable? Significantly better, but maybe not as better as you would like. A typical cable for this application—used by at least one 802.11 vendor—is Times Microwave LMR-400. LMR-400 is a very high-quality cable, but it still has a loss of 6.8 dB per 100 feet at 2.4 GHz. This means that, in a 100-foot length of cable, over three quarters of your signal is lost. The moral of the story is clear: keep your access points as close as possible to your antennas. Minimize the length of the transmission line. If you want a roof-mounted antenna, perhaps to cover a courtyard where people frequently have lunch, don't stick your access point in a wiring closet in the basement and run a cable to the roof. If possible, put your access point in a weatherproof enclosure on the roof. If that's not possible, at least put the access point in an attic or crawlspace. There is no substitute for keeping the transmission line as short as possible. Also, keep in mind that transmission lines have a strange ability to shrink when they are routed through walls or conduits. I've never understood why, but even if you measure carefully, you're certain to find that your cable is two feet short. More to the point: the straight-line distance from your access point to the antenna may be only 20 feet, but don't be surprised if it takes a 50-foot cable to make the trip. The cable will probably have to go around corners and through conduits and all sorts of other misdirections before it arrives at its destination.

If you decide to use an 802.11a product, which operates at 5-GHz, be aware that cable loss will be an even more significant issue. Losses increase with frequency, and coaxial cable isn't particularly effective at 2.4 GHz, let alone 5 GHz.

Finally, there's the matter of antenna connectors. All wireless vendors sell cables in various length with the proper connectors and adapters. I strongly recommend taking the easy way out and buying cables with the connectors preinstalled. Connector failure is one of the most common causes for outages in radio systems, particularly if you don't have a lot of experience installing RF connectors.

Antenna diversity

One common method of minimizing multipath fading is to have *antenna diversity*. Rather than making the antenna larger, radio systems can use multiple antennas and choose the signal from the antenna with better reception. Using multiple antennas does not require sophisticated mathematical theory or signal-processing techniques.

Several wireless LAN vendors have built multiple antennas into wireless network cards. Some vendors even offer the ability to connect multiple external antennas to network cards intended for access points. Antenna diversity is recommended by the 802.11 standard, but it is not required. For environments with large amounts of interference, antenna diversity is a worthwhile option to consider when selecting vendors.

Bring on the heat

Amplifiers are available for increasing your transmitting power. Transmitting amplifiers often incorporate preamplifiers for receiving, helping to improve your weak signal sensitivity. Is an amplifier in your future? It depends. The basic problem is that, as you cover a larger and larger territory, there are more and more stations that can potentially join your network. However, the number of stations that can be handled by any given access point is fairly limited (see the following section). All in all, more low-power access points provide better service than a smaller number of access points with high-power amplifiers. There may be some applications that are exceptions to the rule (community networks or ISPs in remote areas, for example), but in most situations, high power sounds like a better idea than it really is.

However, if you want to check around and see what's available, SSB Electronics (*www. ssbusa.com/wireless.html*) and HyperLink Technologies (*http://www.hyperlinktech.com/ web/amplifiers_2400.html*) sell high-power amplifiers for 802.11b service. However, remember:

- To stay within the legal power limit, both for absolute power and ERP.
- That 802.11 is an unlicensed service. If you interfere with another service, it's your problem, by definition. And if a licensed service interferes with you, it's your problem, by definition. Interference is more likely to be a problem if your network covers a large service area and if you are using high power.
- To use equipment that is approved for 802.11 service. Other amplifiers are available that cover the frequency range, but using them is illegal.

The FCC does enforce their rules, and their fines are large. If you're in violation of the regulations, they won't be amused, particularly if you're in excess of the power limit or using unapproved equipment.

A word about range

It's tempting to think that you can put up a high-gain antenna and a power amplifier and cover a huge territory, thus economizing on access points and serving a large number of users at once. This isn't a particularly good idea. The larger the area you cover, the more users are in that area—users your access points must serve. Twenty to 30 users for each wireless card in your access points looks like a good upper bound. A single access point covering a large territory may look like a good idea, and it may even work well while the number of users remains small. But if your network is successful, the number of users will grow quickly, and you'll soon exceed your access point's capacity.

Conducting the Site Survey

When working on the site survey, you must duplicate the actual installation as much as possible. Obstacles between wireless LAN users and access points decrease radio strength, so make an effort to replicate exactly the installation during the site survey.

If access points need to be installed in wiring closets, make sure the door is closed while testing so the survey accounts for the blocking effect of the door on radio waves. Antennas should be installed for the test exactly as they would be installed on a completed network. If office dwellers are part of the user base, make sure that adequate coverage is obtained in offices when the door is closed. Even more important, close any metal blinds, because metal is the most effective radio screen.

Signal measurements should be identical to the expected use of the network users, with one exception. Most site survey tools attempt to determine the signal quality at a single spatial point throughout a sequence of several points in time, and thus it is important to keep the laptop in one location as the measurement is carried out. Taking large numbers of measurements is important because users will move with untethered laptops, and also because the multipath fading effects may lead to pronounced signal quality differences even between nearby locations.

Have several copies of the map to mark signal quality measurements at different tentative access point locations, and note how the antenna must be installed at the location. If multiple antennas were used, note the type and location of each antenna.

Direct-Sequence Channel Layout

Most locations are deploying 802.11 products based on direct-sequence technology because the high–data rate products are based on direct-sequence techniques. Direct

---

sequence underlies both the 2-Mbps DS PHY and the 11-Mbps HR/DSSS PHY. Both standards use identical channels and power transmission requirements.

Direct-sequence products transmit power across a 25-MHz band. Any access points must be separated by five channels to prevent inter-access point interference. Selecting frequencies for wireless LAN operation is based partly on the radio spectrum allocation where the wireless LAN is installed. See Table 15-3.

Table 15-3. Radio channel usage in different regulatory domains

Channel number	Channel frequency (GHz)	US/Canada[a]	ETSI[b]	France
1	2.412	✓	✓	
2	2.417	✓	✓	
3	2.422	✓	✓	
4	2.427	✓	✓	
5	2.432	✓	✓	
6	2.437	✓	✓	
7	2.442	✓	✓	
8	2.447	✓	✓	
9	2.452	✓	✓	
10[c]	2.457	✓	✓	✓
11	2.462	✓	✓	✓
12	2.467		✓	✓
13	2.472		✓	✓

[a] 802.11 allows different rules regarding the use of radio spectrum in the U.S. and Canada, but the U.S. Federal Communications Commission and Industry Canada have adopted identical rules.
[b] Not all of Europe has adopted the recommendations of the European Telecommunications Standards Institute (ETSI). Spain, which does not appear in the table, allows the use of only channels 10 and 11.
[c] Channel 10 is allowed by all regulatory authorities and is the default channel for most access points when they are initially powered on.

Access points can have overlapping coverage areas with full throughput, provided the radio channels differ by at least five. Only wireless LANs in the U.S., Canada, and Europe that have adopted the ETSI recommendations can operate access points with overlapping coverage areas at full throughput.

After locating the access points, make sure that any access points with overlapping coverage are separated by at least five channels. The cellular-telephone industry uses the "hex pattern" shown in Figure 15-6 to cover large areas.

Part of the site survey is to establish the boundaries of access point coverage to prevent more than three access points from mutually overlapping, unless certain areas use multiple channels in a single area for greater throughput.

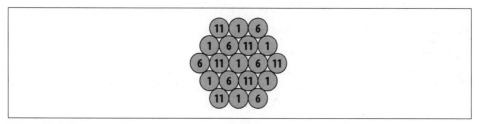

Figure 15-6. Frequency planning

Limitations of direct-sequence channel layout

One of the problems with 802.11 direct-sequence networks and 802.11b Direct-sequence networks is that there are only three nonoverlapping channels. Four channels are required for nonoverlapping coverage in two dimensions, and more channels are required for three dimensions. When laying out frequency channels in three dimensions, always keep in mind that radio signals may penetrate the floor and ceiling.

Application Performance Characterization

As part of the site survey, take some time to work with the "power users" to ensure that the application performance is adequate. Most applications use web frontends and are relatively tolerant with respect to long delays or coverage dropouts because web browsers retry connections. Terminal emulation and other state-oriented client/server applications may be less tolerant of poor coverage. Part of the engineering in installing a wireless LAN is to tailor the areas of overlapping coverage to offer denser coverage when the applications are less tolerant of momentary drops.

The End of the Site Survey: The Report

After the completion of the site survey, the technical details must be provided to installers to complete the network build-out. Consultants may use the site survey in different ways. Some consultants charge for the site survey and allow the customer or a third party to finish the installation. Value-added resellers may take the same approach or use the site survey to put together an installation bid for the customer.

Depending on the customer's requirements, some or all of the following details may be included in a site survey report:

1. A summary of the requirements from the initial preliminary work.

2. Estimated coverage areas based on the site survey measurements. This may be divided into areas with good coverage, marginal coverage, and weak coverage. It may also site potential trouble spots if the signal strength measurements allow for it.

3. A description of the locations of all access points, along with their configuration. Some elements of this configuration are the following:

   a. The access point name

   b. Its operating channel

   c. Approximate coverage area

   d. IP configuration

   e. Antenna type and configuration (including direction for directional antennas)

   f. Any other vendor-specific information

4. If the customer supplied detailed floor plans or physical network maps, those maps can be returned with detailed access point placement information. Estimated coverage areas can be noted on the map and serve as the basis for frequency reuse planning. Any antenna requirements (external antennas, antenna types, and adjustments to default transmission power) for achieving the noted coverage area should be recorded as well.

5. Many customers appreciate an estimate of the work necessary to install drivers onto any affected laptops. The scope of this item depends a great deal on the sophistication of the management tools used by the customer. For many, it will be sufficient merely to include a copy of the driver installation instructions as an appendix to the report. Some clients may require low-level details on the driver installation so that the driver installation can be completely automated down to any necessary registry changes on Windows systems.

Installation and the Final Rollout

After the site survey is finished, there should be enough information available to install a wireless LAN. Actual cabling and physical installation may be contracted out or performed by internal staff.

Recordkeeping

Careful documentation is an important part of any network build-out, but it is especially important for wireless LANs because the network medium is invisible. Finding network components is not always a simple matter of cable tracing! To document a wireless LAN, keep the following list in a safe place with the rest of the network maps:

• The site survey report.

• The annotated building blueprints with access point locations, names, and their associated coverage areas. If possible, the blueprints should also indicate areas of marginal or no coverage.

- A separate list of information about the access points in tabular form, which includes the location, name, channel, IP network information, and any other administrative information.

On the Naming of Access Points

Many institutions have naming policies that may dictate DNS names for wireless LAN access points. Device names should be as descriptive as possible, within reason. Companies that provide network service to other users, such as a "hot spot" provider, may wish to keep information about the detailed location of access points secret from users to keep the physical location of access points secret. Figure 15-7 illustrates a DNS naming convention in which the secrecy of access point locations is not a particular concern, so each name includes the geographic site location, the building name and floor, and the access point number and location on that floor. It also includes the wireless LAN name (SSID).

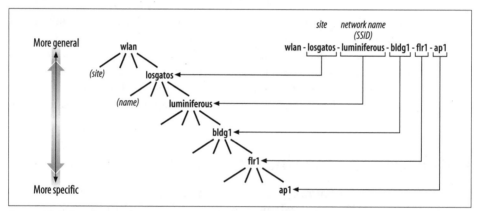

Figure 15-7. Wireless LAN naming convention for access points

All names are prefixed with *wlan-* to indicate clearly that they are associated with an 802.11 network. The next level of hierarchy is the geographic location of the wireless network; it can often be derived from existing site codes in large companies. Each site may compose a campus and have several buildings, but a single extended service area may offer coverage throughout the entire site at anything up through even midsized installations. The next level of hierarchy is the building identifier, which is often clear from existing conventions. Within a building, the floor number and the location of an access point within the floor can be used to further identify an access point. Figure 15-8 shows how the DNS name can be structured for an access point on the luminiferous network on the second floor of building one at a site in Los Gatos, California (*wlan-losgatos-luminiferous-bldg1-flr2-ap1*). In very large buildings, the access point number might even be replaced by a description of the location of the access point on the floor, such as *-ap-nw-4* for the fourth access point in the northwest corner.

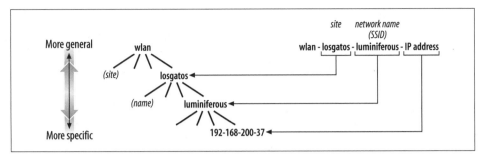

Figure 15-8. Convention for naming wireless LAN stations

To make troubleshooting easier, follow a convention for the naming of wireless LAN stations. A station on the same network as the access point described previously might be *wlan-losgatos-luminiferous-192-168-200-37*, in which the last set of numbers is the IP address.

Security

After installation is complete, you should execute a second test solely for security. Configuring access points can be time-consuming, detail-oriented work, and it is possible to forget to set a software option here and there. Check the following items to be sure your network is as secure as possible:

- If desired, WEP is enabled on all access points to prevent unauthorized association with the network.

- Lists of MAC addresses allowed to associate with the network have been distributed to each access point.

- Any access controllers in place are properly configured to block initial connections, and they can reach authentication servers to allow user access.

- Any VPN software is properly configured to accept connections from associated stations.

- Access points enforce restrictions on stations allowed to connect for management, and passwords are set.

Some vendors are advertising products that support 802.1x security, particularly in high-end access points. 802.1x requires that you set up a RADIUS authentication server, but the additional security is well worth the effort. On the other hand, 1x products are only just appearing as this book goes to press. Because 802.1x is a standard, products should interoperate, in theory—but we don't yet know whether they interoperate in practice. If you're not comfortable buying all your equipment from one vendor, you may want to stay away from 802.1x for a while. It's hard to make predictions that mean anything, but here's a guess: given the amount of attention that security has received lately, I expect that the 802.1x situation will be stabilized by the middle of 2002.

Several vendors have proprietary security solutions to replace or supplement WEP—some appear to be preliminary versions of 802.1x. I do not recommend locking yourself into a proprietary solution when a standard solution is available, or nearly available.

## CHAPTER 16

802.11 Network Analysis

In the 1990s, computer professionals joined doctors as People With Answers. Just as doctors are asked medical questions by complete strangers, computer professionals are asked a bewildering variety of technical questions by complete strangers. When these strangers learn that I work with networks, I am often asked, "Why does the Internet break so often?" The more I contemplate the question, the more I believe that the question should be, "Why doesn't the Internet break *more* often?"

While I could never hope to answer either question in a single chapter of a book, it is obvious that network problems are a fact of life. Networks break, and wireless networks are no exception. Wireless LANs can improve productivity, but they also carry a larger risk of complete outage, and the limited bandwidth is almost sure to be overloaded. After building a wireless LAN, network engineers must be ready to investigate any problems that may arise.

As in many other network types, the trusty network analyzer is a key component in the engineer's toolbox. Network analyzers already exist for the wired backbone side of the wireless network and can be used productively in many troubleshooting scenarios. Wireless network troubleshooting depends on having a network analyzer for exactly the same reason. Sometimes, you just need to have a way of seeing what is on the airwaves. This chapter is devoted to tools that allow network engineers to do just that. Several commercial analyzers are available, and there are free tools that run on Linux. Before diving into the tools, though, it may help to consider why wireless network analyzers are a practical requirement for the network administrator.

Why Use a Network Analyzer?

In spite of the shared heritage, 802.11 is not Ethernet. It has a number of additional protocol features, each of which can cause problems. Fixing problems on 802.11 networks sometimes requires that a network administrator get down to the low-level protocol details and see what is happening over the airwaves. Network analyzers have long been viewed as a useful component of the network administrator's toolkit on wired networks for their ability to report on the low-level details. Analyzers on wireless networks will be just as useful, and possibly even more important. More things can go wrong on an 802.11 network, so a good analyzer is a vital tool for quickly focusing troubleshooting on the likely culprit.

Avoiding problems begins at the planning stages. Some analyzers can report detailed statistics on RF signal strength, which can help place access points. Analyzers can help network administrators avoid creating dead zones by ensuring that there is enough overlap at the edges of BSSs to allow for timely transitions. As wireless networks grow in popularity, they may need to support more users. To avoid performance problems, administrators may consider shrinking the size of access point coverage areas to get more aggregate throughput in a given area. In the process of shrinking the coverage areas, network administrators may go through large parts of the deployment plan all over again and depend once again on their analyzer.

With the limited bit rates of wireless networks, performance is likely to be a problem sooner or later. Performance problems can be caused by cramming too many users into too few access points, or they can be related to problems happening at the radio layer. The designers of 802.11 were aware of the problems that could be caused by the radio transmission medium. Frame transmissions succeed reliably. Most implementations will also retransmit frames with simpler (and slower) encoding methods and fragment frames in the presence of persistent interference.

Interference is a major problem for 802.11 network performance. In addition to the direct effect of trashing transmitted frames that then require retransmission, interference has two indirect effects. Poor transmission quality may cause a station to step down to a lower bit rate in search of more reliable radio link quality. Even if slower transmissions usually succeed, some measure of throughput is lost at the lower bit rates. 802.11 stations may also attempt to fragment pending frames to work around interference, which reduces the percentage of transmissions that carry end user data. 802.11 headers are quite large compared to other LAN protocols, and fragmentation increases the amount of header information transmitted for a fixed amount of data.

On many networks, however, only a few applications are used. Do performance complaints indicate a general network problem, or a problem with a specific application? Network analyzers can help you find the cause of the problem by examining the distribution of packet sizes. More small packets may indicate excessive use of fragmentation in the face of interference. Some analyzers can also report on the distribution of frames' transmission rates on a wireless network. 802.11b networks are capable of transmitting at 11 Mbps, but frames may be transmitted at slower rates (5. 5 Mbps, 2 Mbps, or even 1 Mbps) if interference is a problem. Stations capable of high-rate operation but nonetheless transmit at lower rates may be subject to a large amount of interference.

To solve interference problems, you can attempt to reorient the access point or its antenna, or place a new access point in a zone with poor coverage. Rather than waiting for users to report on their experience with the changes in place, you can use an analyzer to get a quick idea of whether the changes will help alleviate the problem. Some analyzers can provide extensive reports on the RF signal quality of received frames, which can help you place hardware better the first time around. Avoiding repeated experimentation directly with end users makes you look better and makes users happier. Shortening troubleshooting cycles has always been a strength of network analyzers.

Analyzers also help network administrators check on the operation of unique features of the 802.11 MAC. While it is possible to capture traffic once it has been bridged on to a wireless backbone network and analyze it there, the problem could always be on the wireless link. Are frames being acknowledged? If they are not, there will be retransmissions. Are the direct-sequence bits set correctly? If they are not, then address fields will be misinterpreted. If a malformed packet is seen on the wired side of an access point, it could be mangled at several points. A wireless analyzer can look at frames as they travel through the air to help you pin down the source of the mangled packet. Malformed frames may be transmitted by the client or mangled by the access point, and it is helpful to pin down the problem before requesting assistance from the vendor.

Security is a major concern for wireless networks, and wireless analyzers can be used to monitor wireless networks for security problems. They can look at the MAC addresses of all stations to look for unknown addresses, though this may or may not be all that useful in practice. It is probably impossible to know all the MAC addresses used on your network, though it might be possible to spot cards from manufacturers of hardware that is not part of a standard build. It may be more effective to look for failed attempts to authenticate to your access points.

Some installations will rely on WEP for security, either totally or in part. Some commercial analyzers offer the ability to decrypt frames processed by WEP, provided they are given the shared WEP key. 802.11 frames have enough information to enable a sniffer in possession of the key to do real-time decryption. This ability allows network administrators to peer into frames protected by WEP to perform higher-level protocol analysis and to check that WEP processing is not mangling frames. Real-time decryption is a byproduct of the poor design of WEP. Once WEP is replaced by a real security system, real-time decryption may become much more complicated.

802.11 Network Analyzers

802.11 network analyzers are now quite common and should be a part of any wireless LAN administrator's toolbox. Most 802.11 network analyzers are software packages that use an 802.11 network card. No special hardware is required because commodity 802.11 network cards supply all the RF hardware needed to grab packets. The only catch is that each software package usually only works with a limited number of cards on the market.

Commercial Network Analyzers

With the stunning growth of wireless networks, commercial software vendors rushed to introduce wireless versions of successful wired network analyzers. The two main commercial wireless network analyzers are Sniffer Wireless from Network Associates (*http://www.sniffer.com*) and AiroPeek from WildPackets (*http://www.wildpackets.com*). Sniffer Wireless requires the use of wireless LAN cards from either Cisco or Symbol. AiroPeek supports a much broader range, including cards made by 3Com, Cisco, Nortel, Intel, Symbol, and Lucent.

Like their wired relatives, the commercial wireless LAN analyzers have a host of features. In addition to decoding captured frames, they can filter the captured frames based on anything in the 802.11 header, report statistical data on the packet size and speed distributions, monitor the real-time network utilization, and quickly scan all the available channels to detect all networks in the area. If given the key, both can decrypt frames protected by WEP.

A network analyzer should be part of the deployment budget for any wireless network. The choice to buy or build is up to you, though I anticipate that most institutions will rely primarily on commercial products and leave development and bug fixes to the network analyzer vendors, especially because commercial analyzers can be purchased, installed, and made useful much more quickly.

Ethereal

Ethereal is the standard open source network analyzer. Like the proprietary analyzers, it supports a long list of protocols and can capture live data from a variety of network interfaces. Unlike the proprietary analyzers, Ethereal comes complete with a slogan ("Sniffing the glue that holds the Internet together").

Ethereal runs on most Unix platforms as well as Windows. Source code is freely available for both, but modifications are easier to make on Unix because of the availability of free compilers for the Unix programming environment. Like many open source projects, Ethereal is distributed under the terms of the GNU Public License. Protocol decodes are included for many common networking protocols. For the purpose of this section, the important protocols are IEEE 802.11 and LLC, both of which are used on every 802.11 frame. Of course, the TCP/IP suite is included as well.

For 802.11 network analysis with Ethereal, Linux is the platform of choice. The *linux-wlan-ng* driver can be modified to feed raw 802.11 packets to Ethereal, and Ethereal can be modified to decode them in real time. For data capture on Linux, only Intersil-based cards are supported. Of course, Intersil cards can be used to monitor any 802.11 network, including those that use other chipsets.

Compilation and Installation

Binary packages are available from the main project web site at *http://www.ethereal. com*. Because of the required modifications to the code, a binary package is not sufficient.

Prerequisites

Before compiling Ethereal, both *libpcap* and the GTK+ library must be installed. *libpcap* is the packet capture library from *tcpdump*, and the GTK+ library is the GIMP tool kit. For 802.11 network analysis, *libpcap* must be modified, so it needs to be built from source. GTK+ is used unmodified, however, and can typically be installed from a package that came with your Linux distribution. GTK+ source is available from *http://www.gtk.org/* and is built with the standard *./configure*, *make*, and *make install* sequence familiar to most open source software users. If you opt to go the package route, it is necessary to install both the libraries themselves and the – *devel* versions to install the required header files.

Several utility programs must be installed on the system for Ethereal to build properly. Ethereal depends on GNU *make*, which is the default *make* program on Linux systems. Perl is used to assemble the manpages. The modified *libpcap* that grabs raw 802.11 frames needs to build a parser, which requires the *flex* lexical scanner and either *yacc* or *bison*. Users intending to do NetWare Core Protocol (NCP) analysis must have Python installed.*

Ethereal depends on one kernel function. Because it interfaces directly with the kernel to grab packets, it requires that the kernel be built with Packet Socket support (*CONFIG_PACKET*).

Compiling the modified libpcap

The next step is the installation of the slightly modified *libpcap* library. *libpcap* is available from *http://www.tcpdump.org*. Tim Newsham's monitoring patch is intended to be applied against 0.6.2, the latest version as of the writing of this book. At slightly over 200 lines, the patch is fairly lightweight. Its main purpose is to add another type of packet capture to the *libpcap* library for 802.11-specific captures. Essentially, it adds the functionality of *prismdump* to *libpcap*, which makes it much

---

* Network administrators who deal with NCP also have my sympathy.

easier to write programs that manipulate raw 802.11 frames. The patch also defines a data structure that holds miscellaneous data of interest to network analyzers, such as the received signal strength and information on the signal-to-noise ratio.

First, fetch the wireless LAN monitoring patches from *http://www.lava.net/ ~newsham/wlan/*. Get the *wlan-mods.tgz* package, which includes the patch for *libpcap*, the patch for Ethereal, and a new system header file to describe the PRISM capture type:

```
$ patch -p1 < ../wlan-mods/libpcap.patch
patching file Makefile.in
patching file gencode.c
patching file pcap-linux.c
patching file pcap-prism.c
patching file pcap-prism.h
```

The newly modified libpcap depends on the *802.11h* file included in the *wlan-mods* package. *802.11h* includes definitions for the raw PRISM monitoring. Copy it to the main system *include* file location (probably */usr/include*). After applying the patch, building *libpcap* follows the usual routine of configuration, building, and installing:

```
$ ./configure
creating cache ./config.cache
checking host system type... i686-pc-linux-gnu

(many lines of configuration output omitted)

updating cache ./config.cache
creating ./config.status
creating Makefile
creating config.h
$ make
gcc -O2 -I.  -DHAVE_CONFIG_H -c ./pcap-linux.c

(many lines of compilation output omitted)

ar rc libpcap.a pcap-linux.o pcap.o inet.o gencode.o optimize.o nametoaddr.o
etherent.o savefile.o bpf_filter.o bpf_image.o bpf_dump.o pcap-prism.o scanner.o
grammar.o version.o
ranlib libpcap.a
```

Finally, run *make install* to put *libpcap* in its place. With the installation complete, you can proceed to link the modified *libpcap* with Ethereal, which gives Ethereal the ability to work with 802.11 frames.

Building Ethereal itself

You can build Ethereal after installing the modified *libpcap* and the associated header file. Grab the source code for Ethereal from *http://www.ethereal.com* and uncompress it into a working directory:

```
$ tar -xzvf ../ethereal-0.8.17-a.tar.gz
ethereal-0.8.17/
```

```
ethereal-0.8.17/Makefile.in
ethereal-0.8.17/debian/
ethereal-0.8.17/debian/README.debian
```

(many other filenames omitted)

Next, apply Tim's monitoring patch, which is written against Ethereal Version 0.8.
17. The patch does not apply cleanly against later versions, though with some effort
it could undoubtedly be made to do so.

```
$ patch -p1 < ../wlan-mods/ethereal.patch
patching file Makefile.am
patching file capture.c
patching file packet-ieee80211.c
patching file packet-prism.c
patching file packet-prism.h
patching file wiretap/libpcap.c
patching file wiretap/wtap.h
```

You're now ready to begin building the source code. Ethereal ships with an autocon-
figuration script that you run from the root directory of the source tree. The autocon-
figuration script performs a series of tests to assist in the compilation process. On
one of my systems, the configure script had trouble finding the GLIB library, so I had
to point it at the correct location. On Mandrake 7.2, GLIB is installed in */usr/lib*. The
GTK prefix is used to find the *gtk-config* script. I specified */usr* because */bin* will be
appended to the specified path. As a result of my configuration, the Ethereal configuration script looked in */usr/bin* for *gtk-config* and found it:

```
$ ./configure --with-gtk-prefix=/usr/lib --with-gtk-exec-prefix=/usr
creating cache ./config.cache
checking for a BSD compatible install... /usr/bin/install -c
checking whether build environment is sane... yes
```

(many other test results omitted)

```
creating ./config.status
creating Makefile
creating config.h

The Ethereal package has been configured with the following options.
                 Build ethereal : yes
                 Build tethereal : yes
                  Build editcap : yes
                  Build randpkt : no
                   Build dftest : no

                 Install setuid : no
               Use pcap library : yes
               Use zlib library : yes
       Use IPv6 name resolution : no
               Use SNMP library : no
```

Note the summary at the end of the configuration script. When I failed to identify the
location of the GLIB library, Ethereal was perfectly happy to configure for terminal-only

analysis. Check the summary to be sure you are building the features you want. After configuration, run *make*, which builds:

Ethereal
>The X-based graphical analyzer described in the rest of this section.

tethereal
>A terminal-based analyzer that uses the same core packet-analysis code.

editcap
>A program that manipulates capture files and can translate between several common capture formats. By default, it uses the file format used by *libpcap*, though it also supports snoop, Sniffer traces, NetXray, and Microsoft Network Monitor captures. For a complete list of the supported file types, see the manual page for *editcap*.

Finally, install the executables using *make install*, which puts the executable in the location specified by the *Makefile*. If no install directory is explicitly specified in the configuration step, Ethereal is installed in the */usr/local* hierarchy, with executables in */usr/local/bin* and man pages in */usr/local/man*.

Ethereal on Windows

Binary packages are more important in the Windows world because of the lack of a high-quality, free-development environment. Though Ethereal does not provide the same level of 802.11 support under Windows, it can still be a valuable program to have, especially in a day job that requires use of Windows systems. Binary versions of Ethereal for Windows are available from *http://www.ethereal.com*. They require the WinPcap library to provide the *libpcap*-type support on Windows. WinPcap can be downloaded from *http://netgroup-serv.polito.it/winpcap/*. WinPcap is supported only on 32-bit Windows systems (95, 98, ME, NT, and 2000) and is licensed under a BSD-style license. Interestingly enough, WinPcap was supported in part by Microsoft Research.

Running Ethereal

To start Ethereal, run it from the command line. Any user may start Ethereal, but root privileges are required to capture packets. Other users may load Ethereal to analyze capture files and perform analysis, though.

```
[gast@bloodhound ethereal-0.8.17]$ ethereal &
```

Starting Ethereal pops up the main window, which is shown in Figure 16-1. The main window has three panes. The top pane, called the *packet list pane*, gives a high-level view of each packet. It displays each packet's capture time, source and destination address, the protocol, and a basic decode of the packet. The Protocol field is filled in with the final decode, or *dissector*, used to analyze the frame. On 802.11 networks, the final decode may be IEEE 802.11 for management frames, or it may go all the way to the final TCP protocol for analysis, as in the case of an 802.11 frame holding an LLC-encapsulated IP packet with a TCP segment carrying HTTP.

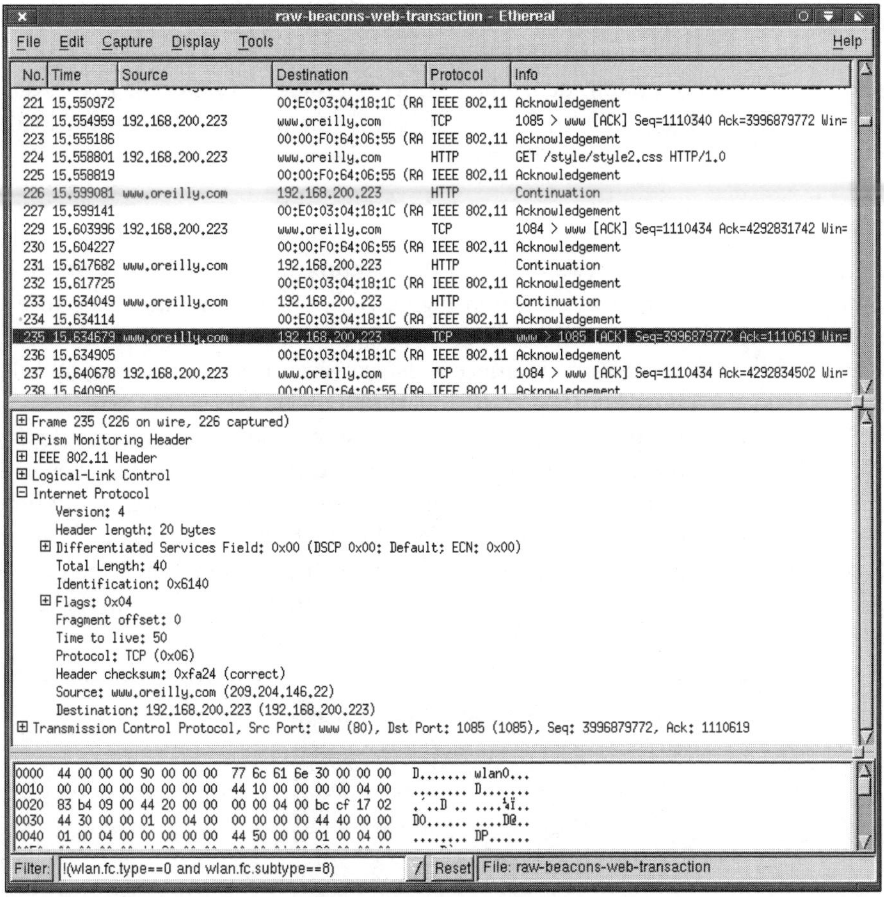

Figure 16-1. Main Ethereal window

The middle pane, called the *tree view pane*, is a detailed view of the packet selected in the packet list. All the major headers in a packet are shown and can be expanded for more detail. All packets have the basic "Frame" tree, which contains details on arrival time and capture length. On 802.11 networks, all frames have the Prism Monitoring header, which contains radio-link data. Data packets on 802.11 networks also have a Logical Link Control (LLC) header. From there, the LLC may contain ARP packets, IP packets, TCP segments, and so on. Ethereal includes dissectors for all the commonly used protocols, so 802.11 frames are fully decoded most of the time. The bottom pane is called the *data view pane*. It shows the raw binary data in the selected packet. It also highlights the field selected in the tree view pane.

At the bottom of the Ethereal window is a bar with four important elements. The leftmost button, **Filter:**, is used to create filters that reduce the captured packet list to the packets of interest. The text box just to the right allows you to enter filters without going through the construction process. Ethereal maintains a filter history list that enables easy switching between filters. At the right is a text field that displays several kinds of information, depending on what Ethereal is doing. It may indicate that Ethereal is currently capturing data, display the name of the capture file loaded, or display the field name currently highlighted in the tree view.

Capturing data

Capturing data is straightforward. Go to the **Capture** menu and choose **Start**. The Capture Preferences window, shown in Figure 16-2, opens. The first thing to do is select the interface you want to monitor. Interface selection has one small wrinkle. Naturally, Ethereal can use any interface it detects, even *wlan0*. However, all Ethernet drivers in the Linux kernel present Ethernet frames. If you choose *wlan0*, you miss out on all 802.11 control and management frames, and the Data frames lose the 802.11 headers by the time they get to Ethereal's capture engine. The reason for applying the patch to Ethereal during compilation is that it creates a pseudo-interface, *prism*, which allows Ethereal to read data directly from the hardware. That way, Ethereal uses the same capture code that *prismdump* does and can display all the 802.11 traffic in the air. *prism* does not appear as an interface in the drop-down box, but it can be typed into the field directly, as in Figure 16-2.

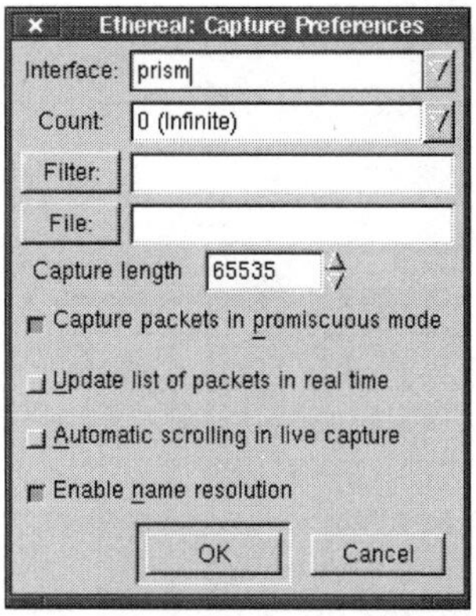

Figure 16-2. Selecting the prism pseudo-interface

Ethereal accepts the *–i* command-line option to specify an interface. If you plan to do all of your analysis on one interface, you can define a shell mapping of *ethereal* to *ethereal –i prism*.

Capture Length is what *tcpdump* calls the *snap length*. It is the amount of data from each packet that will be captured. *tcpdump* uses a short snap length and saves only IP and TCP headers. By default, Ethereal grabs the entire packet, which facilitates much more detailed offline analysis.

I typically turn on "Update list of packets in real time" and "Automatic scrolling in live capture". If the former is left unselected, the trace appears only when the capture stops. If the latter is left unselected, the trace does not scroll to the bottom. Speed is important to real-time analysis. Disabling name resolution eliminates overhead for every packet captured and may allow a station to avoid missing frames in the air.

Saving data to a file

To save data for offline analysis, use the File → Save As option from the menu bar. Selecting it displays the dialog box shown in Figure 16-3.

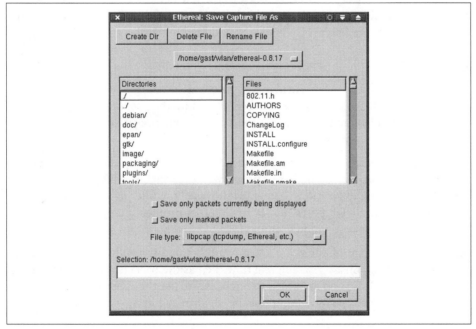

Figure 16-3. Save As dialog box

Choosing a filename is straightforward. The real power of Ethereal is that extraneous packets can be eliminated by using the two checkboxes below the file chooser. "Save only packets currently being displayed" saves only the packets that made it through the display filter, greatly reducing the amount of data in the capture file. "Save only marked packets" saves only packets that you have selected. If neither option is checked, Ethereal saves the entire trace. Saving an entire trace may be necessary at times, but it's worth avoiding; an entire trace could include all the packets that have crossed your network over an extended period. Using a display filter and saving only the displayed packets makes the trace far more manageable.

The file type selection allows the file to be saved to a *libpcap* file format. To imply that there is only one *libpcap* file format would be wrong, though. Four choices are available, including one that allows you to read capture files collected from *tcpdump* on Nokia's IPSO-based network appliances.

Data Reduction

Raw captures can be quite large, and extraneous packets can make finding wheat among the chaff a challenge. One of the keys to successful use of a network analyzer is to winnow the torrent of packets down to the few packets at the heart of the matter. Ethereal provides three ways to reduce the amount of data captured to a manageable amount: capture filters, display filters, and marking packets.

Capture filters

Capture filters are the most efficient way to cut down on the amount of data processed by Ethereal because they are pushed down into the packet sniffing interface. If the packet capture interface discards the packet, that packet does not make it to Ethereal for further processing.

Ethereal uses *libpcap*, so the capture filter language is exactly the same as the language used by *tcpdump*. A number of primitives are available, which can be grouped into arbitrarily long expressions. These primitives allow filtering on Ethernet and IP addresses, TCP and UDP ports, and IP or Ethernet protocol numbers. Many can be applied to source or destination numbers.

All in all, though, capture filters are less powerful than display filters for a simple reason: capture filters must operate in real time (i.e., as the packets are arriving over the network interface). A good approach to filtering is to use the capture filters to make a rough cut, then fine-tune the selection using the display filters.

Display filters

Display filters can be used on any field that Ethereal identifies, which makes them far more powerful than capture filters. Display filters inherit the knowledge of all the dissectors compiled into Ethereal, so it is possible to filter on any of the fields in any of the protocols that Ethereal is programmed to recognize. Wireless LAN administrators can filter frames based on anything in the 802.11 or LLC headers. Examples specific to 802.11 are presented later in this chapter.

Marking packets

You can mark any packet by pressing Ctrl-M. Marking is essentially a manual filter. Marked packets are highlighted in the packet view pane. The only reason to mark a packet is to perform a manual reduction of a trace to a few interesting packets. When eliminating large amounts of data, automated filters are faster.

Analysis Tools

Several additional tools are available for Ethereal users. Packets can be colorized according to protocol. This chapter does not take advantage of the feature because the traces presented in the case study sections are short, and colorization doesn't help much.

Ethereal can reconstruct a TCP stream. For example, a reconstructed HTTP transaction would likely show several objects being fetched from a web page, as well as the HTML text used to create the page.

Summary statistics are available for each capture loaded into Ethereal as well. Administrators can view the details of the capture file, which includes information such as the length of time the capture covers and the amount of traffic on the network. It is also possible to see how much data falls into each level of the protocol hierarchy.

Using Ethereal for 802.11 Analysis

Several Ethereal features are handy when applied to 802.11 networks. This section lists several tips and tricks for using Ethereal on wireless networks, in no particular order.

Display filters

Ethereal allows filtering on all fields in the 802.11 header. Frame fields are structured hierarchically. All 802.11 fields begin with *wlan*. Two subcategories hold information on the Frame Control field (*wlan.fc*) and the WEP Information (*wlan.wep*) field. Figure 16-4 shows the variable names for 802.11 header components; in the figure, each field is labeled with a data type. Boolean fields are labeled with a B, MAC addresses with MA, and unsigned integers with U plus the number of bits. Table 16-1 shows the same information, omitting the Ethereal display fields that are unlikely to be useful for filtering.

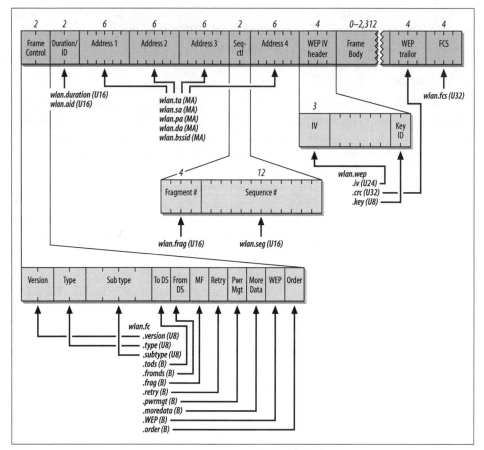

Figure 16-4. Header component variables

Table 16-1. Ethereal fields for 802.11 header components

802.11 header field	Ethereal field
Header fields	
Duration	*wlan.duration*
Association ID	*wlan.aid*
Transmitter address	*wlan.ta*
Source address	*wlan.sa*
Receiver address	*wlan.ra*
Destination address	*wlan.da*
BSSID	*wlan.bssid*
Fragment number	*wlan.frag*

Table 16-1. Ethereal fields for 802.11 header components (continued)

802.11 header field	Ethereal field
Sequence number	wlan.seq
Frame control subfields	
Version	wlan.fc.version
Frame type	wlan.fc.type
Frame subtype	wlan.fc.subtype
ToDS flag	wlan.fc.tods
FromDS flag	wlan.fc.fromds
Fragment flag	wlan.fc.frag
Retry flag	wlan.fc.retry
Power management flag	wlan.fc.pwrmgt
More Data flag	wlan.fc.moredata
WEP flag	wlan.fc.wep
Order flag	wlan.fc.order
WEP fields	
Initialization vector	wlan.wep.iv
Key identifier	wlan.wep.key

Fields can be combined using operators. Ethereal supports a standard set of comparison operators: == for equality, != for inequality, > for greater than, >= for greater than or equal to, < for less than, and <= for less than or equal to. An example of a display filter would be wlan.fc.type==1 to match Control frames.

Logical operators and and or are supported; as in many programming languages, the exclamation point is used for logical negation. Boolean fields can be tested for existence, so Control frames with WEP enabled would be matched by the display filter wlan.fc.type==1 and wlan.fc.wep.

Figure 16-5 shows a complete 802.11 header in the tree view. Selecting the 802.11 header in the tree view highlights the bits that comprise the 802.11 header in the ASCII view at the bottom. Expanding the 802.11 header tree decodes all the fields in the 802.11 header.

Compared to Control and Data frames, 802.11 Management frames have a great deal of structure. Ethereal decodes Management frames into two parts. *Fixed Parameters* in the tree view pane correspond to the fixed fields of 802.11 management frames. *Tagged Parameters* are the variable fields and are decoded in the tree view pane. Table 16-2 shows the fixed fields that can be searched on in Ethereal, as well as the capability flags.

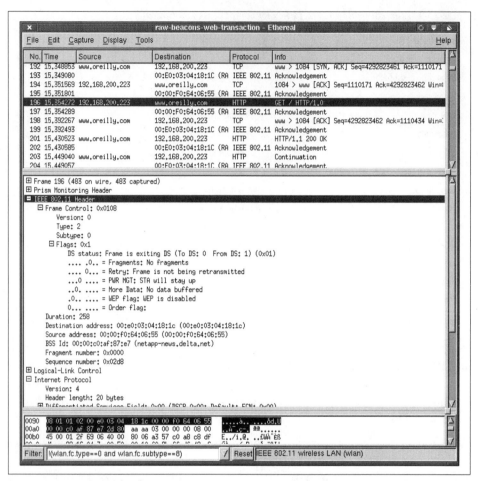

Figure 16-5. An 802.11 header in tree view

Table 16-2. Fixed Management frame components

802.11 management field	Ethereal field
Fixed fields	
Authentication Algorithm Number	*wlan_mgt.fixed.auth.alg*
Authentication Transaction Sequence Number	*wlan_mgt.fixed.auth_seq*
Beacon Interval	*wlan_mgt.fixed.beacon*
Current AP address	*wlan_mgt.fixed.current_ap*
Listen Interval	*wlan_mgt.fixed.listen_ival*
Association ID	*wlan_mgt.fixed.aid*
Timestamp	*wlan_mgt.fixed.timestamp*

Table 16-2. Fixed Management frame components (continued)

802.11 management field	Ethereal field
Reason Code	*wlan_mgt.fixed.reason_code*
Status Code	*wlan_mgt.fixed.status_code*
Capability info	
ESS flag (is the BSS part of an ESS?)	*wlan_mgt.fixed.capabilties.ess*
IBSS flag (is the BSS independent?)	*wlan_mgt.fixed.capabilities.ibss*
Contention-free station polling bit	*wlan_mgt.fixed.capabilities.cfpoll.sta*
Contention-free AP polling bit	*wlan_mgt.fixed.capabilities.cfpoll.ap*
Privacy flag (is WEP implemented?)	*wlan_mgt.fixed.capabilities.privacy*
Preamble (is 802.11b short preamble implemented?)	*wlan_mgt.fixed.capabilities.preamble*
PBCC (is 802.11b PBCC coding implemented?)	*wlan_mgt.fixed.capabilities.pbcc*
Channel Agility (is 802.11b Channel Agility implemented?)	*wlan_mgt.fixed.capabilties.agility*

In the tree view pane, the fixed and variable fields show up in different trees. Variable information elements are decoded under the tagged tree item according to their type. Figure 16-6 shows the decoding of the information elements in a Beacon frame. The access point generating the Beacons is indeed an access point for the Hack Me network on direct-sequence channel 11. It supports both the older 1-Mbps and 2-Mbps encodings in addition to the faster 802.11b encoding schemes.

At the end of the Beacon is a variable field with a reserved tag number that the wireless card's vendor uses to hold the access point's name, and possibly the access point's load factor. The ASCII dump displays the word Outside clearly, which is, in fact, the name of this access point.

Excluding Beacon frames

Beacon frames can get in the way when working with a raw 802.11 trace. The sheer number of frames obscures patterns in the data. Therefore, it's common to exclude those frames from display. Frame type information is carried in the Frame Control field of the 802.11 header. Beacon frames are identified by a Type code of 0 for Management frames, with a subtype of 8 for Beacon. The filter matching the Type code is `wlan.fc.type==0`, and the filter matching the Subtype code is `wlan.fc.subtype==8`. Therefore, to discard frames that match both these conditions, one possible filter is `!(wlan.fc.type==0 and wlan.fc.subtype==8)`.

PRISM monitoring header

The modifications to *libpcap* add a PRISM pseudo-header to any captured frames. Some of the information in this header corresponds to the information that would be kept in the PLCP header. Figure 16-7 shows the pseudo-header on a frame.

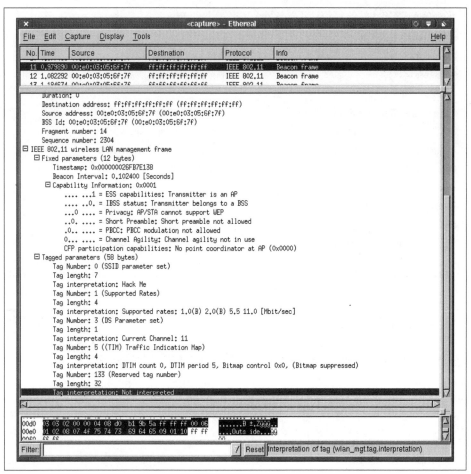

Figure 16-6. Beacon frame decode

Four fields of note are reported by the PRISM capture:

MAC Time
  A timestamp added by the MAC counter to each received frame.

Signal
  Indicates the signal strength of the received packet.

Noise
  Quantifies background noise during the packet time. Calculating the signal-to-noise ratio is straightforward from these two fields.

Rate
  Encoded according to the MAC framing conventions described in Chapter 4. In Figure 16-7, the network is operating at 2 Mbps because the rate field is 0x04.

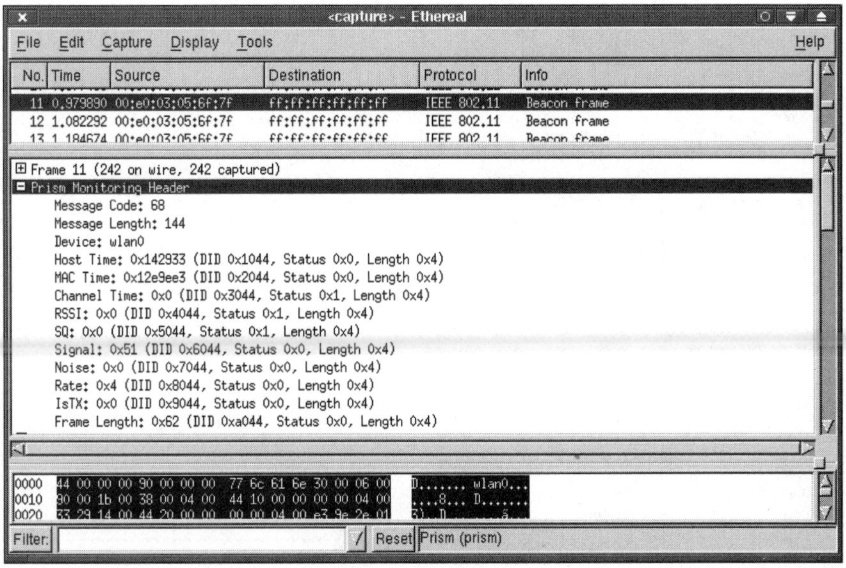

Figure 16-7. PRISM monitoring header

Understanding the LLC header

To multiplex higher-level protocol data over the wireless link, 802.11 uses the LLC SNAP encapsulation. (SNAP encapsulation was described at the end of Chapter 3.) 802.11 does not include a protocol field, so receivers cannot discriminate between different types of network protocols. To allow multiple protocols, an 8-byte SNAP header is added. The SNAP header is decoded in Ethereal's tree view, as shown in Figure 16-8.

Highlighting the LLC header in the tree view shows the corresponding 8-byte header in the packet dump. The eight bytes in the SNAP header are clearly visible in the data view pane. Five fields make up the header:

The destination service access point (DSAP)
    This is always set to 0xAA for SNAP encapsulation.

The source service access point (SSAP)
    This is always set to 0xAA for SNAP encapsulation.

Control
    This is derived from HDLC. Like all data transfer using HDLC, it labels the data following the LLC header as unnumbered information. Unnumbered information indicates the use of a connectionless data transport and that the data need not be sequenced or acknowledged.

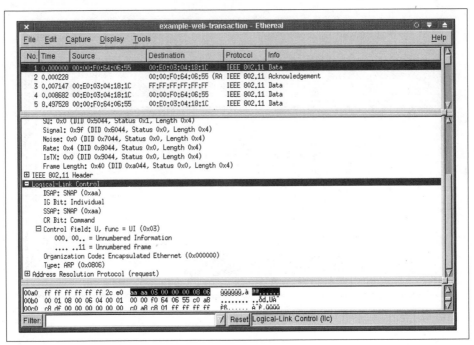

Figure 16-8. LLC SNAP header

An organizationally unique identifier (OUI)
> This is used to determine how to interpret the following bytes. IP is encapsulated in LLC using the standard in RFC 1042, which specifies the use of the OUI 0x00-00-00. (Some vendors may use an assigned OUI for proprietary communications.)

Protocol Type
> This is copied from the corresponding Ethernet frame. The Type field matches the Ethernet type codes. On IP networks, it will be either 0x0800 for IP or 0x0806 for ARP.

LLC encapsulation is required by the 802.11 specification because it saves the 802.11 frame from having to carry protocol information directly.

802.11 Network Analysis Examples

To illustrate how a network analyzer can aid network engineers in looking at wireless LAN traffic, this section presents three detailed examples network analyzers to answer questions about a wireless LAN. The examples are contrived, but nonetheless show the types of operations that are common with network analyzers. The examples are described specifically for Ethereal but can be carried out with any of the commercial alternatives described earlier.

Case Study 1: Access Point Name and Workload Information

As an example of how to use Ethereal, consider the typical driver display on Windows. Usually, there is a function within the driver that allows a card to display the name of an access point supplied by the same vendor. As an example, consider the transmission of access point name and workload information by the Nokia A032. The trace in Figure 16-9 was taken in the vicinity of a Nokia A032 with no stations associated with it. Naturally, there are many Beacon frames announcing the A032's existence.

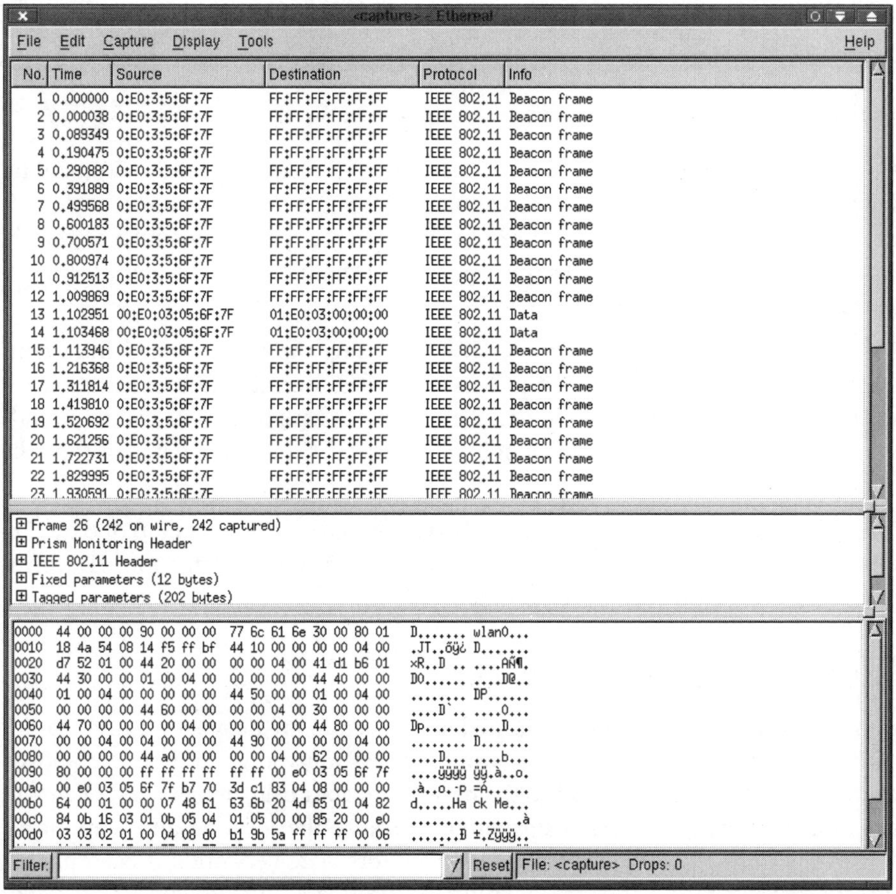

Figure 16-9. Trace of idle 802.11 network

At this point, it is best to get rid of the Beacon frames because they are getting in the way of what we actually want to see. The easiest way to do this is to use the filter expression that excludes Beacon frames: !(wlan.fc.type==0 and wlan.fc. subtype==8). After adding the filter, a few stray Data frames are left; Figure 16-10 shows the remaining Data frames in couplets approximately every three seconds.

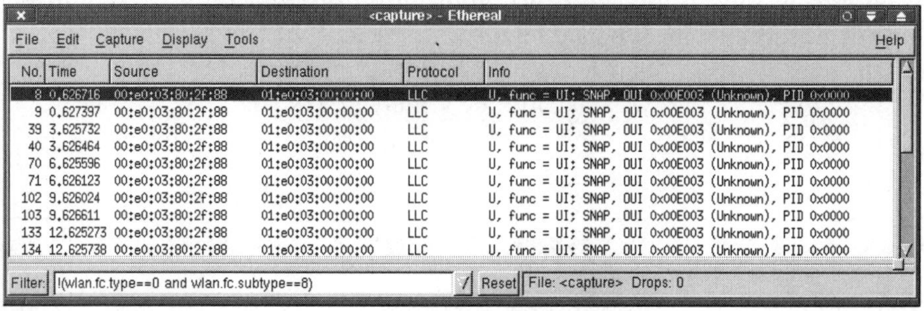

```
┌──────────────────────────────────────────────────────────────────────────────────────────┐
│ ✕                                    <capture> - Ethereal                          ○ ▼ ▲  │
├──────────────────────────────────────────────────────────────────────────────────────────┤
│ File   Edit   Capture   Display   Tools                                             Help   │
├──────────────────────────────────────────────────────────────────────────────────────────┤
│ No. Time       Source              Destination         Protocol   Info                 ⌃  │
│   8 0.626716   00:e0:03:80:2f:88   01:e0:03:00:00:00   LLC        U, func = UI; SNAP, OUI 0x00E003 (Unknown), PID 0x0000 │
│   9 0.627397   00:e0:03:80:2f:88   01:e0:03:00:00:00   LLC        U, func = UI; SNAP, OUI 0x00E003 (Unknown), PID 0x0000 │
│  39 3.625732   00:e0:03:80:2f:88   01:e0:03:00:00:00   LLC        U, func = UI; SNAP, OUI 0x00E003 (Unknown), PID 0x0000 │
│  40 3.626464   00:e0:03:80:2f:88   01:e0:03:00:00:00   LLC        U, func = UI; SNAP, OUI 0x00E003 (Unknown), PID 0x0000 │
│  70 6.625596   00:e0:03:80:2f:88   01:e0:03:00:00:00   LLC        U, func = UI; SNAP, OUI 0x00E003 (Unknown), PID 0x0000 │
│  71 6.626123   00:e0:03:80:2f:88   01:e0:03:00:00:00   LLC        U, func = UI; SNAP, OUI 0x00E003 (Unknown), PID 0x0000 │
│ 102 9.626024   00:e0:03:80:2f:88   01:e0:03:00:00:00   LLC        U, func = UI; SNAP, OUI 0x00E003 (Unknown), PID 0x0000 │
│ 103 9.626611   00:e0:03:80:2f:88   01:e0:03:00:00:00   LLC        U, func = UI; SNAP, OUI 0x00E003 (Unknown), PID 0x0000 │
│ 133 12.625273  00:e0:03:80:2f:88   01:e0:03:00:00:00   LLC        U, func = UI; SNAP, OUI 0x00E003 (Unknown), PID 0x0000 │
│ 134 12.625738  00:e0:03:80:2f:88   01:e0:03:00:00:00   LLC        U, func = UI; SNAP, OUI 0x00E003 (Unknown), PID 0x0000 ⌄│
├──────────────────────────────────────────────────────────────────────────────────────────┤
│ Filter: !(wlan.fc.type==0 and wlan.fc.subtype==8)        ✓ Reset  File: <capture>  Drops: 0 │
└──────────────────────────────────────────────────────────────────────────────────────────┘
```

Figure 16-10. The leftover Data frames

With a filter active, the 802.11 Data frames are fully decoded, and the Protocol field is given the value of the protocol dissector for the highest possible layer. In this case, the Protocol field in Ethereal is set to LLC because the data is contained as raw data within an LLC header. After selecting one of the Data frames for further analysis, the tree view displays Figure 16-11.

The data is encapsulated in a raw LLC frame using the Unnumbered Information header. The OUI used is assigned to Nokia Wireless Business Communications, the wireless LAN product unit of Nokia. (The listing of assigned OUIs can be found at *http://standards.ieee.org/regauth/oui/oui.txt.*) In the LLC data, the name of the access point, Outside, is plainly clear.

The other Data frame, shown in Figure 16-12, also encapsulates a blob of data. I can only assume that this Data frame encapsulates workload information, though the data doesn't make obvious which protocol is in use.

Case Study 2: Joining a Network

Joining a network is a more complicated affair than many people ever need to think about. Stations wishing to access network services must locate a desirable network, prove their identity, and connect to the network to start using its services. On a wired network, the joining process seems simple because the location and identification steps are performed by the network administrators. The network has been built out to network jacks throughout the building, so locating a network consists of looking

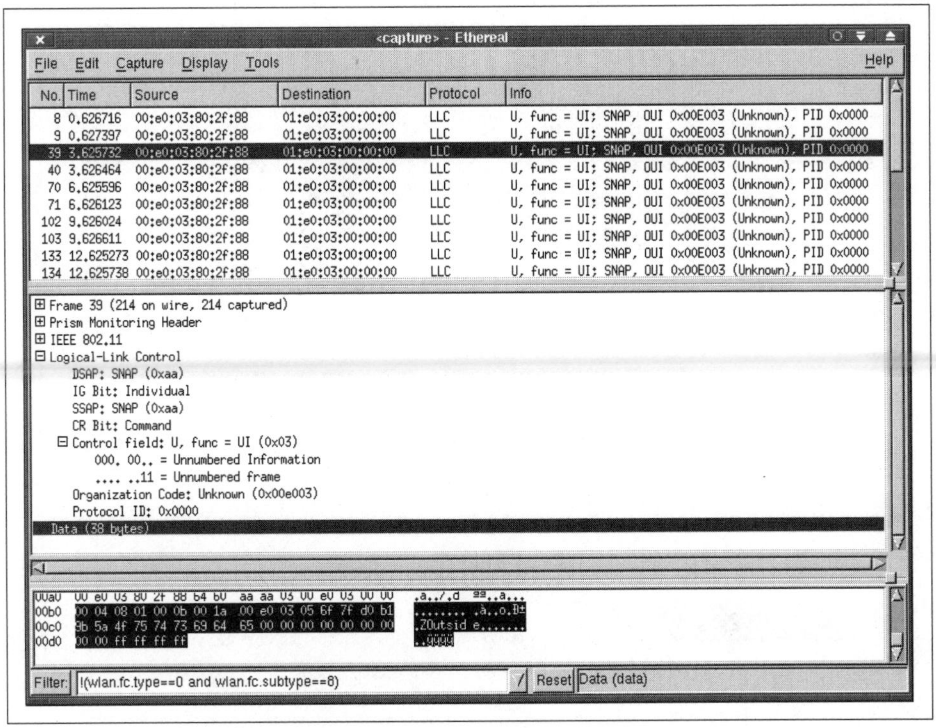

Figure 16-11. One of the random 802.11 Data frames and its LLC data

around for a jack. Proving identity is based on physical access control and personal interaction. Connecting to the network consists of plugging in the cable. Joining an 802.11 network consists of the same steps, but the elimination of the cable means the steps take a different form. To find the network, you must actively scan for other stations to link up with. Authentication cannot be based on physical access control but on cryptographic authentication. Finally, the connection to the network is not based on establishing a physical connection but on the logical connection of an association. The second case study examines the trace of a station joining a network after filtering out extraneous frames to present a clear picture of the exchange.

Scanning

Scanning may be active or passive. Passive scans are carried out by listening to Beacon frames in the area and are not be displayed on a network analyzer because the analyzer cannot tell whether a given Beacon was heard by a wireless station. Active scans rely on Probe Request and Probe Response frames, which are recorded by an analyzer.

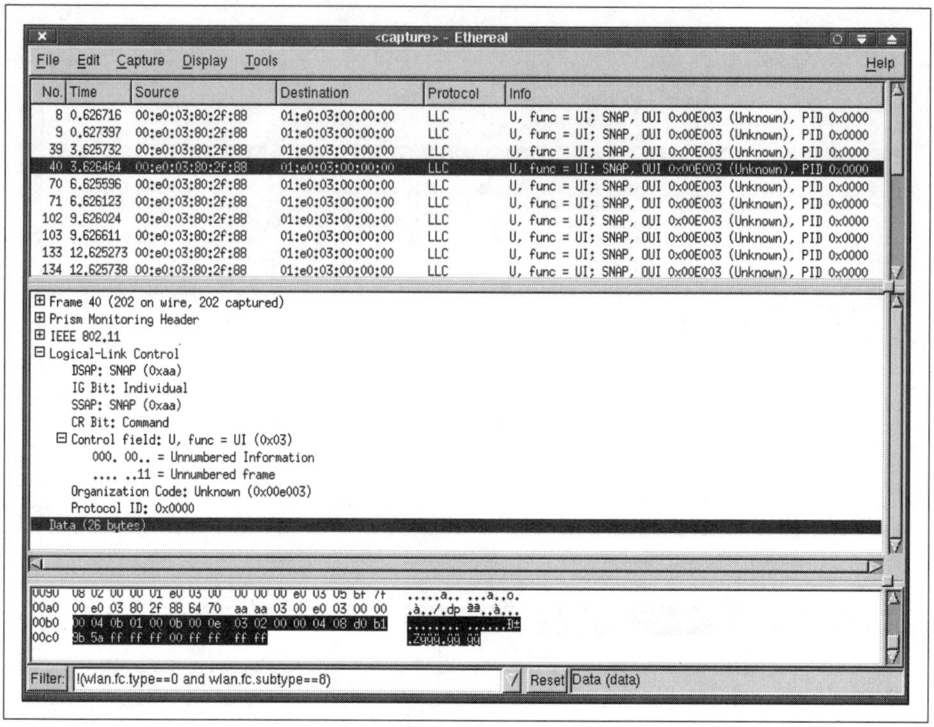

Figure 16-12. The second random 802.11 Data frame and its LLC data

Figure 16-13 shows a Probe Request frame sent by a station seeking access to a network. Probe Request frames carry only two variable information elements in the frame body: the desired SSID and the supported data rates. Probe Requests are broadcast in two senses. First, they are sent to the all-1s destination address ff:ff:ff:ff:ff:ff. However, the frame filtering rules in 802.11 would prevent such a frame from being passed to higher protocol layers if the BSSID did not match. Therefore, the frame is also a broadcast in the sense that it is sent to BSSID ff:ff:ff:ff:ff:ff. Ethereal has also decoded the information elements to determine that the SSID parameter was set to Luminiferous Ether. Probe Requests frequently use a zero-length SSID to indicate that they are willing to join any available network, and any receiving network is responsible for sending a Probe Response. However, this Probe Request is sent specifically to one network. Finally, the Probe Request indicates that the station supports 1-Mbps, 2-Mbps, 5.5-Mbps, and 11-Mbps operation, which is what is expected from an 802.11b card.

In response to the probe request, access points in the SSID named Luminiferous Ether should respond with a Probe Response. Indeed, that is the next frame in the trace. Figure 16-14 shows the expanded view of the Probe Response frame in Ethereal's tree

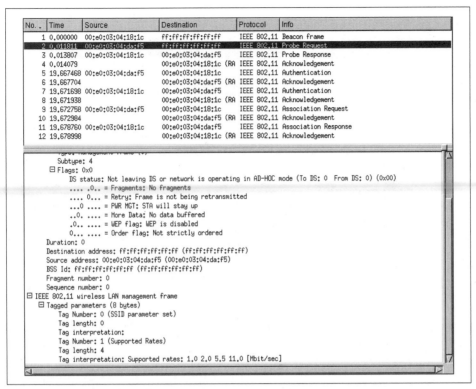

No.	Time	Source	Destination	Protocol	Info
1	0.000000	00:e0:03:04:18:1c	ff:ff:ff:ff:ff:ff	IEEE 802.11	Beacon frame
2	0.011811	00:e0:03:04:da:f5	ff:ff:ff:ff:ff:ff	IEEE 802.11	Probe Request
3	0.013807	00:e0:03:04:18:1c	00:e0:03:04:da:f5	IEEE 802.11	Probe Response
4	0.014079		00:e0:03:04:18:1c (RA	IEEE 802.11	Acknowledgement
5	19.667468	00:e0:03:04:da:f5	00:e0:03:04:18:1c	IEEE 802.11	Authentication
6	19.667704		00:e0:03:04:da:f5 (RA	IEEE 802.11	Acknowledgement
7	19.671698	00:e0:03:04:18:1c	00:e0:03:04:da:f5	IEEE 802.11	Authentication
8	19.671938		00:e0:03:04:18:1c (RA	IEEE 802.11	Acknowledgement
9	19.672758	00:e0:03:04:da:f5	00:e0:03:04:18:1c	IEEE 802.11	Association Request
10	19.672984		00:e0:03:04:da:f5 (RA	IEEE 802.11	Acknowledgement
11	19.678760	00:e0:03:04:18:1c	00:e0:03:04:da:f5	IEEE 802.11	Association Response
12	19.678998		00:e0:03:04:18:1c (RA	IEEE 802.11	Acknowledgement

```
          Subtype: 4
        ⊟ Flags: 0x0
             DS status: Not leaving DS or network is operating in AD-HOC mode (To DS: 0  From DS: 0) (0x00)
             .... .0.. = Fragments: No fragments
             .... 0... = Retry: Frame is not being retransmitted
             ...0 .... = PWR MGT: STA will stay up
             ..0. .... = More Data: No data buffered
             .0.. .... = WEP flag: WEP is disabled
             0... .... = Order flag: Not strictly ordered
          Duration: 0
          Destination address: ff:ff:ff:ff:ff:ff (ff:ff:ff:ff:ff:ff)
          Source address: 00:e0:03:04:da:f5 (00:e0:03:04:da:f5)
          BSS Id: ff:ff:ff:ff:ff:ff (ff:ff:ff:ff:ff:ff)
          Fragment number: 0
          Sequence number: 0
  ⊟ IEEE 802.11 wireless LAN management frame
     ⊟ Tagged parameters (8 bytes)
          Tag Number: 0 (SSID parameter set)
          Tag length: 0
          Tag interpretation:
          Tag Number: 1 (Supported Rates)
          Tag length: 4
          Tag interpretation: Supported rates: 1.0 2.0 5.5 11.0 [Mbit/sec]
```

Figure 16-13. Probe Request frame

view pane. Probe Response frames contain three fixed fields. Timestamps are included so that the probing station can synchronize its timer to the access point timer. The Beacon interval is included because it is a basic unit of time for many power-saving operations. It is expressed in time units, though later versions of Ethereal convert it to seconds. The third fixed field is capability information. The access point transmitting the frame does not implement WEP and is not an 802.11b access point, so most of the Capability field flags are set to 0. The CFP capabilities are set to 0 because this access point, like all access points I am aware of, does not implement contention-free service. After the fixed-length fields, the variable-length fields describe the network. Parameters are the same as in the Probe Request frame, with the addition of the DS Parameter Set to identify the current operating channel.

Probe Responses are unicast frames and must be acknowledged by the receiver. Following the Probe Response, the receiver sends an acknowledgment to the access point. No source address is listed because the only address included in an 802.11 acknowledgment frame is the receiver address.

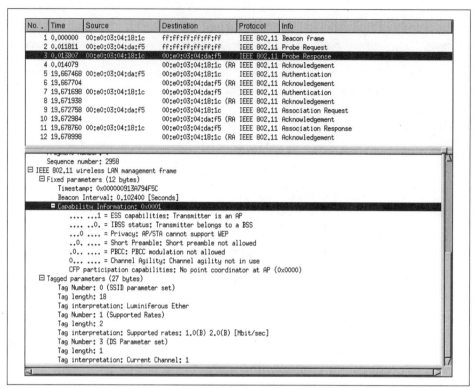

```
No. .  Time      Source             Destination        Protocol   Info
    1  0.000000  00:e0:03:04:18:1c  ff:ff:ff:ff:ff:ff  IEEE 802.11  Beacon frame
    2  0.011811  00:e0:03:04:da:f5  ff:ff:ff:ff:ff:ff  IEEE 802.11  Probe Request
    3  0.013807  00:e0:03:04:18:1c  00:e0:03:04:da:f5  IEEE 802.11  Probe Response
    4  0.014079                     00:e0:03:04:18:1c (RA IEEE 802.11  Acknowledgement
    5  19.667468 00:e0:03:04:da:f5  00:e0:03:04:18:1c  IEEE 802.11  Authentication
    6  19.667704                    00:e0:03:04:da:f5 (RA IEEE 802.11  Acknowledgement
    7  19.671698 00:e0:03:04:18:1c  00:e0:03:04:da:f5  IEEE 802.11  Authentication
    8  19.671938                    00:e0:03:04:18:1c (RA IEEE 802.11  Acknowledgement
    9  19.672758 00:e0:03:04:da:f5  00:e0:03:04:18:1c  IEEE 802.11  Association Request
   10  19.672984                    00:e0:03:04:da:f5 (RA IEEE 802.11  Acknowledgement
   11  19.678760 00:e0:03:04:18:1c  00:e0:03:04:da:f5  IEEE 802.11  Association Response
   12  19.678998                    00:e0:03:04:18:1c (RA IEEE 802.11  Acknowledgement

     Sequence number: 2958
 ⊟ IEEE 802.11 wireless LAN management frame
   ⊟ Fixed parameters (12 bytes)
        Timestamp: 0x000000913A794F5C
        Beacon Interval: 0.102400 [Seconds]
      ⊟ Capability Information: 0x0001
          .... ...1 = ESS capabilities: Transmitter is an AP
          .... ..0. = IBSS status: Transmitter belongs to a BSS
          ...0 .... = Privacy: AP/STA cannot support WEP
          ..0. .... = Short Preamble: Short preamble not allowed
          .0.. .... = PBCC: PBCC modulation not allowed
          0... .... = Channel Agility: Channel agility not in use
          CFP participation capabilities: No point coordinator at AP (0x0000)
   ⊟ Tagged parameters (27 bytes)
        Tag Number: 0 (SSID parameter set)
        Tag length: 18
        Tag interpretation: Luminiferous Ether
        Tag Number: 1 (Supported Rates)
        Tag length: 2
        Tag interpretation: Supported rates: 1.0(B) 2.0(B) [Mbit/sec]
        Tag Number: 3 (DS Parameter set)
        Tag length: 1
        Tag interpretation: Current Channel: 1
```

Figure 16-14. Expanded view of Probe Response frame

Authentication

After finding a network, the next step is to authenticate to it. The network in this example is using simple open-system authentication. This greatly simplifies interpreting the trace because open-system authentication requires exchanging only two authentication frames.

First, the station requests authentication with the first frame in the authentication sequence, shown in Figure 16-15. Authentication requests occur only after the station has matched parameters with the network; note that the BSSID now matches the source on the Beacon frames. The first frame specifies authentication algorithm 0 for open system. (Ethereal decodes the field improperly; when highlighted, the data pane clearly shows that the algorithm number is set to 0.) Finally, the status code indicates success because it is too early in the sequence to fail. There is a big time gap between the fourth and fifth frames in the sequence because the driver on the client station was configured to prompt the user to determine which ESS should be joined.

Authentication requests are unicast Management frames and must be acknowledged under the rules of the DCF. The access point sends an acknowledgment immediately after receiving the first Authentication frame. The access point may then choose to

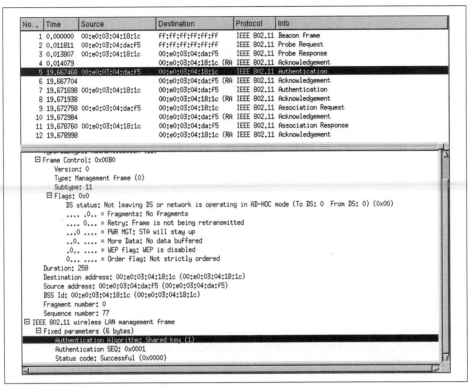

No.	Time	Source	Destination	Protocol	Info
1	0.000000	00:e0:03:04:18:1c	ff:ff:ff:ff:ff:ff	IEEE 802.11	Beacon frame
2	0.011811	00:e0:03:04:da:f5	ff:ff:ff:ff:ff:ff	IEEE 802.11	Probe Request
3	0.013807	00:e0:03:04:18:1c	00:e0:03:04:da:f5	IEEE 802.11	Probe Response
4	0.014079		00:e0:03:04:18:1c (RA	IEEE 802.11	Acknowledgement
5	19.667468	00:e0:03:04:da:f5	00:e0:03:04:18:1c	IEEE 802.11	Authentication
6	19.667704		00:e0:03:04:da:f5 (RA	IEEE 802.11	Acknowledgement
7	19.671698	00:e0:03:04:18:1c	00:e0:03:04:da:f5	IEEE 802.11	Authentication
8	19.671938		00:e0:03:04:18:1c (RA	IEEE 802.11	Acknowledgement
9	19.672758	00:e0:03:04:da:f5	00:e0:03:04:18:1c	IEEE 802.11	Association Request
10	19.672984		00:e0:03:04:da:f5 (RA	IEEE 802.11	Acknowledgement
11	19.678760	00:e0:03:04:18:1c	00:e0:03:04:da:f5	IEEE 802.11	Association Response
12	19.678998		00:e0:03:04:18:1c (RA	IEEE 802.11	Acknowledgement

```
   Type/Subtype: Authentication (11)
 ⊟ Frame Control: 0x00B0
      Version: 0
      Type: Management frame (0)
      Subtype: 11
    ⊟ Flags: 0x0
         DS status: Not leaving DS or network is operating in AD-HOC mode (To DS: 0  From DS: 0) (0x00)
         .... .0.. = Fragments: No fragments
         .... 0... = Retry: Frame is not being retransmitted
         ...0 .... = PWR MGT: STA will stay up
         ..0. .... = More Data: No data buffered
         .0.. .... = WEP flag: WEP is disabled
         0... .... = Order flag: Not strictly ordered
      Duration: 258
      Destination address: 00:e0:03:04:18:1c (00:e0:03:04:18:1c)
      Source address: 00:e0:03:04:da:f5 (00:e0:03:04:da:f5)
      BSS Id: 00:e0:03:04:18:1c (00:e0:03:04:18:1c)
      Fragment number: 0
      Sequence number: 77
 ⊟ IEEE 802.11 wireless LAN management frame
    ⊟ Fixed parameters (6 bytes)
         Authentication Algorithm: Shared key (1)
         Authentication SEQ: 0x0001
         Status code: Successful (0x0000)
```

Figure 16-15. First authentication frame

allow or deny the request. Open systems are supposed to accept any authentication request, as this one does (Figure 16-16). The second frame concludes the open-system authentication exchange, and, as expected, the result is successful. Once again, the sequence number is highlighted in the data view pane. Like the previous Management frame, the second Authentication frame is a unicast management frame and must be acknowledged.

Association

After authentication is complete, the station is free to attempt association with the access point. Figure 16-17 shows the frame expanded in the tree view. Most of the parameters in the association request are familiar by this point. Capability information is present, along with the SSID and supported rates of the station.

Association Request frames must be acknowledged. Following the 802.11 acknowledgment, the access point decides whether to allow the association. The main reason for rejecting an association is that a busy access point may not have sufficient resources to support an additional node. In this case, the association was successful.

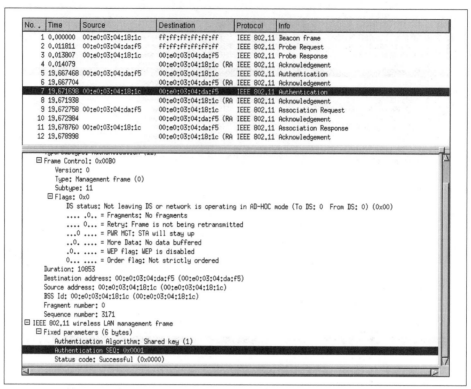

No.	Time	Source	Destination	Protocol	Info
1	0.000000	00:e0:03:04:18:1c	ff:ff:ff:ff:ff:ff	IEEE 802.11	Beacon frame
2	0.011811	00:e0:03:04:da:f5	ff:ff:ff:ff:ff:ff	IEEE 802.11	Probe Request
3	0.013807	00:e0:03:04:18:1c	00:e0:03:04:da:f5	IEEE 802.11	Probe Response
4	0.014079		00:e0:03:04:18:1c (RA	IEEE 802.11	Acknowledgement
5	19.667468	00:e0:03:04:da:f5	00:e0:03:04:18:1c	IEEE 802.11	Authentication
6	19.667704		00:e0:03:04:da:f5 (RA	IEEE 802.11	Acknowledgement
7	19.671698	00:e0:03:04:18:1c	00:e0:03:04:da:f5	IEEE 802.11	Authentication
8	19.671938		00:e0:03:04:18:1c (RA	IEEE 802.11	Acknowledgement
9	19.672758	00:e0:03:04:da:f5	00:e0:03:04:18:1c	IEEE 802.11	Association Request
10	19.672984		00:e0:03:04:da:f5 (RA	IEEE 802.11	Acknowledgement
11	19.678760	00:e0:03:04:18:1c	00:e0:03:04:da:f5	IEEE 802.11	Association Response
12	19.678998		00:e0:03:04:18:1c (RA	IEEE 802.11	Acknowledgement

```
⊟ Frame Control: 0x00B0
    Version: 0
    Type: Management frame (0)
    Subtype: 11
    ⊟ Flags: 0x0
        DS status: Not leaving DS or network is operating in AD-HOC mode (To DS: 0  From DS: 0) (0x00)
        .... .0.. = Fragments: No fragments
        .... 0... = Retry: Frame is not being retransmitted
        ...0 .... = PWR MGT: STA will stay up
        ..0. .... = More Data: No data buffered
        .0.. .... = WEP flag: WEP is disabled
        0... .... = Order flag: Not strictly ordered
    Duration: 10853
    Destination address: 00:e0:03:04:da:f5 (00:e0:03:04:da:f5)
    Source address: 00:e0:03:04:18:1c (00:e0:03:04:18:1c)
    BSS Id: 00:e0:03:04:18:1c (00:e0:03:04:18:1c)
    Fragment number: 0
    Sequence number: 3171
⊟ IEEE 802.11 wireless LAN management frame
    ⊟ Fixed parameters (6 bytes)
        Authentication Algorithm: Shared key (1)
        Authentication SEQ: 0x0001
        Status code: Successful (0x0000)
```

Figure 16-16. Second authentication frame

As part of the response, which is shown decoded in Figure 16-18, the access point assigns an Association ID.

Case Study 3: A Simple Web Transaction

Now we'll look at a higher-level operation: a trace of a machine browsing the Web. If you ask most network engineers how a connection to a web server works, the reply would go something like this:

1. Before it can make an HTTP request, a host must locate the HTTP server by making a DNS request. Because the DNS server is probably not attached to the same IP subnet as the host, the host issues an ARP request to find its default gateway.

2. Once it receives the ARP reply, the host sends a DNS query to resolve the name of the web server (*www.oreilly.com*). It receives a reply with the IP address of the web server (209.204.146.22).

3. The client opens a standard TCP connection to port 80 on the web server and sends an HTTP request for the specified page.

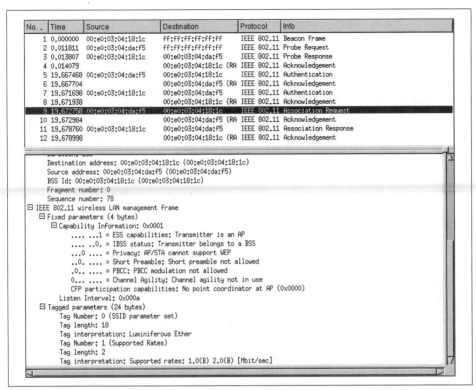

```
No. .  Time      Source             Destination        Protocol  Info
    1  0.000000  00:e0:03:04:18:1c  ff:ff:ff:ff:ff:ff        IEEE 802.11 Beacon frame
    2  0.011811  00:e0:03:04:da:f5  ff:ff:ff:ff:ff:ff        IEEE 802.11 Probe Request
    3  0.013807  00:e0:03:04:18:1c  00:e0:03:04:da:f5        IEEE 802.11 Probe Response
    4  0.014079                     00:e0:03:04:18:1c  (RA   IEEE 802.11 Acknowledgement
    5  19.667468 00:e0:03:04:da:f5  00:e0:03:04:18:1c        IEEE 802.11 Authentication
    6  19.667704                    00:e0:03:04:da:f5  (RA   IEEE 802.11 Acknowledgement
    7  19.671698 00:e0:03:04:18:1c  00:e0:03:04:da:f5        IEEE 802.11 Authentication
    8  19.671938                    00:e0:03:04:18:1c  (RA   IEEE 802.11 Acknowledgement
    9  19.672758 00:e0:03:04:da:f5  00:e0:03:04:18:1c        IEEE 802.11 Association Request
   10  19.672984                    00:e0:03:04:da:f5  (RA   IEEE 802.11 Acknowledgement
   11  19.678760 00:e0:03:04:18:1c  00:e0:03:04:da:f5        IEEE 802.11 Association Response
   12  19.678998                    00:e0:03:04:18:1c  (RA   IEEE 802.11 Acknowledgement
```

```
     Destination address: 00:e0:03:04:18:1c (00:e0:03:04:18:1c)
     Source address: 00:e0:03:04:da:f5 (00:e0:03:04:da:f5)
     BSS Id: 00:e0:03:04:18:1c (00:e0:03:04:18:1c)
     Fragment number: 0
     Sequence number: 78
  ⊟ IEEE 802.11 wireless LAN management frame
     ⊟ Fixed parameters (4 bytes)
        ⊟ Capability Information: 0x0001
              .... ...1 = ESS capabilities: Transmitter is an AP
              .... ..0. = IBSS status: Transmitter belongs to a BSS
              ...0 .... = Privacy: AP/STA cannot support WEP
              ..0. .... = Short Preamble: Short preamble not allowed
              .0.. .... = PBCC: PBCC modulation not allowed
              0... .... = Channel Agility: Channel agility not in use
              CFP participation capabilities: No point coordinator at AP (0x0000)
        Listen Interval: 0x000a
     ⊟ Tagged parameters (24 bytes)
        Tag Number: 0 (SSID parameter set)
        Tag length: 18
        Tag interpretation: Luminiferous Ether
        Tag Number: 1 (Supported Rates)
        Tag length: 2
        Tag interpretation: Supported rates: 1.0(B) 2.0(B) [Mbit/sec]
```

Figure 16-17. Association request

On an 802.11 network, this simple, well-understood process requires 24 frames. Figure 16-19 shows these frames in the packet summary pane. A display filter has been applied to remove SSH traffic that was in the air at the same time, as well as the vendor-specific access point name advertisements using the raw LLC encapsulation. References to frame numbers throughout this section use the frame numbers from Figure 16-19.

The ARP request

The first step in the process is an ARP request to get the MAC address of the default router, 192.168.200.1. ARP requests are normally broadcast to the local network. On a wireless network, though, different procedures apply. To start with, the ARP request takes more than one frame on the wireless network. The first frame, shown in Figure 16-20, kicks off the exchange. The 802.11 header has several expected fields. The frame is a Data frame because it is carrying a higher-layer packet. It is bound for the distribution system in the AP, so the ToDS bit is set, and the FromDS bit is clear. Like all ARP requests, it is sent to the broadcast address. However, the BSSID keeps the broadcast from being replicated to wireless stations attached to other BSSs in the area.

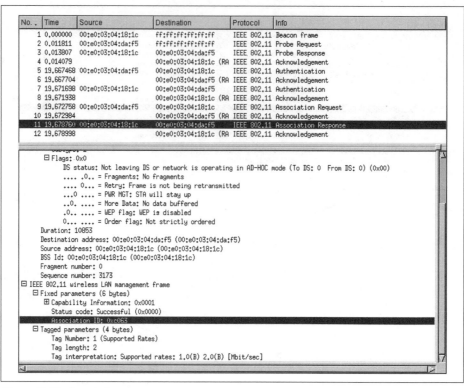

Figure 16-18. Association response

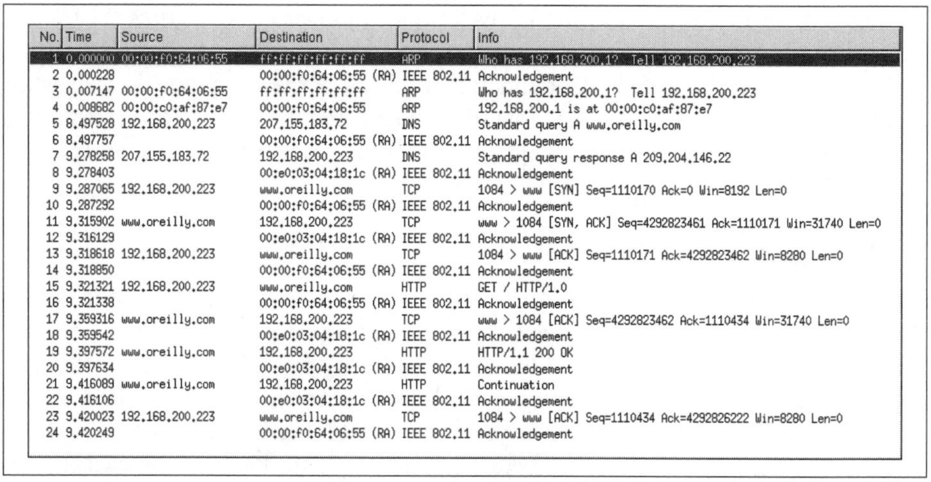

Figure 16-19. Full web site trace

Although the frame is destined for a broadcast address, the wireless LAN station has no way of sending a broadcast directly onto the wired network. The access point converts the frame into a broadcast on the wired network. Like any packet on the

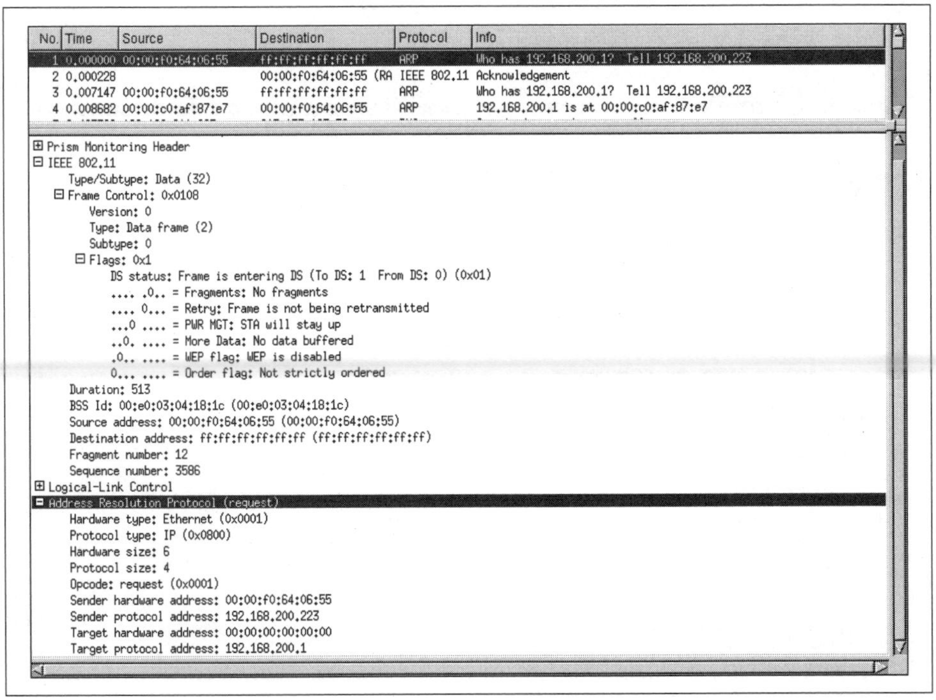

No.	Time	Source	Destination	Protocol	Info
1	0.000000	00:00:f0:64:06:55	ff:ff:ff:ff:ff:ff	ARP	Who has 192.168.200.1? Tell 192.168.200.223
2	0.000228		00:00:f0:64:06:55 (RA	IEEE 802.11	Acknowledgement
3	0.007147	00:00:f0:64:06:55	ff:ff:ff:ff:ff:ff	ARP	Who has 192.168.200.1? Tell 192.168.200.223
4	0.008682	00:00:c0:af:87:e7	00:00:f0:64:06:55	ARP	192.168.200.1 is at 00:00:c0:af:87:e7

```
⊞ Prism Monitoring Header
⊟ IEEE 802.11
     Type/Subtype: Data (32)
     ⊟ Frame Control: 0x0108
          Version: 0
          Type: Data frame (2)
          Subtype: 0
          ⊟ Flags: 0x1
               DS status: Frame is entering DS (To DS: 1  From DS: 0) (0x01)
               .... .0.. = Fragments: No fragments
               .... 0... = Retry: Frame is not being retransmitted
               ...0 .... = PWR MGT: STA will stay up
               ..0. .... = More Data: No data buffered
               .0.. .... = WEP flag: WEP is disabled
               0... .... = Order flag: Not strictly ordered
     Duration: 513
     BSS Id: 00:e0:03:04:18:1c (00:e0:03:04:18:1c)
     Source address: 00:00:f0:64:06:55 (00:00:f0:64:06:55)
     Destination address: ff:ff:ff:ff:ff:ff (ff:ff:ff:ff:ff:ff)
     Fragment number: 12
     Sequence number: 3586
⊞ Logical-Link Control
⊟ Address Resolution Protocol (request)
     Hardware type: Ethernet (0x0001)
     Protocol type: IP (0x0800)
     Hardware size: 6
     Protocol size: 4
     Opcode: request (0x0001)
     Sender hardware address: 00:00:f0:64:06:55
     Sender protocol address: 192.168.200.223
     Target hardware address: 00:00:00:00:00:00
     Target protocol address: 192.168.200.1
```

Figure 16-20. Initial ARP request

wired network, the access point checks to see whether the broadcast must be relayed to the wireless network. Frame 3 is the ARP request after it is processed by the access point. Note that the FromDS bit is set to indicate that the frame originated on the distribution system. In this case, the frame originated on the wired network (the distribution system medium).

The ARP reply

Once the frame reaches the wired network, the default router can reply. The ARP reply of Frame 4 is shown in Figure 16-21. The Reply frame originates from the wired network, so the FromDS bit is set. The frame retains its source address from the wired network.

The DNS request

The DNS request of Frame 5 is shown in Figure 16-22. It is sent using the same BSSID used throughout this example, with a source address of the wireless LAN station and a destination of the default router. The frame originates on the wireless network and must be bridged to the wired side, so the ToDS bit is set. Ethereal's tree view shows summary decodes on the source and destination IP addresses and UDP ports. Finally, the DNS decode is called, which shows the request for the address of *www.oreilly.com*.

```
No. Time      Source             Destination         Protocol  Info
  1 0.000000  00:00:f0:64:06:55  ff:ff:ff:ff:ff:ff   ARP       Who has 192.168.200.1? Tell 192.168.200.223
  2 0.000228                     00:00:f0:64:06:55 (RA IEEE 802.11 Acknowledgement
  3 0.007147  00:00:f0:64:06:55  ff:ff:ff:ff:ff:ff   ARP       Who has 192.168.200.1? Tell 192.168.200.223
  4 0.008682  00:00:c0:af:87:e7  00:00:f0:64:06:55   ARP       192.168.200.1 is at 00:00:c0:af:87:e7

⊞ Frame 4 (226 on wire, 226 captured)
⊞ Prism Monitoring Header
⊟ IEEE 802.11
      Type/Subtype: Data (32)
   ⊟ Frame Control: 0x0208
         Version: 0
         Type: Data frame (2)
         Subtype: 0
      ⊟ Flags: 0x2
            DS status: Frame is exiting DS (To DS: 0  From DS: 1) (0x02)
            .... .0.. = Fragments: No fragments
            .... 0... = Retry: Frame is not being retransmitted
            ...0 .... = PWR MGT: STA will stay up
            ..0. .... = More Data: No data buffered
            .0.. .... = WEP flag: WEP is disabled
            0... .... = Order flag: Not strictly ordered
      Duration: 25898
      Destination address: 00:00:f0:64:06:55 (00:00:f0:64:06:55)
      BSS Id: 00:e0:03:04:18:1c (00:e0:03:04:18:1c)
      Source address: 00:00:c0:af:87:e7 (00:00:c0:af:87:e7)
      Fragment number: 6
      Sequence number: 3083
⊞ Logical-Link Control
⊟ Address Resolution Protocol (reply)
      Hardware type: Ethernet (0x0001)
      Protocol type: IP (0x0800)
      Hardware size: 6
      Protocol size: 4
      Opcode: reply (0x0002)
      Sender hardware address: 00:00:c0:af:87:e7
      Sender protocol address: 192.168.200.1
      Target hardware address: 00:00:f0:64:06:55
```

Figure 16-21. ARP reply

Frame 6 is an 802.11 acknowledgment of the DNS request. It is a Control frame of type Acknowledgment. Acknowledgment frames are extraordinarily simple, containing only the address of the sender of the previous frame. It is shown in Figure 16-23.

The DNS reply

The DNS system queried in the previous step responds with Frame 7, which is shown in Figure 16-24. The frame comes from the distribution system, so the FromDS bit is set. The source MAC address of the frame is the default router and is transmitted using the BSSID of the network. Like all unicast Data frames, the DNS reply must be acknowledged by the 802.11 MAC layer. Frame 8 is the required acknowledgment.

The TCP three-way handshake

The TCP three-way handshake is shown in the packet view pane in Figure 16-25. Note that each TCP segment involved is embedded in a unicast 802.11 data and must be acknowledged, so the exchange requires six frames.

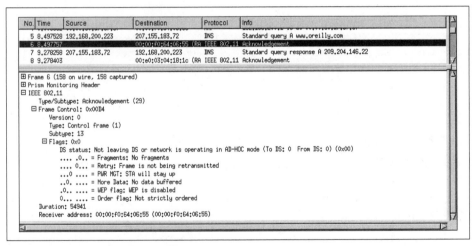

```
No. Time        Source            Destination        Protocol  Info
   5 8.497528   192.168.200.223   207.155.183.72     DNS       Standard query A www.oreilly.com
   6 8.497757                     00:00:f0:64:06:55 (RA IEEE 802.11 Acknowledgement
   7 9.278258   207.155.183.72    192.168.200.223    DNS       Standard query response A 209.204.146.22
   8 9.278403                     00:e0:03:04:18:1c (RA IEEE 802.11 Acknowledgement

⊟ IEEE 802.11
    Type/Subtype: Data (32)
    ⊟ Frame Control: 0x0108
        Version: 0
        Type: Data frame (2)
        Subtype: 0
        ⊟ Flags: 0x1
            DS status: Frame is entering DS (To DS: 1  From DS: 0) (0x01)
            .... .0.. = Fragments: No fragments
            .... 0... = Retry: Frame is not being retransmitted
            ...0 .... = PWR MGT: STA will stay up
            ..0. .... = More Data: No data buffered
            .0.. .... = WEP flag: WEP is disabled
            0... .... = Order flag: Not strictly ordered
        Duration: 513
        BSS Id: 00:e0:03:04:18:1c (00:e0:03:04:18:1c)
        Source address: 00:00:f0:64:06:55 (00:00:f0:64:06:55)
        Destination address: 00:00:c0:af:87:e7 (00:00:c0:af:87:e7)
        Fragment number: 13
        Sequence number: 1282
  ⊞ Logical-Link Control
  ⊞ Internet Protocol, Src Addr: 192.168.200.223 (192.168.200.223), Dst Addr: 207.155.183.72 (207.155.183.72)
  ⊞ User Datagram Protocol, Src Port: 1083 (1083), Dst Port: domain (53)
  ⊟ Domain Name System (query)
        Transaction ID: 0x000a
    ⊞ Flags: 0x0100 (Standard query)
        Questions: 1
        Answer RRs: 0
        Authority RRs: 0
        Additional RRs: 0
    ⊟ Queries
        ⊞ www.oreilly.com: type A, class inet
```

Figure 16-22. DNS request

```
No. Time        Source            Destination        Protocol  Info
   5 8.497528   192.168.200.223   207.155.183.72     DNS       Standard query A www.oreilly.com
   6 8.497757                     00:00:f0:64:06:55 (RA IEEE 802.11 Acknowledgement
   7 9.278258   207.155.183.72    192.168.200.223    DNS       Standard query response A 209.204.146.22
   8 9.278403                     00:e0:03:04:18:1c (RA IEEE 802.11 Acknowledgement

⊞ Frame 6 (158 on wire, 158 captured)
⊞ Prism Monitoring Header
⊟ IEEE 802.11
    Type/Subtype: Acknowledgement (29)
    ⊟ Frame Control: 0x00D4
        Version: 0
        Type: Control frame (1)
        Subtype: 13
        ⊟ Flags: 0x0
            DS status: Not leaving DS or network is operating in AD-HOC mode (To DS: 0  From DS: 0) (0x00)
            .... .0.. = Fragments: No fragments
            .... 0... = Retry: Frame is not being retransmitted
            ...0 .... = PWR MGT: STA will stay up
            ..0. .... = More Data: No data buffered
            .0.. .... = WEP flag: WEP is disabled
            0... .... = Order flag: Not strictly ordered
        Duration: 54941
        Receiver address: 00:00:f0:64:06:55 (00:00:f0:64:06:55)
```

Figure 16-23. ACK of DNS request

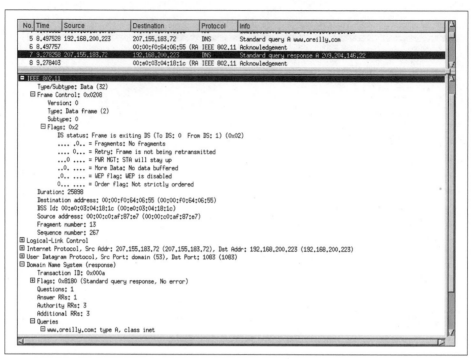

```
No. Time        Source            Destination      Protocol  Info
  5 8.497528  192.168.200.223     207.155.183.72     DNS      Standard query A www.oreilly.com
  6 8.497757                      00:00:f0:64:06:55 (RA IEEE 802.11 Acknowledgement
  7 9.278258  207.155.183.72      192.168.200.223    DNS      Standard query response A 209.204.146.22
  8 9.278403                      00:e0:03:04:18:1c (RA IEEE 802.11 Acknowledgement
```

```
□ IEEE 802.11
    Type/Subtype: Data (32)
    □ Frame Control: 0x0208
        Version: 0
        Type: Data frame (2)
        Subtype: 0
        □ Flags: 0x2
            DS status: Frame is exiting DS (To DS: 0  From DS: 1) (0x02)
            .... .0.. = Fragments: No fragments
            .... 0... = Retry: Frame is not being retransmitted
            ...0 .... = PWR MGT: STA will stay up
            ..0. .... = More Data: No data buffered
            .0.. .... = WEP flag: WEP is disabled
            0... .... = Order flag: Not strictly ordered
        Duration: 25898
        Destination address: 00:00:f0:64:06:55 (00:00:f0:64:06:55)
        BSS Id: 00:e0:03:04:18:1c (00:e0:03:04:18:1c)
        Source address: 00:00:c0:af:87:e7 (00:00:c0:af:87:e7)
        Fragment number: 13
        Sequence number: 267
  ⊞ Logical-Link Control
  ⊞ Internet Protocol, Src Addr: 207.155.183.72 (207.155.183.72), Dst Addr: 192.168.200.223 (192.168.200.223)
  ⊞ User Datagram Protocol, Src Port: domain (53), Dst Port: 1083 (1083)
  □ Domain Name System (response)
        Transaction ID: 0x000a
      ⊞ Flags: 0x8180 (Standard query response, No error)
        Questions: 1
        Answer RRs: 1
        Authority RRs: 3
        Additional RRs: 3
      □ Queries
          □ www.oreilly.com: type A, class inet
```

Figure 16-24. DNS reply

```
No. Time        Source            Destination      Protocol  Info
  8 9.278403                      00:e0:03:04:18:1c (RA IEEE 802.11 Acknowledgement
  9 9.287065  192.168.200.223     www.oreilly.com    TCP      1084 > www [SYN] Seq=1110170 Ack=0 Win=8192 Len=0
 10 9.287292                      00:00:f0:64:06:55 (RA) IEEE 802.11 Acknowledgement
 11 9.315902  www.oreilly.com     192.168.200.223    TCP      www > 1084 [SYN, ACK] Seq=4292823461 Ack=1110171 Win=31740 Len=0
 12 9.316129                      00:e0:03:04:18:1c (RA) IEEE 802.11 Acknowledgement
 13 9.318618  192.168.200.223     www.oreilly.com    TCP      1084 > www [ACK] Seq=1110171 Ack=4292823462 Win=8280 Len=0
 14 9.318850                      00:00:f0:64:06:55 (RA) IEEE 802.11 Acknowledgement
 15 9.321321  192.168.200.223     www.oreilly.com    HTTP     GET / HTTP/1.0
```

Figure 16-25. TCP three-way handshake

The TCP data transfer

The HTTP connection itself lasts much longer than everything we've seen so far, but everything past the three-way TCP handshake is boring. Figure 16-26 illustrates the exchange, which consists of a series of packets in the following pattern:

1. An 802.11 Data frame containing a maximum-sized TCP segment from the web server, carrying data from TCP port 80 on the server to the random high-numbered port chosen by the client. The frame's source address is the default router, but its transmitter address is the access point.

2. An 802.11 acknowledgment from the client to the access point to acknowledge receipt of the frame in step 1.

3. An 802.11 Data frame carrying a TCP acknowledgment from the client to the server acknowledges the receipt of the data in the frame in step 1. However, the acknowledgment in this step is a TCP segment, which is higher-layer data to the MAC layer. The source MAC address of this frame is the client, and the destination MAC address is the default router. However, the default router is on a wired Ethernet, and an access point is required for bridging, so the receiver address is the MAC address of the wireless interface in the access point.

4. The access point sends an 802.11 acknowledgment for the frame in step 3 to the client.

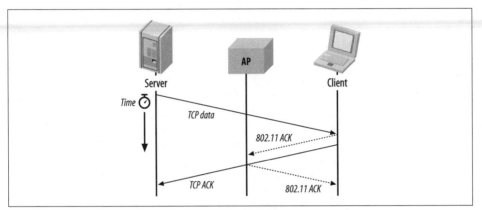

Figure 16-26. Frames corresponding to the bulk transfer of an HTTP connection

AirSnort

Technically, AirSnort is not a network analysis tool. It is a tool that every wireless network administrator should be familiar with, though, because it allows a malicious attacker to retrieve the WEP keys from an active network simply by collecting enough traffic. AirSnort was released with some fanfare in August 2001 as the first public implementation of the Fluhrer/Mantin/Shamir attack against WEP.

Prerequisites

Before attempting to configure AirSnort, you need to have a configured kernel source tree, a configured PCMCIA source tree, and a compiled *linux-wlan-ng* driver capable of raw packet captures. If you have already built Ethereal for use with a PRISM-2 card, all the prerequisites should be met. Download and unpack the code from *http:// airsnort.sourceforge.net*; the current version as this chapter was written was 0.0.9. Unlike Adam Stubblefield's attack, the code for AirSnort is publicly available under the GPL.

AirSnort can be used to recover either standard 40-bit keys or what it refers to as 128-bit keys. However, as noted in Chapter 5, the label of 128-bit WEP is a slight misnomer because it refers to the size of the RC4 key. After subtracting the 24-bit initialization vector, only 104 bits are secret. To be accurate, then, AirSnort can be used to recover 40-bit secret keys and 104-bit secret keys, which correspond to the two most common WEP implementations currently on the market. Some vendors have WEP implementations that use longer keys; for example, Nokia uses 128 secret bits in addition to the 24-bit IV, and this vendor's long key-length WEP cannot currently be attacked with AirSnort. However, the longer key length doesn't provide any real protection against this attack. If the history of open source development is a guide, future versions of AirSnort will be able to attack longer keys.

Compiling

AirSnort is written in C++. Some Linux distributions do not install a C++ compiler by default, so you may need to fetch the C++ compiler package before proceeding. Simply run *make* in the top-level directory to build the package:

```
$ make
make -C src
make[1]: Entering directory `/home/gast/wlan/airsnort-0.0.9/src'
g++  -g  -c -o capture.o capture.cc
g++  -g  -c -o PacketSource.o PacketSource.cc
g++ -o capture capture.o PacketSource.o  -lncurses
g++  -g  -c -o crack.o crack.cc
g++  -g  -c -o RC4.o RC4.cc
g++  -g  -c -o crc-32.o crc-32.cc
g++ -o crack crack.o RC4.o crc-32.o
g++  -g  -c -o gencases.o gencases.cc
g++ -o gencases gencases.o RC4.o crc-32.o
g++  -g  -c -o decrypt.o decrypt.cc
g++  -g  -c -o utils.o utils.cc
g++ -o decrypt decrypt.o RC4.o crc-32.o utils.o
make[1]: Leaving directory `/home/gast/wlan/airsnort-0.0.9/src'
```

The final product of the compilation is two executable files:

capture

A program that interfaces with low-level device drivers to capture raw packets as they come in. The sole argument to *capture* is the filename used to store "interesting" packets for later processing.

crack

A program that takes the interesting packets saved by *capture* and runs them through the cryptographic attack.

Running AirSnort

AirSnort depends on promiscuous capture, so start by using *wlanctl-ng* to enable promiscuous mode capture on the channel you want to monitor:

```
# wlanctl-ng wlan0 lnxreq_wlansniff channel=5 enable=true
message=lnxreq_wlansniff
  enable=true
  channel=5
  resultcode=success
```

Next, fire up AirSnort's *capture* program. *capture* grabs all the incoming frames and looks for frames with a weak initialization vector. Those frames are saved for further analysis. *capture* takes one argument: the name of the file for saving captured frames. *capture* always appends data to the saved file, so a file can collect the traces from several sniffing sessions before attempting analysis. The –c option displays statistics on the number of packets captured, the number of encrypted packets analyzed, and the number of weak IVs saved. It also displays the last IV received, which allows you to check for vulnerability to the "IV increments from zero" design flaw identified by the Berkeley team. *capture* won't run if the driver is not in sniffing mode.

```
$ ./capture -c 40bits.1

AirSnort Capture v0.0.9
Copyright 2001, Jeremy Bruestle and Blake Hegerle

Total Packets:       70550
Encrypted Packets:   22931
Interesting Packets: 5
Last IV = 8f:1b:1e
```

To attempt key recovery, run the *crack* program against the capture output file. *crack* takes one argument, which is the name of the capture file. There are two options. The –b option controls the *breadth* of the analysis and ranges from 1 to 5. Wider breadths take more CPU time but may be able to guess the key earlier. The second option is the key length, specified as –l. *crack* can attempt to recover 40-bit keys and 128-bit keys (with 104 secret bits), which are specified with –l 40 and –l 128, respectively. Note that higher breadths can require vastly more CPU time at long key lengths. As a practical matter, all breadths are fine for 40-bit keys. For 128-bit keys, a breadth of 2 requires about 30 seconds of run time, and a breadth of 3 takes so long to complete, it's impractical.

When *crack* is unsuccessful, it simply prints the number of samples received. Each IV is associated with the key byte it is used to attack. *crack* categorizes the samples against each key byte; the authors of AirSnort suggest that approximately 115 samples are needed for each key byte to mount a successful key recovery:

```
[gast@bloodhound airsnort-0.0.9]$ time ./crack -b 5 40bits.1
Reading packets
```

```
Performing crack, keySize=40 bit, breadth=5
Key Byte 0: 8 samples
Key Byte 1: 12 samples
Key Byte 2: 9 samples
Key Byte 3: 8 samples
Key Byte 4: 11 samples
Check samples: 10

FAILED! r=1
0.29user 0.14system 0:00.42elapsed 100%CPU (0avgtext+0avgdata 0maxresident)k
0inputs+0outputs (152major+16minor)pagefaults 0swaps
```

When a *crack* run is successful, it prints the key at the end of the run. Some vendors simply take an ASCII string and use the ASCII representation for the WEP key, so *crack* prints both the hexadecimal and textual representations of the key string:

```
[gast@bloodhound airsnort-0.0.9]$ time ./crack -b 5 40bits.1

Reading packets
Performing crack, keySize=40 bit, breadth=5
Key Byte 0: 143 samples
Key Byte 1: 149 samples
Key Byte 2: 132 samples
Key Byte 3: 127 samples
Key Byte 4: 128 samples
Check samples: 10

GOT KEY!
Hex = 9c:3b:46:20:97
String = '.;F .'
0.00user 0.01system 0:00.01elapsed 62%CPU (0avgtext+0avgdata 0maxresident)k
0inputs+0outputs (153major+21minor)pagefaults 0swaps
```

(Although it is probably meaningless to do so, I have changed the key on my wireless LAN from 9c:3b:46:20:97.)

Key Recovery Time Estimates

There are two components to recovering a key. First, enough frames with weak IVs must be gathered to mount an attack, which I refer to as the *gathering time*. Second, a successful attack must be run against the stored frames, which I refer to as the *analysis time*.

In my experience, the time required to gather enough data to mount the attack dominates the CPU time required to run the attack. With enough samples to successfully attack, the analysis time is only a few seconds. The analysis time scales linearly, so the protection afforded by longer keys is only a few seconds. By doubling the key length, the CPU time required for the attack will double, but doubling a few seconds is still only a few seconds.

In my real-world trials against my home network, only a few hours of gathering time were required, and longer keys did not dramatically increase the gathering time. While longer keys require more weak IVs, more IVs are weak at longer key lengths. WEP IVs are three bytes long and are often written in the byte-delimited, colon-separated format commonly used for MAC addresses. Weak IVs have a middle byte that is all 1s; that is, they can be written in the form B+3:FF:N, in which B and N may take on different values. In the Fluhrer/Mantin/Shamir attack, N may be any value from 0 to 255 and is not constrained. Each weak key helps recover a particular byte in the secret portion of the key. B is the byte number, starting from 0, of the secret portion of the key. Thus, a weak IV of the form 4:FF:N helps recover key byte 1. The number of weak IVs is the product of the key length in bytes multiplied by 256; Table 16-3 shows how the fraction of weak keys increases with key size. As the fraction of weak keys increases, the requisite number of weak keys may be gathered more quickly.

Table 16-3. Number of weak packets as a function of key length

Secret key length	Values of B+3 in weak IV (B+3:FF:N)	Number of weak IVs	Fraction of IV space
40 bits	3 <= B+3 < 8 (0 <= B < 5)	1,280	0.008%
104 bits	3 <= B+3 < 16 (0 <= B < 13)	3,328	0.020%
128 bits	3 <= B+3 < 19 (0 <= B < 16)	4,096	0.024%

Two opposing forces work on the gathering time. Longer keys require more samples of weak IVs but also expose more IVs as weak. In my experience, these two effects offset for the most part, though longer keys may slightly increase the gathering time. In theory, the two effects should offset each other. In fact, the number of weak IVs that need to be collected is directly proportional to the key size. In my testing, about 100 weak IVs per key byte were necessary before the key recover could be successful. The fraction of weak IVs is also a direct function of the key size in bytes, so there is reason to believe that the gathering time is independent of key size.

In my experimental runs, I generated a 30% load on an 11-Mbps 802.11b network. I was always able to recover keys in eight hours, though I could occasionally recover shorter keys in as few as five. Many production wireless LANs may run at higher loads, which would certainly decrease the required gathering time. If the network load was 60%, which would not be outrageous for an 11-Mbps shared medium, keys could easily be recovered within a single working day. AirSnort conclusively demonstrates that any information flowing over a wireless LAN and protected with standard WEP should be treated as fully exposed.

CHAPTER 17
802.11 Performance Tuning

Until now, wireless network administrators have probably received a bit of a free ride. Wireless is new and cool, and people do not know what sort of service they should expect. Users are happy that it works at all, and it is both easy and correct to tell them that they should not expect the same performance they would see on a 100BaseT Ethernet. Most wireless installations do not have large user communities and therefore do not have dozens or hundreds of stations trying to associate with a small number of access points. Furthermore, most wireless networks are logically subordinate to existing wired networks. 802.11 was designed to complement existing LANs, not replace them. When the wired LAN is the primary network, people can still get the job done without the wireless network, and it is seen as less critical. Most likely, your biggest problems are positioning your access points so you have coverage everywhere you want it, installing drivers, and keeping your WEP keys up to date.

However, networks have a way of growing, and users have a way of becoming more demanding. Your network's performance "out of the box" is probably fairly poor, even if no one but you notices. Changing the physical environment (by experimenting with access point placement, external antennas, etc.) may alleviate some problems, but others may best be resolved by tuning administrative parameters. This chapter discusses some of the administrative parameters that can tuned to improve the behavior of your wireless network.

Tuning Radio Management

As with other types of wireless networks, the most precious resource on an 802.11 network is radio bandwidth. Radio spectrum is constrained by regulatory authority and cannot be easily enlarged. Several parameters allow you to optimize your network's use of the radio resource.

Beacon Interval

Beacon frames serve several fundamental purposes in an infrastructure network. At the most basic level, Beacon frames define the coverage area of a basic service set (BSS). All communication in infrastructure networks is through an access point, even if the frame is sent between two stations in the same BSS. Access points are stationary, which means that the distance a Beacon frame can travel reliably won't vary over time.* Stations monitor Beacon frames to determine which Extended Service Sets (ESSs) offer coverage at a their physical location and use the received signal strength to monitor the signal quality.

Transmitting Beacon frames, however, eats up radio capacity. Decreasing the Beacon interval makes passive scanning more reliable and faster because Beacon frames announce the network to the radio link more frequently. Smaller Beacon intervals may also make mobility more effective by increasing the coverage information available to mobile nodes. Rapidly moving nodes benefit from more frequent Beacon frames because they can update signal strength information more often.† Increasing the Beacon interval indirectly increases the power-saving capability of attached nodes by altering the listen interval and the DTIM interval, both of which are discussed in the section "Tuning Power Management." Increasing the Beacon interval may add an incremental amount of throughput by decreasing contention for the medium. Time occupied by Beacon frames is time that can't be used for transmitting data.

RTS Threshold

802.11 includes the RTS/CTS clearing procedure to help with large frames. Any frame larger than the RTS threshold must be cleared for departure from the antenna by transmission of an RTS and reception of a CTS from the target. RTS/CTS exists to combat interference from so-called hidden nodes. The RTS/CTS exchange minimizes interference from hidden nodes by informing all stations in the immediate area that a frame exchange is about to take place. The standard specifies that the RTS threshold should be set to 2,347 bytes. If network throughput is slow or there are high numbers of frame retransmissions, enable RTS clearing by decreasing the RTS threshold.

In Chapter 3, I said that a hidden node was a node that wasn't visible to all the stations on the network. Under what sorts of situations can you expect hidden nodes? Just about any, really. In almost any network, there are bound to be places where two nodes can reach the access point but not each other. Let's consider the simplest

---

* Multipath interference may cause odd time-dependent interference patterns. A particular spot may be within range of an access point at one instant in time and subject to multipath fading seconds later. However, such a spot has marginal coverage and should not be considered a part of a basic service area.

† 802.11 is not designed to support high-speed mobility, though. Cellular-based, wide-area technologies are more effective.

network imaginable: one access point in the middle of a large field with nothing to cause reflections or otherwise obstruct the signal. Take one mobile station, start at the access point, and move east until the signal degrades so that communication is just barely possible. Now take another station and move west. Both stations can communicate with the access point, but they are invisible to each other.

The previous thought experiment should convince you that invisible nodes are a fact of life. I would expect invisible nodes to be common in buildings with a great deal of metal in the walls and floors, lots of surfaces capable of reflecting radio waves, and lots of noise sources. In general, the harsher the radio environment, the greater the probability that a significant number of nodes are invisible to each other. All environments have hidden nodes. The question is how many there are and how many collisions result. Hidden nodes are likely to be more of a problem on highly populated networks, where more stations have the opportunity to transmit and cause unwanted collisions, and on busy networks, where there are more network communications that can be interrupted by unintended collisions.

Fragmentation Threshold

MAC-layer fragmentation is controlled by the fragmentation threshold variable. Any frames longer than the fragmentation threshold are sliced into smaller units for transmission. The default fragmentation threshold is the smaller of 2,346 or the maximum MAC frame length permitted by the physical layer. However, the RF-based physical layers usually have a maximum MAC frame length of 4,096 bytes, so this parameter generally defaults to 2,346. The common value immediately implies that fragmentation and RTS/CTS clearing are often used in tandem.

In environments with severe interference, encouraging fragmentation by decreasing this threshold may improve the effective throughput. When single fragments are lost, only the lost fragment must be retransmitted. By definition, the lost fragment is shorter than the entire frame and thus takes a shorter amount of time to transmit. Setting this threshold is a delicate balancing act. If it is decreased too much, the effective throughput falls because of the additional time required to acknowledge each fragment. Likewise, setting this parameter too high may decrease effective throughput by allowing large frames to be corrupted, thus increasing the retransmission load on the radio channel.

Retry Limits

Every station in a network has two retry limits associated with it. A retry limit is the number of times a station will attempt to retransmit a frame before discarding it. The *long retry limit*, which applies to frames longer than the RTS threshold, is set to 4 by default. A frame requiring RTS/CTS clearing is retransmitted four times before it is discarded and reported to higher-level protocols. The *short retry limit*, which applies to frames shorter than the RTS threshold, is set to 7 by default.

Decreasing the retry limit reduces the necessary buffer space on the local system. If frames expire quicker, expired frames can be discarded, and the memory can be reclaimed quicker. Increasing the retry limits may decrease throughput due to interactions with higher-layer protocols. When TCP segments are lost, well-behaved TCP implementations perform a slow start. Longer retry limits may increase the amount of time it takes to declare a segment lost.

Tuning Power Management

From the outset, 802.11 was designed for mobile devices. To be useful, though, mobile devices cannot be constrained by a power cord, so they usually rely on an internal battery. 802.11 includes a number of parameters that allow stations to save power, though power saving is accomplished at the expense of the throughput or latency to the station.

Listen Interval

When stations associate with an access point, one of the parameters specified is the listen interval, which is the number of Beacon intervals between instances when the station wakes up to received buffered traffic. Longer listen intervals enable a station to power down the transceiver for long periods. Long power-downs save a great deal of power and can dramatically extend battery life. Each station may have its own listen interval.

Lengthening the listen interval has two drawbacks. Access points must buffer frames for sleeping stations, so a long listen interval may require more packet buffer space on the access point. Large numbers of clients with long listen intervals may overwhelm the limited buffer space in access point hardware. Second, increasing the listen Interval delays frame delivery. If a station is sleeping when its access point receives a frame, the frame must be buffered until the sleeping station is awake. After powering up, the station must receive a Beacon frame advertising the buffered frame and send a PS-Poll to retrieve the frame. This buffering and retrieval process can delay the time the frame spends in transit. Whether this is acceptable depends on the traffic requirements. For asynchronous communications such as email, lengthening the listen Interval isn't likely to be a problem. But in other applications that require synchronous, time-sensitive communications (such as securities market data feeds today or an IP phone with an 802.11 interface in the future), a longer interval might not be acceptable. Certain applications may also have trouble with the increased latency. Database applications, in particular, are significantly affected by increased latency. A task group is working on MAC enhancements to provide quality of service for transmissions on 802.11 networks, but no standard has emerged yet.

DTIM Period

The DTIM period is a parameter associated with an infrastructure network, shared by all nodes associated with an access point. It is configured by the access point administrator and advertised in Beacon frames. All Beacon frames include a traffic indication map (TIM) to describe any buffered frames. Unicast frames buffered for individual stations are delivered in response to a query from the station. This polled approach is not suitable for multicast and broadcast frames, though, because it takes too much capacity to transmit multicast and broadcast frames multiple times. Instead of the polled approach, broadcast and multicast frames are delivered after every Delivery TIM (DTIM).

Changing the DTIM has the same effect as changing the listen Interval. (That should not be a surprise, given that the DTIM acts like the listen Interval for broadcast and multicast frames.) Increasing the DTIM allows mobile stations to conserve power more effectively at the cost of buffer space in the access point and delays in the reception. Before increasing the DTIM, be sure that all applications can handle the increased delay and that broadcasts and multicasts are not used to distribute data to all stations synchronously. If the application uses broadcast or multicast frames to ensure that all mobile stations receive the same blob of data simultaneously, as would be the case with a real-time data feed, increasing the DTIM will likely have adverse effects.

ATIM Window

In an infrastructure network, access points provide most of the power-saving support functions. In an independent or ad hoc 802.11 network, many of those functions move into the network interface driver. In ad hoc networks, stations are required to power up for every Beacon transmission and remain powered up for the duration of the Announcement TIM (ATIM) window, which is measured in time units (TUs).

Decreasing the ATIM window increases the power savings because the required power-on time for the mobile stations is reduced. Stations can power down quickly and are not required to be active during a large fraction of the time between Beacons. Increasing the ATIM window increases the probability a power-saving station will be awake when a second station has a frame. Service quality is increased, and the required buffer space is potentially smaller.

Decreasing or disabling the ATIM window would probably have the same effect on synchronous or real-time applications as increasing the DTIM timer on an infrastructure network—that is, it is likely to cause problems with less reliable communications or applications that depend on real-time data. One of the most obvious examples of a real-time application of ad hoc networking is gaming, but it is far more likely that ad hoc gaming networks would be tuned for low delay and high through-put than for low-power operation.

Timing Operations

Timing is a key component of 802.11 network operations. Several management oper-ations require multistep processes, and each has its own timer.

Scan Timing

To determine which network to join, a station must first scan for available networks. Some products expose timers to allow customization of the scanning process. In products that expose timers, both an *active scan timer* and a *passive scan timer* may be exposed. The active timer is the amount of time, in TUs, that a station waits after sending a Probe Request frame to solicit an active response from access points in the area. Passive scanning is simply listening for Beacon frames and can take place on several radio channels; the passive scan timer specifies the amount of time the receiver spends listening on each channel before switching to the next.

Timers Related to Joining the Network

Once a station has located an infrastructure network to join, it authenticates to an access point and associates with it. Each of these operations has a timeout associ-ated with it. The *authentication timeout* is reset at each stage of the authentication process; if any step of the process exceeds the timeout, authentication fails. On busy networks, the timeout may need to be increased. The *association timeout* serves a similar function in the association process.

Dwell Time (Frequency-Hopping Networks Only)

The amount of time that an FH PHY spends on a single hop channel is called the dwell time. It is set by local regulatory authorities and is generally not tunable, except by changing the network card driver to a different regulatory domain.

Physical Operations

Most wireless LAN hardware on the market includes antenna diversity and user-selectable power levels, though neither option is strictly required by the specifica-tion. Some products implementing these features offer configuration options to con-trol them.

Antenna Diversity

Multiple antennas are a common way of combating multipath fading. If the signal level at one antenna is bad due to multipath effects, a second antenna a short distance away may not be subject to the same fade. Some products that implement antenna diversity allow it to be disabled, though there is little reason to do so in practice.

Transmit Power Levels

All common 802.11 products implement multiple transmission power levels. Boosting the power can overcome fading because the power does not fall below the detection threshold. Power level selection may not be available in all products and may depend on the country in which you use the product; the transmitted power must comply with local regulatory requirements. Consult your manufacturer's documentation or support organization for details.

Lower power can be used to intentionally increase the access pont density. Increasing the access point density can increase the aggregate wireless network throughput in a given area by shrinking the size of the BSSs providing coverage and allowing for more BSSs. Depending on the number of access points required by 802.11a equipment, reducing the transmit power on access points might also be useful in reducing the coverage area as part of a move to 802.11a.

Summary of Tunable Parameters

For quick reference, Table 17-1 summarizes the contents of this chapter, including the effect of changing each of the tuning parameters.

Table 17-1. Summary of common tunable parameters

Parameter	Meaning and units	Effect when decreased	Effect when increased
Beacon Interval	Number of TUs between transmission of Beacon frames.	Passive scans complete more quickly, and mobile stations may be able to move more rapidly while maintaining network connectivity.	Small increase in available radio capacity and throughput and increased battery life.
RTS Threshold	Frames larger than the threshold are preceded by RTS/CTS exchange.	Greater effective throughput if there are a large number of hidden node situations .	Maximum theoretical throughput is increased, but an improvement will be realized only if there is no interference.
Fragmenttion Threshold	Frames larger than the threshold are transmitted using the fragmentation procedure.	Interference corrupts only fragments, not whole frames, so effective throughput may increase.	Increases throughput in noise-free areas by reducing fragmentation acknowledgment overhead.

Table 17-1. Summary of common tunable parameters (continued)

Parameter	Meaning and units	Effect when decreased	Effect when increased
Long Retry Limit	Number of retransmission attempts for frames longer than the RTS threshold.	Frames are discarded more quickly, so buffer space requirement is lower.	Retransmitting up to the limit takes longer and may cause TCP to throttle back on the data rate.
Short Retry Limit	Number of retransmission attempts for frames shorter than the RTS threshold.	Same as long retry limit.	Same as long retry limit.
Listen Interval	Number of Beacon intervals between awakenings of power-saving stations.	Latency of unicast frames to station is reduced. Also reduces buffer load on access points.	Power savings are increased by keeping transceiver powered off for a larger fraction of the time.
DTIM Window	Number of Beacon intervals between DTIM transmissions (applies only to infrastructure networks).	Latency of multicast and broadcast data to power-saving stations is reduced. Also reduces buffer load on access points.	Power savings are increased by keeping transceiver powered off for a larger fraction of the time.
ATIM Window	Amount of time each station remains awake after a Beacon transmission in an independent network.	Increases power savings by allowing mobile stations to power down more quickly after Beacon transmission.	Latency to power-saving stations is reduced, and the buffer load may be decreased for other stations in the network.
Active Scan Timer	Amount of time a station waits after sending a Probe Response frame to receive a response.	Station moves quickly in its scan.	Scan takes longer but is more likely to succeed.
Passive Scan Timer	Amount of time a station monitors a channel looking for a signal.	Station may not find the intended network if the scan is too short.	Scan takes longer but is more likely to succeed.
Authentication Timeout	Maximum amount of time between successive frames in authentication sequence.	Authentications must proceed faster; if the timeout is too low, there may be more retries.	No significant effect.
Association Timeout	Maximum amount of time between successive frames in association sequence.	Associations must proceed faster; if the timeout is too low, there may be more retries.	No significant effect.

## CHAPTER 18

The Future, at Least for 802.11

It's hard to make predictions,
especially about the future.
—Yogi Berra

This completes our picture of the current state of 802.11 networks. In this chapter, we'll get out a crystal ball and look at where things are heading. First, we'll look at standards that are currently in the works and close to completion. Then we'll take a somewhat longer-term look and try to draw conclusions about where wireless local networks are heading.

Current Standards Work

Publication of the 802.11 standard was only the beginning of wireless LAN standardization efforts. Several compromises were made to get the standard out the door, and a great deal of work was deferred for later. The 802.11 working group conducts its business publicly, and anybody can view their web site at *http://grouper.ieee.org/ groups/802/11/* to get an update on the progress of any of these revisions to 802.11.

Revisions to the standard are handled by Task Groups. Task Groups are lettered, and any revisions inherit the letter corresponding to the Task Group. For example, the OFDM PHY was standardized by Task Group A (TGa), and their revision was called 802.11a.

Task Group D

802.11 was written with only North American and European regulatory agencies in mind. Expanding the wireless LAN market beyond these two continents required that the 802.11 working group study regulatory requirements for other locations. TGd was chartered for this purpose, and the required revisions were approved in June 2001 as 802.11d.

Task Group E: Quality of Service

TGe works on generic MAC enhancements, including both quality of service (QoS) and security. Security issues took on a life of their own, though, and were eventually split off into TGi, leaving only quality of service revisions for TGe. Work on the draft is currently being letter balloted; once any outstanding issues are worked out, the draft will be sent to the IEEE Standards Association for review.

Task Group F: A Standard IAPP

Right now, roaming between access points is possible only if all the access points in the BSS come from the same vendor. Before roaming between access points supplied by different vendors can become a reality, a standardized Inter-Access Point Protocol (IAPP) is required. With most of the bugs worked out of existing wireless LAN products on the market, customers are now turning to the challenge of expanding existing networks. Lack of a vendor-neutral IAPP is hindering these efforts and is a major driver behind the standardization work.

Task Group G: Higher ISM Data Rates

Now that we have reached the third millenium, data rates of 2 Mbps or even 11 Mbps can be considered "slow" for LAN applications. Many customers have invested in site surveys to identify potential problems with the RF environment on an ISM-band wireless LAN. Building a wireless LAN in the 2.4-GHz spectrum is reasonably well understood. Customers would like to take advantage of this existing work in understanding the ISM band with even higher data rates. The project authorization request that set up TGg specifies a target data rate of at least 20 Mbps.

The encoding mechanisms used by 802.11b are more sophisticated than the initial 802.11 draft, but they still leave a great deal of room for improvement. In May 2001, the Texas Instruments proposal to use Packet Binary Convolution Coding (PBCC) was removed from consideration; the surviving proposal to use OFDM in the ISM band made by Intersil looks likely to succeed, although it has not yet attained enough support to reach draft status.

Task Group H: Spectrum Managed 802.11a

Spectrum Managed 802.11a (SMa) incorporates two additional features into the 802.11a standard: dynamic channel selection and transmit power control. Both features are designed to enhance 802.11a networks; additionally, both are required to obtain regulatory approval for 802.11a devices in Europe. Dynamic channel selection improves the ability to coexist with other users of the 5-GHz bands because devices can select channels based on real-time feedback. One likely application of dynamic channel selection is selecting lower-powered channels for short-range indoor situations while transparently switching to a higher-power channel when longer ranges are required. Transmit power control enables dense network deployments by allowing administrators to control the area that an access point services by tuning the power to achieve the desired size. Preliminary implementations of TGh enhancements have already been developed by vendors and will likely be revised to comply with the final standard.

Task Group I: Improving 802.11 Security

Security has been the most visible flaw in current 802.11 implementations and, as a result, has grabbed the headlines. Weak security was long suspected, and these suspicions became reality with the successful attempt to break WEP's cryptosystems. Initially, TGi had contemplated simply lengthening the key, but the success of the Fluhrer/Mantin/Shamir attack means that such an approach is also doomed to fail. TGi has refused to mandate any authentication protocols or key distribution mechanisms but has adopted the 802.1x framework and is moving forward.* Several proposals that have been made involve the use of PPP's Extensible Authentication Protocol (EAP) to authenticate users; EAP is specified in RFC 2284, which was in turn updated by RFC 2484. It is unclear what will come out of TGi, but the possibility that manual keying will remain the only method for key distribution leaves a great deal of room for third-party security products, especially if TGi does not finish standardization before 802.11a products are produced in volume.

The Longer Term

What does the picture look like over the longer term? 802.11 has already killed off other wireless efforts aimed at the home market (such as HomeRF), and it seems likely to severely constrain deployment of Bluetooth as well—which is unfortunate, because Bluetooth and 802.11 can coexist and serve different needs.

The larger issues for the long term are in areas such as wireless mobility and security, both of which present problems that aren't easily solved.

Mobility

Wireless networks are fundamentally about mobility. 802.11 deployments have successfully demonstrated that users are interested in mobility and that mobile connectivity is a long-felt need in the networking world. After all, users move, but network jacks do not.

However, 802.11 offers only link-layer mobility, and that is possible only when the access points can all communicate with each other to keep track of mobile stations.

---

* The recent discovery of flaws in 802.1x makes it seem likely that this story is far from over.

Standardization of the IAPP by Task Group F should make it easier to deploy networks by facilitating interoperability between multiple vendors. Standardization of the IAPP will also make it easier to merge multiple distinct wireless networks into each other.

A lot of planning is required if you want to deploy a wireless LAN with a substantial coverage area, especially if seamless mobility through the entire coverage area is a requirement. In most deployments, the requirement for centralized planning is not in and of itself a hurdle. With community networks, however, loose cooperation is the watchword, and centralized command-and-control planning makes it hard to build a functional network. Furthermore, community networking groups do not have the resources to purchase big Ethernet switches, extend VLANs between houses, and create a neighborhood fiber backbone. Community networks are typically a federation of access points that offer Internet access through NAT. Without centralized addressing, mobile users will need to obtain new DHCP addresses when roaming throughout a network.

It's easy to overlook the problems that mobility causes at the IP level. It's easy to say that a wireless node should receive a new IP address when it moves from one part of a larger network to another, but in practice, it isn't simple. How do you get the node to notice that it should abandon its current address and ask for a new one? What happens to network connections that are open when the node's IP address changes?

Avoiding the NAT requirement and the need to periodically change addresses requires mobility at the network layer. Mobile IP has been standardized to a reasonable degree, but an open source Mobile IP implementation of choice has yet to emerge. Barring a large commercial driving force, it is likely that community networking will drive future open source Mobile IP implementation. When Mobile IP can be deployed without significant headaches, there may be another burst in the market as network managers discover that deployment of wireless networks can happen without painful readdressing or Ethernet switching games.

Wireless LANs are likely to borrow a few concepts from mobile telephony. When European telephony experts wrote the standards on which modern second-generation cellular networks are built, it was explicitly recognized that no single telecommunications carrier had the resources to build a pan-European cellular network. Wireless telephony had previously been held back by a plethora of incompatible standards that offer patchwork coverage throughout parts of Europe. Experts realized that the value of carrying a mobile telephone was proportional to the area in which it could be used. As a result, the GSM standards that were eventually adopted emphasized roaming functions that would enable a subscriber to use several networks while being billed by one network company. As public-access wireless LANs become larger, authentication and roaming functions are likely to be a larger focus in both the 802.11 working group and the IETF. Network sharing is another concept that will likely be borrowed from the cellular world. The incredible cost of third-generation licenses has pushed a number of cellular carriers to the brink of bankruptcy. In reponse, groups of carriers are now planning to share the data-carrying infrastructure to share the cost and risk of an expensive third-generation network build-out. The high costs of building a wide-scale 802.11 network are likely to have the same effect, with the surviving "hot zone" players regrouping around one set of multitenant access points in the coverage area.

Security

Wireless networks have all been tarred with the brush of poor security. Weaknesses in the Wired Equivalent Privacy (WEP) standard made the news with a great deal of regularity in 2001, culminating with a total break partway through the year. Even against this backdrop, though, the market for 802.11 network equipment has exploded. Better security mechanisms are needed to usher in centrally coordinated rollouts at large, security-conscious institutions, but the apparent security weaknesses in current equipment have not prevented the market from forming and growing rapidly.

Many observers long suspected that WEP was fundamentally broken. (It was humorously derided as "Wiretap Equivalence, Please" by several commentators.) WEP suffers from several fatal design flaws, and it is now clear that something far better is needed. One common tactic to address the shortfalls of WEP is to require the use of stronger encryption technology over the wireless link. Unfortunately, this only shifts the problem elsewhere. Adding VPN client software moves the problem from security weaknesses in the wireless link to managing desktop software images. System integration of VPN client software is difficult on the best of days. Integration so far has proven too large a hurdle for most users. Moving forward, 802.11 will need to incorporate public-key mutual authentication of stations and access points and random session keys. Neither is a new idea, and both have been used for years in both *ssh* and IPSec.

Most importantly, though, different access controls are needed for the future. Right now, most wireless LANs are used to extend corporate LANs throughout the office. Existing authentication concepts were designed for a known, static user group, such as a group of employees. Just as in cellular telephony, the promise of wireless networks is installation in hard-to-reach spots or places where users are on the move. Designing an 802.11 network for an airport or train station requires dealing with the question of who is allowed to use the network. These problems aren't trivial; service providers need to think about how to protect users from each other and how to authenticate users to access points and other services on the network.

Radio Resources

So far, wireless networks have had a free ride. They are fairly exotic, and wireless cards still aren't common (though they're selling quickly and, as a result, becoming less expensive), so wireless networks tend to have relatively few users, and the networks themselves are physically relatively far apart. What happens when they're stressed? What would a wireless network be like if it had, say, 1,000 users (which can easily be supported by a well-designed wired network)? What would it be like in a large office building, where you might have half a dozen companies, each with its own network, in the space of two or three floors?

We don't really have the answers to these questions yet. As wireless becomes more common, we'll be forced to answer them. It is clear, though, that there are resource constraints. Current technologies will suffer from overcrowding within the unlicensed 2.4-GHz band. 802.11a and other technologies will move to the 5-GHz band, but crowding will eventually become an issue there, too. Meanwhile, commercial users are fighting for additional frequency space, and it's not likely that governments will allocate more spectrum to unlicensed users.

There are a few ways out of this problem. Improved encoding techniques will help; the use of directional antennas may make it possible for more devices to coexist within a limited space. Directional antennas aren't without cost: the more effective a directional antenna is, the harder it is to aim. It's all very nice to imagine sitting at a picnic table in front of your company's office with your portable antenna aimed at the access point on the roof; but what if somebody else sits down and knocks over the antenna? How much of a pain will it be to reorient it?

Other solutions have already been mentioned in the discussion of continuing standards work. We'll certainly see cards that can switch between high-power and low-power transmission, possibly even changing channels on the fly as power requirements change.

Deployment

One of the major problems faced by the architects of public-access wireless networks is that the service is quite generic. In the absence of any constraints, anybody can put up an antenna and offer Internet access via 802.11 equipment. Mobile telephony coped with this problem by licensing the spectrum so that only one carrier had the right to transmit in a given frequency band. A similar solution is not possible with 802.11 because it explicitly uses the unlicensed bands. Competition between network providers therefore shifts to the political layer of the OSI model; an example is a network provider that leases space from the building owner for the exclusive right to deploy a wireless network in a given area. Airports are a leading proponent of this new approach, though many observers believe that allowing genuine competition would better serve the interests of users.

Other deployment problems faced by wireless LAN builders are common throughout the industry: obtuse command lines, the need for extensive attention to individual desktops, and the lack of large-scale automation. Vendors are concentrating on large-scale management frameworks to ease the pain of network administrators stuck with managing tens or hundreds of access points. Better analysis tools, both for the site survey phase and the troubleshooting/deployment phase, are required by network engineers.

The End

And that's it. The future of wireless networking isn't without its problems, but that's no different from any other technology. The price of network cards is dropping rapidly—they now cost about half what they did when I started writing, and it wouldn't be surprising if they were eventually little more expensive than the typical Ethernet card. While it's probably true that equipment that stays fixed will benefit from a fixed network—it's hard to imagine backing up a large database over a wireless network, for example—we will certainly see more and more computer users accessing their networks through wireless links, leaving their desks and working in the park, the library, or wherever they're most comfortable.

802.11 MIB

802.11 contains extensive management functions to make the wireless connection appear much like a regular wired connection. The complexity of the additional management functions results in a complex management entity with dozens of variables. For ease of use, the variables have been organized into a management information base (MIB) so that network managers can benefit from taking a structured view of the 802.11 parameters. The formal specification of the 802.11 MIB is Annex D of the 802.11 specification.

The Root of the Matter

The 802.11 MIB is designed by the 802.11 working group. Like other MIBs, it is based on a global tree structure expressed in Abstract Syntax Notation 1 (ASN.1) notation. Unlike SNMP MIBs, though, the 802.11 MIB has a different root: *.iso.member-body. us.ieee802dot11* (.1.2.840.10036). (For simplicity, the prefix will be omitted from any objects described in this appendix, much as *.iso.org.dod.internet* is omitted from SNMP object names.)

The basic structural overview of the 802.11 MIB is shown in Figure A-1. Four main branches compose the MIB:

dot11smt
Contains objects related to station management and local configuration

dot11mac
Composed of objects that report on the status of various MAC parameters and allow configuration of them.

dot11res
Contains objects that describe available resources

dot11phy
Report on the status of the various physical layers

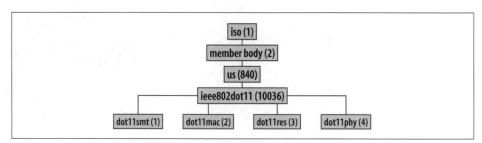

Figure A-1. The 802.11 MIB root and its main branches

Station Management

Station management is the term used to describe the global configuration parameters that are not part of the MAC itself. Figure A-2 shows a high-level view of the station management branch of the MIB. Six subtrees organize information on global configuration, authentication, and privacy, and provide a means for automated notification of significant events.

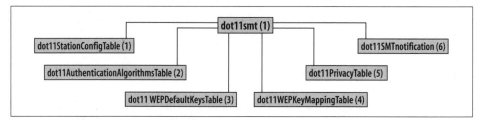

Figure A-2. Main branches of the station management (SMT) tree

The Station Configuration Table

The main table in the station management tree is the global configuration table, *dot11StationConfigTable*, which is shown in Figure A-3. All entries in the station configuration table start with the prefix *dot11smt.dot11StationConfigTable.
dot11StationConfigEntry* (1.1.1):

dot11StationID (MacAddress)
  The bit string in this object is used to identify the station to an external manager. By default, it is assigned the value of the station's globally unique programmed address.

dot11MediumOccupancyLimit (integer, range 0–1,000)
  This object has meaning only for stations that implement contention-free access using the point coordination function. It measures the number of continuous time units (TUs) that contention-free access may dominate the medium. By default, it is set to 100 TUs, with a maximum value of 1,000 (1.024 seconds).

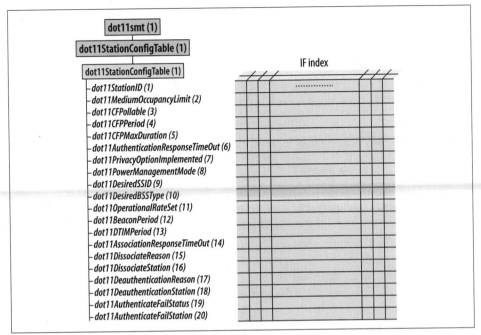

Figure A-3. The station configuration table dot11StationConfigTable

Making this value larger increases the capacity allocated to contention-free service. Decreasing it reduces the amount of time available for contention-free service. Network managers can tune this value appropriately once products implementing contention-free service are produced.

dot11CFPollable (TruthValue: a defined type set to 1 for true or 2 for false)
This object reports whether a station can respond to contention-free polling messages. Because the ability to respond to CF-Poll messages is a function of the software installed, this object is read-only.

dot11CFPPeriod (integer, range 0–255)
Contention-free periods always begin on a DTIM message. This object is the number of DTIM intervals between contention-free periods. DTIM messages are always a part of a Beacon frame, so the time between contention-free period starts can be obtained by multiplying the CFP period value in this object by the DTIM interval.

dot11MaxDuration (integer, range 0–65,535)
This object describes the maximum duration of the contention-free period when a new BSS is created. The reason for the difference in the allowed range of values between this object and the *dot11MediumOccupancyLimit* is a mystery.

dot11AuthenticationResponseTimeout (integer, range 1–4,294,967,295)
At each step of the station authentication process, the station will wait for a timeout period before considering the authentication to have failed. This object

contains the number of TUs that each step is allowed to take before failing the authentication.

dot11PrivacyOptionImplemented (TruthValue)
If the station implements WEP, this object will be *true* (1). By default, it is *false* (2). It is read-only because a software update to the station is required to implement WEP. This object does not report whether WEP is in use, only whether it is available.

dot11PowerManagementMode (enumerated type)
This object reports whether a station is *active* (1) or in a *powersave* (2) mode. When queried by an external manager, it will always return active because a station must be powered up to send the response frame. This object is far more useful for a local management entity, which can poll the object periodically to determine how often a station is active.

dot11DesiredSSID (string, maximum length 32)
During the scan procedure, stations may be configured to look for a particular network, which is identified by its service set ID (SSID). Management entities may set this value to modify the scanning process to preferentially associate with a certain network.

dot11DesiredBSSType (enumerated)
Like the previous object, this object is also used to configure the scanning procedure. By setting this object, a manager can force association with an *infrastructure* (1) network, an *independent* (2) BSS, or *any* (3) BSS.

dot11OperationalRateSet (string, maximum length 126)
Initially, this described the data rate as a number that was the number of 500-kbps increments for the data rate. Recent standardization work is likely to make them simple labels because the range of 1–127 allows only a maximum rate of 63.5 Mbps.

dot11BeaconPeriod (integer, range 1–65,535)
This object contains the length of the Beacon interval, in TUs. Once a BSS has been established with the Beacon interval, the value may be changed. However, it will not take effect until a new BSS is created.

dot11DTIMPeriod (integer, range 1–255)
This object contains the number of Beacon intervals between DTIM transmissions.

dot11AssociationResponseTimeOut (integer, range 1–4,294,967,295)
At each step of the association process, the station will wait for a timeout period before considering the association attempt to have failed. This object contains the number of TUs that each step is allowed to take before failing the association.

dot11DisassociateReason and dot11DeauthenticateReason (integer, range 0–65,535)
This object contains the reason code from the most recently transmitted Disassociation or Deauthentication frame. If no such frame has been transmitted, the value is 0. For a complete list of reason codes, see Chapter 3 or clause 7.3.1.7 of 802.11.

dot11DisassociateStation and dot11DeauthenticateStation (MacAddress)

This object contains the MAC address of the station to which the most recently Disassociation or Deauthentication frame was transmitted. If there is no such frame, the value is 0. By using either of these objects in combination with the corresponding Reason object described previously, a manager can track which station was kicked off the network and why.

dot11AuthenticateFailStatus (integer, range 0–65,535)

This object contains the status code from the most recently transmitted Authentication Failure frame. If no such frame has been transmitted, the value is 0. For a complete list of status codes, see Chapter 3 or clause 7.3.1.9 of 802.11.

dot11AuthenticateFailStation (MacAddress)

This object contains the MAC address of the station to which the most recent Authentication Failure frame was transmitted. If there is no such frame, the value is 0.

Authentication Algorithms Table

The authentication algorithms table reports on which authentication algorithms are supported by the station on each interface. It is best thought of as the three-dimensional array shown in Figure A-4.

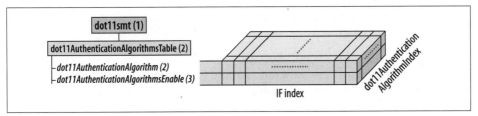

Figure A-4. The authentication algorithms table

In addition to the ifIndex index variable, an auxiliary index variable is used. The reason for the auxiliary variable is that multiple authentication algorithms exist, and the table should report on all of them. For each index, the auxiliary index allows several cells to report on one authentication algorithm each. Each cell has two component objects:

dot11AuthenticationAlgorithm (enumerated type)

This object is set either to *openSystem* (1) or *sharedKey* (2) to report on the authentication algorithm.

dot11AuthenticationAlgorithmsEnable (TruthValue)

This object reflects whether the corresponding authentication algorithm noted by the previous object is supported by the interface that indexes the table. By default, it is set to *true* (1) for open-system authentication and *false* (2) for shared-key authentication.

WEP Key Tables

Two tables report on the status of WEP key information. Both use the *WEPKeytype* defined data type, which is simply a 40-bit string. The WEP key tables are shown in Figure A-5. WEP key tables are supposed to be write-only, but a security advisory was issued in June 2001 against one vendor who exposed the keys to queries using SNMP.

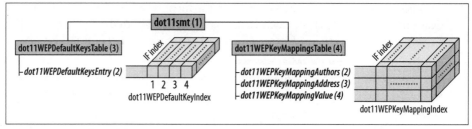

Figure A-5. WEP key tables

WEP default key table

The default key table is quite simple. Each interface has a maximum of four default keys associated with it because the WEP specification allows for four default keys per network. When transmitted in frames over the air, the WEP key ID for the default key runs from 0–3. In this table, however, the index runs from 1–4. Each cell in the table has just one object:

dot11WEPDefaultKeyValue (WEPKeytype)
  A 40-bit string that holds the default key for the interface and default key ID specified by the location in the table.

WEP key-mapping table

WEP supports using a different key for every MAC address in the world. Keys can be mapped to the unique pair of (transmitter address, receiver address). For each interface on the system, an arbitrary number of address and key pairs can be associated with that interface. Each interface uses an auxiliary index to identify all the MAC addresses associated with keys, plus information about each address. The following three objects are used to describe a key-mapping relationship. A fourth object in the row gives the row status, but the row status indicator is used only when creating or deleting table rows.

dot11WEPKeyMappingAddress (MacAddress)
  This is the "other" address of the address pair for which a key-mapping relationship exists.

dot11WEPKeyMappingWEPOn (TruthValue)

This object is set to *true* (1) when WEP should be used when communicating with the key-mapping address. If WEP should not be used, this object is set to *false* (2).

dot11WEPKeyMappingValue (WEPKeytype)

This is the 40-bit keying information used as the shared secret for WEP. Logically, this cell in the table should be write-only, but not all implementations will obey that convention.

MAC Management

The MAC branch of the 802.11 MIB provides access to objects that allow administrators to tune and monitor MAC performance and configure multicast processing. It is divided into three main groups as shown in Figure A-6.

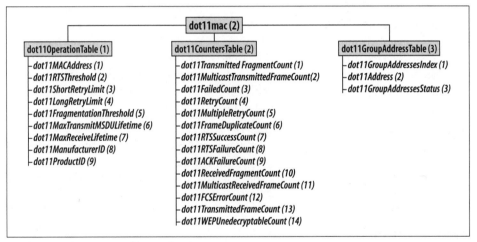

Figure A-6. The MAC attributes subtree

The dot11OperationsTable

The main table in the station management tree is the global configuration table, *dot11OperationTable*, which is shown in Figure A-6. All entries in the station configuration table start with the prefix *dot11mac.dot11OperationTable.dot11OperationEntry* (2.1.1) and are indexed by a system interface:

dot11MACAddress (MacAddress)

This object is the MAC address of the station. By default, it is the globally unique address assigned by the manufacturer. It may, however, be overridden by a local manager.

dot11RTSThreshold (integer, range 0–2,347; default value is 2,347)

Any unicast data or management frames larger than the RTS threshold must be transmitted using the RTS/CTS handshake exchange. By default, the value is 2,347, which has the effect of deactivating RTS/CTS clearing before transmission. Setting the object to 0 activates the RTS/CTS handshake before every transmission.

dot11ShortRetryLimit (integer, range 1–255; default value is 7)

The short retry limit is applied to frames that are shorter than the RTS threshold. Short frames may be retransmitted up to the short retry limit before they are abandoned and reported to higher-layer protocols.

dot11LongRetryLimit (integer, range 1–255; default value is 4)

The long retry limit is analogous to the short retry limit but applies to frames longer than the RTS threshold.

dot11FragmentationThreshold (integer, range 256–2,346; default value is vendor-specific)

When a unicast frame exceeds the fragmentation threshold, it is broken up. MAC headers and trailers count against the threshold limits.

dot11MaxTransmitMSDULifetime (integer, range 1–4,294,967,295; default value is 512)

This object is the number of TUs that the station will attempt to transmit a frame. If the frame is held by the MAC longer than the lifetime, it is discarded, and the failure is reported to higher-level protocols. By default, it is set to 512 TUs, or about 524 ms.

dot11MaxReceiveLifetime (integer, range 1–4,294,967,295; default is 512)

When MAC-layer fragmentation is used, the receiver uses a timer to discard "old" fragments. After the reception of the first fragment of a frame, the clock starts running. When the timer expires, all fragments buffered for reassembly are discarded.

dot11CountersTable

Counters allow a local or external management entity to monitor the performance of a wireless interface. One of the major uses of data from the counters is to make informed performance-tuning decisions. All entries in this table begin with *dot11mac.dot11CountersTable.dot11CountersEntry* (2.2.1):

dot11TransmittedFragmentCount (Counter32)

This counter is incremented for all acknowledged unicast fragments and multicast management or multicast data fragments. Frames that are not broken up into pieces but can be transmitted without fragmentation also cause this counter to be incremented.

dot11MulticastTransmittedFrameCount (Counter32)

This counter is incremented every time a multicast frame is sent. Unlike the previous counter, acknowledgement is not necessary.

dot11FailedCount (Counter32)

When frames are discarded because the number of transmission attempts has exceeded either the short retry limit or the long retry limit, this counter is incremented. It is normal for this counter to rise with increasing load on a particular BSS.

dot11RetryCount (Counter32)

Frames that are received after requiring a retransmission will increment this counter. Any number of retransmissions will cause the counter to increment.

dot11MultipleRetryCount (Counter32)

Frames that require two or more retransmissions will increment this counter. As such, it will always be lesser than or equal to the retry count.

dot11FrameDuplicateCount (Counter32)

Duplicate frames arise when acknowledgements are lost. To provide an estimate of the number of lost acknowledgements from the station, this counter is incremented whenever a duplicate frame is received.

dot11RTSSuccessCount (Counter32)

Reception of a CTS in response to an RTS increments this counter.

dot11RTSFailureCount (Counter32)

When no CTS is received for a transmitted RTS, this counter is incremented.

dot11ACKFailureCount (Counter32)

This counter directly tracks the number of inbound acknowledgements lost. Whenever a frame is transmitted that should be acknowledged, and the acknowlegment is not forthcoming, this counter is incremented.

dot11ReceivedFragmentCount (Counter32)

This counter tracks all incoming data and management fragments. Full frames are considered fragments for the purpose of incrementing this counter.

dot11MulticastReceivedFrameCount (Counter32)

This counter tracks incoming multicast frames.

dot11FCSErrorCount (Counter32)

If the frame check calculation fails, this counter is incremented. This is one of the main counters that give network administrators an idea of the health of a BSS.

dot11TransmittedFrameCount (Counter32)

The transmitted frame count is the number of successfully transmitted frames. Part of the definition of successful transmission is that an expected acknowledgement is received.

dot11WEPUndecryptableCount (Counter32)

This counter is incremented when an incoming frame indicates that it is encrypted using WEP, but no decryption is possible. Naturally, this number will increment rapidly on stations that do not implement WEP when WEP frames are used on the network. It can also increment rapidly when the key mapping key is invalid or the default key is incorrect.

Group Addresses Table

The group addresses table maintains a list of multicast addresses from which the station will accept frames. The table is a list of *dot11Address* objects of type *MacAddress*, indexed by an auxiliary variable and the interface index. The table is shown in Figure A-6.

Physical-Layer Management

Physical-layer management is divided into 11 tables, as shown in Figure A-7. Certain tables are specific to a certain product, or the implementation highly vendor-dependent, so those tables are not described in this appendix. There is a table for the infrared physical layer, but that table is omitted as well because no products on the market implement the infrared physical layer.

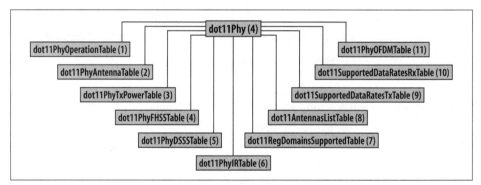

Figure A-7. Physical-layer MIB branches

Physical-Layer Operations Table

Overall operational status is reported by the physical-layer operations table, *dot11phy.dot11PhyOperationTable* (4.1) (Figure A-8). Each interface creates corresponding entries in the operation table, which allows a manager to determine the physical-layer type and access the appropriate related branch in the physical-layer subtree. All entries in the physical-layer operation table begin with *dot11phy. dot11PhyOperationTable.dot11PhyOperationEntry* (4.1.1):

dot11PHYType (enumerated)
    This object is set to *fhss* (1) for frequency-hopping radio systems and *dsss* (2) for direct-sequence radio systems. It may also be set to *irbaseband* (3) if IR systems

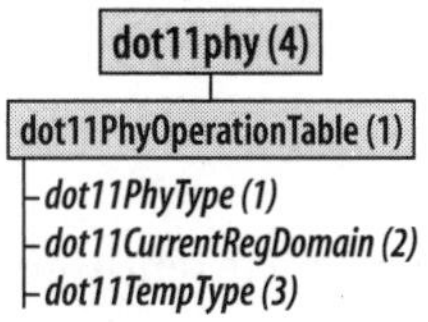

Figure A-8. Physical-layer operations table

are ever implemented and will be set to *ofdm* (4) for the OFDM PHY specified in 802.11a.

dot11CurrentRegDomain (enumerated)

This object is set to the current regulatory domain of the system. Several values are possible, as shown in Table A-1.

Table A-1. Regulatory domains in the 802.11 MIB

Value	Regulatory authority	Regulatory area
fcc (16)	U.S. Federal Communications Commission	United States
doc (32)	Industry Canada	Canada
etsi (48)	European Telecommunications Standards Institute	Europe, excluding France and Spain
spain (49)		Spain
france (50)		France
mkk (64)	Radio Equipment Inspection and Certification Institute	Japan

dot11TempType (enumerated)

This object is set to *tempType1* (1) for a commercial operating temperature range of 0–40 degrees Celsius and *tempType2* (2) for an industrial operating temperature range of 0–70 degrees Celsius.

FHSS Table

The MIB table for FH PHYs is shown in Figure A-9. Entries in the frequency-hopping table begin with *dot11phy.dot11PhyFHSSTable.dot11PhyFHSSEntry (4.4.1)*:

dot11HopTime (integer, set to 224)

The time, in microseconds, required for the frequency-hopping PMD to change from channel 2 to channel 80. This is fixed by the specification, so the corresponding MIB definition is also fixed.

dot11CurrentChannelNumber (integer, range 0–99)

This object is set to the current operating channel. In a frequency-hopping system, the operating channel changes frequently.

dot11MaxDwellTime (integer, range 1–65,535)

The maximum amount of time the transmitter is permitted to use a single channel, in TUs.

dot11CurrentSet (integer, range 1–255)

The number of the hop pattern set currently employed by the station.

dot11CurrentPattern (integer, range 0–255)

The current hopping pattern in use by the station.

dot11CurrentIndex (integer, range 1–255)

The index in the current hop pattern that determines the current channel number. This index will select the hop frequency in *dot11CurentChannelNumber*.

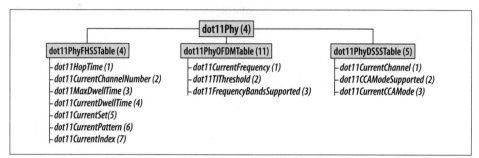

Figure A-9. Physical-layer attribute tables

DSSS Table

The direct-sequence table is also shown in Figure A-9. All entries in the direct-sequence table are indexed by the interface number and begin with *dot11phy. dot11PhyDSSSTable.dot11PhyDSSSEntry* (4.5.1):

dot11CurrentChannel (integer, range 1–14)

This object reports the current operating channel. Valid channels range from 1–14.

dot11CCAModeSupported (integer, 1–7)

Three main clear-channel assessment options can be used to determine the status of a direct-sequence operating channel: energy detection (ED), carrier sense (CS), or a combination of both. The three options are assigned numerical values and added up to produce the value reported by this object. Only energy detection is assigned the value 1. Only carrier sense is assigned the value 2. Using both in combination is assigned the value 4. A system that supports all three modes reports a value of 7 in this object.

dot11CurrentCCAMode (enumerated)

This object is set to *edonly* (1) if only energy detection is used to assess channel clarity. If only the MAC carrier sense functions are used, the object is set to *csonly* (2). If both are employed, the object is set to *edandcs* (4).

OFDM Table

When the OFDM PHY was standardized in 802.11a, a corresponding table was added in the MIB to report on its status. All entries in the OFDM table, which is also shown in Figure A-9, begin with *dot11phy.dot11PhyOFDMTable.dot11PhyOFDMEntry* (4.11.1). The table is indexed by interface number.

dot11CurrentFrequency (integer, range 0–99)

This is the current operating-frequency channel number of the OFDM PHY.

dot11TIThreshold (Integer32)

This medium will report as busy if a received signal strength is above this threshold.

dot11FrequencyBandsSupported (integer, range 1–7)

The OFDM PHY is designed for the U-NII frequency bands. The lowest band (5.15–5.25 GHz) is assigned the value 1, the midband (5.25–5.35 GHz) is assigned the value 2, and the high band (5.725–5.825 GHz) is assigned the value 4. The values corresponding to the supported frequency bands are added to produce the value returned by a query to this object.

802.11 on the Macintosh

Apple Computer has been a key player in establishing the market for 802.11 equipment. Most companies in the 802.11 market saw their contributions in terms of standards committee activity and technology development. Apple contributied by distilling complex technology into an easy-to-use form factor and applying its mass-marketing expertise.

In 1999, 802.11 was a promising technology that had demonstrated its value in a few narrow markets. 802.11 interfaces cost around $300, and access points were around $1,000. Apple saw the promise in the technology and moved aggressively, releasing $300 access points and $99 interfaces. With a new competitor suddenly pricing the gear at a third of the prevailing price, other vendors were forced to drop prices dramatically, and the market took off. Prices have been dropping over the last year. 802.11 will probably never be as cheap as Ethernet, but it's easy to imagine 802.11 interfaces under $50 and access points under $100.

This appendix was made possible by a generous equipment loan from Apple. Apple loaned me an iBook running Mac OS X 10.1, the dual Ethernet version of the Air-Port Base Station, and their software tools for configuration and management. Unfortunately, it arrived too late for me to include in the discussion of Apple's hardware; that will have to wait for the second edition. The late delivery also prevented me from presenting the Software Base Station, a MacOS 9 application that turns any Macintosh with an AirPort card into a base station. (It was not available for MacOS X as this book went to press, so time constraints prevented its inclusion.)

The AirPort Card

Apple offers tightly integrated systems because the hardware and the software are designed in tandem. Unlike the chaotic IBM-compatible world, with Apple one company is responsible for both the hardware and software, and it shows. You can install the hardware and software and connect to an existing network in only a few minutes.

If an AirPort card is plugged in during system installation, this can be done as part of the initial configuration

Hardware Installation

AirPort interface cards are specialized 802.11 interfaces designed to be inserted into an AirPort slot, a feature on every machine Apple has introduced since 2000. AirPort-capable Macintoshes contain an antenna in the machine's case, so the AirPort card can use a much larger antenna than most PCMCIA interfaces in the PC world. With the antenna integrated into the case, it also eliminates the hazard of a protruding antenna. I have also found that the integrated antenna has better range than many PCMCIA-based 802.11 interfaces used with Windows.

Installing the AirPort card into an iBook is a relatively simple procedure. The iBook should be powered down, unplugged, and have its battery removed. The AirPort slot is underneath the keyboard. Lift up the keyboard, slide the card in, and connect the computer's built-in antenna cable to the card. Other machines are just as straightforward. PowerBooks work the same as iBooks. The AirPort slot on iMacs is under the bottom panel; tower machines have a slot readily available under the cover. The external antenna connector is the same connector used by Lucent products, so users who really want an external antenna can use Lucent gear.

Software Installation

Drivers for the AirPort are included in OS 9.1 and later, so there is no need to download and install drivers. If the AirPort card is installed before the system first boots, the first-time boot configuration utility will allow you to configure the AirPort interface out of the box by selecting a network name and choosing how to configure TCP/IP. For a network that uses DHCP, the configuration instructions are only a few screens long.

AirPort cards added after the system first boots can be configured by the AirPort Setup Assistant.* After inserting the card, run the Setup Assistant. When it starts, you will see the dialog box in Figure B-1.

Choose to configure the AirPort card and click Continue. The next step, shown in Figure B-2, is to select the network you wish to join. Every network within range is displayed in the pop-up menu. Figure B-2 shows the user selecting the Little Green Men network.

---

* Cards can also be configured with the System Preferences application. For completeness, this appendix discusses the Setup Assistant first and the System Preferences application later in terms of monitoring and changing the configuration. However, there is no reason why you cannot configure the card straight from the System Preferences application.

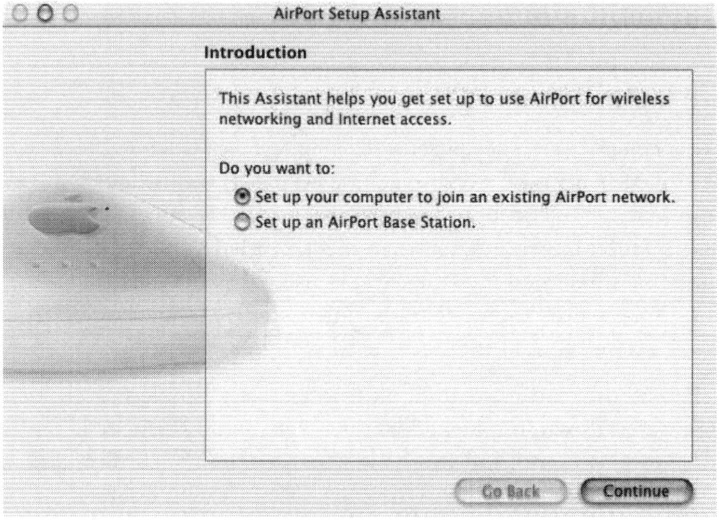

Figure B-1. Initial AirPort Setup Assistant screen

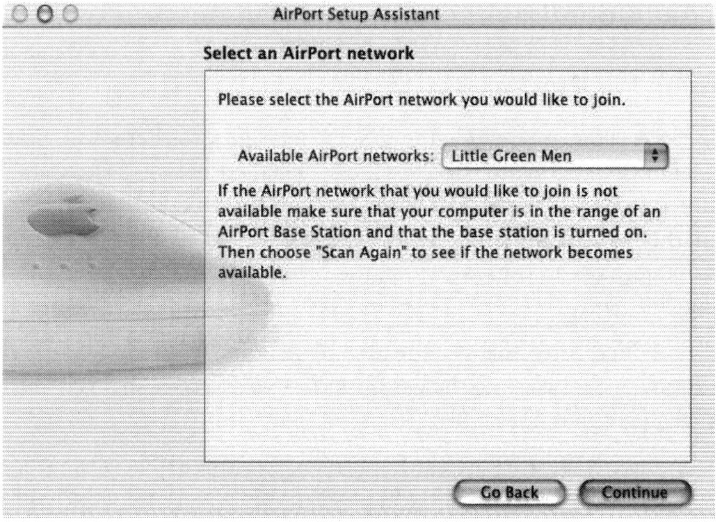

Figure B-2. AirPort card network selection

Once the network is selected, you can move on to the third step: entering the network password. This is the WEP configuration. To make matters easier for users, Apple has allowed administrators to input WEP keys as variable-length passwords. The ASCII text of the password is then hashed into a WEP key of the appropriate length. WEP keys can also be entered in hexadecimal by prefacing them with a dollar sign, such as $EB102393BF. Hex keys are either 10 hex digits (40-bit) or 26 hex digits

(104-bit). Interpretation of the input string can be forced to ASCII by enclosing the key in double quotes.* Input the key, if any, into the box in Figure B-3, then move on by clicking the Continue button.

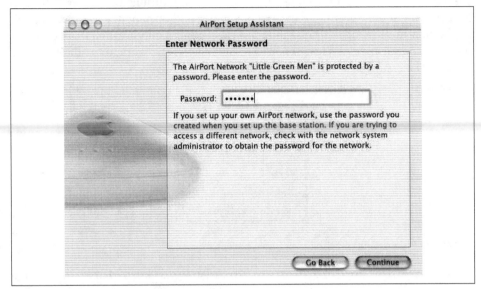

Figure B-3. AirPort network password entry

After these three steps are performed, the setup is complete, and you will be joined to the wireless network. Subsequent screens inform the user that the network configuration is complete.

Configuring and Monitoring an AirPort Interface

You may need to change the AirPort configuration from time to time. You may move between different 802.11 networks (ESSs) or need to change the WEP keys or IP settings. Once the card is installed, you can change its configuration with the configuration tools provided with OS X. Apple's configuration programs do not allow users to change any of the more complex 802.11 parameters. All the information needed to join a network, for example, is broadcast in the Beacon frames. Apple decided that in most cases, it is sufficient to simply present the user with network names and prompt for a password if needed.

Basic configuration with the AirPort status icon

Once configuration is complete, the AirPort status icon is displayed in the upper-right corner of the screen, next to the speaker volume, battery, and clock icons, provided

---

* For more information, see article 106250 in Apple's Knowledge Base at *http://kbase.info.apple.com*.

you haven't turned off those icons. The AirPort icon also indicates radio strength. In Figure B-4, there are several solid wavefronts on the icon. As you move farther from the access point and the signal degrades, the number of bars decreases. When it is clicked, a drop-down command list offers the option of turning the power to the Air-Port card on or off, selecting or creating networks, and opening the Internet Connect application to monitor the radio interface. It is quite handy for users to be able to turn off the card at will. When you are out of range of a network, or just not using it, the card can easily be powered down to save battery power.

Figure B-4. AirPort status icon

In Figure B-4, there are two networks within range: Little Green Men and Luminiferous Ether. The checkmark by Little Green Men indicates that it is the network to which the user is currently connected, though the user can switch between the two networks simply by selecting a preference. Any other network can be selected by using the Other... option and entering the name of the network.

An IBSS can be created by going to the Create Network option and selecting the basic radio parameters shown in Figure B-5. The computer is set to create an IBSS with the network name of Very Independent BSS; the radio channel defaults to 11 but can be changed to any of the 11 channels acceptable in North America and Europe. Every computer taking part in the IBSS must use the same channel. After you've set up an independent network, the system adds a new section titled "Computer to Computer Networks" to the drop-down list, as shown in Figure B-6. The AirPort status icon also changes to a computer in the pie wedge shape to indicate that the network is an IBSS rather than an infrastructure network.

Configuration with the System Preferences application

If you move between different ESSs, you can create a "location" for each and use this to configure the ESS/password pair, which you can then pick from a menu as you move to a different location. You can also preconfigure an ESS/password pair if you're not currently on the network for which you are setting up.

The System Preferences application allows you to configure many system attributes, including those that are network-related. Figure B-7 shows the network panel of the

Figure B-5. IBSS parameter setup

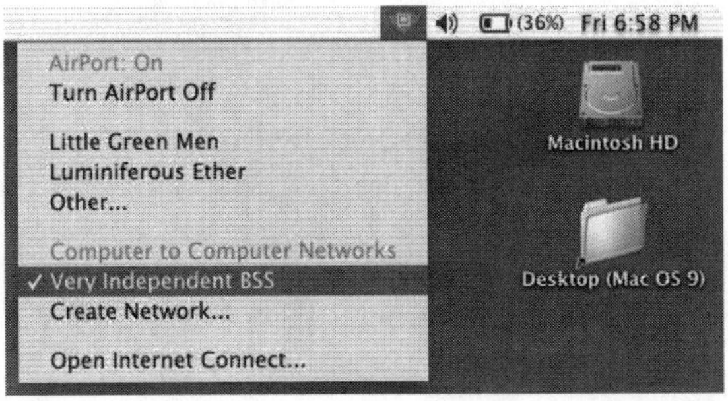

Figure B-6. Network preferences panel of the System Preferences application

System Preferences application. The Show pop-up list can be set to any of the network interfaces in the system. Naturally, when set to AirPort, it enables the fourth tab, as shown in the figure. The default tab is TCP/IP (Figure B-7), which can be set to configure interfaces manually or with the assistance of DHCP or BootP. When set to DHCP, as in the figure, the leased address is shown. Although the DHCP server on my network provided DNS servers, the server IP addresses are not shown. (They are, however, placed in */etc/resolv.conf*, as with any other common Unix system.)

The other network panel worthy of note is the AirPort tab (Figure B-8), which can set the network and password, though it involves more pointing and clicking than the menu associated with the AirPort status icon.

Monitoring the wireless interface

The wireless-interface status can be monitored with the Internet Connect application. The Internet Connect application can be launched from either the Applications folder on the hard disk or from the AirPort status icon. It can be used to display the signal strength of the nearest access point, as well as change the network with which the station is associated.

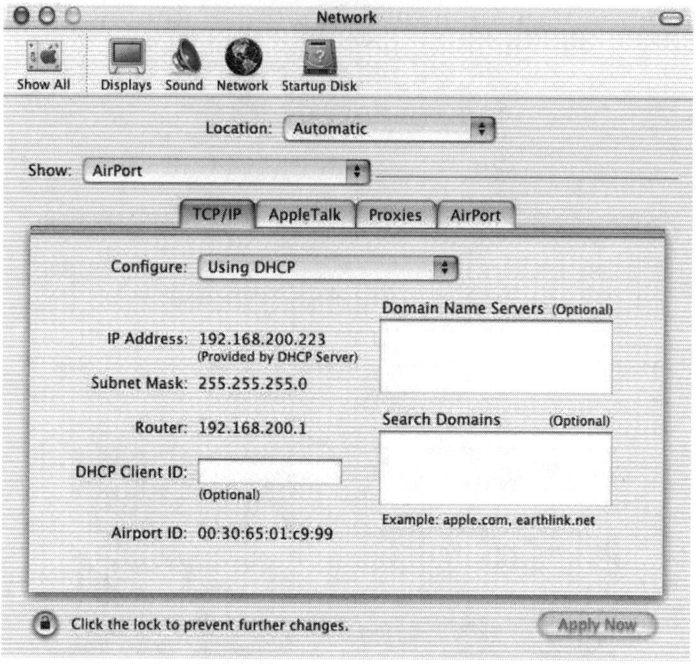

Figure B-7. TCP/IP preferences tab of the Network Preferences settings

The AirPort Base Station

The AirPort Base Station is a model of industrial design. It looks like a flying saucer. There are three lights: for power, wireless activity, and Ethernet activity. The most recent AirPort Base Station model has two Ethernet ports: a 56-KB modem port and a built-in wireless interface. On first-generation AirPort Base Stations, the wireless interface was a Lucent-branded card, complete with a Lucent label; second-generation AirPort Base Stations use Apple-branded AirPort cards.* The AirPort Base Station has a built-in antenna that is good, though not as good as some of the external antennas used with other access points.

In addition to bridging between a wireless and a wired network, the Airport Base Station is designed to connect all network users to the Internet via a cable modem, DSL

---

* Although the AirPort card is an Apple-branded product, a lookup of the FCC ID, IMRWLPC24H, indicates that it was made by Agere (Lucent). In first-generation AirPort Base Stations, the wireless interface was a Lucent Silver card (64-bit WEP). Several web pages show how to dismantle the AirPort Base Station to replace the Silver card with the Gold card (128-bit WEP) for improved security. Many of the same sites also show how to hook up an external antenna by drilling through the AirPort's plastic case. That is not likely to be as big a deal with the second-generation AirPort, since it uses the external antenna connector to use a larger antenna just under the top of the external case.

Figure B-8. AirPort preferences tab of the Network Preferences settings

modem, or a standard 56-KB modem. One of the Ethernet ports is a 10baseT port designed for a connection to a cable modem or DSL modem. The second Ethernet port is a Fast Ethernet port that can be used to connect to an existing LAN.

The AirPort Base Station was developed with assistance from Lucent, and it shows. The configuration of the two access points is quite similar to the configuration of Lucent access points. The AirPort Setup Assistant is used for basic out-of-the-box configuration. The AirPort Utility can then be used to set additional parameters. (Both applications were available only on Mac OS as I wrote this appendix, though Apple announced a Windows configuration application after the submission of the manuscript.) The Lucent access point hardware is commonly used, and there are configuration tools available for both Windows and Linux.

The low price of the AirPort has led many observers to classify it as a consumer device. Certainly, it has a great deal in common with the generic profile of a consumer access point: the price is relatively low, and it is a single unit with an integrated antenna. However, it is more capable than a number of consumer devices and support roaming users. From that standpoint, the AirPort would not be out of place in a small office.

First-Time Setup

The first-time setup is done with the same AirPort Setup Assistant application that configures new wireless interfaces. AirPort Base Stations fresh out of the shrink wrap broadcast their existence to the world so that a MacOS client can be used for configuration. Mac OS X 10.1 shipped with older versions of the configuration utilities, and they required an upgrade. The process is a straightforward software installation from the included CD-ROM. With the release of OS X 10.1.1, the new utilities should be included with the base operating-system installation.

The first step after launching the AirPort Setup Assistant is to select the method by which the AirPort will connect to the Internet. The four choices are shown in Figure B-9. For illustrative purposes, I show the configuration of an AirPort on an existing LAN. The questions asked by the assistant, however, are quite similar for each method.

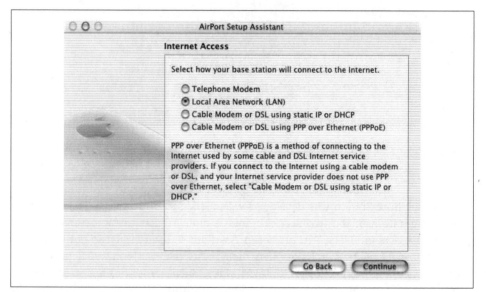

Figure B-9. Network selection methods

After selecting the connection type, the next step is to configure the Ethernet interface for the AirPort. It can be configured automatically with DHCP, or manually. Setting these parameters should be familiar to anyone who has set up a network.

After configuring the Ethernet interface, you proceed to configuring the wireless interface. You must supply the network name and a password. The password is an ASCII seed for the WEP key and can be left blank to run an open network that does not require WEP authentication. Figure B-10 shows the configuration screen for the network name and password.

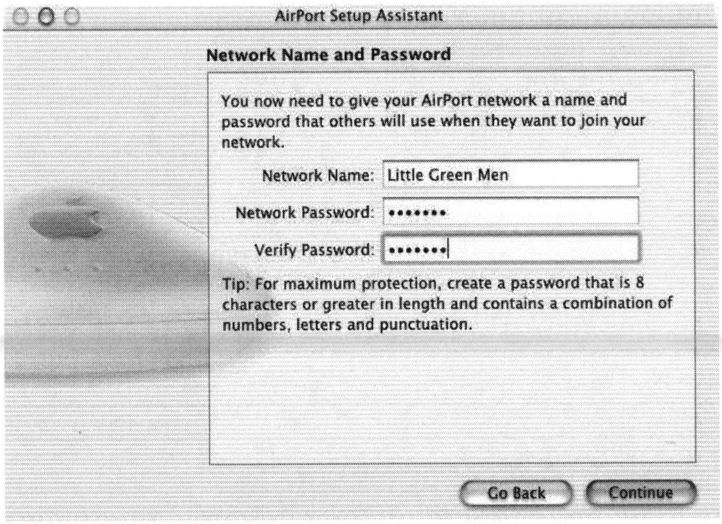

Figure B-10. Network name and password

The AirPort Base Station itself can use the same password as the network, or a different password. As the Setup Assistant itself notes, keeping the passwords separate is a practical requirement for network administrators who must maintain security separate from users. A dialog box lets you make this choice. If a separate password is configured, there is one additional screen in which to enter the base station password before the Setup Assistant terminates.

The Management Interface

Once the bootstrap configuration is done with the Setup Assistant, the AirPort Base Station is on the network and must be configured with the AirPort Utility (Figure B-11). This is a separate configuration utility that will feel vaguely familiar after seeing Lucent's AP Manager. When it is started, the AirPort Admin Utility searches all the AirPort base stations on the network and displays them in a list. Individual base stations can be selected for further configuration. When changes are made, the base station must be restarted for the changes to take effect. The **Other** button at the top allows configuration of any AirPort Base Station that the manager can send IP packets to. Far-away base stations may not appear on the browse list, but by clicking on **Other** and entering an IP address, the Manager can configure any base station to which it has IP connectivity.

Configuring the wireless interface

When a base station is selected for configuration, the configuration screen will pop up. Several tabs are used to group configuration information into logical subsets, and

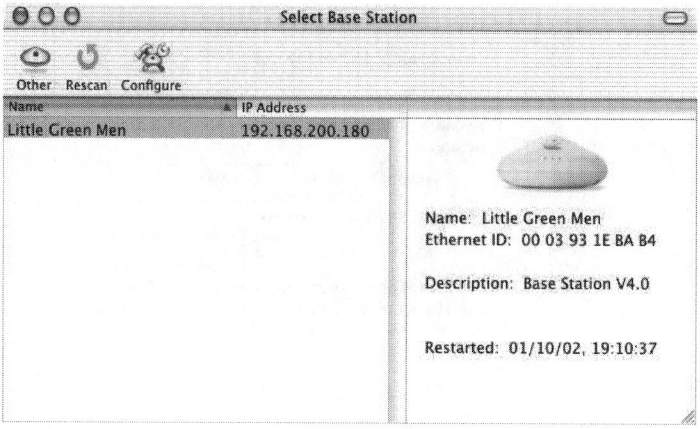

Figure B-11. AirPort Admin Utility main screen

the wireless interface configuration is available by default. Across the top, there are buttons to restart the access point, upload new firmware, return the base station to factory defaults, and change the password. (New firmware is distributed as part of the Admin Utility package.)

The AirPort configuration is shown in Figure B-12. The "AirPort Network" settings are comparable to the Lucent settings of the same name, with the exception of the WEP configuration. Only one password is supported by the AirPort Base Station.

AirPorts were designed to be compatible with other vendors' 802.11 equipment. Most other vendors, however, require that users enter WEP keys as hexadecimal strings. The Password icon at the top of the toolbar will print out the raw WEP key for use in other products. Figure B-13 shows the WEP key that results from entering an ASCII string of Book Key as the text seed.[*]

Configuration of the WAN interface

The Internet configuration tab presents no surprises. When set to Ethernet, it uses the "WAN" Ethernet port to connect to the outside world. You can configure the standard network settings (IP address, network mask, DNS server, router) manually, or you can select automatic configuration via DHCP. The AirPort is compatible with cable modems that use the Point to Point Protocol over Ethernet (PPPoE) and DSL modems. PPPoE configuration requires a username and password supplied by your ISP. Modem access can be set up using either a generic dial-in or a script provided by Apple to make the AirPort Base Station compatible with America Online.

---

[*] Chally Microsolutions (*http://www.chally.net*) distributes a tool called WEP Key Maker that will generate a WEP key of a specified length from a long pass phrase.

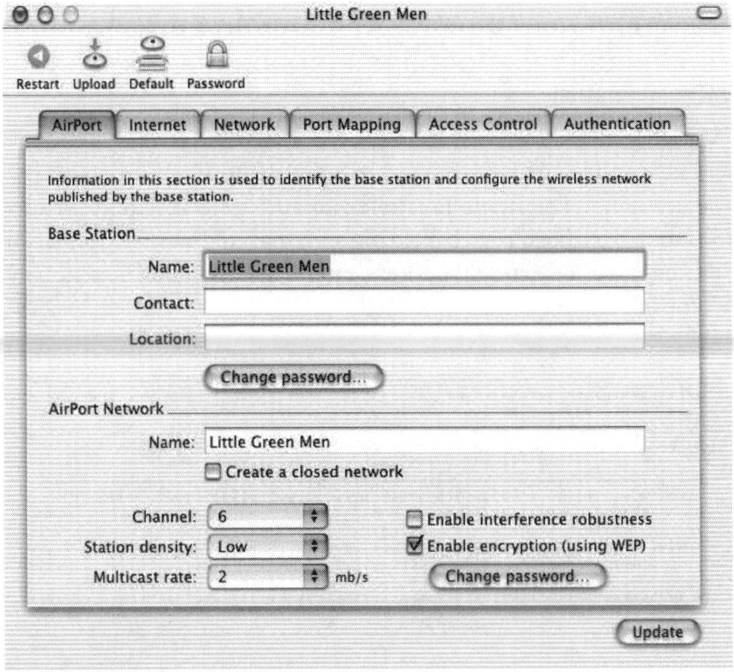

Figure B-12. Wireless interface configuration

Figure B-13. Printing out the WEP key in hexadecimal for use by non-Apple 802.11 stations

Configuration of the LAN interface

The AirPort can be used as the central connection device in a home network by connecting the 10-Mbps Ethernet port to a broadband connection and using the 100-Mbps Ethernet port to connect other LAN stations. Client computers can be statically addressed by the network administrator, or the built-in DHCP server can be turned on and assigned a range of addresses to assign to clients. When NAT is used to hide several computers behind one IP address, the address specified in the Internet properties is used as the public address. The wired LAN interface is given the private address 10.0.1.1, and DHCP is used to lease out addresses from 10.0.1.2 to 10.0.1.200 (in this case, you can't select the range of addresses for the DHCP server to give out). The AirPort base station can be connected to wired networks by its Fast Ethernet LAN port if the DHCP server is disabled.

Inbound NAT configuration

The Port Mapping tab, shown in Figure B-14, can be used to add inbound static port mappings. The public port is translated to the private IP address and port number listed in the mapping. The figure illustrates an address translation for inbound web services to port 80 on host 10.0.1.201. No external address is specified in the Port Mapping tab because the external address can be assigned in different ways depending on the type of Internet connection used.

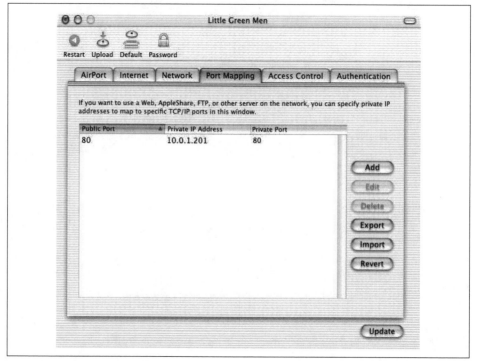

Figure B-14. Port Mapping tab

Access control

Like most other products, the AirPort Base Station supports filtering by client MAC address. The Access Control tab lets you identify clients by their AirPort ID (MAC address) and add them to a list of allowed clients, together with a description.

Authentication

The AirPort allows a RADIUS server, which can provide an external authentication mechanism for MAC addresses. When authentication of a client MAC is required, the base station will pass the request on to the RADIUS servers defined in the tab shown in Figure B-15.

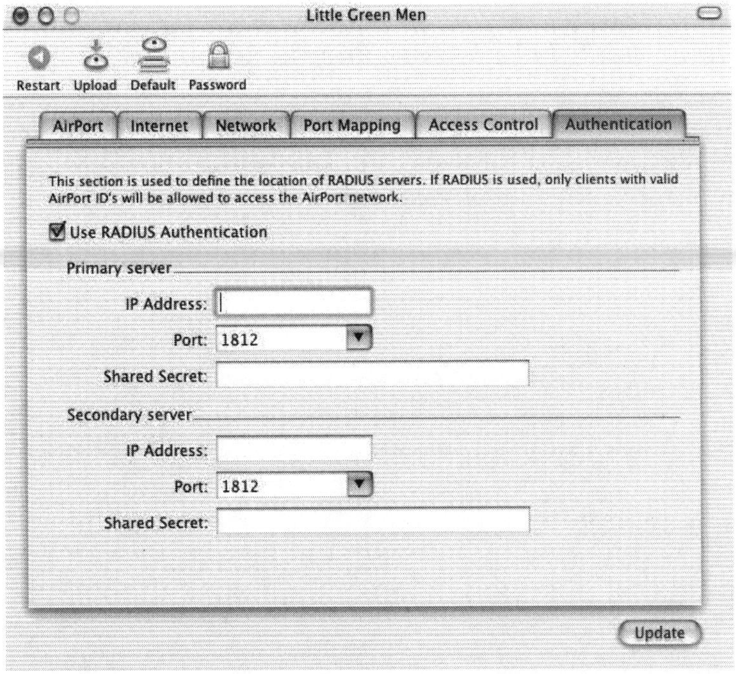

Figure B-15. RADIUS authentication tab

Links to More Information

Official sites

http://www.apple.com/airport/ (sales and marketing)

http://www.info.apple.com/usen/airport/ (support; registration required)

Repairing first-generation AirPorts

http://www.vonwentzel.net/ABS/Repair.html

First-generation AirPort Base Stations tend to fail due to capacitor failure. This site explains the problem and shows how to repair the base station, though the procedure almost certainly voids the warranty.

AirPort hardware hacking

http://www.msrl.com/airport-gold/

Older AirPort base stations use Lucent cards. By changing the card from the stock Silver card to a Gold card, longer WEP keys can be used.

http://jim.chronomedia.com/Airportmod/

First-generation AirPort Base stations run hot. This site shows how to add a cooling fan to the case.

Linux on AirPort Base Stations

http://www-hft.ee.tu-berlin.de/~strauman/airport/airport.html

Early versions of the AirPort firmware did not support PPPoE. One response to this was to run Linux on the AirPort Base Station and use the Linux PPPoE driver. Although recent enhancements to the firmware now support PPPoE, the project may be interesting for some readers.

Glossary

access point
See AP.

ACK
Abbreviation for "Acknowledgment." ACKs are used extensively in 802.11 to provide reliable data transfers over an unreliable medium. For more details, see "Contention-Based Data Service" in Chapter 3.

Acknowledgment
See ACK.

ad hoc
A network characterized by temporary, short-lived relationships between nodes. See also IBSS.

AID
Association Identifier. A number that identifies data structures in an access point allocated for a specific mobile node.

AP
Access Point. Bridge-like device that attaches wireless 802.11 stations to a wired backbone network. For more information on the general structure of an access point, see Chapter 14.

ASN
Abstract Syntax Notation. The formal description of the grammar used to write MIB files.

association identifier
See AID.

ATIM
Announcement Traffic Indication Message. ATIMs are used in ad hoc (independent) 802.11 networks to announce the existence of buffered frames. For more details, see Chapter 7.

basic service set
See BSS.

BER
Bit Error Rate. The number of bits received in error. Usually, the number is quite low and expressed as a ratio in scientific notation. 10^{-2} means one bit in 100 is received in error.

BPSK
Binary Phase Shift Keying. A modulation method that encodes bits as phase shifts. One of two phase shifts can be selected to encode a single bit.

BSS
Basic Service Set. The building block of 802.11 networks. A BSS is a set of stations that are logically associated with each other.

BSSID
Basic Service Set Identifier. A 48-bit identifier used by all stations in a BSS in frame headers.

CCITT
Comité Consultatif International Télégraphique et Téléphonique. A UN body responsible for telephone standardization. Due to a reorganization, it is now called the International Telecommunication Union-Telecommunication Standardization Sector (ITU-T).

CCK

Complementary Code Keying. A modulation scheme that transforms data blocks into complex codes and is capable of encoding several bits per block.

CF

Contention Free. Services that do not involve contention for the medium are contention-free services. Such services are implemented by a Point Coordinator (PC) through the use of the Point Coordination Function (PCF). Contention-free services are not widely implemented.

CFP

Contention-Free Period. Even when 802.11 provides contention-free services, some contention-based access to the wireless medium is allowed. Periods controlled by a central authority are called contention-free periods (CFP).

CRC

Cyclic Redundancy Check. A mathematical checksum that can be used to detect data corruption in transmitted frames.

CSMA

Carrier Sense Multiple Access. A "listen before talk" scheme used to mediate the access to a transmission resource. All stations are allowed to access the resource (multiple access) but are required to make sure the resource is not in use before transmitting (carrier sense).

CSMA/CA

Carrier Sense Multiple Access with Collision Avoidance. A CSMA method that tries to avoid simultaneous access (collisions) by deferring access to the medium. 802.11 and AppleTalk's LocalTalk are two protocols that use CSMA/CA.

CTS

Clear to Send. The frame type used to acknowledge receipt of a Request to Send and the second component used in the RTS-CTS clearing exchange used to prevent interference from hidden nodes.

DA

Destination Address. The MAC address of the station the frame should be processed by. Frequently, the destination address is the receiver address. In infrastructure networks, however, frames bridged from the wireless side to the wired side will have a destination address on the wired network and a receiver address of the wireless interface in the access point.

DBPSK

Differential Binary Phase Shift Keying. A modulation method in which bits are encoded as phase shift differences between successive symbol periods. Two phase shifts are possible for an encoding rate of one data bit per symbol.

DCF

Distributed Coordination Function. The rules for contention-based access to the wireless medium in 802.11. The DCF is based on exponentially increasing backoffs in the presence of contention as well as rules for deferring access, frame acknowledgment, and when certain types of frame exchanges or fragmentation may be required.

DHCP

Dynamic Host Configuration Protocol. An IETF standard used by network administrators to automatically configure hosts. Hosts needing configuration information may broadcast a request that is responded to by a DHCP server. DHCP was the Internet community's admission that the Internet was growing so fast that network administrators had lost control over what was plugged into networks.

DIFS

Distributed Inter-Frame Space. The inter-frame space used to separate atomic exchanges in contention-based services. See also DCF.

distributed coordination function

See DCF.

distributed inter-frame space

See DIFS.

DQPSK

Differential Quadrature Phase Shift Keying. A modulation method in which bits are encoded as phase shift differences between successive symbol periods. Four phase shifts are possible for an encoding rate of two data bits per symbol.

DS

Distribution System. The set of services that connects access points together. Logically composed of the wired backbone network plus the bridging functions in most commercial access points. See Figure 2-6

DSSS

Direct-Sequence Spread Spectrum. A transmission technique that spreads a signal over a wide frequency band for transmission. At the receiver, the widespread signal is correlated into a stronger signal; meanwhile, any narrowband noise is spread widely. Most of the 802.11-installed base at 2 Mbps and 11 Mbps is composed of direct-sequence interfaces.

DTIM

Delivery Traffic Indication Map. Beacon frames may contain the DTIM element, which is used to indicate that broadcast and multicast frames buffered by the access point will be delivered shortly.

EIFS

Extended Inter-Frame Space. The longest of the four inter-frame spaces, the EIFS is used when there has been an error in transmission.

EIRP

Effective Isotropic Radiated Power. An antenna system will have a footprint over which the radio waves are distributed. The power inside the footprint is called the effective isotropic radiated power.

ERP

Effective Radiated Power. Used to describe the strength of radio waves transmitted by an antenna.

ESS

Extended Service Set. A logical collection of access points all tied together. Link-layer roaming is possible throughout an ESS, provided all the stations are configured to recognize each other.

ETSI

European Telecommunications Standards Institute. ETSI is a multinational standardization body with regulatory and standardization authority over much of Europe. GSM standardization took place under the auspices of ETSI. ETSI has taken the lead role in standardizing a wireless LAN technology competing with 802.11 called the High Performance Radio LAN (HIPERLAN).

extended inter-frame space

See EIFS.

FCC

Federal Communications Commission. The regulatory agency for the United States. The FCC Rules in Title 47 of the Code of Federal Regulations govern telecommunications in the United States. Wireless LANs must comply with Part 15 of the FCC rules, which are written specifically for RF devices.

FCS

Frame Check Sequence. A checksum appended to frames on IEEE 802 networks to detect corruption. If the receiver calculates a different FCS than the FCS in the frame, it is assumed to have been corrupted in transit and is discarded.

FH

Frequency Hopping. See FHSS.

FHSS

Frequency Hopping Spread Spectrum. A technique that uses a time-varying narrowband signal to spread RF energy over a wide band.

GFSK

Gaussian Frequency Shift Keying. A modulation technique that encodes data based on the frequency of the carrier signal during the symbol time. GFSK is relatively immune to analog noise because most analog noise is amplitude-modulated.

HR/DSSS

High-Rate Direct-Sequence Spread Spectrum. The abbreviation for signals transmitted by 802.11b equipment. Although similar to the earlier 2-Mbps transmissions in many respects, advanced encoding enables a higher data rate.

IAPP

Inter-Access Point Protocol. The protocol used between access points to enable roaming. In late 2001, each vendor used a proprietary IAPP, though work on a standardized IAPP was underway.

IBSS

Independent Basic Service Set. An 802.11 network without an access point. Some vendors refer to IBSSs as ad hoc networks; see also ad hoc.

ICV

Integrity Check Value. The checksum calculated over a frame before encryption by WEP. The ICV is designed to protect a frame against tampering by allowing a receiver to detect alterations to the frame. Unfortunately, WEP uses a flawed algorithm to generate the ICV, which robs WEP of a great deal of tamper-resistance.

IEEE

Institute of Electrical and Electronics Engineers. The professional body that has standardized the ubiquitous IEEE 802 networks.

IR

Infrared. Light with a longer wavelength and lower frequency than visible red light. The wavelength of red light is approximately 700 nm.

ISI

Inter-Symbol Interference. Because of delays over multiple paths, transmitted symbols may interfere with each other and cause corruption. Guarding against ISI is a major consideration for wireless LANs, especially those based on OFDM.

ISM

Industrial, Scientific, and Medical. Part 15 of the FCC Rules sets aside certain frequency bands in the United States for use by unlicensed Industrial, Scientific, and Medical equipment. The 2.4-GHz ISM band was initially set aside for microwave ovens so that home users of microwave ovens would not be required to go through the burdensome FCC licensing process simply to reheat leftover food quickly. Because it is unlicensed, though, many devices operate in the band, including 802.11 wireless LANs.

ITU

International Telecommunications Union. The successor to the CCITT. Technically speaking, the ITU issues recommendations, not regulations or standards. However, many countries give ITU recommendations the force of law.

IV

Initialization Vector. Generally used as a term for exposed keying material in cryptographic headers; most often used with block ciphers. WEP exposes 24 bits of the secret key to the world in the frame header, even though WEP is based on a stream cipher.

LLC

Logical Link Control. An IEEE specification that allows further protocol multiplexing over Ethernet. 802.11 frames carry LLC-encapsulated data units.

MAC

Medium Access Control. The function in IEEE networks that arbitrates use of the network capacity and determines which stations are allowed to use the medium for transmission.

MIB

Management Information Base. An ASN specification of the operational and configuration parameters of a device; frequently used with SNMP or other network management systems.

MPDU

MAC Protocol Data Unit. A fancy name for frame. The MPDU does not, however, include PLCP headers.

MSDU

MAC Service Data Unit. The data accepted by the MAC for delivery to another MAC on the network. MSDUs are composed of higher-level data only. For example, an 802.11 management frame does not contain an MSDU.

NAV

Network Allocation Vector. The NAV is used to implement the virtual carrier sensing function. Stations will defer access to the medium if it is busy. For robustness, 802.11 includes two carrier-sensing functions. One is a *physical* function, which is based on energy thresholds, whether a station is decoding a legal 802.11 signal, and similar things that require a physical measurement. The second function is a *virtual* carrier sense, which is based on the NAV. Most frames include a nonzero number in the NAV field, which is used to ask all stations to politely defer from accessing the medium for a certain number of microseconds after the current frame is transmitted. Any receiving stations will process the NAV and defer access, which prevents collisions. For more detail on how the NAV is used, see "Contention-Based Data Service" in Chapter 3.

OFDM

Orthogonal Frequency Division Multiplexing. A technique that splits a wide frequency band into a number of narrow frequency bands and inverse multiplexes data across the subchannels. Both 802.11a and the forthcoming 802.11g standards are based on OFDM.

OSI

Open Systems Interconnection. A baroque compendium of networking standards that was never implemented because IP networks actually existed.

PBCC

Packet Binary Convolution Coding. An alternative method of encoding data in 802.11b networks that has not been widely implemented. PBCC was also proposed for consideration for 20+ Mbps networks, but was rejected.

PC

Point Coordinator. A function in the access point responsible for central coordination of access to the radio medium during contention-free service.

PCF

Point Coordination Function. The set of rules that provides for centrally coordinated access to the medium by the access point.

PCMCIA

Personal Computer Memory Card International Association. An industry group that standardized the ubiquitous "PCMCIA card" form factor and made it possible to connect a wide variety of peripherals to notebook computers. 802.11 interfaces are available almost exclusively in the PCMCIA form factor. Also expanded humorously as People Who Can't Manage Computer Industry Acronyms because of its unwieldy length and pronunciation.

PDU

See protocol data unit.

PER

Packet Error Rate. Like the bit error rate, but measured as a fraction of packets with errors.

PHY

Common IEEE abbreviation for the physical layer.

physical-layer convergence procedure

The upper component of the PHY in 802.11 networks. Each PHY has its own PLCP, which provides auxiliary framing to the MAC.

PIFS

PCF Inter-Frame space. During contention-free service, any station is free to transmit if the medium is idle for the duration of one PCF inter-frame space.

PLCP

See physical-layer convergence procedure.

PMD

Physical Medium Dependent. The lower component of the MAC, responsible for transmitting RF signals to other 802.11 stations.

PPDU

PLCP Protocol Data Unit. The complete PLCP frame, including PLCP headers,

MAC headers, the MAC data field, and the MAC and PLCP trailers.

protocol data unit

Layers communicate with each other using protocol data units. For example, the IP protocol data unit is the familiar IP packet. IP implementations communicate with each other using IP packets. See also service data unit.

PS

Power Save. Used as a generic prefix for power-saving operations in 802.11.

PSDU

PLCP Service Data Unit. The data the PLCP is responsible for delivering, i.e., one MAC frame with headers.

PSK

Phase Shift Keying. A method of transmitting data based on phase shifts in the transmitted carrier wave.

QPSK

Quadrature Phase Shift Keying. A modulation method that encodes bits as phase shifts. One of four phase shifts can be selected to encode two bits.

RA

Receiver Address. MAC address of the station that will receive the frame. The RA may also be the destination address of a frame, but not always. In infrastructure networks, for example, a frame destined for the distribution system is received by an access point.

RC4

A proprietary cipher algorithm developed by RSA Data Security and licensed for a great deal of money. Also used as the basis for WEP and prevents open source WEP implementations from existing because of the fear of lawsuits by RSA.

RF

Radio Frequency. Used as an adjective to indicate that something pertains to the radio interface ("RF modulator," "RF energy," and so on).

RTS

Request to Send. The frame type used to begin the RTS-CTS clearing exchange.

RTS frames are used when the frame that will be transmitted is larger than the RTS threshold.

SA

Source Address; as disinct from TA. Station that generated the frame. Different when frame originates on the distrbution system and goes to the wireless segment.

SDU

See service data unit.

Service Data Unit

When a protocol layer receives data from the next highest layer, it is sending a service data unit. For example, an IP service data unit can be composed of the data in the TCP segment plus the TCP header. Protocol layers access service data units, add the appropriate header, and push them down to the next layer. See also protocol data unit.

SFD

Start of Frame Delimiter. The component of the frame header that indicates when synchronization has concluded and the actual frame is about to start.

SIFS

Short Inter-Frame Space. The shortest of the four inter-frame spaces. The SIFS is used between frames in an atomic frame exchange.

SSID

Service Set Identity. A string used to identify a service set. Typically, the SSID is a recognizable character string for the benefit of users.

SYNC

Short for Synchronize. Bits transmitted by the PLCP to allow senders and receivers to synchronize bit timers.

TA

Transmitter Address. Station that actually put the frame in the air. Often the access point in infrastructure networks.

TIM

Traffic Indication Map. A field transmitted in Beacon frames used to inform associated stations that the access point has buffered. Bits are used to indicate both buffered unicast frames for each associated station as well as the presence of buffered multicast frames.

WEP

Wired Equivalent Privacy. Derided as Wiretap Equivalence Protocol by its critics. A standard for ciphering individual data frames. It was intended to provide minimal privacy and has succeeded in this respect. In August 2001, WEP was soundly defeated, and public code was released.

Wi-Fi and Wi-Fi5

The Wireless Ethernet Compatibility Alliance started the Wi-Fi ("wireless fidelity") certification program to ensure that equipment claiming 802.11 compliance was genuinely interoperable. Wi-Fi–certified equipment has demonstrated standards compliance in an interoperability lab. Originally, the term was applied to devices that complied with 802.11b (11-Mbps HR/DSSS). The newer term, Wi-Fi5, is applied to 802.11a (54-Mbps OFDM) equipment that passes a similar certification test suite.

Index

We'd like to hear your suggestions for improving our indexes. Send email to *index@oreilly.com*.

authentication timeout, 373
Authentication Transaction Sequence
        Number field, 69, 121
availability
    data security attribute, 299
    through redundancy, 299

B

backbone networks
    distribution system as, 10
    ESS and, 12
    limitations in choosing access points, 14
backoff timers, 138
backoff window, 33
bandwidth
    802.11a standard, 206
    carriers and, 199
    direct-sequence modulation and, 178
    FCC rules for frequency-hopping
            systems, 168
    frequencies and, 3
    limitations with wireless LANs, 3
    network speed and, 5
Barker sequence, 179
Barker words, 178, 189
basic rate set, 119
basic service area
    active scanning and, 117
    BSS and, 10
    no transition and, 20
    overlapping, 16
    reassociation and, 18
    SSIDs and, 75
    TSF and, 137
basic service set (see BSS)
basic service set ID (see BSSID)
batteries
    802.11 standard and, 268
    high-frequency devices and, 181
    maximizing life of, 133
    mobile devices and, 128
Beacon frames
    ATIM window and, 135
    BSS and, 369
    case study example, 349–350
    CF Parameter Set elements and, 149
    CFP and, 40, 141
    dot11CFPPeriod, 385
    excluding from Ethereal analysis, 345
    features of, 79
    as management frames, 45

passive scanning and, 115, 116, 351
    purpose of, 67
    sleeping periods and, 48
    TBTT and, 138
    TIM and, 49, 129, 132
    timestamps, 168
    timing synchronization and, 137
Beacon interval
    frame buffering and, 130
    Listen intervals and, 371
    management frames and, 69
    tunable parameter, 369
Beacon period
    buffer management and, 137
    dot11BeaconPeriod, 386
    dot11DTIMPeriod, 386
    power management and, 128
Beacon Period scanning parameter, 118
BER (bit error rate), 204
Berra, Yogi, 376
binary phase shift keying (see BPSK)
bison, Ethereal and, 333
bit error rate (BER), 204
Bitmap Control field (TIM), 78
Bitmap Offset field (TIM), 78
bits
    defined, 177
    DS bits, 53–56
    order of, 36
    padding, 205
Bluetooth standard, 5, 378
Bohr, Niels, 86
BPSK (binary phase shift keying), 211
bridges
    access points as, 13, 14, 262
    wireless features, 15
bridging
    802.1d specification, 8
    access points and, 10
    example, 14
    Nokia A032 and, 280, 282
broadcast BSSID, 55
broadcast frames
    ATIM window and, 135
    contention-free service and, 150
    defined, 40
    DTIM and, 132
    frame exchanges and, 44
    mobile stations and, 133
broadcast SSID, 75, 117
Bruestle, Jeremy, 96

OUI (organizationally unique identifier)
Ethereal example, 350
LLC header component, 348
SNAP and, 43

P

p2req_ command, 248
packet binary convolution coding (see PBCC)
packet error rate (see PER)
packet sniffers, 23
packets
filtering, 299
key length and, 367
marking, 341
Pad field, 211
parabolic antennas, 319
parameters
802.11a choices, 206
command-line, 281
DS PHY, 189
FH PHY, 175
HR/DS PHY, 197
Nokia driver, 224
OFDM PHY, 212
performance tuning, 374
power management, 371–373
radio management, 368–371
for scanning, 115
timing operations, 373
timing parameters, 119
tuning for 802.11 standard, 258
wvlan_cs driver, 259
Parity bit, 210
passive scan timer, 373
passive scanning, 115, 116, 351
Path MTU Discovery (RFC 1191), 42
PBCC (packet binary convolution coding)
802.11b option, 196
management frames and, 70
Task Group G, 377
PBCC field, 70
PCF (point coordination function)
atomic exchanges and, 44
contention-free service with, 27, 140–150
dot11MediumOccupancyLimit, 384
features of, 27
throughput using, 311
PCF interframe space (see PIFS)

PCMCIA
cards
access points and, 263
AP-1000 and, 269
common I/O ports, 243
common IRQ settings, 242
enterprise gateways and, 265
Card Services
Linux support, 238–244
linux-wlan and, 245
linux-wlan-ng, 247, 249, 253
PER (packet error rate), 315
performance tuning
dot11CountersTable, 390
power management, 371–373
project planning, 309
radio management, 368–371
timing operations, 373
tunable parameters, 374
wireless networks, 23
Perl, Ethereal and, 333
phase shift keying (PSK)
DBPSK, 183
DQPSK, 184, 194
encoding data, 182
physical-layer convergence procedure (see
PLCP)
physical-layer management entity (see PLME)
physical-medium dependent (see PMD)
physical (PHY) layer, 119, 392
802.11 MAC and, 10, 24
802.11 standard, 8, 152, 164
interframe space times and, 30
MIB and, 115, 392–395
PMD and, 151
radio waves as, 9
PIFS (PCF interframe space), 30
PIN Unlocking Key (PUK), 226
ping tool, 264, 291
PINs, 226, 227
planning, project, 307–314
PLCP (physical-layer convergence procedure)
802.11 specification, 9
DS PHY, 185–186
frequency hopping and, 171–174
HR/DS, 190–193
MAC frames and, 9
OFDM, 208–211

T

Tail field, 210, 211
target Beacon transmission time (see TBTT)
Task Group D (TGd), 376
Task Group E (TGe), 377
Task Group F (TGf), 377, 378
Task Group G (TGg), 377
Task Group H (TGh), 377
Task Group I (TGi), 378
TBTT (target Beacon transmission
        time), 138
TCP
    three-way handshake, 360
    web transaction example, 362
tcpdump, 339
TCP/IP
    cheap access points and, 263
    Ethereal and, 332
    Mobile IP and, 22
    network performance requirements, 309
telephony (see mobile telephony)
telnet connections, 283
temperature range, 393
Texas Instruments, 377
TFTP (trivial file transfer protocol)
    access control and, 299
    address filtering and, 121
    NID mappings and, 287
throughput
    direct-sequence modulation and, 178
    direct-sequence systems and, 181
    expectations for, 311
    frequency-hopping systems and, 168
    guard time and, 202
    project planning, 308
    retry limits and, 371
TIM (traffic indication map)
    Beacon frames and, 79
    buffered frames and, 372
    frame delivery, 129
    power and, 49
TIM information element, 77, 130
time units (TUs)
    active timer and, 373
    ATIM frames, 78
    ATIM window and, 372
    contention-free periods and, 149
    defined, 69
    dot11MaxTransmitMSDULifetime, 390
    dwell time and, 76
    scanning parameter and, 116, 118

timeouts
    dot11AssociationResponseTimeOut, 386
    dot11AuthenticationResponseTimeout,
        385
    joining networks and, 373
    linux-wlan-ng problems, 254
timer synchronization
    802.11 networks, 137–139
    frequency hopping and, 119
Times Microwave (LMR-200), 320
Times Microwave (LMR-400), 320
Timestamp field
    management frames and, 72
    timing parameter, 119
    timing synchronization and, 137
timestamps
    Beacon frames on frequency-hopping
        networks, 168
    rules for, 138
    scanning and, 352
    TSF and, 137
timing operations
    802.11 MAC, 27–31
    performance tuning, 373
timing synchronization function (see TSF)
ToDS bit
    ARP requests and, 357
    control frames and, 61
    DNS request and, 359
    frames from distribution systems, 59
    specifics, 38
Token Ring, 8
traceroute tool, 264, 291
Traffic Indication Map (see TIM)
traffic indication map information element
        (see TIM information element)
transceivers
    802.11 direct-sequence networks, 187
    power conservation and, 128
transmission
    802.11 MAC rules for, 31
    from access points, 142–143
    acknowledgment and, 45
    authentication and, 83–85
    contention-free periods and, 40
    direct-sequence, 176–182
    dot11MaxTransmitMSDULifetime, 390
    dot11TransmittedFrameCount, 391
    DS PHY, 187
    DS PMD, 187
    FH PMD, 174
    frequency-hopping, 165–169

About the Author

Matthew S. Gast is a renaissance technologist. In addition to his demonstrated expertise on a variety of network technologies, he is relentlessly inquisitive about the interconnected and interdependent world around him. After graduating from college, his interests in routing, security, and cryptography pulled him towards Silicon Valley to participate in scaling the mountainous network engineering challenge called the Internet. In addition to his technology interests, Matthew is a voracious reader on science and economics and a lifelong supporter of the scientific method.

Matthew is also a Registered Patent Agent before the United States Patent and Trademark Office. Patent agents assist in the drafting and prosecution of patent applications, which has been called the most demanding task in the United States legal system by the Supreme Court. Matthew has co-written two patent applications, one of which was for his own invention.

Colophon

Our look is the result of reader comments, our own experimentation, and feedback from distribution channels. Distinctive covers complement our distinctive approach to technical topics, breathing personality and life into potentially dry subjects.

The animal on the cover of *802.11 Wireless Netowrks: The Definitive Guide* is a horseshoe bat (*Rhinolophus hipposideros*). This rare and globally endangered species is the smallest of the European horseshoe bats; they typically weigh only 4–10 grams and have a wingspan of 19–25 centimeters. Horseshoe bats get their name from the horseshoe-shaped, leaflike plate of skin around the nose. This nose-leaf helps modify and direct the ultrasonic sounds they emit through their nostrils (a method of sensory perception known as echolocation) to orient themselves to their surroundings, detect obstacles, communicate with each other, and find food. Bats' echolocation systems are so accurate that they can detect insects the size of gnats and objects as fine as a human hair.

Lesser horseshoe bats are found in a variety of habitats, ranging from the British Isles to the Arabian Peninsula and Central Asia, and from Morocco to Sudan. The lesser horseshoe bat was originally a cave-roosting bat, but many summer maternity colonies now occupy the roofs of old rural houses and farm buildings. These bats also sometimes roost in hedgerows and hollow trees. Maternity colonies of 30 to 70 are normal, but roosting mothers have been known to form colonies of as many as 200 bats. Lesser horseshoe bats hibernate, sometimes in large groups, from October until late April or early May. Their winter roosts are usually underground, in caves or tunnels. They hang by their feet with their wings wrapped around their bodies, often in open and exposed positions but rarely in large clusters.

Matt Hutchinson was the production editor and proofreader, and Leanne Soylemez was the copyeditor for *802.11 Wireless Networks: The Definitive Guide*. Sarah Sherman and Darren Kelly provided quality control. Lucie Haskins wrote the index.

Ellie Volckhausen designed the cover of this book, based on a series design by Edie Freedman. The cover image is a 19th-century engraving from the Dover Pictorial Archive. Emma Colby produced the cover layout with QuarkXPress 4.1 using Adobe's ITC Garamond font.

Melanie Wang designed the interior layout, based on a series design by David Futato. Neil Walls converted the files from Microsoft Word to FrameMaker 5.5.6 using tools created by Mike Sierra. The text font is Linotype Birka; the heading font is Adobe Myriad Condensed; and the code font is LucasFont's TheSans Mono Condensed. The illustrations that appear in the book were produced by Robert Romano and Jessamyn Read using Macromedia FreeHand 9 and Adobe Photoshop 6. The tip and warning icons were drawn by Christopher Bing. This colophon was written by Rachel Wheeler.